CALGARY

CANADA'S
FRONTIER METROPOLIS

An Illustrated History
by Max Foran and Heather MacEwan Foran

"Partners in Progress" by John D. Balcers

Introduction by J.W. Grant MacEwan

Advisory Editor Hugh Dempsey

Sponsored by

THE CALGARY CHAMBER OF COMMERCE

Windsor Publications, Inc.

Windsor Publications, Inc.
History Books Division

Publisher: John M. Phillips
Editorial Director: Lissa Sanders
Administrative Coordinator: Katherine Cooper
Senior Picture Editor: Teri Davis Greenberg
Senior Corporate History Editor: Karen Story
Production Manager: James Burke
Art Director: Alexander D'Anca
Art Production Manager: Dee Cooper
Composition Manager: E. Beryl Myers

Staff for *Calgary: Canada's Frontier Metropolis*

Editor: F. Jill Charboneau
Textual Editors: Carol V. Davis, Barbara Marinacci
Picture Editor: Annette Igra
Editorial Assistants: Todd Ackerman, Susan Block,
   Phyllis Gray, Mary Mohr, Susan Wells
Compositors: Shannon Mellies, Barbara Neiman
Proofreaders: Jeff Leckrone, Ruth Hoover
Designer: John Fish
Layout: John Fish, Shannon Strull, Melinda Wade
Production Artists: Janet Bailey, Beth Bowman,
   Ellen Hazeltine
Lettering: Janet Bailey

Courtesy, Glenbow-Alberta Institute.

CONTENTS

THE FRONTIER LEGACY

There are, perhaps, 10 major Canadian cities in terms of size and economic importance. In this small assemblage, Calgary stands alone, almost in typical maverick fashion. First of all, its links with the past are short and tenuous. Few headstones with dates in the 1880s are to be found in the neat, well-kept cemeteries, and certainly none before 1875. Unlike other Canadian cities, the cultural lineage of colonial England or France makes no contribution in the form of crumbling or preserved architecture, familial connections, or historic tradition. Nor is there the salty, ageless romance of the sea. Even the fur trade, which some Canadian historians have seen as the most formative force in Canadian history, was of little consequence in Calgary. Yet, though Calgary has been denied the richness of a long past, the romance of a maritime legacy, or a niche in the fur trading saga of river highways and folklore, this southern Alberta city has been able to cultivate a singular character unsurpassed by any other major Canadian urban centre. For Calgary has had its own unique blend of site and circumstance, which has perpetuated a frontier image of individualism, freedom, and opportunity set in big sky country. In this respect, the history of Calgary has tended to mirror the ebullience and unpredictability of the frontier experience.

Calgary is the only Canadian city to rest in the shadow of the Rockies. The mountains rise suddenly about 150 kilometres to the west and extend the length of the horizon in an endless, ever-changing line of jagged peaks. On a clear winter day, their white starkness provides a breathtaking vista of unparalleled beauty. In the summer, they assume a blue-grey haziness that recedes into the azure mist of a July Alberta sky. Sometimes, and particularly in the vanguard of violent weather change, they brood ominously before being obscured by rolling, angry clouds. Few who have seen a true Chinook arch can forget the visual impact of this winter weather phenomenon. On Chinook days, a grey arch of cloud stretches like a giant canopy to frame the sky and mountains below. The white fingers of mountain protruding into a blue, almost mauve, sky produce a contrast of awesome grandeur. Calgary's proximity to the Rockies and to Canada's mountain playgrounds has long been regarded as an incomparable asset. Both in real and psychic terms, Calgary's association with the mountains has been an enduring component of its urban life.

But though the romance of the mountains and Calgary are inseparable, the city does not really belong to an alpine environment. It is located in a fertile river valley, and its immediate hinterland is foothill and prairie rather than mountain. The rolling green meadows to the south and west constitute some of the best cattle grazing land in the world. A few miles to the east, away from the Bow River valley, are the flat, semi-arid prairies that during the short summer months become a golden sea of waving wheat. Calgary sits where prairie meets foothills, and for years depended on both for its economic survival. For most of its short history, Calgary's fortunes have been irrevocably bound up with those of its agricultural and ranching hinterland. In this context, the impressive backdrop of Rocky Mountains has been more a bonus than a formative force in determining the nature and extent of the city's development.

Calgary's site therefore is unmatched by any Canadian city. And Calgary is alone in drawing on the enduring appeal of alpine scenery, mountain trails, lakes, and streams, as well as on its romantic association with cattle ranching, an industry long enshrined in North American folklore. Its bracing climate is modified by warm, dry winter winds that do much towards tempering the harshness of the feared Canadian winter. Its newness and wealth add an air of prosperity and dynamism that is compatible with its majestic surroundings. There can be but one Calgary in the pantheon of present or emerging Canadian cities.

A succinct analysis of Calgary's history would probably pay short shrift to the city's inauspicious origin as a North West Mounted Police fort in 1875. It would definitely place much more credence on Calgary's position on Canada's first transcontinental railroad and its subsequent role as the chief distributing centre for the agricultural and ranching hinterlands of south and south central Alberta. A historical discussion would also acknowledge the importance of the immigration boom of 1909-1912, which peopled Western Canada and which thrust Calgary from a small railroad centre to moderate city status. Further, it would equate Calgary's modest growth between 1913 and 1945 with international and national factors embracing global conflicts, economic depression, and declining immigration. Finally, the same analysis would link Calgary's rapid growth after 1947 to its position in the forefront of Canada's burgeoning petroleum and natural gas industry. With these considerations, the history of Calgary will be seen in the light of the frontier experience as it relates to urban life. It is hoped that the uniqueness of Calgary's character and historical experience will unfold as a consequence.

The influence of the frontier manifested itself in three different ways, all of which contributed to Calgary's historical development and urban character. As a police outpost in an untamed wilderness, and later as a small settlement on the outskirts of civilization, Calgary's initial function was to temper the raw harshness of the frontier. By providing social refinements, an opportunity for cultural exchange, and, above all, communication links with the outside world, Calgary filled a role vastly disproportionate to its small size. Even after the frontier era, 1875-1905, Calgary continued to be the social and cultural entrepot to a largely undeveloped and sparsely populated hinterland.

The last 20 years of the 19th century saw the establishment of the second frontier influence, an open range cattle industry in southern Alberta. Calgary emerged as the urban expression of the ranching frontier with all its economic and cultural implications. The interdependence between Calgary and the cattle industry, especially before 1906-1907, was quite remarkable. It was manifested in the town's first manufacturing base, in the erection of elegant sandstone structures financed by ranching capital, but most of all in the growing ethos that symbolized Calgary's self-proclaimed commitment to a romantic but often unstable and always unpredictable industry. The Calgary Stampede, espoused by its strident boosters as the greatest outdoor show on earth, epitomizes the city's enduring attachment to the memory of the ranching frontier. Few Calgarians realize or care that their celebrated Stampede originated in 1912 as a conscious nostalgic memorial to a dying way of life. Instead, the Calgary Stampede provides an annual opportunity for Calgarians to show the world that the legacy of cattle and the old west sets their city apart from others. The link with ranching days is preserved in more permanent ways as well. The white Stetson is Calgary's official emblem; main roads are called trails, while the phrase "good Alberta beef" has taken on a mystical connotation that has little to do with either protein content or dollar value.

But the frontier closed as quickly as it had opened. By 1913 Calgary's phenomenal growth had slowed perceptibly, and a year later, with the outbreak of World War I, the ebullience of the frontier disappeared, leaving in its wake a legacy of piling debts and shattered dreams. For the next 30 years, the ethos of the frontier was scarcely discernible in Calgary's urban life. Governmental restraints and other institutional strictures, combined with prolonged economic adversity, tended to mute the voice of individualism. More significant, however, was the absence of the residual optimism characteristic of the frontier. In its place came a cautious, pragmatic vision of the future. This antithesis of the frontier was consolidated during the Depression of the 1930s when increased government intervention emphasized the collective voice and the uncertainty of individual endeavour. In this sense the "dirty thirties" marked the deepest period in the dormancy of the frontier experience in Calgary.

Calgary's phenomenal growth following the Second World War has been due almost entirely to its position as the headquarters of Canada's vigorous oil and natural gas industry, a third echo of frontier existence. Indeed, it has been Calgary's successful experience in the mining frontier of fossil fuel extraction that has earned for the city its long-envisaged big-city status. The intoxicating appeal of "black gold" first touched Calgarians in May 1914 with the success of the historic Dingman "Discovery Well" at Turner Valley, a few miles southwest of the city. Since that memorable date, Calgary has marched in step with the fortunes of an industry unsurpassed in terms of its economic or emotional impact on individual and national life. The towering skyscrapers that reach into the blue Alberta sky are the most visible indication of Calgary's newfound status as the undisputed financial centre of Western Canada, and a potential rival to the national hegemony traditionally exerted by Montreal and Toronto.

Calgary is a youthful city whose affinity for the outdoors is reinforced by its singular location relative to Canada's most scenic recreational areas. This outdoor ethic has been buttressed materially by its long-standing relationship with two industries associated with the frontier. Furthermore, the traditions of both cattle ranching and oil have many similarities, embracing individualism, volatility, and a thinly veiled contempt for bureaucratic controls. It cannot be denied that Calgary has developed historically in response to the demands, limitations, and opportunities provided by its nonurban hinterland. Nevertheless, the very uniqueness of Calgary's special combination of site and circumstance relative to the frontier has contributed markedly to its distinctive urban character.

Max Foran
Calgary, Alberta

Southern Alberta ranch hands drive a team of greys toward a stack where they will unload their rack of fresh hay, circa 1893. A hay mower lies idle to the right, and behind it a team of bays pulls a two-wheel dump rake. Courtesy, Glenbow-Alberta Institute.

INTRODUCTION

Calgarians are not the most modest people in the world. Like St. Paul when addressing the Romans, they would want everybody to know that they are "citizens of no mean city." Even before the community was incorporated, local leaders were proclaiming confidence in their picturesque site becoming that of a great metropolis.

When there came a rumor of the discovery of a nearby "mountain of iron ore," citizens were sure their town would become "the Pittsburgh of Canada." When Pat Burns built his first slaughterhouse close to the junction of the Elbow and Bow rivers, they could immediately see their city becoming the Canadian counterpart of Chicago in the meat trade, and after the oil discoveries at Leduc, the unfailing Calgary optimists were sure Calgary would emerge as the Houston of the Northwest.

Strikingly enough, the Alberta city did become the Canadian leader its optimistic pioneers envisioned and did it in surprisingly short time. The community that had fewer than 500 residents in 1883 had over half a million 100 years later and was showing no sign of slowing down. Year after year, Calgary had the distinction of being Canada's fastest growing city.

It was small wonder that the distinctive city personality, accompanied by phenomenal growth and development, won admiration and fame. The city's history, marked by numerous triumphs and a few failures, repeated booms and a few "busts," and almost steady progress in spite of setbacks, could not fail to hold interest and inspiration and lessons for those who came later. It is a story with color and romance. In its birth Calgary was a child of the North West Mounted Police and in its adolescence it was the frontier city of ranchers and cowboys.

When it undertook to perpetuate the spirit of the range, which was so prevalent in its early years, the city made the Calgary Stampede into a rangeland classic enjoying international attention. When Calgarians celebrated their 100th anniversary, it was with typical Calgary flourish, revealing true pride in their achievements and history, their good fortune in location near the Rocky Mountains and other great natural playgrounds, their rich gifts in Chinook winds, and abundant supplies of mountain water and scenery. They would not forget to point to the conspicuous monuments celebrating their achievements in the new Calgary skyline.

The unusually rich story was too good to be lost. It had to be recorded and shared with readers of this and future generations. Nobody was better qualified to capture that city history and present it in highly readable form than Dr. Maxwell Foran, who had previously elected to conduct the essential research and write his doctoral thesis in the same general area. May I add my personal gratitude for his efforts and to the publishers who wanted to prepare and present this book to the public.

Grant MacEwan
Calgary, Alberta

PART I
THE FIRST FRONTIER: 1850 - 1914

CHAPTER ONE
FUR TRADING AND MISSIONARIES

For centuries the vastness of Western Canada was home only to the Indian who fished the innumerable lakes, trapped in the cold fur-bearing streams, and hunted the shaggy buffalo of the plains. By the 17th century, this pristine existence had been disturbed by European penetration, as French and English fur traders extended their influence across the northern expanses, seeking the luxuriant pelts highly prized by fashion-conscious Europeans. They had reached the Great Divide by the end of the 18th century, and had established a trading network that used the vast river highways of the Great Northwest. By comparison, the short grass country of the southern plains remained largely undisturbed.

There were two main reasons for the fur traders' relative disenchantment with the south. First, with decreased fur potential of southern waterways compared with more northerly streams, commercial penetration into the southern plains had proven both tenuous and impermanent. In 1809, the North West Company had established Chesterfield House near the confluence of the Red Deer and South Saskatchewan rivers. Some time later, probably in the late 1820s or early 1830s, the Hudson's Bay Company built a post on the Bow River about 50 miles west of present-day Calgary. That both posts were subsequently abandoned was not due entirely to their relative unprofitability. The menacing presence of the warlike and unpredictable Blackfoot Indians added an emotional dimension to the more rational economic arguments for the abandonment of the short grass country.

The Blackfoot Confederacy consisted of five distinct Indian groups, each with its own tribal organization and structure. The last major Indian body of the interior to confront the white man, the Blackfoot was a formidable adversary. According to contemporary comment, the Blackfoot was considered more intelligent and therefore less pliable than other Indian tribes. Their tribal discipline was complemented by the mobility afforded them through their possession of the horse. Indeed, their reputation as fighting horsemen had no peer in

THE IMPORTANCE OF THE FUR TRADE

It would be almost impossible to overemphasize the importance of the fur trade in Canada's development before Confederation. During the French regime, and for a couple of generations after the British conquest of 1763, the trade for furs was the staple of the colony's economy. First the French and then the British, with their well-organized companies, probed the streams for the exotic pelts that had suddenly become fashionable, especially among the European hat makers.

The fur traders were responsible for setting the first settlement and exploration patterns. Traders pushed out from Hudson's Bay after 1670, and into the country north and west of the Great Lakes, forever seeking fresh sources and new routes. Anthony Henday saw the Rockies in 1754 and the Pacific four years later, all well before the famous American continental crossing by the Lewis and Clark expedition.

Though the leaders of the Hudson's Bay Company and the North West Company did take some measures to encourage small-scale agriculture around their posts, the fur traders generally fostered a pessimistic view of the harsh land they had entered. Well into the 19th century, the prevailing belief that Western Canada, or Rupert's Land as it was more commonly known, was unfit for anything but the fur trade held sway in the minds of colonial politicians. Indeed, Sir George Simpson, powerful governor of the Hudson's Bay Company, told a British Royal Commission in 1857 that the West should be left forever to the trapper and trader. In this respect, one cannot deny that Canadian reluctance to purchase Rupert's Land from the Hudson's Bay Company in 1869 for $300,000 was partly linked to a belief in the limited potential of the area.

The fur trade revealed the role of the Indians in a different light from the unhappy state we usually associate with their dealings with white men. Historians have shown how the Indians were conscious of their strong position as middlemen, and were thus not the mere savage pawns of predatory whites. Under the strong central authority of the two big fur trading companies, the Indian was eased into the white man's economic ways over a long period of time. Furthermore, the interaction between white and Indian in the fur trade led to intermarriage and the birth of the Metis people of Canada. The degradation and exploitation of the Indian belonged later—to the 19th century when the influence of the big centralized companies had given way to the depredations of less scrupulous private, often illegal, traders.

In a way it is a pity that the fur trade has not figured more prominently in developing a national folklore. The fur traders' stupendous feats of endurance, and their colourful life-styles, form the stuff from which legends are made. The fur traders were the first Europeans to come to grips with a vast new land on its own terms. They made little attempt to tame or change it. They spread themselves across the northern reaches of Canada like a giant hand, and in doing so made an imprint more uniquely Canadian than the beaver they sought.

Facing page, top: *Indians dressed in their ceremonial best don fur and skin clothing, as well as white men's cloth garments. Ceremonial suede and leather garments were frequently decorated with beautiful beadwork and embroidery. Courtesy, Glenbow-Alberta Institute.*

Bottom: *Men operate a Hudson's Bay Company fur press. Furs were compressed so they could be packed into compact, firm bundles that could be transported more easily to Eastern markets. Courtesy, Glenbow-Alberta Institute.*

After the Indians acquired horses in the 18th century, they adapted them for hunting, and the Metis people became experts in hunting from horses. The buffalo hunt was conducted as a huge annual or semiannual community event, in which the settlers and Metis cooperated. George Catlin depicted one such exciting event in Buffalo Hunt, Chase. *Courtesy, Glenbow-Alberta Institute.*

the Canadian experience. Furthermore they nursed an implacable enmity toward the northern Crees who traditionally had functioned as the chief middlemen for the big fur trading companies. For centuries, these proud warriors of the plains had lived by the buffalo hunt, pursuing the shaggy monarch of the plains in a life-style as unrestricted as the sea of grass that stretched westward to the Rocky Mountains. The Blackfoot Confederacy was at the height of its power in the first quarter of the 19th century, before the ravages of smallpox and the social evils of white depredation decimated their ranks and humbled their proud spirit.

Actual visitations by white men to the Calgary area before 1850 were both sparse and poorly documented. Records reveal that as early as 1787 fur traders from both of the great fur trading rivals, the Hudson's Bay Company and the North West Company, had traversed the Bow River country in their restless search for new sources and mountain routes to the Pacific. Yet even then such visitations were rare and sporadic. In his historic journey in 1754, which resulted in a view of the Rocky Mountains, Anthony Henday of the Hudson's Bay Company passed well to the north of Calgary. Peter Fidler of the same company only skirted the Calgary region in his foray into southern Alberta in 1792. Credit for being the first white man to set foot on Calgary's eventual site is usually given to David Thompson, the accomplished car-

tographer and intrepid employee of the North West Company. In 1787, Thompson wintered in an Indian encampment on the Bow River near Calgary. According to Thompson, the river was named because of the species of yew nearby that afforded excellent wood for Indian weapons. Fourteen years later Thompson was back in Blackfoot country. After crossing the Bow near Calgary, Thompson made his way to the country of the Highwood River to the south and west before returning to his base at Rocky Mountain House. He was never to return to the Calgary area again.

It seems fitting that this brief discussion of Calgary's prehistory should contain a dose of local apocrypha. References in certain French journals and memoirs of the colonial period attest to the establishment of a Fort La Jonquiere or Des Prairies by French fur traders in 1751. This spot supposedly marked the most westerly penetration of French fur trading activity, and was reputed to have been erected at the foot of the Rocky Mountains near where Calgary stands today. Credence for a possible Calgary location of Fort La Jonquiere comes from three quarters. First, the Bow River was mentioned in contemporary French notations. Second, the governor of New France, the Marquis De La Jonquiere, had issued instructions that a post be erected 300 leagues west of the fort located near where La Pas, Manitoba, is today. Finally, in 1875, following the establishment of Fort Calgary, Inspector Ephrem Brisebois

Frederic Remington sketched Indians trading at a Hudson's Bay Company store with a North West Mounted Policeman in the background. Hudson's Bay Company established a post on the Bow River in the late 1820s-early 1830s. Courtesy, Glenbow-Alberta Institute.

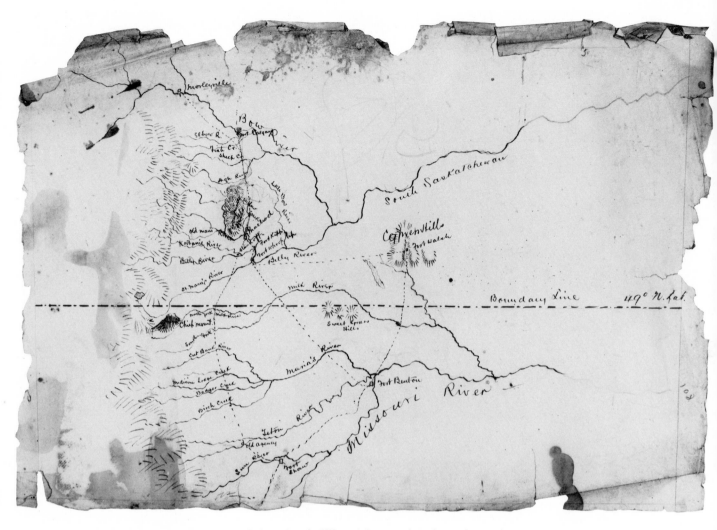

North West Mounted Police artist R.B. Nevitt made this unique map showing Calgary's geographical location relative to the United States, rather than to the rest of Canada. Courtesy, Glenbow-Alberta Institute.

of the North West Mounted Police claimed to have discovered the ruins of Fort La Jonquiere.

The story of Fort La Jonquiere at Calgary, however, is easier to dispel than prove. Historians agree that had such a fort been established in Blackfoot country, mention of it would have emerged in subsequent dialogue with the Indians. The fact that no reference or hint of such a fort has been gleaned from later traders' and missionary recollections is evidence of its non-existence. The Indians, it appears, loved to revel in wild and fanciful stories, and could not have failed to report something as exciting as a crumbling relic of the white man's past. The decaying logs discovered by Brisebois were scarcely more than 20 years old and were in all probability the remains of a hastily built American trading post. Finally, Professor Arthur Silver Morton, long regarded as the most reliable source on fur trading routes, has concluded that if Fort La Jonquiere was actually established, it was probably just west of Fort La Corne near present-day Kinistino, Saskatchewan. Certainly it is possible that the wild and venturesome French fur traders reached Alberta before the middle of the 18th century. Conclusive evidence, however, is lacking, and for the present at least, David Thompson stands undisputed as Calgary's first European visitor.

Following the amalgamation of the North West Company into the Hudson's Bay Company in 1821, the business of the fur trade became more effi-

CANADA

POSTES
5¢
POSTAGE

DAVID
THOMPSON
1770 — 1857

David Thompson, considered to have been the first European to visit Calgary, is depicted with a map of Western Canada on this Canadian postage stamp designed by G.A. Gunderson of Ottawa. The stamp was engraved and printed in sheets of two hundred. Courtesy, Glenbow-Alberta Institute.

cient and selective. The southern plains did not figure in the newly centralized operations of an increasingly expensive and limited industry. The result was a 30-year reprieve for the Indian and the buffalo, both of whom continued to congregate in the beautiful Bow River valley, their pristine existence undisturbed and seemingly not threatened by the world outside.

Between 1850 and 1870, several factors led to a renewed interest in the southern prairies and ultimately to the permanent arrival of the white man. The first set of forces may be described broadly as imperial in nature, as it was basically a change of attitude on the part of Great Britain that led to a new role for Western Canada. The second was more economic, and involved the emergence of a market in the United States for buffalo robes and wolf skins.

Essentially, all of the Canadian Northwest, including Manitoba, Saskatchewan, Alberta, and British Columbia, had been under the jurisdiction of the Hudson's Bay Company since 1670. Known as Rupert's Land, this vast, forbidding area was considered of little value commercially except as a source of furs. As late as 1857, Sir George Simpson, all-powerful governor of the Hudson's Bay Company, told a select committee of the British House of Commons that it was highly unlikely that Western Canada would ever be successfully converted to agriculture. Simpson's claim was borne out in part by an expedition to Western Canada led by Captain John Palliser. Palliser's expedition was basically a fact-finding mission, and indicated, if nothing else, Great Britain's changing attitude towards the Northwest. In any case, Palliser's journeys occupied three years, 1857-59, and were sufficiently diverse and scientific to enable the preparation of a comprehensive report on the agricultural, mineral, and economic potential of Western Canada. Palliser's conclusions on the plains area were inescapably pessimistic. According to Palliser, the region embraced by southern Alberta and southwest Saskatchewan was of marginal arable value and could never be converted to successful agriculture or commercial enterprise.

The British interest in Rupert's Land did not diminish despite the negativism of Palliser and the fur traders. The emergence of the North Pacific as a focal point of international interest placed Western Canada in a strategic position. The discovery of gold in California and British Columbia, the opening of Japan to the western world, the Russian drive for a year-round seaport at Vladivostok, the "Manifest Destiny" doctrine of the dynamic and potentially dangerous United States were all factors that worried Britain's astute senior government officials. The presence of the Americans was particularly disquieting. The westward movement of the American frontier was well under way

Captain John Palliser (left) explored Western Canada in 1857-1859, accompanied by Sir James Hector (right). Courtesy, Glenbow-Alberta Institute.

THE PALLISER EXPEDITION, 1857 - 1859

The Palliser expedition was a British-sponsored enterprise that explored the vast region between Lake Superior and the Pacific Ocean from 1857 to 1859. Though its leader was a dashing young Irish adventurer, the expedition itself was scientifically oriented with specific duties to map the region, examine possible transportation routes, and assess agricultural and mineral potential. It was the first of its kind to enter Western Canada, and in a way typified the fruitful blend of 19th century adventurism with an emerging interest in scientific field observations.

The expedition was the brainchild of a wealthy Irish landowner, John Palliser, who in an earlier visit to the American West had become fascinated by the wild environment of the Great Plains. Palliser in many ways exemplified the brilliant amateur adventurer of mid-Victorian Britain. His versatility was astounding, and he was both courageous and passionately enthusiastic for stirring pursuits of knowledge. He persuaded the Royal Geographic Society to back him in what he hoped was to be a one-man information-gathering mission to British North America.

The Geographic Society was impressed with Palliser's credentials and enthusiasm, but felt that individuals with specific scientific expertise should accompany him. Accordingly, a geologist, botanist, astronomical observer, and magnetic observer were added to form the Palliser expedition. Financial government support was solicited from the Colonial Office, which, fortunately

Fur traders traveled through Western Canada, where fur-bearing animals such as beaver could be found in ample supply. From Horace Martin, Castorologia, 1892. Courtesy, Glenbow-Alberta Institute.

for Palliser, was headed at the time by men interested both in scientific observations and in an all-British route in North America from the Atlantic to the Pacific.

The daily record of the various journeys was kept faithfully by Palliser himself or by his geologist-doctor, James Hector. The journal provides fascinating reading, replete with innumerable facts and adventurous accounts. Wildlife behaviour, Indian life, changing scenery, not to mention mishaps, are described in a lively narrative, particularly by Palliser, who wrote quite well.

The findings of the expedition deserve mention. Hector's geological observations were extraordinarily accurate, and laid the basis for future geological surveys. Palliser was enthusiastic about the agricultural merits of the Red Deer and Saskatchewan river valleys. He was pessimistic, however, about the agricultural potential of the most arid section of the plains known as "Palliser's Triangle." He also foresaw difficulties with the Indians and half-breeds pending white settlement. Time proved him right on both counts. On the merits of the transportation route, Palliser stressed that adverse geographical factors would make it extremely difficult if not impossible to construct a transcontinental railroad without entering American territory.

The Palliser Report was published in 1863 and presented to the British House of Commons, where it received scant interest or attention. Few British politicians were interested in Western Canada; and the report was altogether too formidable and contained too much dry information for quick reading. The saga of wolves and grizzly bears, dangerous river crossings and tortuous mountain trails, buffalo stampedes and physical privation was locked away in the pages of a bulky blue book where it would long gather the dust of neglect.

Sir James Hector accompanied the Palliser expedition as Palliser's principal assistant. Although he was trained for medicine, his interests lay primarily in geology and biology. Courtesy, Glenbow-Alberta Institute.

and would be consolidated by a transcontinental railroad by 1869. Britain doubted its ability to withstand a potential northern movement of the American frontier to embrace the grain-growing areas of Manitoba or the mineral resources of British Columbia. Britain's solution was to consolidate Rupert's Land by disengaging it from the Hudson's Bay Company and incorporating it into the nascent nation of Canada. Throughout the 1860s, therefore, Great Britain was very active in promoting the cause of confederation and the subsequent inclusion of the Northwest into the new nation. In 1867, Canadian nationhood was achieved, and two years later a somewhat reluctant Canadian government yielded to British pressure and ensured true continental sovereignty when it purchased Rupert's Land from the Hudson's Bay Company for £300,000. By 1869, Rupert's Land, or the great Northwest, had become in actual fact, Western Canada.

Historical judgement has been largely positive on the role of the big fur trading companies, particularly with respect to Indian relations. The strong centrallizing character of the Hudson's Bay Company and the North West Company produced consistent and generally fair policies. Conservative in temper, and ultimately pragmatic in their operations, the senior resident fur

The Last of the Buffalo by famous "cowboy artist" Charles Russell depicts plains Indians seated in front of their tepee with buffalo bones scattered nearby. Courtesy, Glenbow-Alberta Institute.

traders realized only too well the fragility of their position and their interdependence with the Indians. While the presence of the fur traders produced some social dislocation among the Indian tribes, and indeed irrevocably transformed certain aspects of Indian life, there was little of the shocking impact that accompanied the arrival of a much different breed of trader to southern Alberta in the 1860s.

After 1860, traders from Montana began their incursions into the hunting grounds of the Blackfoot, lured on by the promise of a lucrative profit from the resale of wolf and, particularly, buffalo hides. Some were legitimate entrepreneurs like the I.G. Baker Company, which established permanent operations at Fort Benton, Montana, as early as 1855. Indeed, the westward extension of the railroad into the American West made it more expedient for the fur trading posts in northern Alberta to secure their supplies from the United States rather than by way of the traditional, but often tortuously slow, river highway system. Throughout the 1860s, the familiar sight of oxen and Red River carts moving north from Fort Benton to Edmonton was a clear indication that the old east-west route of voyageur canoes and portages had been replaced by an overland north-south axis.

The Calgary-Edmonton stagecoach made its five-day trip once a week. The fare each way was $25, and a passenger could take up to one hundred pounds of baggage. Courtesy, Glenbow-Alberta Institute.

Of far more significance than the legitimate traders were the less scrupulous adventurers who put the cause of a quick profit above any moral considerations. These were the infamous whisky traders who plied their heinous trade from a string of illegal posts erected throughout southern Alberta, where, safe from the less than vigilant eyes of the American law, they freely sold vile alcoholic concoctions to the eager Blackfoot in exchange for the readily marketable buffalo robes. The largest post, appropriately named Fort Whoop-Up, was situated between the Belly and St. Mary rivers about 12 miles from today's Lethbridge. Other posts included Stand-Off, on the Belly River southwest of Whoop-Up, and Slide-Out, a few miles down the Belly. Fort Kipp was near the mouth of the Oldman River. Other smaller posts were situated on Sheep Creek and the Highwood River, while the colourful Fred Kanouse had a post on the Elbow River within the corporate limits of present-day Calgary.

The whisky traders had few illusions about their precarious position among the Indians. Their posts were strongly fortified where possible. Fort Whoop-Up, strategically located between two streams, bore the high stockades and bastions of a defensive outpost. With its huge cottonwood pallisades, high windows, low earth roofs, barred chimneys, brass warning bell, two ancient muzzle-loading cannon, and distinctive flag, Whoop-Up represented a crude parallel to the fortified posts that marked the American presence in Indian country.

The whisky traders clearly were convinced of the need to subjugate the Indians through intimidation. Aside from their menacing posts, the traders employed a motley cavalry of wolf hunters who supplemented their trade by acting as roving troubleshooters among the Indians. This determination to cow the Indians led to individual acts of terrorism and finally culminated in the Cyprus Hills massacre of 1872, in which some 30 Assiniboine Indians were killed and mutilated by a gang of whisky traders seeking vengeance for acts of horse stealing.

Right: *Fort Whoop-Up, located a few miles from present-day Lethbridge, was considered the whisky traders' capital until the trade in firewater with the Indians was suppressed when the NWMP came to the area in 1874. Courtesy, Glenbow-Alberta Institute.*

Facing page, top: *Indians clad in blankets and moccasins pose in 1881 at Fort Whoop-Up, an interesting log structure. Courtesy, Glenbow-Alberta Institute.*

Throughout the 1860s and early 1870s, the unbridled presence of the whisky traders in southern Alberta contributed to the economic and moral degeneration of the plains Indian. In this respect, the Cyprus Hills massacre provided the final impetus in prompting a reaction from the newly formed Canadian government. The result was the organization of the North West Mounted Police in 1873, whose arrival in the west a year later effectively ended the whisky traders' depredations and heralded a new era on the Canadian frontier.

The whisky trade depended for its existence chiefly on the buffalo robe industry, which flourished as the prime economic sector of the southern plains between 1860 and 1878. The latter year is particularly significant, as it marked the virtual disappearance of "the shaggy one" from Western Canada. For centuries the buffalo had been the staple of Indian life, providing him with food, clothing, shelter, and even weapons, in short all the necessities of his livelihood. The numbers of buffalo were thought to be limitless. Contemporary accounts refer to dark seas of rustling bodies stretching as far as the eye could see. One observer as late as 1875 wrote of seeing a herd of half a million or more a few miles west of Calgary. The boundary survey party in 1874 noted how on two occasions the freight waggons had to be bunched together as closely as possible with everyone remaining for several hours to permit the buffalo to pass. Estimates of total numbers are, of course, extremely subjective, but it is probable that when the white hunter appeared on the scene, as many as 50 million head roamed the western plains. The large-scale slaughter of these magnificent beasts began around 1860 and continued to their near extermination less than 20 years later. A good hunter was expected to kill about 2,500 buffalo a season. In some years as many as 4,000 and upwards were killed by a single hunter. In 1875 the I.G. Baker Company alone shipped 250,000 robes to the United States. The trade was certainly lucrative; hunters received between 50 cents and one dollar per skin, which was re-sold by middlemen for five dollars, and so the price escalated. Scarcely a voice was raised to protest the slaughter, which was partly rationalized on the grounds that the Indians would never really accept the reservation system as long as they could follow the buffalo.

Below: *A Hudson's Bay Company train of Red River carts laden with $75,000 worth of furs stops in Calgary in 1888. The all-wood vehicles were popular and advertised their presence by a loud screeching noise from their greaseless axles. Courtesy, Glenbow-Alberta Institute.*

Facing page: *Millions of bison inhabited the prairie until the late 1870s, after which they came close to total extinction. Happily, a remnant was saved and the biggest wild herd has been bred inside park fences at Wainwright. Various other small park herds were established from the Wainwright bison, including these animals at Banff. Courtesy, National Film Board.*

BUFFALO BONES

Strangely enough, economic interest in the buffalo did not disappear with their demise. In the 1880s a new and profitable enterprise enabled many a homesteader to supplement his meagre income. The bleached bones of the innumerable carcasses half-buried in the shifting soils of the plains suddenly assumed a marketable significance. With this new awareness the buffalo-bone trade was born.

The bone trade actually began in the early 1880s in the United States, and by 1883 had spread to Canada. Soon thousands of tons of bones were being shipped from various railway points in Saskatchewan and Alberta to the United States, where they were used in the fertilizer industry and for bleaching purposes. With a ton of bones bringing between $6.00 and $8.00, the trade invited widespread participation on both a large and small scale. Many original homesteaders bought food and accumulated the capital for farm implements through the sale of buffalo bones. In the towns and cities, local businessmen turned a tidy profit as commission agents for large American companies. Large-scale pickers with basket racks and horse teams often hauled up to 2,500 pounds per trip.

Buffalo jumps were a particularly good source of bones. These jumps were in coulees where Indians stampeded the buffalo to their deaths, and were veritable graveyards. A good buffalo jump might yield between 40 and 50 tons of bones.

It is difficult to estimate the total volume of trade in Western Canada. According to one approximation, over 3,000 carloads of bones were shipped from Saskatoon alone. Considering the fact that each carload contained about 20 tons, this would represent the skeletal remains of some 750,000 buffalo.

The bone trade reached its peak in the early 1890s, but by 1893 the depressed conditions that gripped North America generally had their inevitable effects on this popular and profitable rural pastime. Also, the bones were becoming more difficult to find and transport easily, and as a result the farmers came less and less to trade them for groceries. As for the buffalo bones, time has taken its toll. They lie buried and forgotten, and if unearthed are, at best, of passing interest to all but the avid collector.

Below left: *Buffalo bones comprised the first harvest to bring cash returns for many prairie homesteaders. Buffalo had almost completely disappeared by 1880, leaving no trace of their numbers except the bones for which industrial uses were found. Courtesy, Glenbow-Alberta Institute.*

Below right: *Buffalo bones were piled up for loading on Canadian Pacific Railway boxcars in the late 1800s. The buffalo-bone trade flourished throughout the West following the extermination of the mammoth beasts, and many early settlers supplemented their incomes by engaging in the bone trade. Courtesy, Glenbow-Alberta Institute.*

Pupils of the Calgary Indian Industrial School pose in 1907. Industrial schools for young Indians were part of a federal government policy aimed at bringing young natives into the new society. Courtesy, Glenbow-Alberta Institute.

Aside from the whisky trader and his legitimate counterpart, and buffalo and wolf hunters, few other white men had come to the valley of the Bow and Elbow rivers by 1875. By that year, two missions had been established in the area to minister to the spiritual and often physical needs of the Indian. Father Albert Lacombe, an Oblate missionary who first came to work among the Crees at St. Albert near Edmonton, moved south to be with the Blackfoot in early 1857. The reputation earned by this remarkable man was incredible, both in terms of his success in Christianizing the Indians, and in the profound influence he exerted over them. By 1875, his Mission of Our Lady of Peace on the Elbow River west of Calgary, with its three priests and lay brother, was the centre of the Roman Catholic Church in southern Alberta.

Also active among the Indians were the Methodists. The Reverend George McDougall had established the Victoria Mission near Edmonton in 1863, and in 1872 his son John was sent to the southwest. In 1873 he and his bride came to the Morley Flats on the Bow River 50 miles west of Calgary. Over the years the Reverend John McDougall laboured long and hard among the Stony Indians at Morleyville. Like Father Lacombe, his name became synonymous with frontier Christianity and, like his Catholic colleague, the Reverend John McDougall became an outspoken observer of western life and a keen critic of government policies detrimental to the well-being of his beloved native people.

ROBERT TERRILL RUNDLE: EARLY MISSIONARY IN WESTERN CANADA

Calgarians are familiar with the name Rundle. It is a suburb in northeast Calgary, and the name of one of Alberta's best known and most identifiable mountains. Calgary's first public hospital bore the name Rundle Lodge in the twilight of its existence. The man Robert Rundle is less well-known, and though not relevant to Calgary specifically, the story of this modest missionary in many ways typifies the trials of the frontier churchman more than the successful exploits of the McDougalls or the Lacombes.

The missionary followed the fur trader into the wilderness of Western Canada. Initially at least, the churchmen were restless souls who laboured haphazardly to bring the message of Christianity to the heathen savage. Robert Rundle was one such pioneer. Though this young Wesleyan minister came to Fort Edmonton in 1840 as a Hudson's Bay Company chaplain, he also acted as an itinerant preacher, bringing the word of God to the scattered Blackfoot and Cree Indian tribes. But after eight long and difficult years, Rundle had little to show for his efforts beyond frustration, official disapproval, and a few scattered converts. His well-kept journal reveals with startling clarity the vicissitudes facing the pioneer missionary in Western Canada.

The image of the missionary as superhuman spiritual athlete was very real in this period, especially among the Indians, who regarded ministers with awe. Consequently, an imposing physical appearance and authoritative demeanour were considerable assets. Unfortunately for Rundle he possessed neither. His youthful features belied his 30-odd years, and in his eagerness to bring God to the Indians, he threw off the mantle of clerical sedateness. Furthermore, he liked to laugh and indulge in frivolous conversation with Indians and other social "inferiors." His natural humility resulted in social indiscretions that had little place in the hierarchical structure of a Hudson's Bay Company trading post.

Chief factor John Rowand was not uncritical of Rundle's efforts at Fort Edmonton. Rowand himself was a tough, gregarious Irishman, a man totally in his element in directing a business operation among a primitive people in an isolated wilderness. He felt that Rundle's approach was all wrong. Against Rowand's advice, Rundle persisted in leaving the post for months at a time visiting far-flung Indian encampments. The merits of these visits were doubtful, particularly in the early days when Rundle was ignorant of Indian dialects and had to work through temperamental and unreliable interpreters. In 1841 for example, on a visit to a Blackfoot camp, Rundle was prevented from holding service by an uncooperative interpreter. The incident greatly embarrassed Rundle and did much to undermine the Indians' confidence in him as a missionary.

Rundle's chief asset was his boundless zeal. He cheerfully endured terrible privations on his many journeys. Periodically, he traveled for weeks in the depths of an Alberta winter in a dog travois, seeking out an isolated Indian camp. He was never sure of his reception; while on some occasions he was greeted joyously, sometimes he faced indifference or downright hostility, especially if the Roman Catholic priests had preceded him. The rivalry between the Protestant and Catholic missionaries for Indian souls was an unfortunate aspect of the Christian presence in Western Canada. Each viewed the other's efforts to Christianize Indians with contempt.

Probably Robert Rundle was unsuccessful in achieving what he hoped for in his eight years in Western Canada. His journal entries reveal his frustrations quite clearly. Yet one wonders whether any missionary labouring in this period experienced any greater measure of success. The giants of missionary endeavour, the McDougalls and Father Lacombe, came more than a generation later when the focus of church activity depended less on itinerancy and the fur trade. It is perhaps appropriate that Rundle's memory is best preserved in a mountain that bears his name, or that his most enduring contribution should be the valuable journal in which he faithfully chronicled his lonely quest in the name of God.

... But let the dew descend in copious streams into my poor parched soul .... Is it faith I want, or what is the cause? Stay, thou insulted spirit, stay. Though I've done thee such despite. Cast me not from thy Presence, O Lord, nor take thy Holy Spirit from me. March 1, 1845.

In the 1840s the Reverend Robert T. Rundle, shown with his wife, laboured with little success to Christianize Indians in the Edmonton area. A Calgary suburb and a mountain peak now carry his name. Courtesy, Glenbow-Alberta Institute.

John Glenn came from Ireland and crossed the United States by waggon train. As a gold-seeker, Glenn participated in the rush on Fraser River. He traveled eastward from there over the mountains to Fort Edmonton and then to Fish Creek (later Midnapore), where he served as postmaster and was an active pioneer farmer. He reached the Calgary area just before the North West Mounted Police arrived to build Fort Calgary. Courtesy, Glenbow-Alberta Institute.

By 1875 there were at least two individuals who believed that the Bow River valley could be used for successful agriculture. Two bewhiskered Irishmen, Sam Livingstone and John Glenn, were both years ahead of their time. The former grew fruit trees on his farm, now covered by the Glenmore Reservoir, while John Glenn successfully used the waters of Fish Creek to irrigate crops on his farm at Midnapore. Livingstone and Glenn arrived in the Calgary area to begin squatting in 1873 and 1875, respectively. They were both colourful characters who in previous years had lived the life of footloose adventurers, seeking gold in California, and brushing death on more than one occasion. In a sense, their lonely yet self-reliant and imaginative efforts in farming the virgin soil symbolized the genesis of Calgary's later corporate ethos.

So while there was no Calgary at the beginning of 1875, the area seemed ready for settlement. For generations, the Indians and animals had been drawn to the Bow and Elbow rivers by the promise of fresh water and shelter. Similarly the white man, too, seemed attracted to the region. The presence of Fred Kanouse's whisky post, Father Lacombe's mission, the farms of Sam Livingstone and John Glenn were indications that this verdant valley was a natural place for man to congregate. All that was needed was an act of fate, some physical phenomenon that would bring things together in permanence. The North West Mounted Police, already ensconced at Fort Macleod by the winter of 1874-1875, were soon to provide the necessary catalyst.

Left: *John Glenn, one of the first two farmers in the Calgary district, should be remembered as the first irrigator in the country for taking water from Fish Creek to irrigate the flat land by his ranch. Like his contemporary and friend, Sam Livingstone, he arrived before the NWMP. Courtesy, Glenbow-Alberta Institute.*

Below: *In about 1882 the Marquis of Lorne sketched this view from a hill near Fort Calgary. From Picturesque Canada. Courtesy, Glenbow-Alberta Institute.*

THE FIRST FRONTIER

CHAPTER TWO
THE NORTH WEST MOUNTED POLICE

The role of the North West Mounted Police in easing the way for the orderly settlement of the Canadian West has been well documented in both academic and popular historical works. Indeed, the scarlet-coated Mountie has become associated with efficient law enforcement over the years and has earned a worldwide reputation for fairness and integrity. As the actual founders of Calgary, the North West Mounted Police rightly deserve a special place in the city's history. However, it should be added that these men were more than the mere originators of the corporate entity now known as the city of Calgary. Just as they left an indelible mark on the social and cultural fabric of southern Alberta, their influence also modified and even redefined the urban character of frontier Calgary.

North West Mounted Police arrest whisky traders in this drawing by noted Western artist Charles Russell. From Forty Pen and Ink Drawings, 1947. Courtesy, Glenbow-Alberta Institute.

The North West Mounted Police came into being in 1873 as the brainchild of Canada's founding statesman, John A. Macdonald. Macdonald had perceived the need for a special type of paramilitary force with the judicial authority to bring law and order to the Canadian West and end the infamous regime of the whisky traders. Concern was also felt over the Indians and over the necessity of controlling them while preparing the way for eventual settlement. Also, Macdonald was forever sensitive to the potential threat posed by Canada's aggressive neighbour, and doubtless felt that the possibility of

unrestrained American expansion northward over the 49th parallel would in large part be thwarted by the presence of a truly Canadian armed force.

The force was recruited in Eastern Canada in the fall and winter of 1873-1874. By the summer of 1874, it had assembled at Fort Dufferin, Manitoba, under Lieutenant Colonel George A. French and was ready for the march west to the Rocky Mountains. On July 8, 1874, some 275 men in six troops, each identified by the colour of its horses, began their 900-mile trek. Spread over five miles, the cavalcade of men, horses, and waggons battled the summer heat, dust, flies, mosquitoes, grasshoppers, prairie fires, and short rations. Luckily, however, the expected encounters with unfriendly Sioux or other Indians did not materialize. By the middle of September, the force was in the foothills with the exception of one troop that had turned north to Fort Edmonton. Drenched by rain and sleet, and hampered by hunger, fatigue, and starving animals, the straggling troops were close to exhaustion when they reached the haven of the Sweet Grass Hills. After a short rest, B, C, and F troops under Colonel James Macleod were directed to seek out Fort Whoop-Up. Finding the fort abandoned, they followed the advice of their half-breed guide, Jerry Potts, and proceeded to a sweeping arm of the Oldman River, where, on a

Top: Six Months in the Wilds of the Northwest: The Start from Fort Dufferin *by artist Henri Julien shows the general chaos of the Mounted Police's departure from Fort Dufferin, Manitoba, in July 1874, when they started their 900-mile trek to what would become Fort Macleod in Western Canada. Courtesy, Glenbow-Alberta Institute.*

Bottom: *Most of the rookie Mounted Policemen and their horses left Toronto in two special trains on June 6, 1874, to travel West by way of Chicago and St. Paul. Special arrangements were made with the U.S. authorities to travel the American route with the understanding that the policemen would not be wearing their uniforms and that their guns would be sealed. Drawings by Henri Julien. Courtesy, Glenbow-Alberta Institute.*

THE NORTH WEST MOUNTED POLICE AND THE INDIAN

When the North West Mounted Police came to Western Canada, the surveillance and protection of the Indian was one of their chief mandates. Considering the many sad bloodbaths that marked Indian encounters with the American law, one can well appreciate the success of the North West Mounted Police in maintaining a peaceful frontier.

Part of the reason for the Mounties' success in Indian relations lay in their system of small patrols and interaction with the most respected Indian chiefs. One has only to note the sensitive relationship between Inspector James Morrow Walsh and the renegade Sitting Bull of the Sioux to realize that the bonds of empathy bridged the gulf created by race and culture. Following the Custer massacre in 1876, Sitting Bull and his warriors crossed into Canadian territory, leaving the cream of the Sioux nation amid the bodies of the American Seventh Cavalry. Canadian authorities were alarmed at Sitting Bull's presence among the volatile Canadian tribes. Their fears proved unfounded. Inspector Walsh at Fort Walsh in the Cyprus Hills handled the potentially explosive situation by gaining Sitting Bull's confidence and respect, and as long as he was on Canadian soil, Sitting Bull honoured the wishes of the colourful, tempestuous Mountie. For his part, Walsh respected the conquered warrior and in many ways could sympathize with the Sioux's hopeless cause.

Crowfoot of the Blackfoot was another who welcomed and respected the Police. Though his high opinion of them did diminish somewhat over the years, Crowfoot held to the opinion that the "scarlet coats" were generally just and tolerant in their enforcement of the "Great White Mother's" wishes.

The Mounted Police were not afraid to employ bravado to make a point with the Indians. One such incident occurred at Calgary in November 1880, when some 500 starving Sarcee Indians, under their recalcitrant chief, Bull's Head, descended on Fort Calgary demanding winter rations. For some days they terrorized the settlement, firing shots and uttering threats of violence and

Crowfoot addresses Colonel Macleod (seated) and Governor Laird (seated, in civilian dress) on the Blackfoot Treaty of 1877. Painting by A. Bruce Stapleton. Courtesy, Glenbow-Alberta Institute.

pillage. Until the arrival of 30 reinforcements under Inspector Cecil Denny, the four resident Mounties were powerless to act. Subsequent attempts at reason had little effect on the Indians, who stubbornly refused to move. Eventually the Police informed Bull's Head that rations at Fort Calgary were insufficient and that adequate supplies were available at Fort Macleod should the Sarcees agree to trek to a winter camping ground on the Oldman River. With matters at an explosive stalemate, Denny decided to act. After securing the loan of horses and carts to assist a mass removal, he and a fellow officer proceeded to pull down the Sarcee tepees. The bluff worked. After a few tense moments, the Indians agreed to leave, and, accompanied by the Police, made an 11-day journey through intense cold to the proposed winter camp.

The North West Mounted Police also did not make the mistake of enforcing white man's justice with all the rigour the law demanded. Instead, by imposing a double standard—one for Indian and one for white—the police were able to ease the Indian into a more realistic acceptance of foreign standards. Records show that the Indian crime rate remained constant throughout the period 1875-1900, compared with the general level, which rose considerably over the same period.

Finally, one could argue that the Indian would not have accepted the controversial reservation system so easily were it not for the North West Mounted Police, who assured them of the legitimacy of the white man's intentions. But perhaps in this role, the Mounties inadvertently contributed to the decline of a culture they originally came to protect.

Below left: *R.B. Nevitt's sketches, published in 1881, depict life, personalities, and events in the Fort Calgary and Fort Macleod area. Fort Calgary on the Bow River flies its flag above a sketch of tepees at a Blackfoot camp. Courtesy, Glenbow-Alberta Institute.*

Below right: *North West Mounted Police artist R.B. Nevitt sketched vignettes depicting life in Western Canada. In 1881 these scenes of Blackfoot Indians, Fort Macleod, and other Western sights were published. Courtesy, Glenbow-Alberta Institute.*

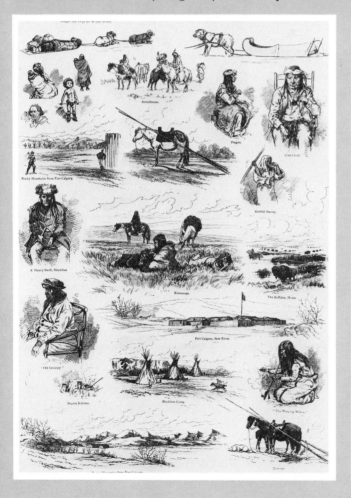

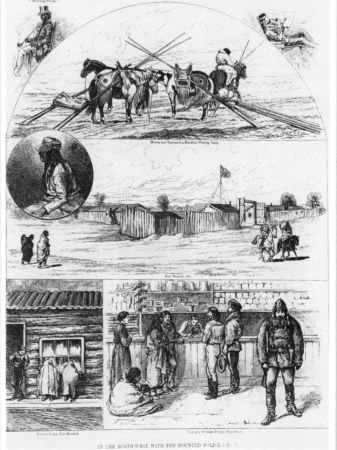

North West Mounted Police dump out illegal whisky in October 1874. Actions such as this soon discouraged the illegal whisky-trading operations that had flourished prior to the arrival of the NWMP. Painting by R.B. Nevitt. Courtesy, Glenbow-Alberta Institute.

brisk October day, the 150 ragged horsemen finally reached the end of their historic trek. With the building of Fort Macleod in the fall of 1874, the North West Mounted Police announced their permanent presence in the Canadian West.

Following the establishment of Fort Macleod, the whisky traders became less brazen in their defiance of the law. Instead, they extended their operations farther into Blackfoot country where they found it easier to evade the police and slip back into American territory unmolested. Fort Calgary was conceived as part of the North West Mounted Police's counterplans to establish a chain of posts in Indian country.

The area around the confluence of the Bow and Elbow, or Swift, rivers was considered ideal for a fort site because Indians were attracted there by the wintering buffalo. Also, the Bow River often did not freeze over completely, and the high river banks afforded excellent protection from the winter winds. In early summer 1875, a Mounted Police guide visited the area, selected a fort site, and marked it by a buffalo robe staked in the ground. (The proposed fort location was in the vicinity of the area currently occupied by the Holy Cross Hospital.)

The mandate to establish Fort Calgary in the late summer of 1875 was given to Inspector Ephrem Brisebois and the men of F Troop, following their

return from the Red Deer River and a meeting with Sir Edward Selby-Smythe, commander in chief of the Canadian Militia Forces. The actual date of F Troop's arrival at the junction of the Bow and Elbow rivers is not known. Pertinent police records have been lost, and none of the later reminiscences refers to a specific date of arrival. It was probably one afternoon in late August or early September when the men of F Troop reached the north hill just east of the present Centre Street Bridge and looked down on the scene below them. Corporal George Clift King, later Calgary's second mayor and longtime postmaster, was dispatched to find a suitable fording place for the 50 men and waggons to cross. King splashed his way across the Bow near the Langevin Bridge area, and in so doing became the first Mounted Policeman to set foot on the original site of Calgary. By evening small tents were pitched beside the Elbow River. The Mounties had arrived.

F Troop of the NWMP stands at attention at Fort Calgary in 1876. Note the upright position of the logs used to construct the buildings. Courtesy, Glenbow-Alberta Institute.

Work on building the permanent fort began almost immediately upon the arrival of the building contractors, the I.G. Baker Company from Fort Benton, Montana. Led by their foreman, D.W. Davis, later Alberta's first representative in the Canadian House of Commons, the Baker men first cut logs upstream and floated them down the Elbow River. These 14-foot pine and spruce logs were placed upright in 3-foot trenches to form a 200-foot square within which were constructed men's quarters, storerooms, blacksmith's shop, stables for 50 horses, officers' quarters, and guardroom. The floors were bare earth; the logs were chinked with clay and the pole roofs were packed down with solid earth. Local half-breeds helped in the wall construction, while the stone fireplaces were built by local squatter John Glenn. By Christmas 1875, Fort Calgary was ready for permanent habitation. The cost of construction to the Canadian government was $2,476.

Dr. R.B. Nevitt, an assistant surgeon with the NWMP on the march West, recorded his impressions of the Northwest in diaries and in paintings, such as this sketch of Fort Calgary on the Bow River. He remained in the force until 1878. Courtesy, Glenbow-Alberta Institute.

Above: *Following his resignation from the force, Colonel James F. Macleod became a judge and lived in Calgary, and the house he occupied still stands in Heritage Park. The marriage of Macleod's daughter to rancher A.E. Cross was the beginning of one of southern Alberta's best-known and widely respected families. Courtesy, Glenbow-Alberta Institute.*

Below right: *Frederic Remington sketched the I.G. Baker and Company store showing an old Indian trading post on the Elbow River constructed out of logs. From* Harper's Weekly, *January 25, 1890.*

Facing page: *William M. Herchmer became a captain in the militia in Winnipeg and then joined the NWMP. In 1881 he led the police detachment that accompanied the Marquis of Lorne on his tour of the West. In 1876 Herchmer became the commander of Fort Calgary and was appointed NWMP assistant commissioner in 1881. He died suddenly in Calgary in 1900. Courtesy, Glenbow-Alberta Institute.*

The new post was unofficially referred to as Bow River Fort, pending the selection of a permanent name. Then at the first Christmas dinner held in the fort, the brash, somewhat impolitic Inspector Ephrem Brisebois proposed a toast to the new post, which he referred to as Fort Brisebois. This misuse of authority was too much for Brisebois' superiors, especially given his uncertain reputation within the force. The name was changed to Fort Calgary and was selected for occupation by Colonel James Macleod. The origin of the name is Gaelic and probably had ancestral relevance for Macleod. For years it was believed that Calgary meant "clear running water," and in that sense seemed an ideal name for a post situated by two glacially fed mountain streams. However, it is more probable that the word Calgary may be translated more accurately as meaning bay farm or bay pasture.

As the trouble over the choice of name presaged, Fort Calgary was not long in producing controversy. Predictably, the key figure was Ephrem Brisebois. The morale of F Troop was not high during the winter of 1875-1876. Living conditions were far from ideal. The men were forced to live in trenches until December, pending the construction of the fort, which subsequently proved to be inadequately heated and insulated. In these trying circumstances, Brisebois' leadership proved sadly lacking, scarcely surprising since he had been previously relieved of his command of B Troop for similar reasons. In any case, following a series of overt acts of disobedience and defiance, the men of F Troop openly mutinied and dispatched a delegation to headquarters at Fort Macleod. The list of complaints cited against Brisebois included his commandeering of the only iron stove to warm himself and his Metis mistress. Brisebois was not relieved of his command, although it was obvious that he had fallen completely out of favour, and it was only a matter of time before he was replaced. In August 1876, William Macaulay Herchmer assumed command of the post at Fort Calgary.

For the rest of the 1870s, Fort Calgary functioned as an outpost of civilization in hostile Indian country. As such it furnished protection while acting as a focal point for regional economic and social activity.

Soon after constructing the fort in 1875, the I.G. Baker Company built its own store and trading post a few hundred yards away, the first of several enterprises that would constitute an emerging town. The Hudson's Bay Company abandoned its small post on the Ghost River west of Calgary and relocated on the east side of the Elbow River opposite the fort. Father Lacombe moved his Our Lady of Peace Mission to its permanent location in the appropriately named Mission District of Calgary. The Reverend John

EPHREM BRISEBOIS

Historian Hugh Dempsey has referred to Ephrem Brisebois as Calgary's forgotten founder, and considering the role he played in establishing Calgary, and the vagueness of his memory, the title seems most appropriate. Brisebois was perhaps the true founder of Calgary. After all it was under his direction that Calgary's site was chosen, and the fort itself was constructed while he was in command of the post. He was in fact commanding officer at Calgary for almost a year. Today his name is perpetuated only in a single street name of fairly recent origin. Indeed, if he is popularly remembered at all, it is usually in association with his injudicious action in naming the fort after himself. However, little is known of Brisebois the man, and it might be appropriate to consider in some depth the life of an individual so involved in the origins of Calgary.

Ephrem Brisebois was born in South Durham, Quebec, in 1856 to reasonably well-to-do Catholic parents. His father was influential in local affairs and was an active member of the federal Conservative Party. The young Brisebois had a taste for adventure, and as a 15-year-old boy tried to enlist in the American Civil War. Between 1867 and 1870 he was in Italy as a member of the Canadian Zouaves, a papal regiment fighting for Pope Pius IX in the civil wars that preceded the unification of Italy.

Following his return to Canada, Brisebois was employed as a clerk during the Dominion Government's first census, and when the North West Mounted Police were organized in 1873, he was one of the first recruits from Quebec. His immediate appointment as sub-inspector showed the political influence of his father. Following his commission, Brisebois spent the winter of 1873-1874 as a recruiting officer in the Maritimes.

Brisebois was in Dufferin in the summer of 1874 to begin the march west, and it was during this trek that he began to exhibit some of the qualities that were to prove his later undoing. First, he had difficulty handling men, and apparently was unable to gain their respect or confidence. He was also something of an idealist, caught up in the grand design of the Mounted Police mission, but insensitive to the practical realities of life in the west. It is fairly certain that even before he went to Calgary in the late summer of 1875, Brisebois had diminished in stature in the eyes of his superior officers.

Thus it is not surprising that following the trouble at Fort Calgary in the winter of 1875-1876, Brisebois was censured severely for his lack of leadership, and over the next few months he found himself thoroughly discredited. The result was his resignation from the force in August 1876 and a return to Quebec.

Between 1877 and 1880, Brisebois was an ardent campaign worker for the Conservative Party in Quebec; and he was apparently very successful. In fact, his strong work for the Conservative candidate led to a narrow defeat of the rising young Liberal Wilfrid Laurier in Brisebois's home-constituency of Drummond-Arthabaska in 1877. Then in 1880, he was appointed registrar of land titles for the federal district of Little Saskatchewan. When that area was incorporated into the province of Manitoba, Brisebois's office was provincially directed, and he took up permanent residence in Minnedosa.

The next few years were the most rewarding of Brisebois's life. He performed his duties well and earned the respect and even affection of the small community. He organized a Home Guard during the Riel Rebellion of 1885 and revisited Calgary before the cessation of hostilities in Saskatchewan. His good fortunes, however, were short-lived. In 1889 his position was abolished following the accession to office of the Liberal Party under Thomas Greenway. He left Minnedosa in January 1890. Six months later he was dead, a victim of a sudden heart attack at age 49.

Ephrem Brisebois was a tragic figure in many ways. While he was misplaced as a field officer in the NWMP he probably would have served quite well in a less personalized administrative capacity. He was, however, instrumental in the founding of Calgary, and is of historical significance as a consequence. And though Calgary was not called Brisebois, it very well could have been.

McDougall held Sunday services, first at the barracks and then at the I.G. Baker store before erecting a permanent church in 1877. The first recreational building held a billiard table installed by an enterprising former whisky trader. Several halfbreeds put up shacks in the vicinity of Fort Calgary where they provided freighting services to the police. Indeed, Fort Calgary became a major stopover on the route from Fort Benton to Edmonton. Oxen teams would ply their way north from Fort Benton, but were replaced by Red River carts at Calgary to accommodate the softer, yielding soils that characterized the Calgary-to-Edmonton trail.

I.G. Baker and Company, an American Trading Enterprise operating out of Fort Benton, Montana, had an important role in early Calgary's history. I.G. Baker and Company men built the first Fort Calgary in 1875, and the company's store and trading post was a leading commercial enterprise prior to town incorporation. Courtesy, Glenbow-Alberta Institute.

The arrival of an oxen train was a lively and keenly anticipated event. These trains usually consisted of six or eight units or waggons with eight pairs of oxen yoked to each waggon. A fully loaded train might carry as much as 60 tons of freight. One can imagine the impressive spectacle provided by more than 100 lumbering, powerful beasts pulling waggons stretched over a quarter of a mile and urged on by bull whackers employing profanity as lustily as they wielded their 16-foot bullwhips.

It was customary for a dance to follow the arrival of an oxen train. These frontier occasions of musical festivity were lively affairs, usually lasting well into the night. They were held in the Baker store or "Kamoose" Taylor's billiard hall and attracted a familiar array of frontier characters. All the ladies, for example, were half-breed or Indian girls who danced with much more gusto than skill. An observer at one of these dances in 1882 commented that only one white woman was there to dance to the music of violin and flute and that furthermore the belle of the ball was "a big half-breed named Steamboat Kate." Not surprisingly, these dances were rarely accompanied by the acts of violence typical of the frontier. The looming presence of the police fort nearby proved more than an adequate deterrent.

By the late 1870s, the future of Fort Calgary was uncertain to say the least. The disappearance of the whisky trade and the seeming acceptance by the Indian of the reservation system lessened the need for a strongly manned and fortified post like Fort Calgary. By 1880 only four policemen were stationed at Calgary, which functioned as a sub-post of Fort Macleod. The disappearance of the buffalo meant an end to the buffalo robe industry. Freighting trade slackened, and the Hudson's Bay Company seriously considered abandoning its Calgary post. There was even talk of the permanent removal of the police themselves. So while the North West Mounted Police were instrumental in establishing Calgary they were unable to sustain it. The transformation from isolated police outpost to town was dependent on other forces. The railroad and the cattle industry were soon to take over from the NWMP in advancing the future of Calgary.

Left: *I.G. Baker and Company's store in Calgary was located on 12th Avenue, the site of Old Calgary General Hospital. Mortimer's Home-Baked Vienna Bread advertisements were posted outside the door. Courtesy, Glenbow-Alberta Institute.*

Below: *Anglican minister A.L. Harkness, seated on the load of firewood, rides on a sleigh drawn by a team of oxen. The arrival of freight by oxen train was an occasion for celebration in frontier Calgary. Courtesy, Glenbow-Alberta Institute.*

By 1882, news of the impending transcontinental railroad's proposed route through the southern plains had emphasized a new but important role for the North West Mounted Police. Their diplomacy and strength were needed in the foreseeable encounters with the Indians, whose territorial prerogatives were to be vitally affected by the railroad. Furthermore, the supervisory presence of the police was essential to control the influx of humanity engendered by railroad construction. The entourage of traders, gamblers, prostitutes, fortune-seekers and squatters merging with the construction crews along the main line presented the Mounted Police with problems far greater than those associated with the whisky traders seven years earlier.

Accordingly, in August 1882, plans were made to rebuild Fort Calgary in anticipation of a permanent police division. The contract was given to Major James Walker, a former Mounted Police officer who had left the force to go into business for himself, first as a ranch manager, and then as a lumber merchant. His Bow River Saw and Planing Mill was one of the first manufacturing enterprises in Calgary.

Walker's contract called for the construction of several buildings, including a barracks room, a guardroom with 12 cells, hospital, recreation room, officers' quarters, sergeants' mess, facilities for tradesmen—tailor, shoemaker,

Calgary, viewed from Fraser's Hill looking west, was sketched by F.B. Strange, a retired soldier-turned-rancher, in 1882. At that time there was extensive settlement on the east side of the Elbow River. Courtesy, Glenbow-Alberta Institute.

harness maker, armourer, carpenter, blacksmith and baker—and stables for 68 horses. Log construction was to be used in all buildings except the officers' quarters. Cost of the new facilities was estimated at $35,000. With the construction of the new barracks in 1883, and the installation of a permanent division of the force, the NWMP had become an integral part, but not the prime focus, of Calgary's fledgling urban life.

However, the continuing presence of the Mounted Police in Calgary had an incalculable effect on the urban temper of the community. While it is true that their military and judicial components diminished somewhat in favour of more routine police activities, the role of the NWMP was crucial in defining Calgary's urban climate. They did this in two ways. First, their presence modified the incipient lawlessness characteristic of the frontier. Second, the police acted as cultural agents facilitating the transfer of established values and procedures to a new and harsh environment. Apart from the church, there was no institution more important than the Mounted Police in influencing the cultural and social fabric of the Western Canadian frontier. Certainly Calgary was no exception.

The strong difference between the historical traditions of the American and Canadian frontiers is readily acknowledged at both the academic and

Fort Calgary's NWMP blacksmith shop was constructed from logs set upright. Customers had to approach the shop cautiously to avoid being spattered with mud and water. Courtesy, Glenbow-Alberta Institute.

popular levels. In fact, Canadians sometimes bemoan the fact that their frontier was nowhere near as exciting as the American experience. The old American West seems much more romantic than the Canadian, which for the most part lacked the gun fights, range wars, and violence from which legends are fashioned. Part of the reason is attributed to the Canadians' innate sense of law and order, and respect for institutional authority. The absence of a violent revolutionary tradition in Canada precluded the type of aggressive behaviour characteristic of the American frontier. While these metaphysical arguments are fascinating, and provide a good launching pad for lively debate, the most obvious reason for the more peaceable Canadian frontier lies in the role played by the NWMP. The presence of a tightly-organized, centrallized, paramilitary body with police and judicial authority *in advance* of settlement markedly influenced the social climate of the emerging frontier. Evidence suggests that the collective mentality on the Canadian frontier was not overly dissimilar to that south of the 49th parallel. It was kept in check, however, by the NWMP. The result was that the forces of institutional propriety and order were allowed to flourish unfettered by the individual, spontaneous element characteristic of human behaviour on other frontiers of settlement.

There was much of the popular frontier in the attitudes and behaviour of 19th century Calgarians. The concept of law and order was no exception. Two early police chiefs personified this mentality. One left town hurriedly, owing money and following charges that he operated rigged dice games. Then there was Chief Tom English, a rough-and-tumble character in the classic American tradition who maintained law and order mostly through intimidation. It was held that a kick in the pants from Chief Tom did wonders for the cause of law and order. It was a point of honour with English that he could bring in any man alone. Yet other less imposing members of Calgary's tiny local police force had more difficulty in enforcing the law. They were subject to verbal abuse, and on more than one occasion were hindered by crowds from making arrests.

The task of effective law enforcement was complicated by other factors. Poorly framed bylaws were subject to flagrant abuse. Local justices of the peace were notoriously partisan. Nominal fines were levied for offences that would have brought stiff prison terms in later years. A comic incident involved two local justices of the peace, both accused of a misdemeanour. Each tried the other's case, not to mutual satisfaction apparently, for they began to fight in the courtroom.

On a more serious note, there was also evidence of the partisanship usually associated with American frontier justice. Ugly talk of a lynching followed the arrest of a Negro cook accused of committing Calgary's first murder in 1885. Then in the infamous Rosalie case of 1889, a white man was tried for the hideous murder and mutilation of an Indian prostitute. In spite of overwhelming evidence to the contrary, the Calgary jury found the defendant, a popular local man, not guilty.

As the spokesmen for a clearly defined concept of law and order, the NWMP were not always popular in frontier Calgary. On two separate occasions, the NWMP were involved in incidents that underscored both the volatile nature of 19th-century Calgary and their own crucial but sensitive role in laying the foundation for the peaceable Canadian frontier.

North West Mounted Police line up for a stable parade at Fort Calgary in the 1880s. The three men at left are wearing buffalo-skin coats. Courtesy, Glenbow-Alberta Institute.

The first incident occurred in 1885-86 and involved the controversial and unpopular liquor law. In effect, the sale of liquor in the North West Territories was prohibited unless authorized by a permit signed by the lieutenant-governor. Designed primarily to protect Indians and to salve the rising temperance movement in Eastern Canada, the law was extremely unpopular and subject to flagrant abuse. Liquor was smuggled into the Territories in a variety of devious ways. Bibles concealed flasks, and one individual received a permit in the name of his prize Angus bull. The local police and justices of the peace were openly critical but notoriously lax in their actions against violators. By comparison, the NWMP were much more consistent in enforcing the law, and as a result, by the fall of 1885 they had earned the hostility of many Calgarians.

The trouble erupted in November 1885, when the recently appointed stipendiary magistrate, Jeremiah Travis, imposed a six-month jail sentence on local saloon keeper and town councillor Simon John Clarke for interfering with the Mounted Police in pursuit of their duties. Travis was a teetotalling Baptist whose sense of moral righteousness far outweighed his tact. Clarke, an ex-Mountie himself, had questioned the right of the Mounted Police to search his premises for evidence of liquor, and had demanded validating documentation. In spite of this, and the fact that Clarke was both popular and influential in Calgary, Travis decided that a stiff prison term was warranted. Clarke subsequently was incarcerated in the Mounted Police cells, an instant martyr and town hero.

Shortly thereafter, Travis jailed Hugh Cayley, editor of *The Calgary Herald* and former clerk of the court, for making libellous comments in the press. Cayley made his journey to jail at the Mounted Police barracks accom-

panied by cheering crowds and an improvised band. Then in a final act of dubious legal merit, Travis disqualified the recently elected mayor and town council from holding office. The result was the absence of civic government in the town for most of 1886. Part of the reason for this municipal inactivity was due to the fact that the slate of officials installed by Travis to run the town's civic affairs found that pertinent records had "mysteriously" disappeared.

In the course of these lively events, the Mounted Police were in a difficult position. First, they had to support Travis, who rightly or wrongly seemed intent on forcing confrontations with the pro-liquor interests. Their beleaguered position on an unpopular law was thus compounded by a crusading, tactless magistrate who seemed insensitive to their delicate position *vis-a-vis* Calgary's tiny but legally constituted local police force. At the large public meetings held to plan collective action against Travis, it was felt that the NWMP ought to be excluded from enforcing the law within Calgary's corporate limits.

By the spring of 1886, the issue had been for the most part resolved. As a result of a civic delegation to Ottawa, Travis was suspended and later superannuated following an investigation. Attention was drawn to the liquor law, and though it was to remain in effect for a few more years, its inapplicability was recognized. In 1888 it was modified, and in 1892 was abolished altogether. Travis returned to Calgary in retirement, and later became one of the town's best known and widely heard citizens. He died in 1909 when the Travis (later the Beveridge) Block was under construction. In that same year Simon John Clarke was elected one of Calgary's first two city commissioners.

Simon John Clarke and Hugh Cayley were imprisoned at the Royal Canadian Mounted Police jail (right centre) during the winter of 1885-1886. Judge Jeremiah Travis imprisoned Cayley for making libelous comments in his newspaper, The Calgary Herald. Courtesy, Glenbow-Alberta Institute.

In 1909 Calgary's board of commissioners consisted of A.G. Graves (left), R.R. Jamieson (centre), and Simon J. Clarke (right). Courtesy, Glenbow-Alberta Institute.

The incidents concerning Travis in 1885-1886 showed how a small community could work in concert to redress perceived inequities. It also marked the first tangible manifestation of bitterness against the NWMP. Though no efforts were made to take the law into their own hands, early Calgarians made it quite clear that they were unprepared to respect or even pay lip service to a law that did not work fairly in their interests. As the agents of this law, the Mounties shared the public opprobrium.

In the summer of 1892, the Mounted Police were involved in a serious incident when the fear engendered by an outbreak of the dread disease smallpox crystallized into hostility and violence against the small resident Chinese population. Indeed, were it not for the presence of the Mounted Police, the vicissitudes of mob law may well have prevailed in Calgary's dusty streets.

The smallpox was first detected on June 28, 1892, in a Chinese laundry on Stephen (Eighth) Avenue. The victim had apparently brought the disease with him from the West Coast, and had been shielded from authorities by his countrymen. To their credit, the town authorities took swift and ultimately effective containment measures. A quarantine was established on Nose Creek, and a health committee was appointed to examine possible sources of contagion and to supervise vaccination procedures. Incoming trains from Vancouver were subject to close inspection at points west of the city before being allowed to proceed.

Public anger specifically against the Chinese rose considerably with the first death on July 22 of a white woman following childbirth. The hostility and threats culminated in outright violence on August 2 upon the release of four Chinese from quarantine. Following a cricket match, a drunken mob of some 300 went on the rampage, destroying Chinese premises, seizing money, and manhandling any luckless Chinese it encountered. Doubtless, the physical abuse would have had serious consequences had it not been for the timely interference of the North West Mounted Police. In fact, Inspector A.R. Cuthbert had had prior knowledge of the impending trouble, and further had been threatened with bloodshed if he attempted to interfere. These threats notwithstanding, the Mounted Police had little difficulty in dispersing the unruly mob. Indeed, some of the would be "shedders of blood" left town with such alacrity that they abandoned their horses. Nevertheless, the resentment against the Chinese did not dissipate immediately, and they were clearly terrified. Many spent the nights in the police barracks or in the homes of clergymen. One unfortunate individual was discovered by the NWMP in a weakened condition hiding in a railway culvert near Gleichen.

But while the Chinese continued to be publicly vilified and ridiculed, they suffered no further physical abuse. The only subsequent damage occurred on August 20, when a few unruly drunks kicked in the door of a Chinese laundry, but the vigilance of the Mounted Police provided an adequate deterrent to any incipient violence. The quarantine was guarded by a Mounted Police detachment, and during the height of the unrest, the Police mounted a 24-hour watch over the town. They were well prepared for trouble. According to Inspector Cuthbert, his special attack squad was comprised in part of "old cavalrymen who know how to use a sword."

The restraining hand of the Mounted Police stood in sharp contrast to other more localized institutional forces. Certainly, there were some in Calgary who both deplored and spoke out against the violence. The clergy, for example, were outspoken in their condemnation of unchristian behaviour. For the most part, however, public opinion was either silent or tacitly in support of the anti-Chinese sentiments. For instance, on the night of the riots the lone policeman on duty could not be found. Both the mayor and the Police chief were conveniently out of town at crucial times. Police Chief Tom English was uncooperative and truculent towards the Mounted Police, and on one occasion assaulted a Mounted Police guard who had tried to prevent him from entering the smallpox quarantine. Civic authorities refused to take action against the half dozen ringleaders in the riots even though their identities were well established. One member of the town council ran an advertisement in the local press offering to donate land for a laundry run by whites "so as to make the presence of Mongolians in our midst totally unnecessary." Finally, the heated public feelings were fanned by adverse press editorials and commentaries on the health menace posed by Chinese residing in the community.

By the end of August, the danger from the smallpox epidemic was over. Resentment against the Chinese subsided, and soon it was business as usual in the various laundries and restaurants operated by Chinese merchants. Yet the inescapable fact remained that for a short, tense period, only the presence of the North West Mounted Police protected a disliked minority from mob

Members of the Chinese YMCA pose in front of the Chinese Mission at 120 Second Avenue Southwest. The YMCA provided a viable social avenue for Chinese immigrants in Western Christian tradition and exemplified the close relationship between the church and the Chinese community in Calgary. Courtesy, Glenbow-Alberta Institute.

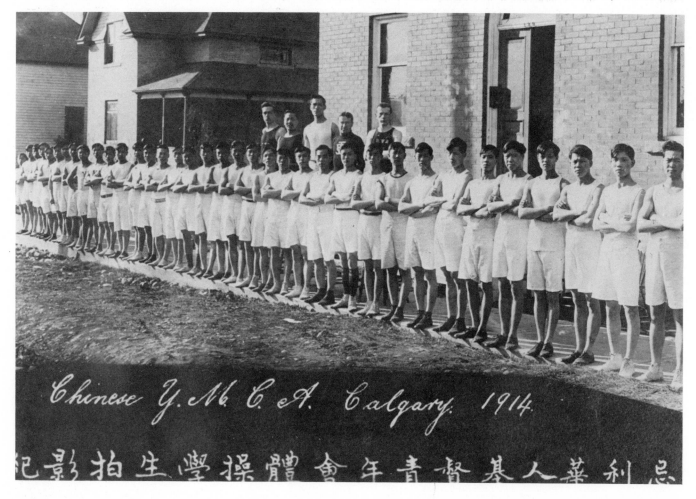

action. More than any other single event in Calgary's history, the smallpox riots of 1892 illustrated how perilously close the peaceable Canadian frontier came to emulating its more lawless American counterpart. And in that context, the pivotal role off the NWMP in maintaining that "peaceable frontier" can be seen to good advantage.

The contribution of the North West Mounted Police to early Calgary extended beyond law and order into the social realm. With their generally superior educational background and military orientation, the NWMP provided a complementary dimension in duplicating the ethos of the British landed gentry in southern Alberta. Manifesting itself in the weekly uniformed parades to the Anglican church, in cricket teams, as well as in the aristocratic sports of polo and the hunt, the influence of the NWMP was clearly discernible in maintaining the distinctive Anglo-Saxon character of 19th-century Calgary.

Police members made contributions to early Calgary's cultural life. The NWMP band provided the town with its first musical refinements. Here the role of Staff Sergeant Fred Bagley was particularly significant. This accomplished musician joined the force at age sixteen and participated in the historic march west in 1874. After leading the NWMP band until his retirement in 1899, Bagley remained in Calgary and continued his active involvement in local musical circles, organizing several proficient military and citizens' bands. Other policemen were involved in the various dramatic, theatrical and

Asian immigrants looking for employment in southern Alberta assemble in about 1910. Courtesy, Glenbow-Alberta Institute.

RACISM AND THE SMALLPOX RIOTS

While the smallpox riots of 1892 were largely induced by fear and even panic, there were unmistakable racist overtones. Antagonism towards Chinese or Orientals or Celestials or John Chinaman, to use contemporary parlance, was part of the frontier experience in 19th century Calgary.

The Chinese first came to Calgary with the construction of the Canadian Pacific Railway. Following completion of the line in 1886, many remained, settling permanently in the urban centres along the main line. By 1892 there were probably fewer than 30 Chinese in Calgary, almost all men who provided the necessary laundry and restaurant service to the predominantly male population.

Though unobtrusive and docile, the Chinese were conspicious wherever they resided. To the Anglo-Saxon mind they were something of an enigma. Many felt that the Oriental impassiveness masked a contempt for the white man. It was further believed that they feigned ignorance while at the same time taking everything but contributing nothing to the society that sustained them. Their seeming impervious attitude towards overcrowding as well as their penchant for gambling and suspected drug use provided additional proof that Oriental standards were both incompatible with and threatening to the western way of life. In short, though the Chinese kept quietly to themselves, their presence evoked strong resident antipathy, which translated readily into outright violence in crisis situations like the smallpox outbreak.

Thus it was not surprising at the height of public tension over the smallpox scare to find strong racist sentiment demanding the exclusion of all Chinese from Calgary and Canada. The chief impetus was provided by Locksley Lucas, secretary of the Anti-Chinese League, who arrived in Calgary from Vancouver to deliver at least two public lectures, and to try to organize a local chapter of the Anti-Chinese League.

Lucas' first address, given in Hull's Opera House on August 16, was full of emotionally charged invective and punctuated by wild histrionics. For instance he called the ministers "black-coated friends of the wily and untrustworthy heathen." He also referred to "the most serious of all Chinese crimes (as being) their lust and sensual passion which showed itself strongest towards white girls, who under the influence of drugs became slaves of Chinamen." In the face of such rhetoric, it is not surprising that the racial flames continued to burn in Calgary.

To Lucas' remarks about drugs, it should be added that his second lecture scheduled for the next evening was cancelled. The reason was both dramatic and ironic. Lucas attempted suicide in his hotel room on the afternoon of August 17 by taking an overdose of morphine. While the exact reasons for his attempt were not established, it was believed that Lucas had been extremely upset by the ridicule he had received for sending his clothes to a Chinese laundry for cleaning. Lucas left town shortly thereafter. As a postscript it might be added that two years later Lucas died in a British Columbia penitentiary where he was serving a prison term for seducing his sister-in-law, a girl under the age of 16.

Facing page, top: *Calgary's Chinese community did not forget its native customs despite Christian and Western influences, and for many years the Chinese were misunderstood and even mistrusted in Anglo-Saxon Calgary. Courtesy, Glenbow-Alberta Institute.*

Bottom: *In the 1920s Hop Wo Laundry was moved from 302 Seventh Avenue West. Chinese immigrants contributed essential services, particularly laundries and restaurants, to Calgary and other Western Canadian communities. Courtesy, Glenbow-Alberta Institute.*

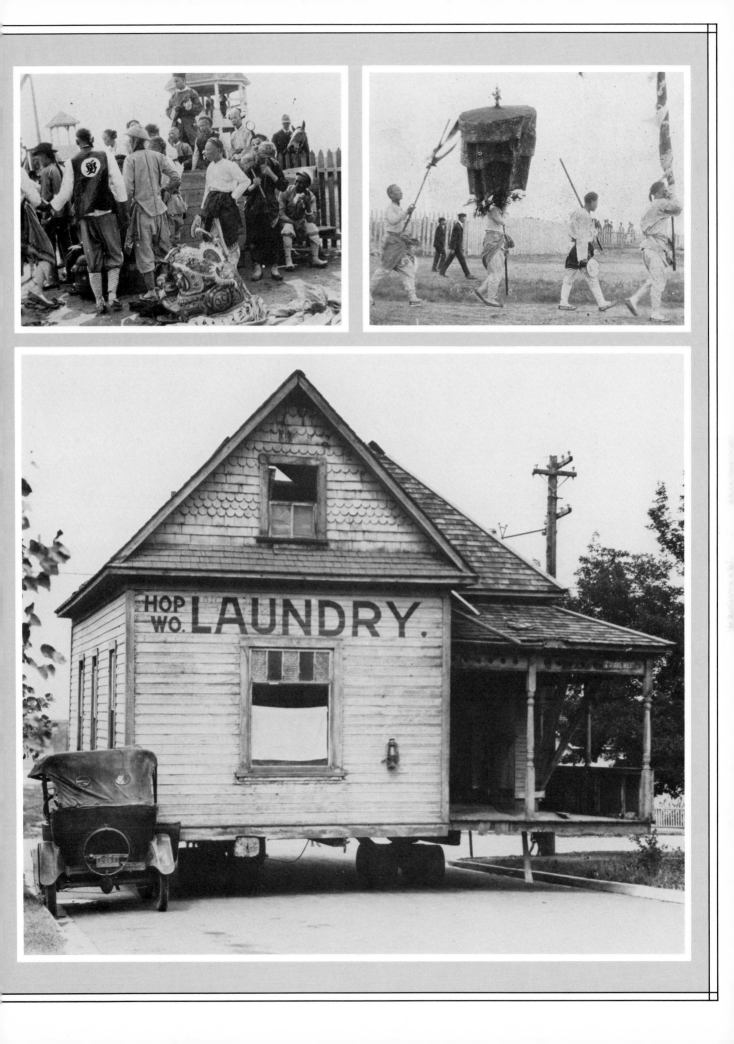

Above: *Frederic Remington depicted the famed musical ride of the Mounted Police as early as 1887. From* Harper's Weekly, *December 24, 1887. Courtesy, Glenbow-Alberta Institute.*

Facing page: *In 1897 North West Mounted Police compiled and hand-lettered a special Christmas card showing scenes from their lives in Western Canada. Courtesy, Glenbow-Alberta Institute.*

literary groups that sprang up in Calgary during the last decade of the 19th century. Still other ex-Mounties became prominent in local business and social circles following their retirement from the force. Included here were James Walker, George Clift King, Simon John Clarke, Cecil Denny, James Macleod and James Burton Deane.

The formation of the province of Alberta in 1905 ended the Territorial period, and with it the dominant role of the North West Mounted Police in overseeing the settlement process. As a result, the Mounties became more associated with typical police functions. Their presence in Calgary lost some of its historical significance when the old barracks ground containing the original site of Fort Calgary was sold to the Grand Trunk Pacific Railway Company in 1914 for $250,000.

The North West Mounted Police are recognized as the founders of Calgary. But they did more than provide the initiative for settlement. For 40 years, they helped fashion the nature of Calgary's law-abiding Anglo-Saxon character. In that context, the recently established Fort Calgary Interpretive Centre, located on the site of the original police post, symbolizes a vital founding force in Calgary's urban life.

THE FORT CALGARY SITE

As has been noted, the original Fort Calgary stood for seven years, 1875-1882, before being demolished to make way for new and enlarged facilities. The stockade was torn down in 1882, and the men's barracks soon thereafter. The last structure, the stores building, was demolished in 1888. Around this time, the original area occupied by the fort was ploughed at least once to allow for a grass parade square. With this development and the collection of the new two-story barracks in 1890, all vestiges of the original Fort Calgary disappeared.

In 1914, the 29.54-acre site was sold by the Canadian government to the Grand Trunk Pacific Railway Company for $250,000. Though the railway company hoped to erect extensive terminal facilities on the site, its plunge into bankruptcy during World War I ended such grandiose plans. However, some railway development occurred on the site. Spur lines and freighting facilities changed the surface topography, burying the remains of Fort Calgary deeper into the prairie soil. Indeed by 1915, a number of industrial enterprises as well as a private residence, used the old Fort Calgary site, including J.Y. Turner Coal and Wood and the Crown Coal Company. Over the next 40 years, similar ventures made their presence felt, among them being the firm of Mac-

Cosham's Storage and Van Lines Ltd., constructed soon after the Second World War. Subsequent spur lines to the warehouse, and a major extension in 1951, completed the destruction of much of the recoverable artifacts and archaeological remains of the original Fort Calgary.

As R. Bruce Wilson has pointed out in his excellent discussion "40 Acres, a Fort and Its Future," public interest in the old fort site was never allowed to die despite its seeming desecration. In 1917, a commemorative cairn known as the "Buffalo Stone" was placed at the east side of the intersection of 8th (Stephen) Avenue and 6th Street East. Eight years later in 1925, a memorial cairn was unveiled in Central Park as part of the city's Golden Jubilee celebrations. Twenty-one years later, a civic furore of sorts erupted over the fate of the "Buffalo Stone" pending the construction of MacCosham's warehouse. Following extensive press coverage and spirited citizen involvement, and negotiations with both MacCosham's and the Canadian National Railways, the cairn was ultimately removed to its present location on the corner of 9th Avenue and 6th Street East.

Below left: *Wooden markers indicate the entrance to the Fort Calgary site, where the NWMP constructed a post in the autumn of 1875. Courtesy, Calgary Herald.*

Interest in Calgary's original site was revived in the late 1960s with civic initiative being provided by local alderman John Ayer. The importance of the site archaeologically was reinforced following a series of digs carried out by the University of Calgary archaeology department and sponsored by the Glenbow-Alberta Institute. Encouraged by progress at these diggings, the city of Calgary officially endorsed the Fort Calgary Project in 1973. Though plans were far from final on the exact development of the site, the first sod-turning ceremony took place in November 1974.

The city originally envisaged an underground interpretive centre where visitors could see the actual reclamations of the original fort. For archaeological and practical reasons, a more "responsible" centre was ultimately decided upon. It was felt that a smaller building set away from the original fort location would enable adequate interior visual re-creations while preserving the openness of the fort site itself. Funded in part by the city of Calgary, the provincial government, and private and corporate organizations, the Fort Calgary Interpretive Centre was opened to the public in 1978.

Above: *Fort Calgary was originally constructed on the site at top right in 1875. The Fort Calgary Interpretive Centre now stands there to commemorate Calgary's beginnings at the confluence of the Bow and Elbow rivers. Courtesy, Calgary Herald.*

THE FIRST FRONTIER

CHAPTER THREE
CALGARY AND RAILWAYS

While Calgary owed its existence to the North West Mounted Police, its growth and development as Alberta's largest city and Western Canada's second major urban centre were due almost entirely to the Canadian Pacific Railway. The railroad transformed Calgary's tenuous economic function as a stopover point on the north-south oxen cart route to a distributing centre with direct links to metropolitan Toronto and Montreal. For decades the steel rails stretching east across the endless prairies, and west through the mountain barrier, effectively demarcated frontier Calgary's only links with the outside world.

A visitor to Calgary in 1900 would have found the influence of the CPR difficult to ignore. Thoroughfares bore the names of CPR officials. Construction had begun on the freighting facilities that had recently made Calgary the most important divisional point west of Winnipeg. As well as being the largest employer in the city, the railway company controlled land development both within and outside the corporate limits. Twelve years later, at the height of Calgary's prewar boom, and with the long-held vision of true city status almost

The Calgary-Edmonton railroad tracks run through the centre of this view looking north from Bow Bend Shack at the turn of the century. General Hospital has since been built on the hill at rear. Courtesy, Glenbow-Alberta Institute.

Ornate lattice work trimmed the roofline of the Hudson's Bay Company store, situated along a wooden sidewalk. Courtesy, Glenbow-Alberta Institute.

a reality, the ubiquitous presence of the CPR was more pronounced than ever. The new, elegant Palliser Hotel, together with the impressive railway station and adjoining gardens, gave visible proof of the CPR as the focal point in Calgary's urban life. Just inside the southeast city limits, the erection of extensive CPR repair facilities at Ogden promised to give Calgary the industrial base to balance its commercial orientation. The presence of the CPR was further evidenced in the numerous spur lines that cut across city streets, in the irrigation ditches that helped green gardens and parks, as well as in the extensive stockyard facilities that advertised Calgary as the livestock centre of Western Canada. There were also the exclusive residential areas like Mount Royal and Sunalta, which owed not only their prestige but their very existence to the CPR. In a sense, the frontier period, 1885-1914, marked the halcyon years when Calgary was only too happy to call itself a CPR town.

The idea of a transcontinental railroad was a concomitant of Confederation in 1867, and of the transfer of the vast Northwest from the Hudson's Bay Company to Canada. The admission of British Columbia to confederation in 1870, combined with the threat to Canadian sovereignty posed by American expansion, led John A. Macdonald, founding statesman and prime minister, to consider the merits of consolidating Canada's new domain by establishing direct railway links from east to west. Attempts to begin the mammoth project were forestalled in the 1870s by financial depression, a political scandal, and differing philosophies respecting construction pursued by Canada's first Conservative (1867-73) and Liberal (1873-78) administrations. When Macdonald was swept back into power in 1878 on the merits of his new National Policy, one of his clear mandates was the construction of the transcontinental line.

In February 1881, the Canadian Pacific Railway Company was incorporated. With the turning of the first sod two months later, one of the most

In the mid-1880s a Canadian Pacific Railway bridge was built across the Elbow River at Calgary. A footbridge spans the river at right, and the NWMP barracks are in the background. Courtesy, Glenbow-Alberta Institute.

ambitious single undertakings ever attempted by a sparsely populated nation was under way. The line was built in sections, under the direction of William Van Horne, a towering personality whose exploits during the four-and-a-half years of construction have been enshrined in Canadian folklore. In the spring of 1882, Van Horne flung 5,000 men and 1,200 teams into action on the prairie section. By October 1882, trains were running from Winnipeg to Regina. The following summer Van Horne relentlessly drove his crews at a record-setting pace. Averaging three-and-a-half miles of track a day, the construction crews reached the east bank of the Bow River on August 9, 1883. Two days later, two engines, "Old 81" and "126," brought the first train of eight boarding and sixteen flat cars into Calgary. Following construction of a bridge across the Elbow River, the first temporary station was set up near where Fourth Street East is today. The establishment of Siding No. 20 at Calgary marked the completion of the prairie section.

A little over two years later, on November 7, 1885, high in the windy Selkirks at Craigellachie, Donald A. Smith (later Lord Strathcona) drove in the last spike. The first transcontinental train left Montreal at 8 p.m., June 28,

In 1884 a Canadian Pacific Railway mail train travels by Calgary at 30 m.p.h. Construction of the railroad into Calgary in 1883 changed many things, none more than mail service. Courtesy, Glenbow-Alberta Institute.

1886, and reached the western terminus at Port Moody on time at noon July 4. With this epic journey, the CPR dream came to fruition with little thought at the time as to whether or not the price paid was too high.

The Canadian Pacific Railway Company, by dictating the precise placement of towns and villages along the right-of-way, effectively determined land settlement patterns. Under terms of contract with the federal government, the CPR had clear title to all odd-numbered sections along its main line to a depth of 24 miles. It was thus in a position to decide arbitrarily where to place stations and townsites regardless of any existing settlement. Calgary was no exception. While it was known that the CPR line was to pass through the Bow River valley, the exact location of Siding No. 20 was less certain. However, it was assumed that the line would pass through Calgary and that a townsite would be located there because a number of settlers, including merchants and businessmen, were already clustered around Fort Calgary on the banks of the Elbow River.

The CPR's secrecy respecting townsite locations was designed to forestall squatters and land speculators who hoped to share in the profitable real estate deals that invariably accompanied railroad construction. With regard to Calgary, the CPR played its guessing game well. Route plans were changed frequently and, as late as March 1883, it was rumoured that the line would bypass Calgary in favour of Nose Creek and Gleichen. In actual fact, however, railway officials had long since decided on a townsite at Calgary, which had been described by Superintendent James Egan as one of the finest natural townsites on the prairie section.

When the rails reached Calgary in August 1883, the CPR found a sizeable settlement including a police fort and two major trading posts located on an even-numbered section (Section 14). The dilemma facing the CPR

Before permanent homes could be erected, many of Calgary's early citizens lived in tents, pending the issuance of land titles. Courtesy, Glenbow-Alberta Institute.

Above: *Mr. McKibbon balances on a ladder while Mrs. McKibbon, clad in a snow-shoeing outfit, sits in the snow outside their tent home in Calgary at what is now the corner of 12th Avenue and First Street West, circa 1883. Courtesy, Glenbow-Alberta Institute.*

Facing page: *Weekly issues of* The Calgary Herald *began appearing in 1883. Its local news and personals offer a look at the interests and activities of early Calgarians. Courtesy, Glenbow-Alberta Institute.*

involved the placement of the station and townsite. Resisting strong local pressure to establish its townsite within the existing settlement by the Elbow River, the CPR temporized before locating its permanent station about three-quarters of a mile west on a railroad-owned section (Section 15).

The laying out of the Calgary Townsite on Section 15 was carried out in December, and a month later the first sale of lots was held. All lots were standardized in price and size. Corner lots cost $450 and all others $100 less. Ballots were drawn for choice, the first going to old-time resident John Glenn. Taking advantage of the CPR's offer of a 50 percent rebate for buildings erected before April 1884, most residents skidded their dwellings across the frozen Elbow River to relocate near the railway station on Atlantic (Ninth) Avenue. One hundred eighty-eight lots were sold that first day, 183 within three blocks of the railway station, with the two blocks directly opposite the station being easily the choicest.

A month later the CPR induced Postmaster James Bannerman to relocate in the new townsite by granting him two free lots and a $100 bonus. Though a residue of commercial activity remained on the original settlement, the town of Calgary began to take permanent shape under the direct auspices of the CPR on Section 15. It was a pattern oft-repeated across the southern plains as the company demonstrated its primary role in the birth of urban Western Canada.

By the end of 1884, Calgary was an incorporated town, the second in the North West Territories, and with a population of 500 possessed all the trappings of permanency. *The Calgary Herald* already had a year of weekly publication to its credit, and the rudiments of institutional life were established

THE CALGARY HERALD.

MINING AND RANCHE ADVOCATE AND GENERAL ADVERTISER.

VOLUME I.   CALGARY, ALBERTA, FRIDAY, AUGUST 31, 1883.   NUMBER 1

LOCAL NEWS.

NEW STOCK.—I. G. Baker & Co. have just received 180 wood and coal stoves, which will be sold cheap.

POLICE HOSPITAL.—The hospital contains at present four patients, three civilians and one policeman.

C. P. CONSTRUCTION.—Tracklaying is being vigorously proceeded with by the C. P. R., about 10 miles west of Calgary.

FIRST ARRIVALS.—The first train of freight for Calgary, carried the plant of the CALGARY HERALD, and some goods for Winder & Co.

IN LIMBO.—The guard-room has but one occupant, an Indian named Cut Lip, who is serving his time for stabbing a white man last winter.

TROOP PHOTOGRAPHED. — Immediately after full dress parade, on Tuesday morning, the troop stationed here was photographed by Mr. Bingham.

ANTHRACITE COAL.—We have been shown some fine specimens of what has been pronounced "anthracite coal," lately brought from the mountains.

BIG DRIVE OF LOGS.—The Bow River Mills are now receiving a drive of about 8000 logs, and are sawing night and day to supply the wants of their customers.

PROSPECTORS.—Some of the prospectors have returned from the mountains, bringing fine specimens with them, and glowing accounts of what they have seen.

THE NAVVIES.—We have to congratulate Mr. G. W. Peterson, of the firm of Peterson & Peterson, Barristers of this place, on his success in securing pesces over the C. P. R., for several hundred of Langdon, Shepherd & Co's men. It seems that when engaging, the men were promised passes back on the completion of the contract, but when the work was completed, and pay day came, these were refused and the men were lying here idle, without any shelter day or night for some time, and but for the clever management of the case by the above named gentlemen, might have caused serious embarassment. Not the least pleasing feature of the affair was the handsome fee received by Mr. Peterson.

TREATY MONEY.—The treaty money is to be paid to the Stony Indians, at Morley, to-morrow. The Sarcees receive theirs on the 10th and the Blackfeet on the 25th prox.

PRESBYTERIAN MISSION.—A meeting was recently held in the Hudson Bay store, for the appointment of Managers in connection with the above Mission, when the following gentlemen were appointed : Major Walker, Dr. Henderson, and Mr. Joseph McPherson. The management have adopted the envelope system for their weekly offering.

REGISTRAR DISTRICTS.—We understand that Alberta has been divided into two registration districts. One office will be established at Calgary, the other at Edmonton.

TRAIN SERVICE.—A passenger train now leaves Calgary, daily for the east, at 10.30 a.m., and one leaves Medicine Hat for Calgary, every morning at 3 a.m., arriving here about 3 p.m.

EXCURSION.—The Brandon Town Officials purpose visiting Calgary, in a few days. Mr. Egan has placed a sleeper at their disposal. Could not something be done towards giving them a public reception ?

FIRST ENGINE.—On the arrival of the first engine into Calgary, the hill sides were crowded with admiring spectators, many of whom had never seen one before, and others who had not been near a railway for eight or ten years.

ROYAL HOTEL.—Mr. Moulton has just closed his popular hotel for the season, owing to the fact that he could obtain no suitable building site, at present. We believe it is his intention to return to Calgary and erect a large hotel, when the town is surveyed. The outfit was sold by auction on Tuesday last, and owing to the successful manner in which Mr. T. S. Burns wielded the hammer, fancy figures were obtained.

GEOLOGICAL SURVEY.—Mr. J. H. Panton, geologist, of the Manitoba Historical and Scientific Society, spent a day in and about Calgary, and reports a very interesting field of study for men of his profession. He has promised to prepare a paper on his researches in this locality for THE HERALD, which we have no doubt will be hailed with interest by our readers. We hope also to be favored with a paper by the Botanist of the Society.

CALGARY HOUSE.—We have had the pleasure of inspecting the new hotel just completed by Dunne & Wright, and find it a perfect model of taste and neatness. It contains a large comfortable parlour, and a number of bed-rooms, all handsomely carpeted and furnished in the best of style. The dining-room has accommodation for about 40 guests, and the reading room is well supplied with the latest papers. Messrs. Dunne & Wright are well and favorably known to the public, and we have no doubt they will receive the large share of public patronage, which they so justly merit.

SABBATH SERVICES.—Divine service is held at the Catholic Chapel every Sunday at 10.30 a.m. and 4.30 p.m.

PRESBYTERIAN SERVICE.—The service in connection with the Presbyterian Mission will be held in a tent near the Calgary House on Sunday next at 7 p.m.

CATHOLIC INDUSTRIAL SCHOOL.—Rev. Father La Combe is waiting for the specifications and forms of tenders from Lieut.-Governor Dewdney for the Indian Industrial School at High River. As soon as they arrive parties wishing to tender will be supplied with blank forms.

HUDSON BAY FORT.—The H. B. Fort, at Calgary has lately been raised to the chief post of the district, from which the supplies for 5 posts in the Edmonton district, 6 in the Peace River district, and 1 in the Athabasca district will be forwarded.

THIEVES. — A number of petty thefts have lately been committed in the vicinity, but the smallest thing we have heard of, was the cutting and stealing of the ropes from the foot bridge across the Elbow. This is a matter of some importance, as strangers coming into town are very liable to get a cold bath gratuitously. We hope the ropes will soon be replaced.

METHODISTICAL.—We are pleased to see that the energetic Methodist missionary of this place, Rev. Mr. Turner, is always equal to the occasion. The hospital of the Mounted Police not being longer available, Mr. Turner has secured a tent, and made it comfortable, and will hold service therein next Sunday at 3 p.m. The tent is situated just east of the Hudson Bay store. There is some talk of securing an organ, and forming a choir.

HOUSE RAIDED.—Information was laid a few evenings since, at Police quarters, that a number of men were engaged in gambling in a certain house on the bank of the Elbow, accordingly Major Dowling, with a detachment of men, proceeded to the place in question and after entering, found eight or nine persons with cards and checks on the table, who arrested the parties and placed them in the guard-room. The next morning they were up for trial before Supt. McIlree, but as no direct evidence, was forthcoming, they were discharged. Mr. Bleecker of Edmonton defended the prisoners.

A MURDEROUS ASSAULT.—On Saturday afternoon, about 3 o'clock, a telegram was received at the Police barracks that a fracas had occurred at the end of the track, by which a man named Torrance had committed a murderous assault on another of the gang, knocking him down and kicking him about the head and face. Afterwards drawing a revolver, he "stood off" some men who interfered, and starting down the track, succeeded in gaining a dense bush. A detachment was sent up to keep guard, and see that he did not escape from the thicket, the night being too dark to search for him then. Sergt. Major Lake, with ten men, proceeded at day-break next morning to scour the bush thoroughly, but unfortunately the man had effected his escape and has not since been heard of. The wounded man is progressing favourably.

RAILWAY SMASH UP.

On Sunday evening about 8.30, Engine No. 80, C. P. R., left Calgary for the east drawing Mr. Ross's car, and a caboose, running about 20 miles per hour. On arriving at the 18th siding, through some one having meddled with the switch, they were turned off the main line and run into a train standing on that material. When the engineer found that they had been switched off, he whistled down brakes, but before the brakes could be reached by the brakemen, they struck heavily against the construction train, injuring more or less every one on board. A telegram was despatched to Calgary for medical aid, a car for the wounded, and a train to clear up the wreck. The services of Dr. Lindsay were secured and accompanied by a Herald reporter, the train drew out for the scene of the catastrophe. On arriving it was found that Mr. Ross had received a contusion on the side of the head and a small cut over the eye. Brakeman E. Green had been crushed about the hips and was suffering severely. Another brakeman had a severe cut in the face, and the engineer and fireman some bruises about the face and head. After the wounds were dressed the patients were brought to Calgary and placed in the C. P. R. hospital.

We are pleased to learn that none of the injuries have proved at all serious—with the exception of the two brakemen, all the parties being able to be around the next day, and they will be out in a short time. The engine and a number of flats were thrown off the track and considerably damaged, and will have to be sent to Winnipeg for repairs. We cannot understand how any on board escaped.

Fergus Falls has an Enoch Arden case. His name is Arnott, and after a long absence from home he returned to find his wife re-married. The wife chose to remain with husband No. 2, and Arnott was left out in the cold.

The Canadian artillery man have scored another success at Shoeburyness. The record of last year's team in the shifting ordnance competition was a great surprise, and this year's team has sustained the reputation gained then.

LAND SPECULATION AND THE CALGARY TOWNSITE

The general uncertainty over CPR townsites and their precise placement was compounded at Calgary by intense speculative activity. Unlike most CPR townsites across the prairies, Calgary was a settled community well before the arrival of the rails, and this, combined with the belief that there was to be a townsite at Calgary, led to a flurry of speculative activity in 1882-1883.

In 1883, a group of eastern Canadian speculators negotiated with a resident squatter to purchase his quarter section east of the Elbow River. The squatter was a half-breed former employee of the Hudson's Bay Company named Louis Rozelle, who in 1880 had been granted permission by the Hudson's Bay Company factor to homestead the quarter section around the post. At the time the land was granted, the Hudson's Bay Company saw little future at Calgary and was seriously considering abandoning its post there. In any case, Rozelle completed homestead requirements before selling to the speculators for $10,000.

With the news of the impending railway, the Hudson's Bay Company suddenly regained its interest in Calgary. In October 1882 it challenged the legality of Rozelle's claim, maintaining that the land had been disposed of wrongfully, and was in point of law still company property. Not to be outmaneuvered by the CPR's well advertised caprice in choosing townsites, the Hudson's Bay Company further sought to claim six sections around Calgary in lieu of other company lands in the North West Territories.

It took over a year to settle the issue in the speculators' favour. By this time, however, the CPR had arrived, and was proceeding to lay out its townsite west of the Elbow River. The entourage of settlers, having no clear title to the disputed land, were easily persuaded to move their temporary dwellings to Section 15 where permanent title was assured. Had the settlers around the Elbow River held clear title to land in 1882-1883, the CPR may have felt more pressured to establish its townsite and station farther to the east; and the physical face of Calgary would have been decidedly different.

There was yet another interested party in this real estate guessing game. In September 1882 the federal government created a government reserve at Calgary. Like the Hudson's Bay Company, the government was clearly anti-

Above: *Calgary's small settlement is shown in this view from Fraser's Hill just prior to town incorporation in late 1884. The rebuilt police barracks can be seen in the centre background. Courtesy, Glenbow-Alberta Institute.*

Facing page, top: *Sparrow's Meat Market is on the right in this view looking east on Stephen Avenue, circa 1885. The NWMP barracks are in the background at the east end of the street. Courtesy, Glenbow-Alberta Institute.*

Bottom: *Calgary's growth accelerated with the great real-estate boom of 1911-1913 and the discovery of oil at Turner Valley in 1914. Courtesy, Glenbow-Alberta Institute.*

cipating the route of the railway. Its reserve included all of Section 15 and an area two miles north of the Bow River. (As late as March 1883, it was believed that the mainline may have bypassed Fort Calgary to the north of the Bow River.) The police maintained that their expanded facilities justified the need for additional pasture lands, and so throughout 1883 they refused to allow squatting or buildings of any kind on the reserved section.

Even following the establishment of the Calgary townsite, the speculative rivalry continued over the direction of town expansion. Landholders of property east of Third Street East and beyond the Elbow River made strenuous efforts to promote an easterly development of commercial and residential activity. They lost the battle, however; by the turn of the century, the downtown core of Calgary had begun to take shape west of Centre Street. By 1912, the intersection of Eighth Avenue and First Street West denoted the heart of the city. At the time of town incorporation in 1884, the hub was located at Ninth Avenue and First Street East.

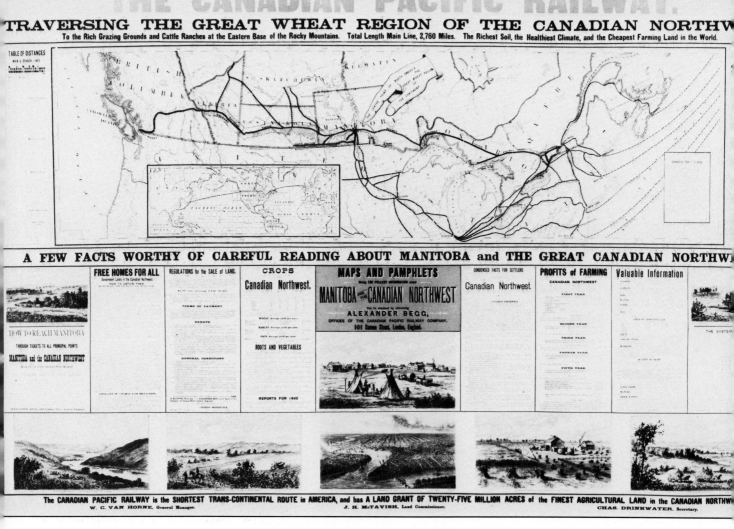

An advertisement posted by the Canadian Pacific Railway in 1882 encourages settlers to come to Manitoba and Western Canada. Courtesy, Glenbow-Alberta Institute.

through permanent churches, banks, municipal government, and various social organizations. Commercial activity was brisk as local businessmen provided some of the services and amenities associated with urban life. Yet this initial growth was due entirely to the demands created by the ongoing railroad construction to the west. At this stage, there was no hinterland to sustain or even justify Calgary's corporate existence. In function, fact, and theory, Calgary was a CPR creation.

The period following the construction of the railroad marked the settlement process in Western Canada. In southern Alberta, the ranching industry was dominant until about 1907 when it was superseded by the inexorable advance of the agricultural frontier and the economy of cash crop farming. Calgary's growth was linked directly with this hinterland development and, indeed, the city continued to function as the urban expression of rural southern Alberta until after the Second World War. Throughout this entire period, and especially before 1912, the railroad was vital in consolidating Calgary's focal position in the agricultural economy of Alberta and Western Canada.

Calgary's interest in railroad development did not dissipate with the construction of the CPR. For the next 30 years the intoxicating foment of railway-related matters figured prominently in local affairs. First there was the speculative element; in the late 19th century the promise of railroad construction conjured up the same visions of limitless prosperity that a major oil strike does today. *The Calgary Herald* once remarked that it was "the duty of every man, woman and child to further the cause of railway development in Alberta."

In the 1890s, local interests in Calgary secured charters from the federal government authorizing the construction of no fewer than five railroads converging in Calgary. Two of these were designed to tap the coal-bearing deposits of central Alberta, and revealed the ambitions of local entrepreneurs to secure a reliable supply of cheap power for industrial purposes. Another line was projected to link up with the United States rail network and provide a short route from San Francisco to Liverpool, England, via Calgary and the Hudson's Bay. This frenzied interest in railroad matters led one disgruntled local resident to remark that he "could circulate a petition praying the Angel Gabriel to build a railway to the moon and get hundreds of signatures to it in Calgary." The depressed conditions of the 1890s, plus the federal government's more cautious policies respecting land grants, kept these railroad lines on paper, and a reality only in the fertile minds of Calgary's frontier visionaries.

The real impact of railway construction, however, received its best expression in the period 1910-1914 with the construction of the two transcontinental lines, the Grand Trunk Pacific and the Canadian Northern. From 1910, when civic authorities petitioned the federal government to compel

A view of First Street West in 1911 included Jim Kee and M.G. George laundries on the right. Courtesy, Glenbow-Alberta Institute.

On July 21, 1890, the Honourable E. Dewdney, lieutenant governor of the Northwest Territories, turns the first sod for the construction of the Calgary and Edmonton Railway at Calgary. The line was constructed in 1890-1891 by the contracting firm of MacKenzie and Mann. Courtesy, Glenbow-Alberta Institute.

both companies to extend branch lines to the city, until 1914, when the first train from Mirror steamed into the temporary terminal near the site of the old Fort Calgary, speculators associated with railroad construction dominated Calgary's urban atmosphere. Land prices around the terminals and the proposed rights-of-way rose dramatically. Prices of over $1,000 per frontage foot were common around the sites of the two proposed stations near the police barracks ground and St. Mary's Cathedral. Real estate men like Fred Lowes made fortunes buying land along the rights-of-way. New residential and industrial subdivisions sprang up along the approach lines to the city. The best example was the present district of Forest Lawn, which owed its existence to the commercial promise provided by its proximity to the Grand Trunk Pacific line. At one point, the proposed plans of the Canadian Northern involved a joint terminal with the CPR, and provided for an entrance route paralleling First Street West and crossing the main thoroughfares via a system of overhead traffic bridges. With all this, Calgary's phenomenal development in the years 1911-1912 was probably due in large part to the speculative confidence inspired by railroad construction.

Yet, like the paper schemes of the 1890s, the two transcontinental lines promised much more than they actually delivered. Both companies were hard hit by the depression following 1913, and could not fulfill their grand

G.C. King and Company's store on Stephen Avenue in Calgary was decorated to celebrate the Honourable E. Dewdney's visit and the commencement of construction on the Calgary and Edmonton Railway in 1890. Courtesy, Glenbow-Alberta Institute.

schemes. In fact the opposite was closer to the truth. When the two transcontinental lines were amalgamated into the Canadian National Railways, Calgary did not figure prominently in the Canadian government's new railroad system. The old Fort Calgary site remained largely undeveloped, while the only passenger terminal operated by the CNR was small and peripherally located in the Mission District of south Calgary.

There was, however, enough real railroad development after 1885 to consolidate Calgary as the major distributing centre of southern and south-central Alberta. The line to Edmonton was constructed in 1890-1891. In 1896 rail connections to Fort Macleod were established, and a few years later were extended to Lethbridge and the American border. The aggressive railroad policies pursued by Alberta's first provincial government after 1905 linked rural Alberta towns and cities with a series of branch lines, and cemented Calgary's focal position as the chief transportation hub west of Winnipeg.

Internally Calgary continued to reflect the influence of the railroad. A wholesale district was clearly in evidence by 1900, marked by warehouses and spur lines along Ninth and Tenth avenues, and stretching from Third Street East to Eighth Street West. In 1898, the civic authorities achieved a *coup* of sorts when they persuaded the CPR to locate freight yards in Calgary in return for a cash grant of $25,000. These facilities were located just east of the existing passenger terminal, and were considered an immeasurable boon to the local economy. In 1907 it was estimated that the yards were worth over one million dollars annually to the city. On an average, 700 cars were switched daily over 20 miles of track, while handling and maintenance of equipment employed over 300 men. Even before the erection of the Ogden Shops in 1912, the CPR was the largest private employer in the city.

Above: *Early Canadian Pacific Railway snow-ploughs clear mountain tracks, circa 1893. Courtesy, Glenbow-Alberta Institute.*

Above right: *In the 1890s the Canadian Pacific Railway used early rotary snow-ploughs to clear tracks mainly west of Calgary in the Rockies. Courtesy, Glenbow-Alberta Institute.*

The increasing railway activity after 1900 led the CPR to consider the feasibility of building major repair facilities to handle the needs of the western provinces. For years civic officials had waited on visiting CPR dignitaries, regaling them with the merits of a Calgary location for the projected "shops," as they were termed. However, the railway officials had always demurred with vague allusions to future considerations. In reality, the CPR was discouraged by the high cost of power in Calgary, and for a time was more favourably disposed towards Medicine Hat, where cheap power was abundant in the form of natural gas.

Following construction of the Horse Shoe Falls power project by the Calgary Power Company in 1910, the balance tipped in Calgary's favour. With a source of cheap power now available, the CPR entered into negotiations with the city in 1911. Under an arrangement with the city popularly termed the Ogden Shops Agreement, the CPR consented to construct the shops on railway land 4.8 miles from the city in return for certain concessions, which were given willingly by delighted civic officials. These included construction of access roads and bridges, a streetcar service, water and light at cost, as well as a clause that absolved the CPR from all further responsibility respecting the construction of subways or underpasses under its main line in Calgary.

Ground was broken for the shops on April 1, 1912. Less than a year later, the giant 213-acre project was completed, the 12 buildings alone comprising 13.5 acres. The locomotive repair shops were designed to handle between 20 and 25 classified engine repairs per month, while the freight repair facilities had a capacity of 500 cars per month. When fully operational, the Ogden facilities employed over 1,200 men.

The erection of the Ogden Shops was easily the most important single factor in the economic development of Calgary before the post-1945 oil boom, and local interests, recognizing the shops' value, had been united in their efforts to secure them. There was even talk of a boycott of the CPR in favour of the impending Grand Trunk Pacific if the shops did not materialize.

The city also granted generous tax concessions to the CPR in 1912 in return for the construction of the Palliser Hotel. As with the Ogden Shops, the economic advantages were seen as far outweighing the costs to the city. The celebrated Palliser Hotel (which was named after a man who doubted the feasibility of an all-Canadian transcontinental railroad) was impressive. Completed in 1914 at a total cost of almost $2 million, the imposing Palliser with its 300 modern rooms was to dominate Calgary's skyline for over half a century.

Calgary benefited economically from the CPR in another major way. In 1903 the federal government ordered the company to make its final selection of land grants, and in response the railroad was induced to begin a large-scale irrigation project to enhance the marginal value of its lands in southeast Alberta. Over $18 million were spent in the construction of dams and reservoirs, as well as some 4,000 miles of canals and ditches to irrigate a quarter of a million acres. As a result, Calgary became the headquarters for CPR irrigation operations while catering to the demands created by construction and associated irrigation needs.

Erected in 1912, the CPR Ogden Shops represented the most important consolidation of industrial activity in the city. The 213-acre facilities employed over 1,200 workers when fully operational. Courtesy, Glenbow-Alberta Institute.

THE CALGARY IRRIGATION COMPANY

The CPR was not the first organization to attempt irrigation on a large scale in Alberta. An early pioneer was the Calgary Irrigation Company, which in its short life proved beyond doubt the feasibility of irrigation in Alberta.

Irrigation in that province actually dated to 1875 when John Glenn, using only a carpenter's level to strike his elevations, ran a ditch from Fish Creek to his farmlands at Midnapore, now a Calgary suburb. While other individual efforts at irrigation were recorded in the 1880s, they were sporadic, haphazardly financed, and thus of marginal utility. One energetic, far-sighted individual, however, perceived a solution. William Pearce, Dominion Superintendent of Lands and Mines, and an ardent advocate of irrigation, was convinced that only a corporate entity could marshal the financial resources necessary to substantiate the merits of irrigation in Alberta. After trying unsuccessfully to persuade others to form an irrigation company, Pearce finally took

The first irrigation project on the Western Canadian prairie was a ditch in the Midnapore district in south Calgary, now part of Fish Creek Provincial Park. Courtesy, Calgary Herald.

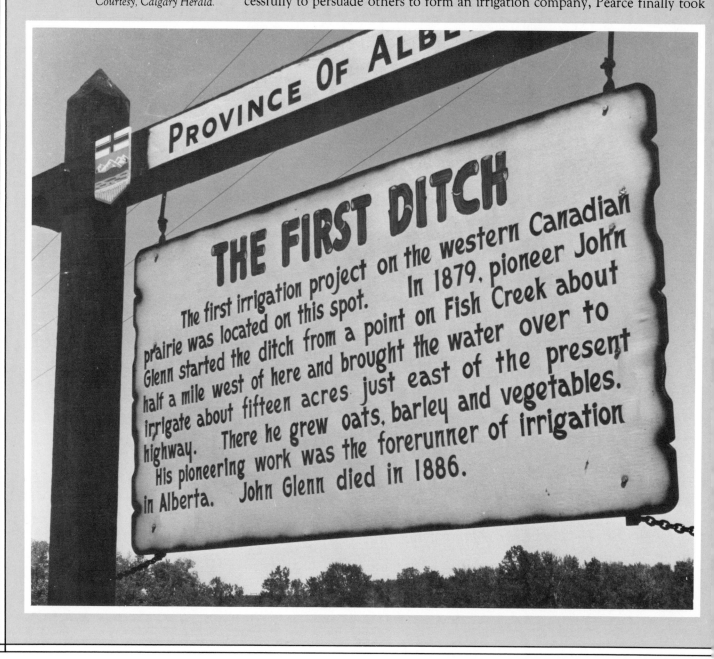

PROVINCE OF ALBE[RTA]

THE FIRST DITCH

The first irrigation project on the western Canadian prairie was located on this spot. In 1879, pioneer John Glenn started the ditch from a point on Fish Creek about half a mile west of here and brought the water over to irrigate about fifteen acres just east of the present highway. There he grew oats, barley and vegetables. His pioneering work was the forerunner of irrigation in Alberta. John Glenn died in 1886.

matters into his own hands. From his colleague, the Minister of the Interior, Pearce secured approval of his scheme to divert water from the Elbow River to irrigate semiarid lands near Calgary. He then formed the Calgary Irrigation Company to implement his proposals. Though still in the employ of the federal government, Pearce wielded control over this company by virtue of his large stockholdings and active involvement.

This control was not to last. Cries of monopoly were raised against the company, particularly by a rival fledgling farmers' group called the Springbank Irrigation League, which in contesting the water rights of the Calgary Irrigation Company came forward with a counter-proposal to divert the waters of the Elbow River. In the ensuing bitter controversy, Pearce's reputation and integrity were challenged, and his right to combine official with private business was brought up for public debate. The federal government finally arbitrated the matter and though its decision went against the Springbank group and vindicated Pearce, the latter was ordered to divest himself from any association with the Calgary Irrigation Company.

The reorganized company began operations in 1895 and by 1896 had over 15,000 acres under irrigation. With more than 60 miles of main canal, and solid customers like the city of Calgary, the company confidently faced the future. Oats, peas, beans, and cereal crops did very well, and on Pearce's Calgary farm, yields were 70 percent better than under conventional farming methods.

After 1897, a period of wet years reduced the need for irrigation. Successful dry-farming techniques convinced many farmers that irrigation was not only expensive but unnecessary. As a result, interest in irrigation declined greatly. Furthermore, floods and inadequate maintenance reduced the whole system to a state of disrepair. Not surprisingly the Calgary Irrigation Company fell into bankruptcy and was dissolved in 1907.

The way had been shown, however. It was obvious that only a powerful corporation backed by government aid could implement irrigation on a practical scale. The experience of the Calgary Irrigation Company simply proved that southern Alberta was worth the effort.

Above: *William Pearce, called the father of irrigation development for the southern Alberta area, formed the Calgary Irrigation Company and diverted water from the Elbow River to semiarid lands near Calgary. As one of Calgary's first conservationists, he was interested in tree planting and soil management. Courtesy, Glenbow-Alberta Institute.*

Below: *The Grand Trunk Pacific Railway bridge over the main irrigation canal near Calgary is shown near an elevator in 1911. Courtesy, Calgary Herald.*

Right: *Well-dressed passengers ride a Canadian Pacific Railway sleeping car in 1892. Hanging lamps, a carpeted aisle, and heavy curtains add to the atmosphere of elegance. Note the "no smoking" sign over the doorway. Courtesy, Glenbow-Alberta Institute.*

It is difficult to exaggerate the importance of the CPR to Calgary's economic development in the 30 years following civic incorporation. Whether a railroad town of 500 in 1884, or a bustling city of almost 50,000 in 1912, Calgary's fortunes were irrevocably affected, and even determined, by the steel rails. In economic terms, they supplied the lifeline to nurture commercial growth. In a social context, they were crucial in transforming Calgary from a frontier town to a vital urban expression of Western Canada.

Aside from its importance in affecting Calgary's economic development, the CPR was also a crucial agent in determining the physical face of the city. Decisions made by the railway company in the early years of urban growth had incalculable and permanent effects for Calgary's later spatial, industrial, commercial, and even residential patterns.

Initially the railroad company chose both the townsite and the exact location of the railway station. In opting for a station on the north side of the tracks, the CPR in effect decreed the precise placement of the commercial centre. Furthermore, by withholding certain lots from sale south of the tracks, the company was able to consolidate wholesale facilities in that area. The CPR also donated land for church, park, and municipal purposes, but reserved the right to choose the locations. For instance, the present location of city hall was not the choice of the founding civic fathers who had favoured a site farther west, closer to the railway station. Access routes to the city centre were also determined by the CPR, which acted arbitrarily and often counter to civic wishes in closing certain level crossings. Originally the railroad was responsible for building subways or underpasses beneath main thoroughfares. The decision to build these at Eighth Street West, First Street West, and First Street East was made arbitrarily, while responsibility for others like the Fourth Street West subway was negated by the Ogden Agreement.

The CPR was instrumental in influencing the differentiation of Calgary's early residential districts, which originally were located adjacent to the business district. Although handsome houses were erected on Seventh, Sixth and Fifth

Below: *In 1905 some of the industries located in east Calgary north of the Canadian Pacific Railway tracks were, from left to right: Calgary Brewing and Malting Company, Western Milling Company, and Alberta Iron Works. Courtesy, Glenbow-Alberta Institute.*

THE HUMAN SIDE

Below: *Employees clad in appropriate business attire work at their desks in the office of Toole Peet and Company at 809 Second Street Southwest in 1926. The real-estate firm was started by William Toole, an Irishman who had worked for the Land Department of the CPR. Courtesy, Glenbow-Alberta Institute.*

Facing page: *Arthur Garnet Graves, Calgary's most perennial and influential civic politician, served almost 25 years as an elected city commissioner after an earlier term as city alderman. He was the unquestioned authority on many civic matters. Courtesy, Glenbow-Alberta Institute.*

Several leading figures in the frontier era were former CPR employees who had come to the West through their association with the railroad company.

William Toole was an Irishman who joined the Land Department of the CPR in 1890; and in 1894 was appointed district agent in charge of land affairs with headquarters in Calgary. His activities over the next 10 years included supervising work in experiments carried out with winter wheat. The highly successful strain Alberta Red was the most significant outcome of this experimentation, and indeed Alberta Red was dominant in southern Alberta until the development of the spring wheat variety Marquis in 1910 transformed the nature of Western Canadian agriculture. Toole left the CPR in 1904 to enter private business, and for his solid service with the company was rewarded by being allowed to administer the CPR townsite holdings in Calgary. In subsequent years, the real estate firm of Toole Peet and Company became prominent as one of Calgary's leading business operations.

Arthur Garnet Graves was employed by the CPR in locomotive work for 10 years, 1897-1907, at Fort Macleod and Calgary. Following a brief period in private business as a real estate agent, as well as a term as city alderman, Graves

Thomas Underwood's family, including Mrs. Underwood, clad in an elegant "walking" outfit, and the baby in the wicker pram, pose in their front yard in 1905. The Underwood home, located at 536 13th Avenue West, was decorated with stained-glass windows. Courtesy, Glenbow-Alberta Institute.

was elected as one of Calgary's first civic commissioners in 1909. Over the next 25 years, Graves worked almost continuously in the city's service, becoming easily the most perennial figure in Calgary's municipal history. Graves's largely unheralded role in determining civic policies between 1909 and 1933 makes him a prime candidate for the title of Calgary's most underrated personality.

Thomas Underwood was a leading figure in commercial and social life for many years, and when he died in 1948 was one of Calgary's oldest continuous residents. He first came to Calgary in the 1890s as a carpenter on the CPR line between Medicine Hat and the Rockies. He entered the contracting business soon after, and later operated the successful Diamond Coal Company. Underwood was once described as "the man who made First Street West," having erected the first commercial building on that street, as well as a handsome edifice that still stands at the intersection with Thirteenth Avenue. Underwood was active in the temperance movement that was fast gaining momentum in the first decade of the 20th century. He was also the chief benefactor of the resident Chinese population, and was active in efforts to Christianize them. The first Chinatown in the vicinity of Tenth Avenue and First Street West was located on land owned by Thomas Underwood. Underwood was

also prominent in civic affairs, serving several years as alderman and one term as mayor.

The superintendent of Underwood's contracting operations was also a former CPR employee. Richard A. Brocklebank has been loosely described as the first working man to secure a position on the city council. A former carpenter with the CPR, Brocklebank eventually took over Underwood's entire contracting business, and was involved in the erection of several major structures including the YMCA building and the Carnegie Library in Central Park.

Reuben R. Jamieson began working for the CPR as a telegrapher in 1883, and reached the position of general superintendent before his retirement in 1908. Part of his career was spent in Calgary where he established the superintendency of the division in 1903. Following his retirement, he returned to Calgary permanently, and was elected mayor the following year (1909). His personal interests were manifested during his two year mayoralty term when Calgary established its municipal street railway system. He was also interested in the ill-fated Alberta Interurban line. Jamieson died prematurely in 1911. His widow, Alice, went on to achieve honours of her own, becoming the first woman judge in the British Empire in 1917.

Thomas Underwood, one of Calgary's early civic and commerical leaders, has been described as "the man who made First Street West." There he built the Underwood block, the dominant feature in Calgary's first commercial nucleus south of the CPR tracks. Courtesy, Glenbow-Alberta Institute.

Pat Burns' uniquely designed residence was built in 1901 at Fourth Street Southwest, where the Colonel Belcher Hospital stands today. Until it was demolished in 1956, the Burns house was among Calgary's most impressive structures. Courtesy, Calgary Herald.

avenues, the most exclusive mansions were to the south along Twelfth and Thirteenth avenues. Included here were the homes of Sir James A. Lougheed, Pat Burns, and William Roper Hull. Lougheed's home, appropriately named Beaulieu, was constructed in 1889 from local sandstone. With its spacious lawns and beautifully crafted interior, Beaulieu was for a time Calgary's showcase residence. While the Lougheed mansion still stands today, the Burns and the Hull residences have been replaced by the Belcher Hospital and the Hull Estates apartment block. The loss of the Hull estate is particularly unfortunate as it was probably the best example of classical architecture among early Calgary residences. Certainly, many of the city's more expensive homes during this period were examples of architectural eclecticism.

By 1909 Calgary's suburban expansion had begun. The extension of the corporate boundaries brought more CPR-owned land into the city. Through the real estate company of Toole Peet and Company, the CPR offered certain subdivisions for sale to prospective home builders. By establishing and enforcing differing building requirements in certain subdivisions, the railroad effectively dictated the pattern for future residential expansion. For instance, the subdivision of Bridgeland was offered for sale to working men. Houses were erected on 25-foot frontages on what was probably the finest scenic land in the city. At the time, however, it was out of the way and of marginal potential, being close to existing manufacturing establishments in east Calgary, and to the non-Anglo-Saxon element at Riverside. On the other hand, the subdivision known as Mount Royal was more favourably located. Here, stringent building restrictions were enforced, with the result that Mount Royal became Calgary's first exclusive suburb. The same applied to the CPR subdivision of Sunalta. By 1912 the residential pattern emerged that was to remain unchanged for 50 years. The dominance of the southwest in residential land values was due almost entirely to policies followed by the CPR between 1909 and 1912.

After 1912, the CPR in Calgary continued to be a dominant, albeit less visible, part of the city's economic life. In the early period, however, the railway acted almost unilaterally in influencing Calgary's physical and commercial development. Overall, the CPR has been as important in determining Calgary's urban growth as any other single element, the oil and natural gas industry notwithstanding.

Lady Lougheed, her daughter Marjorie, and their chauffeur prepare to go for a ride in front of "Beaulieu," the Lougheed mansion, which still stands today. Courtesy, Glenbow-Alberta Institute.

Right and below: *William Roper Hull's magnificent house at 12th Avenue and Sixth Street Southwest was demolished in 1970 to make way for the Hull Estates apartment complex. Courtesy, Calgary Herald.*

THE ALBERTA INTERURBAN RAILWAY COMPANY

Speculative interest in railway development was not confined to the traditional steam locomotive. Between 1909 and 1912, the electric-powered railway captured the interest of several speculators in Calgary. The municipal street railway system was the most popular with investors and in this respect the line to Bowness was the best practical example. Here a group of speculators exchanged island property in the Bow River for a civic commitment to extend the street railway line to Bowness, where a self-sufficient community of wealthy estate owners was envisaged. Another unsuccessful promotion provided for a luxury country club on the shores of Lake Chestermere east of the city limits. Again the main lure to potential investors was the promise of the street railway. Indeed it was believed that the speculators dumped railway ties along the projected right-of-way in order to convince the more sceptical investor of the likelihood of the proposed extension. Probably the most ambitious example of speculative interest in an electric-powered railroad was provided by the Alberta Interurban Railway Company.

The Interurban Railway Company was incorporated in 1912 to build and operate a network of standard-gauge electric lines to Calgary from various points in southern Alberta. While the initial line was to run from Carbon, other towns to be connected included Banff, Taber, Medicine Hat, Strathmore, Lethbridge, and Pincher Creek. In addition to a regular passenger service, the railroad was to carry fresh farm produce daily to the city market on the south side of the Bow River near the present Langevin Bridge. Four of the five directors were local men, including ex-mayor Reuben R. Jamieson and 1911 alderman, William Lathwell. In the ensuing negotiations with the city, the Interurban company was given permission to use the street railway lines within the city limits. Furthermore, 40 city lots were made available to the company for operational purposes at a nominal cost of $1.00 per year.

The Alberta Interurban Railway Company fell victim to the prewar depression, and like similar ventures was never begun, let alone completed. It was a speculative venture spurred on by the promise of limitless prosperity, and rendered feasible by the recent availability of hydroelectric power at Horse Shoe Falls. In a way it represented the final burst of railroad frenzy and, at the same time, the end of an era.

William Lathwell, a lawyer and city alderman, was one of the promoters of the ill-fated Alberta Interurban Railway Company. Courtesy, Calgary Herald.

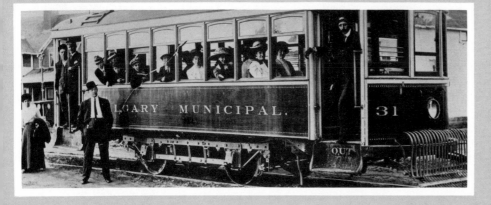

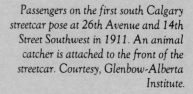

Passengers on the first south Calgary streetcar pose at 26th Avenue and 14th Street Southwest in 1911. An animal catcher is attached to the front of the streetcar. Courtesy, Glenbow-Alberta Institute.

THE FIRST FRONTIER

CHAPTER FOUR
CALGARY AND CATTLE

Calgary has long been generally regarded by Canadians as a cattle town. Though the term is somewhat misleading, it cannot be denied that the ranching frontier provided Calgary with its first economic muscle. Especially before 1907, the ranching hinterland was crucial to Calgary's commercial existence, and early business leaders fully appreciated the implications of their dependence on cattle. Thus it was not surprising to find a conscious identification with the cattle industry emerging very early, and long before the Calgary Stampede popularized Calgary's cowtown image. But while the cattle industry did indeed nurture Calgary's early economic and social life, its overall effects were less positive than those advertised by popular tradition. In fact, the cattle industry infused an unpredictable and often unstable element into the city's economy. Calgary's new status as a major urban centre in Canada's national life has had little to do with cattle, cowboys, meat or stetsons.

A cattle industry in Western Canada was made possible by the demise of the buffalo. Buffalo and cattle could not co-exist on the open range as the more aggressive bison would kill the bulls and take the cows into their own herds. But after 1878 with the virtual disappearance of the buffalo, the idea of using the lush grasses of the foothills for grazing became a tantalizing possibility. Southern Alberta, it appeared, possessed all the ingredients for successful open range operations. Plentiful fresh water and adequate sheltered areas complemented the highly favourable and fast-growing prairie grasses. It was thus only a matter of time before the ranching frontier moved north across the 49th parallel into Canada. The Marquis of Lorne was reputed to have once said that had he not been Governor General of Canada, he would be a cattle rancher in Alberta.

The earliest ranching operations were sporadic affairs designed to cater to the local demand for beef created by the arrival of the North West Mounted Police in Alberta in 1874. The first serious attempts to introduce cattle to Alberta occurred in 1877 when Tom Lynch and George Emerson brought a small herd to Fort Macleod for sale to retired Mounted Police officers who hoped to begin their own ranches. Then in 1879, Lynch and Emerson moved 1,000 head from Montana into the Highwood country. But while it had been proven that cattle ranching was possible in Alberta, the organization of permanent large-scale commercial operations had to wait for a systematic method of land disposal. Beginning about 1880, wealthy eastern Canadian and British cattle breeders, together with the ubiquitous entrepreneurial element, began to pressure the federal government to sanction the establishment of formal cattle

Facing page: Bar U Ranch cowboys participated in the general roundup of cattle in southern Alberta on May 31, 1901. A North West Mounted Policeman, wearing his shiny buttoned uniform, stands at centre. Courtesy, Glenbow-Alberta Institute.

ranching in southern Alberta.

In 1881, the federal government introduced its controversial lease system, which provided for 21-year leases at one cent per acre per year. Prospective lessees were expected to stock their land within three years with one head of cattle per 10 acres. One of the first to take advantage of the new lease system was Senator Matthew Cochrane, a wealthy Quebec cattle breeder. Following a visit to Alberta, the internationally known Cochrane secured a lease of 100,000 acres of rolling land at Big Hill northwest of Calgary. Cochrane bought 3,000 head of mixed cattle for $16.00 a head in Montana, and paid an additional two dollars and fifty cents a head to have them delivered at Calgary to James Walker, his ranch manager, who in turn drove them to the ranch site in the present town of Cochrane. There the haggard, unbranded beasts, their numbers depleted by the long hard drive, faced the bitter western winter in a state of pathetic unpreparedness. When spring came, the coulees were filled with carcasses. By any yardstick, the Cochrane experiment and the cattle industry had made a most inauspicious debut.

Ranchers brand cattle through a "squeeze" at Bar U Ranch in southern Alberta, circa 1905. A "squeeze" is a device used to secure an animal in the chute for branding and vaccinating. Squeezes have changed from primitive types consisting of hinged gates, which operators squeezed by pressure, to modern mechanical devices that can be installed in chutes. Courtesy, Glenbow-Alberta Institute.

Cochrane tried again unsuccessfully before moving his ranch operations south to the area between the Waterton and Oldman rivers in 1883. Fortunately his setbacks did not deter others from bringing cattle to the Canadian range. In 1882, the colourful Fred Stimson brought 3,000 head for the North West Cattle Company to the Highwood country. Later known by its more famous name, the Bar U, this ranch became one of Alberta's largest and most famous cattle operations. In 1883 another 3,000 head were brought in to stock the equally famous Oxley Ranch on Willow Creek. By the end of 1883 there were more than 25,000 head of cattle between the Bow River and the American boundary. A year later 1.7 million acres were under lease to 41 assorted companies. Southern Alberta had become cattle country.

The period 1886-1906 roughly marks the golden age of the open range industry. By the end of that time, three million acres were under lease. There were almost 1,000 leases and about one million head of cattle in Alberta. Economically, ranching was a profitable enterprise. For example, in 1896 the Walrond Ranch Company declared over $133,000 in clear profit.

STOCKING THE SOUTHERN ALBERTA RANGE

The rangelands of southern Alberta were stocked between 1881 and 1886 mainly with cattle purchased in Montana. Evidence presented by Professor Simon Evans suggests that the original herds were of superior quality, which might seem surprising to those who envisaged the Alberta cattle industry as a haphazard extension of its American counterpart.

Much of the Montana stock had its origins in the Pacific Northwest. Here, high quality bulls from a Durham-shorthorn cross had been imported to accommodate the mining market of the Northwest. By the time the Montana cattle barons were building up their herds in the 1870s, the Durham-shorthorn cross had become acclimatized to the more extreme conditions of mountainous areas. This, combined with other selective breeding practices, resulted in good quality stock being available to the new Alberta leaseholders in 1891.

Cowboys at Mosquito Creek round up cattle bearing brands of the Quorn, Bar U, Oxley, 44, A7 and 25 ranches. Courtesy, Glenbow-Alberta Institute.

While the origins of the first Cochrane herd are somewhat obscure, the second herd of about 4,000 was considered among the finest in Montana. The Oxley Ranch and North West Cattle Company were stocked with herds of better than average quality. Also, the Walrond Ranch purchased its original herd from T.C. Power, an eminent Montana cattle breeder.

Montana was not the only source looked to by pioneer Alberta cattlemen. Pedigreed stock was purchased elsewhere. For instance in 1881, 125 Herefords and 21 polled Angus bulls were bought in Chicago for the Cochrane Ranch and the North West Cattle Company, respectively. Other consignments were received from Great Britain and Eastern Canada, with the result that when shipments of Alberta beef began to reach distant markets in 1887, they elicited favourable comments and commanded good prices.

Thus the beginnings of the Alberta cattle industry were on solid foundations. For the most part the business acumen and expertise of early ranchers ensured good quality herds to start their operations. As will be noted, the subsequent deterioration in herd quality was due to policies pursued in later years.

ALFRED ERNEST CROSS TELLS OF THE ROUNDUP OF 1887

In December 1923, Mr. A.E. Cross of the A7 Ranch, founder of the Calgary Brewing and Malting Company, addressed a meeting of the Calgary Historical Society. In his talk entitled "The Roundup of 1887," Mr. Cross described some of his recollections of an early Alberta roundup, which in the days of the open range were large cooperative ventures. The following are some excerpts from that address reprinted in its entirety in the spring 1965 issue of the *Alberta Historical Review*.

"It was about June 1, 1887, after the most severe and disastrous winter ever experienced in the cattle ranching history of North America. Few of the ranchers lost less than 40 percent, some losing 100, many losing 75 percent. The roundup met at what was then known as the High River Crossing, composed of a stopping house, a good-sized stable, and a stockade corral, all built of logs. The old stopping house was run by Buck Smith who used to whittle sticks (being one of the habits of many old timers) while he related his wonderful experiences of hunting buffalo. Poker and an occasional bottle of red-eye were the principal attractions. The stage and the mail coach running from Calgary to Fort Macleod called at the Crossing once or twice a week going each way. Men in those days did not seem very much interested even in the mail, being so far removed from the outside world...."

"Bachelor's Hall," a bunkhouse on a southern Alberta ranch, was the working cowboys' home on the ranch. Furnishings include a homemade log chair (right), a wood- or coal-burning stove (centre), and a pitcher and washbasin (left). The bed is occupied by a sleeping dog. Courtesy, Glenbow-Alberta Institute.

Bar U cowboys and a North West Mounted Policeman (seated at left) relax in their tent on June 1, 1901, during a general roundup in southern Alberta. Courtesy, Glenbow-Alberta Institute.

"The general roundup was a large one, each outfit having about 15 riders besides the cook, night herder, and horse wrangler. It looked like a formidable outfit as we rode up to the high ground in the early morning from our various camps. The Captain (Howell Harris of the Circle Ranch) sat in his saddle like a general and picked out the most suitable riders who knew the country. Counting off about 10 riders with each, they were instructed to ride over a certain piece of country, and to bring all the cattle to a certain point further ahead.

"The head rider started over the prairies; the rest followed suit, going in various directions so that all the country was carefully covered and very few cattle were missed. When all the cattle were rounded up they were held in by riders surrounding them. The bunches were kept well apart to permit comfortable working.

"The calves and cows were separated and when the cows had been cut out they were driven to a suitable grazing and watering place where their particular outfit was camped. This started the herd which was moved and added to each day as the roundup moved on. The herd reached about 2,000 and an outfit was sent to drive them onto their range."

Mr. Cross went on to describe some of the individual ranching operations that took part in the roundup. In a few brief pages he referred to several outfits and characters who, like Cross himself, have become synonymous with the early days of cattle ranching in southern Alberta. His article is valuable historically as it is one of the few firsthand accounts of 19th century ranching operations available to the public.

The economic base for a successful open range industry was created by the emergence of a hungry British market and the completion of the Canadian Pacific Railway in 1886. Sales to Britain began in 1888 when 5,000 head brought between $40 and $50 per head. Between 1891 and 1906 an annual average of about 50,000 head of cattle made their way from Alberta ranches to Great Britain. A more favourable American tariff structure in the 1890s resulted in more cattle being shipped south of the border. National figures show a peak of over 90,000 in 1899.

The slow progress of agriculture prolonged the dominance of the cattle industry. Particularly in the early and mid-1890s, popular opinion held that southern Alberta was unsuited to agriculture, and to prove the point, ranchers indicated the widespread presence of rusting barbed wire, rotting fence posts, and abandoned homesteads. Knowledgeable individuals like William Pearce, Dominion Superintendent of Lands and Mines and ardent conservationist, maintained that the natural grass cover, or "prairie wool," was superb for grazing, but disturbing and breaking it to sod could have serious consequences. And as many were to discover during the dust of the Depression, Pearce's predictions proved ominously accurate.

The era after 1906-1907 was paradoxically one of both expansion and

THE WINTER OF 1906 - 1907

It seemed destined to be a bad winter. On the fenced and overstocked ranges, summer prairie fires had taken their toll, with the result that little good grass was available for winter grazing. Then fall began badly with bitterly cold periods compounded by late drenching rains that turned to sleet. The lingering presence of mange in many range cattle added to the problem. Indeed, some beasts were actually hairless when the full force of winter hit. The combination of lack of food, uncured grasses, poor physical condition, and extreme weather was to exact a frightful price. Losses were estimated at over $10 million, while in the Calgary district total herd depletion was said to be over 60 percent.

One of the classic works on Alberta's early cattle days is *The Rangemen*, written by Calgary resident L.V. Kelly in 1913. In his discussion of the winter of 1906-1907, Kelly tells of an incident that graphically illustrates the awful impact of southern Alberta's worst winter in living memory.

"One day in January 1907, just north of Fort Macleod, a dark rustling mass appeared on the horizon, silhouetted against the snow. It was moving slowly towards the town, and as it approached could be identified as thousands of starving cattle. A steady wailing filled the air as the emaciated, wretched beasts staggered blindly along the road allowances. Straight into town they came, gaunt, hairless steers and tottering yearlings, six or eight abreast, lowing piteously for the help that no one could give. And as they made their way through town, past the gaping onlookers, some dropped in exhaustion to

contraction—expansion in numbers of cattle, and contraction in the lands available to carry them. Cash crop farming continued to encroach on former grazing lands and cheap ranges disappeared. Increasingly cattle operations became smaller, and were often combined with other agricultural operations with the result that more stock were sold off farms rather than ranches. With this shift in emphasis, the predominant position of southern Alberta and Calgary in the Canadian cattle industry was weakened.

In fact, the development of the cattle industry in southern Alberta can be interpreted more readily in terms of adversity rather than progress. In the first place, the emphasis on open range operations had serious implications, not the least of which were the vagaries of weather. The winter of 1886-1887, for example, was catastrophic in terms of stock losses, and did much towards reducing the desire of American cattlemen to stock the Canadian range. Even more disastrous was the winter of 1906-1907. The Bar U ranch lost 12,000 of its herd of about 24,000. One rancher spoke of dying cattle lying down for the last time on the bodies of those already dead. It has been said that the winter of 1906-1907 marked the end of an era. In its brutal and uncompromising way, it opened the way to mixed farming more effectively than either changing demands or political decisions.

perish where they lay in front of the stores and businesses that advertised Fort Macleod as a thriving cattle town. Forty-eight carcasses littered the main street before the doomed herd moved out and onto the endless prairie to the oblivion of death in the snow and cold."

Snowy winters treated cattle harshly, and many thousands died in the devastating winter of 1906-1907. Courtesy, Calgary Herald.

Since 1901, the Calgary Bull Sale has become a great annual meeting place for ranchers, farmers, and breeders of purebred cattle. Originally backed by the Northwest Territories Cattle Breeders Association, the sale was recognized for many years as the biggest event of its kind in the world. Courtesy, Calgary Exhibition and Stampede.

The open range factors contributed to a deterioration in stock quality. The importation of inferior bulls, combined with random breeding practices, had adverse effects in sales. Canadian cattle consistently brought less than their American counterparts on the British market. The first provincial bull sale held in Calgary in 1903 represented an attempt by local cattle organizations to upgrade the quality of Alberta beef, and in the ensuing years, top Alberta cattle did well at the prestigious Chicago cattle auction. Here, the efforts of A.E. Cross should be noted, as on four separate occasions his cattle topped the sale.

The pressure to produce an increasingly high quality of stock, especially after World War I, spelled near-disaster to many small operators who, faced with rising operational costs, were forced into debt and into using cost-saving measures. Political decisions, too, had negative effects on the cattle industry.

For example, Alberta cattlemen considered that policies pursued by the federal Liberal government after 1896 did much towards crippling the livestock industry. They felt that unfavourable legislation respecting lease cancellations and stock watering reserves meant an unnecessary end to successful open range operations.

The problem of markets was crucial in retarding the development of the Alberta livestock industry. First, the domestic market was unable to absorb Canadian production, a situation exacerbated in Alberta by the problems created by distance, as well as by the competition from Ontario and Quebec beef producers. Yet the subsequent reliance on foreign markets to accommodate surplus production, estimated at about 150,000 head annually in the 1920s, did not resolve the difficulties. The United States market was particularly vexatious to the Canadian cattlemen, who found their options severely limited by the frequent changes in the American tariff and quota systems. In short, the Alberta cattle industry was neither able nor even allowed to compete with its giant counterpart south of the border.

Canadian marketing difficulties were compounded by the rise of highly competitive cheap-beef producing nations like Australia and Argentina, which were able to take advantage of modern refrigeration technology to offset their disadvantageous location. There were other vagaries. An outbreak of pleuropneumonia in the early 1890s resulted in a British embargo on Canadian cattle. Similarly, the presence of mange in the late 1890s reflected itself in lower prices on overseas markets.

In the late 1920s and during the Great Depression the fortunes of the cattle industry went from bad to worse. The founding of the journal *The Canadian Cattlemen* in 1938 represented in part an attempt to address serious collective concerns. The early issues were replete with pessimistic accounts by livestock authorities on the industry's unstable history to date.

Finally, the nature of Alberta's cattle industry limited Calgary's development as a livestock centre. For though there were several meat packing plants in the city, they catered largely to local and regional demands. Even P. Burns and Company Limited, easily Canada's largest independent meat packing enterprise, was dwarfed by its great American rival, Swift and Company. Aside from its distance from marketing, the most significant reason explaining Calgary's modest development as a meat packing centre was the fact that most Alberta cattle were fattened or finished in Eastern Canada or the United States. Being essentially a marketing and shipping centre, Calgary could scarcely have achieved its wistful ambition of becoming "the Chicago of Canada."

The circumstances of the cattle industry dictated that Calgary become the urban expression of the ranching frontier. In the first place, cattle operations demanded centralized facilities for marshalling, marketing, and processing. Unlike agriculture, there was a sharp division between the managerial and operational functions, especially on the large spreads. The big ranch owners and managers pursued a life-style much different from the cowboys they employed. This tightly knit managerial group was elitist, and contributed a cultural and social dimension that demanded refinements found only in large urban centres. From the outset, the ranching industry cultivated a spirit of cooperation, the best early example of which was the general roundup. In later

A Chinese cook works in a ranch kitchen, papered with pages of periodicals, in southern Alberta in 1905-1906. Kitchen utensils hang on the walls, and a "Tetley's Tea" can sits on the shelf. Courtesy, Glenbow-Alberta Institute.

Before 1920 the proximity of the Calgary Stockyards to the P. Burns and Company packing plant symbolized early Calgary's close association with the ranching frontier. Courtesy, Glenbow-Alberta Institute.

years stockmen were quick to realize the advantages of joint political action to safeguard their interests. For economic, social, and political reasons, then, the cattle industry cultivated an urban extension of itself. Between 1884 and 1906-1907, Calgary rose to prominence primarily because it could cater to the demands created by the ranching frontier.

It is interesting that Calgary was not the initial centre of ranching operations. That honour went to Fort Macleod, which between 1881 and 1885 saw its future in roseate terms. However, the completion of the Canadian Pacific Railway in 1886 effectively shattered Fort Macleod's dream of retaining its position as the headquarters of a fast-growing cattle industry.

The first indication of Calgary's new role came in 1887 when the CPR wanted to locate stockyards to handle the cattle shipments that were increasingly making their way down the Macleod Trail to the railhead. The

decision as to where the stockyards should be located engendered a lively public debate with the town council and the CPR in hot disagreement. A compromise solution was put forward by James Walker, who suggested that the town purchase a quarter of Section 11 from the territorial government. This section was designated school lands and was not open to normal homestead entry or deeded to the CPR. Walker's proposal was accepted. The stockyards were placed in their present location where, according to a relieved *Calgary Tribune,* "the prevailing winds would not blow the offensive effluvia over the town." With the establishment of the stockyard, Calgary gained the nucleus for its subsequent manufacturing base in east Calgary.

Calgary Stockyards Company was organized by the Canadian Pacific Railway and became one of the biggest livestock marketing centres in Canada. Courtesy, Glenbow-Alberta Institute.

W.R. Hull, prominent in Calgary's early development, built his ranch house in Midnapore. Pat Burns later owned the house, whose doorway was flanked by ribs of whales and decorated with suspended vertebrae. Courtesy, Glenbow-Alberta Institute.

Even before the arrival of the CPR stockyards, Calgary butchers met district demands for dressed beef. In 1884, over 250,000 pounds of beef were shipped from Calgary to railway contractors to meet what was described as "the Christmas demand." Calgary's first meat market was established in 1883 by A.G. Sparrow and Company. By 1885 Sparrow's company had butchered 3,500 head of cattle at its slaughterhouse just outside the town limits. Sparrow's meat market catered to regional demands from as far away as Medicine Hat and was described in Calgary's first business directory in 1885 as "the most complete meat market west of Chicago."

Another early participant in the slaughtering and retail meat trade was English-born William Roper Hull, who opened a meat business in Calgary in 1884. Hull soon expanded into ranching, and in its time his Bow River Ranch south of Calgary on Fish Creek was considered the showpiece of the district. Social gatherings at the ranch house were often lavish affairs, and included titled guests, stringed music, lawn entertainment, and of course the inevitable hunt. The ranch house itself still stands, and forms part of the administrative buildings for Fish Creek Provincial Park.

Though he did not remain in the meat business, selling out to Pat Burns in 1905, Hull was prominent in Calgary's early development. He helped organize many local enterprises including the brewery, a pork packing plant, the Turf Club, and the Calgary Irrigation Company. He was also part of a group interested in establishing a street railway system in the city in the early 1890s. Hull was also instrumental in erecting several major buildings in the city. Included were the Victoria Block, Hull's Opera House, and the splendid Grain Exchange Building, completed in 1909 and still standing today. The Hull Home for special-needs children in southwest Calgary is another continuing legacy to this generous, intrepid man of action who once had the daring to drive 1,200 horses from Kamloops to Calgary.

Significantly it was railroad development that brought another "meat man" to Calgary in 1890. The construction of the line to Edmonton in 1890-1891 by the contracting firm of Mackenzie and Mann necessitated beef contracts to feed the hungry crews. Donald Mackenzie looked no further than his boyhood friend, Pat Burns, to do the job. The arrival of the chubby Burns in the city heralded the start of a career that was to elevate the modest but outstandingly astute Irish-Ontarian to a position as Canada's cattle king, and Calgary's best known citizen.

The story of Burns' meteoric rise to success and fortune is incredible. From a small slaughterhouse (which was destroyed by fire in 1892 and rebuilt in east Calgary) Burns supplied meat to regional customers. By 1898, over 600 head per month were needed to fill railway and Indian contracts, to supply emerging towns along the newly constructed railroads, and to feed the lumber and mining camps of British Columbia.

Pat Burns' abattoir in east Calgary was built in 1905-1906. Burns began his meat-packing career in Calgary in 1890, and his business in livestock and meat processing expanded across the country. Courtesy, Glenbow-Alberta Institute.

In 1910 Burns Shamrock Brand was probably the best-known meat in Western Canada. Pat Burns sold his packing interest for $15 million in 1928. Courtesy, Glenbow-Alberta Institute.

The Klondike gold rush in the late 1890s gave Burns another opportunity to display his business aggressiveness in the face of a lucrative but challenging market. Cattle were shipped to Skagway and then driven across forbidding passes where they were slaughtered, wrapped in burlap, and rafted down the Yukon River to Dawson City. The unheard-of price of one dollar per pound made the daring venture worthwhile.

A do-it-yourself man, Burns did most of the cattle buying himself, and so it was only natural that he should consider the possibility of a truly integrated meat business. He already possessed several retail outlets in British Columbia and had begun to deal in meats other than beef. Over the next decade he set out to realize his ambition. He went into ranching in a big way, buying several large spreads. By 1912, he had six large ranches including William Roper Hull's Bow River Ranch at Midnapore. The number eventually reached 12, totalling about half a million acres. With these acquisitions, Burns was able to breed, fatten, and slaughter his own cattle, which, combined with his expanding retail outlets, gave him total involvement in the preparation, marketing and disposal of his product.

Expansion came quickly. Burns' meat packing plants appeared in six other Canadian cities as rival enterprises were incorporated into his growing empire. With the opening of offices in Great Britain, Europe, and Japan to handle exports, the name of Pat Burns had assumed international prominence.

Though his enterprises were dominated by his huge Calgary meat packing plant and slaughterhouses, Burns never lost sight of the need to increase the marketing potential of domestic food animals. He branched into tanneries,

creameries, dairying, and fertilizer plants. Later he attempted to include vegetables in his operations. He dabbled more than occasionally in mining but experienced little success. He was also active in local enterprises including building and real estate speculation, and as usual, he was more astute than most. Records show that he was one of the few who successfully unloaded real estate holdings before the crash in 1913-1914. When Burns sold out to Dominion Securities in 1928 for $15 million, he was already a living legend in Calgary. Local supporters prepared a two-ton cake to mark his 75th birthday in 1931. Burns was elevated to the Canadian Senate the same year, and died in Calgary in 1937.

Burns' business identity is perpetuated in Calgary through Burns Food Ltd. But the name and the meat packing operations are the chief similarities between the modern company and its corporate frontier ancestor. Restructured in 1974, and rescued from the brink of financial disaster by its able chief executive, Arthur Child, the new Burns corporation has diversified on a scale that Pat Burns would have appreciated. Burns Foods Ltd. is a holding company for at least 13 other corporations that handle various kinds of foods as well as dealing in transportation, catering, and the restaurant business. In 1975, annual sales exceeded $622 million, which in turn netted a profit of $4.7 million to company shareholders. Its 73 plants and offices, employing over 6,000 people across Canada, help make Burns Foods Ltd. one of the country's 25 largest private corporations. There are a couple of historical ironies, however. Meat packing operations have been curtailed in the new expansion, while the majority of shares in this former Western Canadian giant are held in Ontario.

Pat Burns, Alberta's leading industrialist, poses at his ranch in Bow Valley in about 1930. He came west from Kirkfield, Ontario, to homestead in Manitoba in 1878, and within a few years he was contracted to furnish beef for construction workers on the Calgary and Edmonton Railway. He settled in Calgary, and as the slaughterhouse he built became an abattoir, he grew to become a meat and cattle king. Courtesy, Glenbow- Alberta Institute.

Pat Burns represents the western success story. He started penniless and with little formal education, but showed how hard work and avowed confidence in a raw, new land could pay handsome dividends. More than any other single individual, it was Pat Burns who solidified Calgary's relationship with the cattle industry. His comment in 1911 that he "had made Calgary," while somewhat irreverent, was not without foundation.

While the Burns enterprises most clearly emphasized Calgary's association with cattle, they represented only one of many manufacturing concerns dependent on the cattle industry for survival. The town's first manufacturing base in the early 1890s provides an example in point. By 1900, there were at least three slaughtering operations, a soapworks, tannery, pork packing plant,

Left: *Men attempt to drive the Calgary Brewing and Malting Company's team of buffalo for the brewery's owner, A.E. Cross (on horseback). Courtesy, Glenbow-Alberta Institute.*

Below: *Bartenders George Clair (left) and Fred Adams worked at the Alberta Hotel at the turn of the century. In the 1950s Picardy's store occupied the site of the bar, reputed to be the longest in Alberta. Courtesy, Glenbow-Alberta Institute.*

and cold storage works. And ranchers invested heavily in other local businesses as well. The best example was the Calgary Brewing and Malting Company Ltd., which began its long association with Calgary in 1892 under the direction of Big Four cattleman Alfred Ernest Cross. For years the Cross home, which still stands in east Calgary, occupied almost a manorial position in the social evolution of the district somewhat graphically known as Breweryville. The celebrated and ostentatious Alberta Hotel, erected in 1889, was financed by ranching interests. The penchant for cattlemen to invest heavily in Calgary, whether it be in business blocks, manufacturing enterprises, or even municipal utilities, was additional evidence of the close interdependence between Calgary and the cattle industry.

Right: *Pat Burns' residence on Fourth Street West, shown just prior to its demolition in 1956, once symbolized Calgary's prosperity. The cattle rancher's splendid home has been replaced by the Colonel Belcher Hospital, which serves war veterans. Courtesy, Calgary Herald.*

Below: *A child rides in a basket chair, designed to fit on a horse, at the Bedingfeld Ranch in Alberta in 1913. The Bedingfeld Ranch at Pekisko was bought by the Prince of Wales and became the E.P. Ranch. Courtesy, Glenbow-Alberta Institute.*

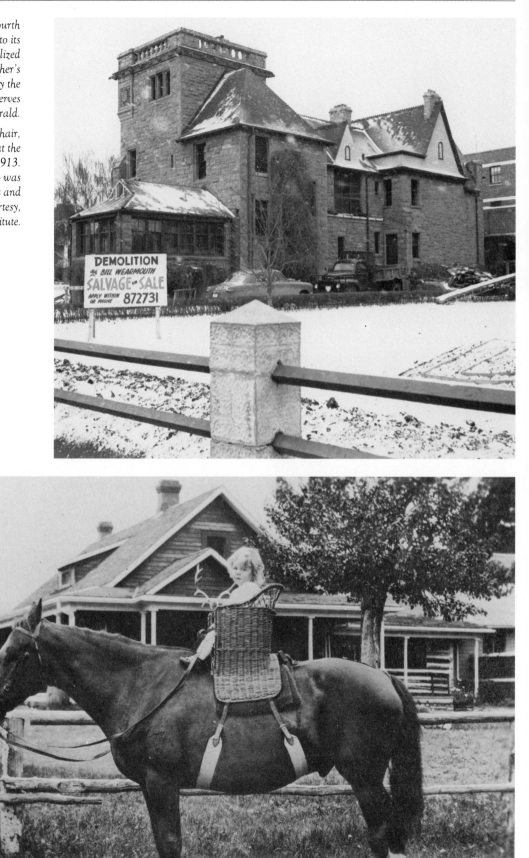

The cattlemen also made their presence felt in Calgary's social life. Their mansions were among the town's most opulent, especially the castle-like structure erected by Pat Burns, or the architecturally aesthetic residence of William Roper Hull. Ranchers were prominent on the elitist board of directors of Calgary's first general hospital, joining such social luminaries as Senator James A. Lougheed, Bishop Cyprian Pinkham, Judge Rouleau, and banker E.B. Braithwaite. Ranching interests enjoyed a prestigious position on the toasting ladder at the banquet table, while the Ranchmen's Club, formed in 1893, with its assorted membership of Calgary professional men and affluent ranchers, represented the apex of Calgary society.

The Ranchmen's Club was based on the St. James Club in Montreal. With a restricted membership and an inordinately high initiation fee of $200, this club preserved the exclusiveness often demanded by wealth and prestige. Features included a library, private dining rooms, exclusive and expensive menus, the London *Times*, and 10-year-old Edinburgh Scotch. Elsewhere, in areas of recreation, the names of ranchers were conspicuous in local cricket and

Hull's Opera House, named after William Roper Hull, was built in 1893 at Centre Street and Sixth Avenue South with a capacity of one thousand people. The Calgary Opera Company and the Calgary Amateur Dramatic Club staged many grand productions in this magnificent building. Courtesy, Glenbow-Alberta Institute.

polo teams as well as in the Turf and Hunt clubs. They, or more specifically their wives, could be seen at gala occasions at Hull's Opera House. Certainly ranchers provided the crucial element in the fusion of town and country life typified by the Calgary of the frontier era.

Right: *Rancher Charles Perrenoud and his son, George, pose at their ranch in Alberta, circa 1905. The frame building at left was added to the original log structure, a construction common in those days. Courtesy, Glenbow-Alberta Institute.*

Below right: *In the 1920s the Prince of Wales chats with Guy Weadick (left) at the E.P. Ranch in Alberta. Guy Weadick, one of the most glamorous cowboys in the Western scene, managed the first Calgary Stampede in 1912 and returned as its permanent director in 1923. Courtesy, Glenbow-Alberta Institute.*

Facing page, top: *Some of Calgary's most prominent citizens gather at the Prince of Wales' E.P. Ranch, circa 1919. They are, from left to right: the Honourable A.J. McLean, A.E. Cross, Dan Riley, Sir W. Peacock, R.B. Bennett, W.L. Carlyle, E.D. Adams, the Prince of Wales, George Lane, Pat Burns, the Honourable P.C. Larkin, Joseph H. "7 U" Brown, Major General Trotter, Colonel James Walker, and Major D. Metcalfe. Courtesy, Glenbow-Alberta Institute.*

Bottom: *If any single plough won the West, it was the walking plough. Farmers welcomed the next development — the one-furrow plough, known as a sulky, which had a seat for the operator. The one-furrow was an intermediate stage between the walking plough and the two-furrow or gang plough. From the Grant MacEwan Collection.*

Between 1881 and 1906-1907, Calgary's close association with the cattle, or more specifically the open range, industry reflected itself in several ways. Economically and commercially, Calgary benefited by the demands created by the ranchers. The cattlemen in turn invested heavily in local enterprise. Culturally, the ranching society contributed to Calgary's social stratification. This close interdependence was modified and changed after 1908 by the increasing advance of agriculture, and by evolutionary developments in the nature of the cattle industry itself. Yet the transformation from open range ranching to more traditional methods of animal husbandry did not lessen the element of instability. So while the romanticism may have disappeared with the open range, the volatility remained.

CALGARY'S FIRST STAMPEDE, 1912

Calgary's first Stampede was held in September 1912, just before the collapse of the real estate boom, and when the fortunes of the foothills city seemed at their peak. It was a bold, speculative venture typical of the age, and proved to be easily the most successful event ever staged in the city. But here was another dimension to the Stampede that in fact represented a conscious "last hurrah" to a vanishing way of life.

The idea of the Stampede was conceived in the fertile mind of a born promoter. Guy Weadick, a well-known American vaudeville cowboy, had in

Bareback and saddle-bronc riding are two of the most popular events at the Calgary Stampede, and they reflect both the Indian and cowboy heritage. Courtesy, Calgary Exhibition and Stampede.

previous visits to the city become convinced of Calgary's potential for an outdoor western show. The dream became a reality when he secured the financial backing of cattlemen George Lane, Pat Burns, A.E. Cross and A.J. McLean (known since as the Big Four). It is fairly certain that the four men were not induced to guarantee the Stampede financially by Weadick's silver tongue, the lure of profits, or even by possible historical immortality. They were, instead, aware of and worried by the changing nature of the cattle industry. The popularity of cash crop farming and adverse legislation had sent the open range industry into full retreat. Lane, Burns, and Cross had gone on record as saying that the old-style cattle industry was as good as dead. Therefore, their guarantee of $100,000 to cover the costs of the Stampede was probably no more than a nostalgic gesture to "the good old days."

The first Stampede was planned on an extravagant scale. Twenty thousand dollars were set aside for rodeo prizes. Two hundred wicked Mexican longhorns were imported, plus 300 of the meanest horses available. Some of the best riders in North America were attracted to the competitions, which

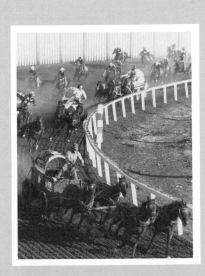

included the new and exciting rodeo sport of bulldogging. Five thousand Indians were in attendance, many in full regalia. There was even a replica of Fort Whoop-Up with old whisky trader Fred Kanouse presiding.

Most of the rodeo honours went to American cowboys, and even though Calgary's Clem Gardner won the all-around Canadian championship, the highlight of the riding events was the victory of Blood Indian Tom Three Persons in the Bucking Horse Contest. His ride on the notorious Cyclone to win the event is vividly described by L.V. Kelly in the following account.

"Straight into the air the animal reared until the Indian's body stood almost horizontal, then like a dog coming from water Cyclone shook himself with a mighty shake that would have dislodged a panther; but the saddle cinches withstood that awful strain and Three Persons stayed firmly in his seat, waving his hat as he 'fanned' his mount to force it into the buck-jumps. Johnny Franklin, judge of the buckers, rode close and watched with an eagle eye as the big brute sunfished, swapped ends, zigzagged, and pitched, but the rider rode by balance and skill, without spurs or roll or reins. A hundred times a minute the thousand pounds of hardened horse muscle humped five feet in the air, and hit the ground with every joltable twist and jar that he was capable of, but the Indian was waving his victorious hat at the thundering grandstand thousands. Finally the animal grew discouraged, bucked a few final plunges and gave up while his owner, Bertha Blanchard of Arizona, wept her disappointment...."

In the ensuing years of depression and war, it is not surprising that the Stampede did not return for some time. It was not until 1923 that the Stampede, complete with Guy Weadick and the added attraction of chuck waggon races became an annual feature in Calgary. Over the years, the famous Stampede has become synonymous with the vibrancy of the city's outdoor ethic, and a fitting advertisement for a unique urban identity.

Left: Chuckwaggon races were instituted as an attraction when the Calgary Stampede was revived in the 1920s. From the Grant MacEwan Collection.

Above: The nucleus of the chuckwaggon races was the "chuck" or cook's waggon, a surviving reminder of the ranching era. Courtesy, Calgary Exhibition and Stampede.

THE FIRST FRONTIER

CHAPTER FIVE
CONSTRUCTION AND REAL ESTATE

The growth of Calgary from a cluster of tents in 1882 to a bustling, modern city within the space of 30 years was accompanied by two closely dependent phenomena. The first was the development of a flourishing construction industry, the most reliable barometer of urban expansion. The second was the ubiquitous presence of speculation in real estate. More than anything else, it was these two activities that most vividly advertised Calgary's frontier environment before 1914. However, since both depended for their existence on the promise of continued growth induced by other economic sectors, they could only reflect prosperity, not sustain it.

From the outset, Calgary was able to capitalise on its location both in terms of transportation and available raw materials, and establish successful

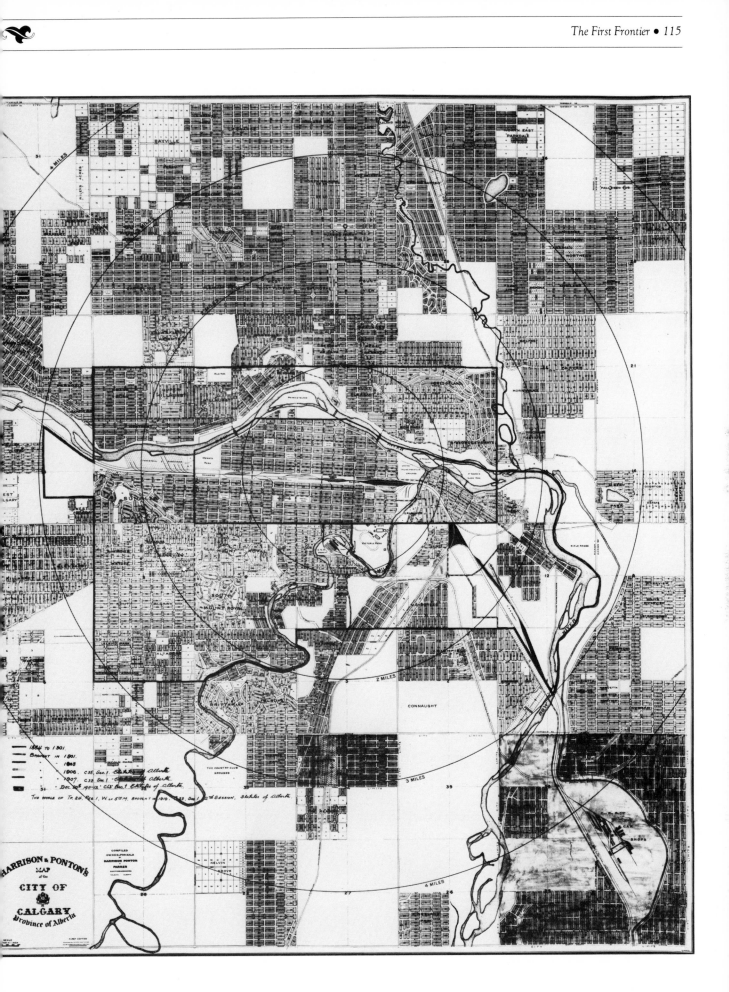

commercial construction enterprises. Over the years, these Calgary establishments expanded in size and number, until by 1914 they were able to meet wide regional demands.

Given Calgary's river location and proximity to the heavily wooded areas of the foothills, it is not surprising that lumber enterprises met with early success. James Walker (later Calgary's Citizen of the Century, 1975) established his Bow River Saw Mills Company in 1881. By 1883 business was so good that he had to advertise for 20 carpenters at three dollars and fifty cents per day. In 1886 an enterprise long associated with Calgary arrived in the form of the Eau Claire Lumber Company. Under its fiery but astute manager, Peter Prince, the Eau Claire mill was established on the Bow River near Prince's Island. Both the Walker and Prince mills flourished and expanded. In 1894 for example, both sold over one million feet of timber. These two lumber operations, together with William H. Cushing's sash and door factory, also established in Calgary in 1885, helped place Calgary in the forefront of Alberta's nascent construction industry.

The accessibility of good building clay and stone facilitated the establishment of brick works and sandstone quarries. The first brickyard was opened in 1885 in the Mission District, and, according to contemporary testimony, used clay superior to almost any found in Canada. The 15-acre plant was able to employ 15 men and 10 horses to supply local and district needs. John (Gravity) Watson also opened a brick and terra cotta works in the 1890s. Another successful brickmaking concern was the Crandell Pressed Brick and Sandstone Company, which took over Watson's plant in 1905. The Crandell operation was most impressive. On some 400 acres west of the city, the village of Brickburn was virtually a company town with homes, boarding houses, stores, a church, and a post office. At its peak Crandell's company produced 45,000 bricks a day from its 15 coal-fuelled kilns. When it finally ceased operations in 1931 the Crandell Pressed Brick and Sandstone Company was one of four

The Eau Claire and Bow River Lumber Company's mill and offices were located on Prince's Island in the Bow River. I.K. Kerr was president of the lumber company and Peter Prince, after whom the island is named, was its general manager. Courtesy, Glenbow-Alberta Institute.

companies in North America processing high quality enamelled brick and caustic tile. Another brick-making operation during this period was owned by W.J. Tregillus. The *News Telegram* reported in 1911 that Tregillus envisaged a plant in Calgary capable of producing 100,000 bricks daily.

Even more impressive than the brick-making works were the sandstone quarries that turned out high quality building stone. Beginning with the Knox Presbyterian Church in 1887, sandstone residential, commercial, and institutional structures appeared in Calgary. Aesthetically pleasing and sturdy, these splendid buildings were a welcome contrast to the clapboard fire traps that had given the town a ramshackle appearance and a horrendous reputation for high fire insurance rates. The self-imposed soubriquet "The Sandstone City" indicated the popularity and distinctiveness of sandstone in defining Calgary's first real urban landscape.

Credit for opening the first sandstone quarry is given to Wesley Fletcher Orr who reportedly operated a quarry as early as 1886. His enterprise was short-lived and Orr soon abandoned the sandstone business for civic politics. Far more successful was John McCallum who opened the Sunny Side Freestone Quarry (near present day Sunnyside). In 1896, McCallum shipped a stone bassinette in a railway flatcar to the Chicago World's Fair, where it won a bronze medallion. The village of Glenbow, near Cochrane, owed its existence entirely to the nearby stone quarry. Stone from the Glenbow quarry was used to build the legislative buildings in Edmonton. The most successful

Stephen Avenue in Calgary was filled with activity in 1892. Looking east from west of Centre Street, the Lougheed block is on the left. Courtesy, Glenbow-Alberta Institute.

CALGARY'S SANDSTONE BUILDINGS

The best available reference guide to Calgary's sandstone heritage is Richard Cunniffe's small booklet entitled "Calgary in Sandstone." Published in 1969 by the Alberta Historical Society, this booklet gives a chronological survey of the sandstone era and attempts to categorize the various structures according to type and time of erection. Cunniffe concludes his discussion by listing some of the more notable of these buildings that were still standing at the time of publication. At least 40 remained in the area bounded by the Bow River and 19th Avenue South, from 6th Street East to 6th Street West, while dozens more were to be found in other parts of the city.

Despite downtown Calgary's modern appearance, it is almost impossible to mistake the visual impact of its sandstone heritage. Schools like McDougall, Sunalta, King Edward, James Walker, Ramsay, and King George; churches like Central United, Knox United, or Cathedral Church of the Redeemer; institutional structures like the old Carnegie Library in Central Park, the Mewata Armouries or even Calgary City Hall are but some of the visual reminders of

At the turn of the century the Bank of Montreal (centre), an example of sandstone architecture common in early Calgary, stood at the corner of Eighth Avenue and First Street West. The bank was built in 1889 at an estimated cost of $50,000. Courtesy, Glenbow-Alberta Institute.

the sandstone era. Residences like the former Lougheed mansion on 13th Avenue and a few more on 15th Avenue are still standing. And of course there are many splendid old commercial blocks. Foremost among these are the Grain Exchange Building and the Alberta Corner.

One pleasing aspect in Calgary's modern downtown redevelopment projects has been the refurbishing of sandstone buildings to accommodate new demands. The old Lancaster Building on 8th Avenue provides an excellent case in point. Here, provision has been made for several modern shopping conveniences within the building without disturbing its original architecture or historic charm.

Calgary's sandstone era was short-lived. By 1914, brick, limestone, and other building stones were coming into vogue. Furthermore the market for rubble and other by-products of the quarries had also declined. High labour costs, too, cut into profit margins. One by one the stone quarries ceased operations. The Mewata Armouries, completed in 1917, was one of the last Calgary buildings to use native sandstone in its construction.

One of the first sandstone buildings constructed in Calgary was located on the Burns block at the corner of Centre Street and Stephen Avenue (later Eighth Avenue). Pat Burns conducted a retail trade in meats at this building, and he became the leading meat merchant in the city and ultimately in the West. Courtesy, Glenbow-Alberta Institute.

Constructed in the early 1900s, the Lancaster Building at Eighth Avenue and Second Street Southwest is a handsome stone structure that has been refurbished for modern use. Courtesy, Calgary Herald.

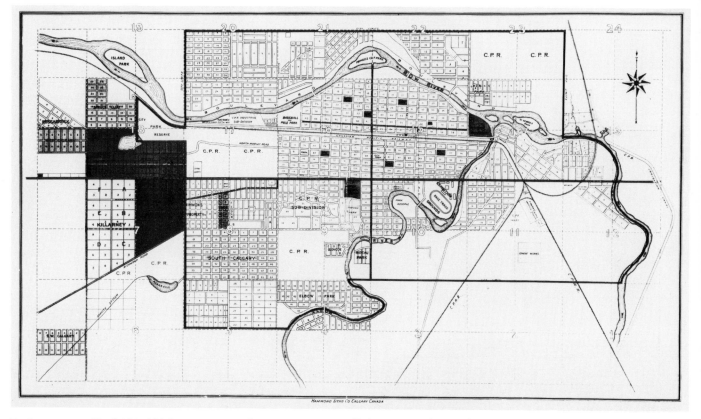

HAMMOND LITHO CO CALGARY CANADA

Real-estate agents Hatfield and McLaren issued this map in 1908 showing the southwest Calgary subdivisions of Killarney, Glengarry, Rosscarrock, Spruce Cliff, West Calgary, South Calgary, Elbow Park, Glencoe, and Rideau Park. Courtesy, Glenbow-Alberta Institute.

sandstone quarry in Calgary was located in the Richmond district, and was owned and operated by William Oliver. Using the soft, easily carved but durable Paskapoo sandstone, Oliver employed 40 men to use mechanized shovels, hoists, derricks, drill, saws, and stripping equipment.

Between 1901 and 1912 Calgary's population increased tenfold. The urban landscape changed dramatically as commercial and wholesale enterprises, manufacturing, and residential subdivisions sprang up to accommodate new demands. Figures released in 1911 showed that Calgary was headquarters to over 150 wholesale, commission, and jobbing houses, not to mention the 18 banks and other extensive financial and related institutions. In 1901, there were 1,689 houses in Calgary. Ten years later the number had grown to 11,350, but a housing shortage still prevailed. Assessment figures jumped from a modest $2.3 million to over $133 million in 1914. Building permits reveal a more astounding statistic. The number of permits issued between 1909-1912 surpassed that for the 16 years 1915-1930, and the 1912 figure was not exceeded until after the Second World War.

One significant result of this phenomenal growth was the emergence of a construction industry heavily disproportionate in strength and size to the city's overall economy. Over 25 percent of the city's labour force was employed directly in the construction industry in 1911. There were more than 200 listed building contractors and more carpenters than workers in any other occupation. Stalwart boosters like real estate man Freddie Lowes exulted in the construction boom, and on one occasion proudly pronounced that the real measure of Calgary's prosperity was evidenced in the continuous sound of hammers. A few more sober souls were not so sure. By 1912 even the usually optimistic board of trade was expressing concern over the city's heavy reliance

Construction on the Hudson's Bay Company store began with excavation of its downtown Calgary site in 1911. Enlarged in 1929, the store has become a downtown landmark. Courtesy, Glenbow-Alberta Institute.

on the construction industry. Its fears proved well founded. The collapse of the boom in 1914 threw thousands out of work with little chance of job reinstatement. In 1915 the *Herald* caustically commented that Calgary's solid war enlistment record was due to the unemployed construction workers who had no other choice than to join the army.

Some of Calgary's best known early business leaders were associated with the construction industry. Individuals like James Walker, William H. Cushing, Peter Prince, I.S.G. Van Wart, Thomas Underwood, James Wheeler Davidson, James Watson, James H. Garden, Richard A. Brocklebank, James Hornby, and R.C. Thomas were among the city's best known and most respected citizens. Like the cattlemen, they invested in real estate and diversified enterprises. Yet unlike the cattlemen, the construction men entered civic politics on a consistent and influential scale. Their influence was so prevalent in this period that it could be argued that the construction industry provided Calgary with the chief nucleus for its first resident, business elite.

At the other end of the spectrum the construction workers indicated the direction Calgary's incipient labour movement was to take. The stonemasons and carpenters were the highest paid and the most numerous occupational groups in the city. With their craft guild mentality, the construction workers gave Calgary's labour organizations a decidedly conservative and somewhat elitist orientation.

A recurring feature in Calgary's growth up to 1914 involved periodic, inordinately heavy activity in the real estate market. In real terms, this phenomenon contributed directly to the city's economy, and even more importantly had long range effects on Calgary's physical growth patterns. Moreover, the real estate firms were the most conspicuous practical examples

Right: *Physician and surgeon Dr. James W. Richardson sits at the desk in his office, located at 138 Seventh Avenue East in the Judge Travis block, in 1915. Courtesy, Glenbow-Alberta Institute.*

Below: *Horses wandering by the river stop for a drink in this circa 1890 view of Calgary taken from North Hill. The spire of the Anglican Pro Cathedral can be seen in the background, right of centre. Courtesy, Glenbow-Alberta Institute.*

of the booster ethic in action. This ethic promised limitless prosperity, and was at its height during the boom period 1906-1912. It was all-pervasive at policy levels in municipal affairs, and in its extravagances led to over-extension and heavy debt outlays. Finally, it was the speculative element in real estate activity that most clearly advertised Calgary's place on the urban frontier. Since land speculators essentially gambled on the promise of potential refinements, they were presuming the inevitable modification of a frontier, in this case Calgary and its environs.

Real estate agencies were needed to bring order to the sale and transfer of lands, and most dealt in improved and unimproved town and country properties. They were also involved in the laying out and disposal of lots in emerging townsites throughout south and south-central Alberta.

Calgary always had a goodly number of real estate agents. Early pioneers in local real estate like T.S.C. Lee, R.H. Moody, G.C. Marsh, and Wesley Orr met with only moderate success before the turn of the century. There was really only one favourable period following the flurry of activity that surrounded Calgary's corporate origins in 1883-1884. This occurred in 1890-1891 and was prompted by the construction of the railroad to Edmonton. It was at this time that Senator James A. Lougheed reaped the rewards of his early land purchases on Eighth Avenue west of Centre Street. The beginnings of commercial expansion in this area pushed land prices up and accrued handsome profits to Lougheed as well as giving him the dubious honour of being the highest individual ratepayer in Calgary.

Beginning around 1906 the long-awaited immigration influx began and ushered in the golden age of the real estate business in Calgary. The next six years were marked by frenzied, unprecedented activity, with the more venturesome real estate men soaring to the heights of fame, prosperity, and even opulence. When the balloon finally burst in 1913-1914, Calgary settled down to a period of dormancy virtually uninterrupted until the post-1950 era. The voices of the real estate men were in effect silent for a long time following their six-year flirtation with success.

If one were asked to encapsulate in a single phrase the prevailing ethos in Calgary commercial life between 1909 and 1912, the answer would have to be "real estate." As early as 1910 the usually conservative *Herald* ran a large caption over its two-page real estate section reading, "Deal in Calgary Real Estate and Grow Wealthy." At that time there were 54 real estate firms offering employment to approximately 250 people. Two years later the number had swelled to 441 licensed real estate establishments, and over 2,200 employees. Lots of all types changed hands with bewildering rapidity. In 1912 an unimproved business lot might change hands four or five times in the space of a couple of months. Astronomical prices were paid for properties on Eighth and Ninth avenues in the heart of the business section, reaching a peak of $3,000 per frontage foot in 1912. Suburban subdivisions were popular as well. As early as 1904-1905 strategic land parcels on the city environs began changing hands. The Richmond area was bought for subdivision purposes in 1905 for $35 per acre. Another well-placed 40 acres two miles from the downtown area was sold in 1905 for $1,000. By 1909 the merits of these early purchases had begun to pay handsome dividends. Investor O.G. Devenish paid $9,500

SUBURBAN CALGARY, 1912

A glance at a 1912 map of the city of Calgary would expose the reader to a variety of subdivision names. Some like Sunalta, Mount Royal, Hillhurst, Glengarry, Killarney, and Belfast are familiarly located where they are today. However, the names of many others like Roseview Gardens, are unrecognizable, the only resemblance to their modern counterparts lying in their somewhat euphemistic ring.

To the south the large subdivision of Meadow Field occupied the area currently taken up by Willow Park. Hiawatha was where Bayview is today, while present day Oakridge was more appropriately called Sarcee Gardens. The Ogden area carried the names of prospective suburbs like Hyde Park, Norwood, Prospect Place, Maryland, Pasadena, and Cossar. Further to the east was Garden Heights, and to the north in the Forest Lawn area were Eldorado, Transcona, and Winchester. The area around the old airport was surrounded by Harbourne Estates, Blackstone Park, Wellesbourne, Columbia Gardens, and Majestic View.

The district of the Glens, Glamorgan, Glenbrook, Glendale, and Glen-

meadow, is in southwest Calgary. In 1912 only Glengarry was located on the map. The others bore the names of Deer Park, Roseview Gardens, Silver Heights, and Von Mielecki Park. Varsity Heights and University Plateau were in the present Strathcona district, and reflected some of the real estate activity associated with Calgary's first but ultimately unsuccessful bid for a university. Indeed it was commonly believed that real estate speculation was behind the effort that resulted in a proposed university site in the Wildwood district.

In the north and northwest the pattern of subdivisions continued. Varsity Acres was originally called The Bronx, and Dalhousie was Berkeley. North of Tuxedo Park were the future residential areas of Ree Heights and La Hoyt. North of Rosedale was Pleasant Heights and farther north again, Highbury, La Grange, and Pullman.

A great majority of these subdivisions existed in name only in that they had been registered and approved by the city. But in actual fact very few were ready for building. Utility services were virtually nonexistent; and the city had no established policy regarding their extension. Access was impeded by a lack of even marginally adequate roads. Suburban Calgary in 1912 was a place where houses rarely interrupted the line of prairie and where gophers outnumbered people by a wide margin.

In the 1940s this aerial view of the Hillhurst district was taken for the Bennette and White Company. Built on land donated by the Honourable E. Riley, this was the first housing project in Calgary. Courtesy, Provincial Archives of Alberta.

In about 1914, the buildings along the Macleod-Calgary Trail in Midnapore were, from left to right, an Anglican church, a Roman Catholic church, and the Samuel W. Shaw residence. Shaw, one of Calgary's early settlers and industrialists, brought milling equipment with him in 1883 and established a woolen mill at Midnapore. The two frame churches have become landmarks. Courtesy, Glenbow-Alberta Institute.

in 1906 for the subdivision known as Capitol Hill. He sold half in 1910 for $50,000. The Hon. E. Riley, MLA for Gleichen, purchased the Hillhurst subdivision in 1904 for $30 to $40 per lot. In 1910 he disposed of it easily at prices between $800 and $1200 per lot.

One aspect of the land speculation binge in this period involved the aggressive policies pursued by some real estate firms. The best individual example on a sustained scale was provided by F.C. Lowes and Company, which led the way in advertising and innovative land development projects. In 1907 a group of investors built the first Centre Street bridge in an effort to enhance the appeal of the new suburb known as Crescent Heights. Another land company sold shares in a luxury aquatic and country club proposed for the shores of Lake Chestermere. But perhaps the prize for single-minded promotional extravagance should go to Englishman John Hextall, who in 1911 paid over $200,000 for 1,700 acres in present day Bowness. To attract buyers to his high priced acreage lots, Hextall built a bridge over the Bow River, provided for electricity and water as well as a professionally laid-out golf course. In 1909, promoters of the Kitsilano subdivision offered buyers of $30 lots generous terms at $10 down and $5 per month plus a chance at prizes including a trip to Europe. The speculative appeal was nurtured and encouraged in the press. At least two newspapers during this period were virtual mouthpieces of real estate interests. Between 1909 and 1912 both *The Calgary Optimist* and the *News Telegram*, by providing extensive commentary on real estate activities, continued to fan the speculative flames.

The frenzied activity in real estate speculation touched all segments of the city's population, and most Calgarians were bitten by the speculative bug. In

Calgary's original municipal industrial district was located on the CPR line to Fort Macleod and Lethbridge. Although it was purchased in 1910, the Manchester Industrial Area remained largely undeveloped until after World War II. Courtesy, Calgary Herald.

1912 hundreds stood all night in the rain waiting to buy a maximum of two lots for $1,100 each in the new Sunalta subdivision. Many prominent business leaders dealt extensively in real estate during this period. Included were Pat Burns, James Walker, William Pearce, A.E. Cross, E.H. Crandell, W.J. Tregillus, W.R. Hull, A. Samis, Arthur Graves, Reuben Jamieson, I.S.G. Van Wart, Simon John Clarke, James H. Garden, Dr. N.J. Lindsay, A.A. Dick, and countless others. The city's building contractors, too, were heavily involved in real estate activity. Indeed it was the close liaison between construction and real estate personnel that led to the most identifiable coalition of sectional interests ever to sit on city council.

The dominance of real estate agents and building contractors in civic politics between 1908 and 1913 contributed markedly to the growth mentality and as a consequence had specific effects on Calgary's physical growth patterns. In the 1912 council, for instance, no fewer than nine of the twelve aldermen were either in the real estate or construction business. The influence

Small houses characterize many of Calgary's older residential districts. The city's policy of allowing construction of residences on 25-foot frontage lots led to the emergence of closely packed residential subdivisions in the period of 1906-1913. Courtesy, Calgary Herald.

F.C. (FREDDIE) LOWES

Few Calgarians in 1912 had not heard of Freddie Lowes. The youthful millionaire's name was as close to a household word as was possible in the frenzied years of rapid growth that preceded World War I. Lowes' meteoric rags-to-riches career, unparalleled in Calgary's history, represented the stuff from which legends were made. In many ways he epitomized the western success story. Similarly, his equally rapid fall from fortune into the abyss of bankruptcy and broken health was a personal illustration of the pitfalls facing those who had the courage to gamble all on the untested promise of a raw new land.

Freddie Lowes was born in Brampton, Ontario, in 1880. After high school, he secured a position in 1899 with the Canada Life Assurance Company of Toronto, and came to Calgary three years later to look after the company's interests in Alberta. Between 1902 and 1906 he served in various senior capacities before resigning to go into the real estate business. His total capital outlay of $400 was sufficient to open a small office on Stephen Avenue.

After surviving the initial bad years 1906-1907, Lowes' fortunes improved dramatically in the wake of the demand for land engendered by rapid settlement. He dealt in urban properties as well as ranch and farm lands, both improved and unimproved. By 1911 he had opened branch offices in five Alberta cities, British Columbia, Saskatchewan, and Spokane, Washington. Later he opened offices in London, England and New York City. Though the 1913 speculation that he was worth $7 million was probably exaggerated, there can be little doubt of Lowes's success. His holdings definitely placed him in the millionaire category. With some 400 employees, the firm of F.C. Lowes and Company was easily Western Canada's largest, and certainly the most ambitious and successful, real estate enterprise.

In 1912 a road crew gathers at the Elbow Park project, developed just before the collapse of the building boom. Elbow Park was one of the Calgary suburbs developed by F.C. (Freddie) Lowes. Courtesy, Glenbow-Alberta Institute.

Real-estate developer Freddie Lowes resided in this house on Elbow Drive in Calgary. Courtesy, Glenbow-Alberta Institute.

The secret to Lowes' success was probably his imaginative daring. His approach to business was aggressive on a large scale. In 1909, for example, he spent $12,000 on advertising, a staggering sum by the standards of the day. He prepared and published promotional literature that he distributed in Canada and overseas. He thought nothing of bringing in a trainload of prospective buyers. He was loquacious and sought out interviews in the newspapers of cities he visited. Lowes was also astute enough to keep himself continually in Calgary's public eye. Bob Edwards of the *Eye Opener* was a staunch admirer, and once devoted almost a whole issue to describing how Freddie had neatly outwitted some American confidence men.

Lowes dealt in big figures. In June 1909 he realized $272,225 in sales. As agent for the Canadian Northern Railway Company, he bought up all the land on the right-of-way in Calgary. His purchase in the 17th Avenue area alone amounted to $300,000. In 1909 he paid $500,000 for land parcels in downtown Edmonton, and in 1912 transacted the biggest sale ever completed in Calgary, when he paid $775,000 for two sections adjacent to the proposed Canadian Pacific Railway shops in Ogden.

Not satisfied with real estate commissions alone, Lowes entered the land development business. He owned and controlled five residential subdivisions in Lethbridge and seven in Calgary. His Calgary holdings included Elbow Park and Glenmore as well as Brittania and Roxborough; and he is responsible for Calgary's growth to the southwest. Lowes had great plans for Brittania, and in 1912 hired a prominent town planner from Seattle to lay out the subdivision.

Lowes' most publicized achievement in land development concerned his Roxborough subdivision, which he bought from the Oblate Fathers for $100,000. The feat involved washing away part of the Mission Hill for levelling and beautification purposes. After hooking up a giant hose to the city water mains, a 3000-pound pump was brought in to supply an extra 200-pound nozzle pressure. In 90 days he washed some 110,000 cubic yards down a 900-foot flume to the base of the Elbow River.

Lowes lived a life in keeping with his cavalier business practices. He was both flamboyant and extravagant. He once spent $2500 in a brief shopping spree in New York. He drove expensive Pierce Arrow automobiles and was reputed to have held the speed record from Calgary to High River. His jumping horses were the pride of Calgary. Out of his string of 20, one held a Canadian record while others were repeated winners at shows across the country. On one occasion the Lowes horses outjumped the premier jumpers owned by Clifford Sifton to the wild delight of an enthusiastic Calgary crowd. Boxing was another interest. He was a capable amateur boxer himself, a qualified referee, and an avid supporter of the rising sport of prize fighting. He supplied the land for Tommy Burns to stage his professional fights in Calgary. Lowes donated generously to various charities as well. He wiped out the YMCA's general debt with a donation of $10,000. One old-time Calgary resident recalls visiting the Lowes' residence as a young boy seeking donations for uniforms for his baseball team. Lowes promptly underwrote the whole cost.

Lowes' inveterate faith in the west proved his undoing. He refused to unload his holdings when advised, scoffing in typical fashion at those fainthearted ones who would "knock" the country in times of temporary adversity. And just as one climbed higher up the ladder of success, so one fell more dramatically. When the bottom fell out of the land market, Lowes was left with bank credits vastly disproportionate to the value of his holdings. He was broke by 1916, and after making a temporary comeback after the First World War he lived on in Calgary in reduced circumstances. His health failed and he slipped into the netherland of mental imbalance. He died in 1950 just as Calgary was preparing to launch itself into another speculative binge.

The Roxborough district of Calgary, shown in this 1909-1910 aerial view, was laid out by Fred Lowes, who intended to incorporate many of his ideas for suburban beautification and amenities in the area. Unfortunately the days of prosperity ended before Lowes had a chance to implement his grand schemes for Roxborough. Courtesy, Glenbow-Alberta Institute.

of this group could be discerned in the civic policies of gross expansion. By 1912 the city's area had swelled to 40 square miles, even though the bulk of commercial and residential development remained within the original corporate boundaries. The presence of exotically named empty residential subdivisions, or the over-extended street railway lines to accommodate at least some of them, were the most tangible manifestations of civic participation in the policies of unrestrained expansion. Then there was the controversial Mawson Report of 1914 in which a British town planner in the "City Beautiful" tradition outlined his elaborate and extravagant plans for Calgary's future development. Calgary's interest in formal town planning was initiated and supported in council by aldermen associated with building and real estate, and so Mawson was subsequently hired by the town planning commission, a body dominated by the same element.

The effects of the construction industry and real estate activity on Calgary's development to 1914 were many and varied. Together with the Canadian Pacific Railway, real estate speculation provided the pivotal force in determining the city's physical growth patterns. The construction industry supplied frontier Calgary with its strongest economic sector, albeit disproportionate and volatile. Similarly, construction was complemented somewhat by activity in the real estate market, although it must be added that the corresponding presence of the speculative element led to inflated land values and contributed a pyramiding effect that was to have later disastrous consequences. The construction industry and real estate produced Calgary's first resident business elite and contributed markedly to the booster ethic of unrestricted optimism characteristic of the open frontier.

Downtown Calgary, looking northwest from the Grain Exchange, had an active commercial centre in 1910. Georgeson and Company, Grocers, is in the left foreground, and Heinzman Pianos and the Alberta Hotel are advertised on the right. Courtesy, Glenbow-Alberta Institute.

THE MAWSON REPORT

Anyone who has seen a copy of the Mawson Report cannot fail to be impressed. The handsome, expensively bound volume with its coloured illustrations and drawings and extravagant prose effectively takes the reader back to a period of residual optimism when many believed that mankind's chief panacea lay in a judicious blend of scientific knowledge with an appreciation of the natural environment. The Mawson Report was a classical example of this type of thinking and represented Calgary's and Canada's first experimentation with the exciting new concept of town planning.

Initially Calgary's interest in town planning did not involve Mawson. A city council motion in late 1911 simply called for a comprehensive town planning scheme, but left the details to the subsequently appointed town planning commission. But Thomas Hayton Mawson was his own best ambassador. On a visit to Calgary in the spring of 1912, as part of a cross-country lecture tour, the noted British landscape architect, author, and self-proclaimed town planning expert impressed a Canadian club audience with his visions of the future. Six months later he was back in Calgary, this time at the special invitation of the town planning commission. Using slides and impassioned rhetoric, Mawson captivated a large audience at Central High School as he proffered the panacea of town planning as there for the having.

The town planning commission was obviously impressed. Mawson was subsequently hired by the city at a salary of $6000 to "complete preliminary plans for controlling the city's growth."

Mawson spent a year researching and preparing his report, details of which arrived in Calgary in late April 1914, together with large reproductions of drawings and sketches, which were subsequently displayed for public viewing in the Elizabethan Room at the Hudson's Bay Company Store. The plans were accompanied by 1000 bound volumes of the report, which were to be sold to the public at a price to be agreed upon. (Any person fortunate enough to possess one of these extant volumes will find its current market value far in excess of the $2.00 charged by the city in 1914.)

The Mawson Report was impressive in its scope and recommendations. Not surprisingly, given Mawson's background, the report called for extensive development of open spaces including parks, and river banks, as well as the beautification of boulevards. Transportation corridors were redefined to follow symmetrical, radial patterns. However, it was Mawson's plans for several elaborate buildings of his own design that evoked the most public commentary. The *Herald* described his design for a civic centre on the Bow River as resembling "St. Peter's, the Kremlin, the Houses of Parliament and the Panama-Pacific Exposition rolled into one." Equally controversial were Mawson's plans for the new Centre Street bridge, which included a massive structure on the north side designed to raise and lower vehicles from bridge to road level.

Though the town planning commission was politely positive in its reception of the report, the commissioners were clearly appalled by its extravagance. With the prosperity of the boom already on the wane, the estimated $10 mil-

Central Park, with its beautifully laid-out and manicured gardens, has been a great source of pleasure for Calgarians for many years. Courtesy, Glenbow-Alberta Institute.

lion bond issue for adequate implementation was out of the question. The report was thus allowed to slip into obscurity, being resurrected on occasions as an item of historical curiosity. Still there is evidence to suggest that the report was not entirely forgotten. The sporadic attempts at river bank beautification in the 1920s, the highway arterial plan of 1930, and the recreational land reservation policies of the city parks department all reflected aspects of Mawson's thinking. It is unfortunate that the practicalities of Mawson's report were pushed into the background by the awesome magnitude of his architectural grand design; he might have been better remembered.

THE FIRST FRONTIER

CHAPTER SIX
POLITICS AND PRESSURE GROUPS

The vibrancy of early Calgary was manifested in the way people organized themselves to combat the challenges of life on the frontier. The need to provide a corporate voice, urban services, and the refinements of civilization for a city limited by isolation, and smallness easily injected the most dynamic element in the rise of a truly urban Calgary by 1914.

The notion of Calgary as a political maverick was established during this period, although certainly not at first. The three founding forces in Calgary's

Mrs. Phillips, a widow, came from Ohio with her family to Calgary, where they lived in tent homes on Seventh Avenue and Second Street West at the turn of the century. The tents' bases were boarded up against cold weather. Courtesy, Glenbow-Alberta Institute.

early development, the North West Mounted Police, the Canadian Pacific Railway, and the ranching industry were all creations of the federal Conservative Party, which remained uninterrupted in power from 1878 to 1896. Important local figures in federal and territorial politics, as well as the civil service, were all strong Conservatives. Here the names of Senator James Lougheed, Hugh Cayley, and William Pearce were the most notable. Before 1896 Alberta's lone representative in the House of Commons was D.W. Davis, a rancher who held property interests in the city. The saying "Tory blue and Calgary skies go together" was coined during this period. The influence of

Baked goods were carried in the back of this horse-drawn waggon from James W. Shelby's bakery at 1113-1118 Eighth Street West to private homes in Calgary every day. A 4X bread waggon is shown standing outside the bakery in about 1910. Courtesy, Glenbow-Alberta Institute.

R.B. Bennett (centre), a Calgary lawyer who became Prime Minister, eats with William Parslow (left) and Pat Burns (right) at the Calgary Stampede in 1928. Parslow was a Calgary merchant, stable proprieter, and former Calgary alderman, and Burns was a local cattle king and meat-packing plant owner. Courtesy, Glenbow-Alberta Institute.

the Conservative Party was so pervasive in Calgary that Dr. James Lafferty, an early banker and civic politician, once remarked that he "and James Reilly were the only two Liberals south of the Bow River."

The accession of Wilfred Laurier's Liberal Party to power in 1896 and the election of Edmonton Liberal Frank Oliver to the House of Commons heralded the beginnings of Calgary's long process of federal political alienation. Some Calgarians viewed Laurier's railway policies as prejudicial to their city's interests. They were also mistrustful of federal discriminatory action against the open range industry. However, nothing deepened an enduring resentment

Above: *The original publishers of* The Calgary Herald *stand outside their first offices in about 1883. Andrew M. Armour (second from left) and Thomas B. Bradon (right) were the newspaper's first editors. Courtesy, Glenbow-Alberta Institute.*

Above right: *On April 14, 1911, Sarcee Indians cook a meal on the present site of Eatons store, near the Courthouse. Sarcees gathered in this place for many years when they came to Calgary. The Sarcee Reserve is located directly to the south and west of the city. Courtesy, Glenbow-Alberta Institute.*

of federal Liberalism as much as the issue surrounding the choice of the capital for the newly created province of Alberta in 1905. The outraged local cries of collusion and gerrymander directed against Oliver, Clifford Sifton, and other Liberal patriarchs were all in vain as Edmonton received the coveted prize Calgarians felt was theirs by right.

Calgary representatives were active in the North West Territories Assembly, which after 1890 worked hard for some form of provincial status for Western Canada. Here, Hugh Cayley, the *Herald* editor, played an important part. Calgary had one member in the first provincial Liberal administration. William H. Cushing was Minister of Public Works until 1910, before resigning in protest over the railway scandal, which almost destroyed the government. Due in part to the peculiar alignment of constituencies, Calgary was politically disadvantaged at the provincial level in favour of Edmonton. This imbalance was felt in 1912 when Calgary was denied the site of the first provincial university, again in favour of an Edmonton location.

During this period of frontier ebullience, Calgary began its tradition of protest. The Mounties in 1876 had not accepted Inspector Ephrem Brisebois's inept leadership. Then, the town had refused to countenance Judge Travis' interpretation of the unpopular liquor law in 1885-86. Similarly, the protests over the capital and the university were unified corporate attempts to counter unfairness and discrimination. These protest sentiments manifested themselves in other social and political dimensions as well. The organization that was to topple the provincial liberals was born in Calgary in 1909 in the form of the United Farmers of Alberta. Earlier, in 1904, the Marxist journal *The Bond of Brotherhood* appeared in Calgary. Replete with all the rhetoric of the class struggle and the evils of the capitalist system, this short-lived weekly was the first socialist journal in Western Canada and represented an extreme wave of the swelling social consciousness that was to wash across North America in a storm a generation later. Yet the most strident voice of social concern was supplied by a much different type of journal. The efforts of Bob Edwards through *The Eye Opener* in documenting societal disequilibrium were couched in some of the best satirical language ever to appear in Canadian journalism. Behind the witticisms and humourous anecdotes that punctuated the infrequent edition of the Calgary *Eye Opener* ran the caustic consciousness of a keen social critic.

In the civic arena, the limitations imposed by the frontier produced their own imbalance, which resulted in the rise of action-oriented pressure and self-help groups. The efforts of these bodies in modifying the impact of the frontier provided Calgary with its most dynamic urban expression.

Broadly stated, the role of local government in the late 19th and early 20th centuries was seen to be relatively specific. It was the city council's job to promote growth and provide for essential services. The latter was usually interpreted to mean fire and police protection, utility services, and thoroughfare extension and maintenance. Areas of social concern were peripheral and best assumed by private or religious bodies supplemented but not supported by the civic purse. This prevailing mentality was buttressed by a restricted property franchise and general acceptance of the idea that civic politics was for businessmen only.

Thus the heavy public emphasis in spending priorities in the frontier period was on promotion and physical amenities. The efforts expended to promote town and district included large advertising campaigns, extensive lobbying for favourable institutions and industries, as well as lavish entertainment for visiting immigration delegations. In the years of prosperity after 1908, the emphasis on publicity and promotion became even more pronounced. The city council and the board of trade were united in their efforts to ensure that

Captain Neil McLaughlin (extreme left) and fellow fire fighters pose with their horse-drawn waggon outside fire station Number Seven in the 1910s. Note the windows decorated with flower boxes. Courtesy, Glenbow-Alberta Institute.

BOB EDWARDS OF "THE EYE OPENER"

Above: *Robert Chambers Edwards founded and edited* The Eye Opener. *At the time of his death in 1922, Bob Edwards was a Conservative MLA. Courtesy, Glenbow-Alberta Institute.*

Right: *Peter J. McGonigle, Esq., the editor of the* Midnapore Gazette, *was a Bob Edwards "character." Although entirely fictitious, and created by Edwards as a vehicle for his satire, McGonigle was so well known that many believed in his actual existence. From the Grant MacEwan Collection.*

The stocky man in the wrinkled suit sat with his three companions in the bar of the Alberta Hotel. They were talking about boxing, and occasionally the musical laughter of Paddy Nolan rang through the gloom of Alberta's most celebrated "watering hole." After a couple of hours the party broke up, and as the men left, one asked if the next *Eye Opener* was on schedule. Bob Edwards just shrugged, tightened his tie, and grinned. "Maybe." They all laughed uproariously and disappeared into the cool Calgary night.

The above account is fiction, though probably representative of the behaviour of Western Canada's best remembered journalist. But while little is known of Edwards's private life the same cannot be said of his public image. As the intemperate editor of a maverick journal known as *The Eye Opener*, Edwards waged his personal war with big business, self-righteous individuals, and rigid institutions. He used words like barbs to puncture bloated egos, to penetrate institutional facades and to prick the conscience of a society that luxuriated in the benefits of progress but that remained insensitive to its growing disequilibriums. Edwards' choice of satire as his most popular vehicle of expression propelled his *Eye Opener* into the forefront of national popular appeal, and earned for him an enduring reputation as one of Canada's keenest literary social critics.

Of all his many venues, Calgary was the favourite of the much-travelled, Scottish-born Edwards. He remained in the city longer than in any other place, and felt at home with its urban dynamism and relative freedom from the oppressive weight of institutional dogmatism.

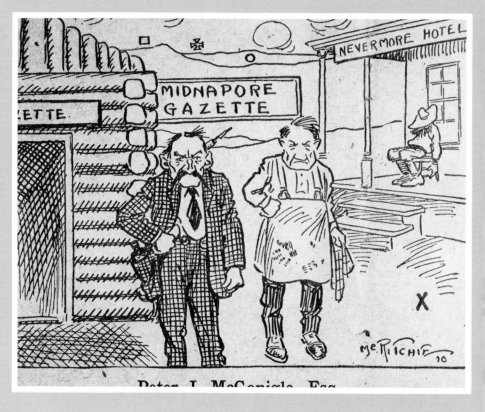

Peter J. McGonigle, Esq.

Certainly he saw enough in Calgary to fuel his smouldering sense of outrage. He criticized churches for their impractical and rigid moralisms, especially towards prostitutes, which Edwards regarded as a classic example of mindless discrimination and religiosity. He championed the cause of women's rights to the franchise and full equality before the law. Edwards's unexpected support of the temperance cause was considered vital in its success during the historic 1916 referendum. Indeed, it was his stance on this issue that showed the often elusive practical side of Edwards' reforming nature. A heavy and compulsive drinker himself, he despised the distillers as the lowest form of humanity, and was outspoken in his support of the alternative three-percent beer. Edwards also campaigned hard for the municipalization of hospitals in 1918, and once referred to the Calgary General Hospital as a place for "sick, rich people." Finally Edwards was emphatic in his assertion that the First World War marked the end of an era, and that the stratified society of the Georgian and Victorian eras would be replaced by one more sensitive to the rights of the common people.

Bob Edwards thus became the champion of the underdog. Many others both despised and feared him, for the fear of an Edwards attack was enough to send chills up the most insensitive of spines. It is a tribute to his literary skills that he was never convicted of libellous public utterances. One was safe if one was poor, generous, or colourful enough to be an individual. Conversely one was a potential target for attack if representative of vested interests, strict religious or governing political institutions—in other words, the status quo. One thing can be said with certainty about Bob Edwards between 1904 and 1922, the year of his death. Calgarians were alternatively delighted, entertained, insulted, and outraged, but never bored by the shy gentle Scot with the vitriolic pen.

In the late 1890s R. Randolph Bruce drew this caricature of Patrick James Nolan. Colourful "Paddy" Nolan, born in Ireland on St. Patrick's Day, 1913, was one of Calgary's first and most celebrated lawyers. He was regarded as the greatest defense lawyer in the Northwest Territories, and it was of him that Bob Edwards said, "All the best criminals go to Paddy Nolan." Courtesy, Glenbow-Alberta Institute.

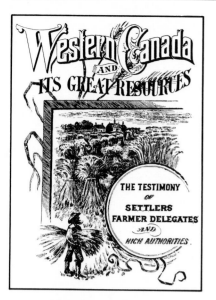

The testimony of settlers, farmers' delegates, and government authorities on farming and natural resources in Western Canada is given in this 1893 federal government booklet. Courtesy, Glenbow-Alberta Institute.

Calgary remained a focal point for both settlement and investment. The close relationship between the two groups during these years was the clearest indication that civic growth was equated with business interests.

In the 1880s the town council had assumed the full functions of the board of trade, a body which did not come into existence until the early 1890s despite unsuccessful attempts at organization as early as 1886. After 1892 the board of trade and city council continued to work in close harmony. In fact, Alexander Lucas was both mayor and board of trade president in 1892. In 1911 the council grant to the board of trade almost equalled the total civic contribution to all charitable and social organizations.

The city of Calgary reflected the heavy civic emphasis on providing "necessary" amenities. The privately owned waterworks was taken over as a public utility in 1900 when it proved inadequate for the growing city's needs. Similarly, the monopoly in the electric power service, enjoyed by Peter Prince of the Eau Claire Lumber Company, was abruptly terminated in 1905 when the city decided to establish its own thermal power plant and operate it as a public utility. The importance of adequate commercial thoroughfares was revealed in the city's heavy expenditure in this area. By the end of the period the city owned and operated its own municipal street paving plant.

On the other hand, matters of a more social nature were considered less favourably by civic groups, and it was this relative indifference that encouraged and even precipitated increasing activity by traditional and emergent private organizations. Here the best example was provided by private efforts in the sadly neglected area of public health, hospital services in particular. The establishment of Calgary's first general hospital in 1895, fully 11 years after incorporation, was primarily due to the determined efforts of an aggressive body of public-minded women known as the "Women's Hospital Aid Society." In

Calgary's first large sanitary sewer ran from the Elbow River east along Eighth Avenue to Fourteenth Street, and then south under the CPR tracks to the Bonnybrook outlet. A sewage disposal plant was built some years after the sewer was constructed. Courtesy, Glenbow-Alberta Institute.

later years active women's groups worked hard to upgrade the general hospital by raising funds for equipment as well as extensions to existing facilities.

In areas of social welfare, the churches and various charitable organizations, usually dominated by women, bore the brunt of responsibility in alleviating the human miseries engendered by social inequities. The prevalent mentality that charity was a matter of individual conscience rather than a corporate responsibility was apparent in the small civic grants to social welfare agencies. Although the urban frontier was geared towards those able to fend for themselves, the prevalence of poverty, untended sickness, and other forms

Members of Calgary's first town council were (from left to right and front to back): Mayor George Murdoch; Treasurer C. Sparrow; Clerk T.T.A. Boys; Councillor S.J. Hogg; Assessor J. Campbell; Solicitor H. Bleeker; Councillor Dr. N.J. Lindsay; Councillor J.H. Millward; Councillor S.J. Clarke; Chief J.S. Ingram; Collector J.S. Douglas; Councillor I.S. Freeze. Courtesy, Glenbow-Alberta Institute.

Members of Calgary's first city council were (from left to right and front to back): A.L. Sifton, city solicitor; J.D. Geddes, clerk; Mayor A. Lucas; Alderman W. Maclean; Alderman E. Watson; Alderman R.J. Hutchings; Alderman J.S. Feehan; Alderman J.H. Millward; T. English, chief of police; S. Cowan, city treasurer; Alderman W.F. Orr. Courtesy, Glenbow-Alberta Institute.

WESLEY FLETCHER ORR: BOOSTER PAR EXCELLENCE

One of the more interesting figures in the early development of Calgary was Wesley Fletcher Orr. In the decade 1888-1898 he was easily Calgary's most ubiquitous and persistent figure in municipal affairs. He was in fact the first elected mayor of the city of Calgary in 1894-1895, and was instrumental in preparing the city charter for ratification by the North West Territories Assembly. Orr was also a promoter, forever seeking ways to advance his own, as well as Calgary's, interests. In a way he represented the true spirit of the frontier as it applied to local government.

Wesley Orr was born at La Chute near Montreal in 1831. His background of Canadian Methodism and political Conservatism included a good education and exposure to the world of commerce and salesmanship; and in 1854 he left home to seek his fortune in the business world. Over the next 30 years Orr worked for financial houses and insurance companies. He manufactured saleratus (a baking ingredient) and sold candles. He taught school, managed stores, and dealt in cattle. During this period, too, he cultivated a habit of writing to various Ontarian newspapers outlining his suggestions for railroads, manufacturing enterprises, and resource development. He became reasonably well-known in federal Conservative circles after 1867 and was rewarded for his work for the party by being appointed coroner for Wentworth and captain of the First Military District of North Wentworth. By 1880 he was managing a lumber company in Barrie, Ontario.

Orr's interest in Calgary was at first purely speculative. Following the advice of knowledgeable Conservatives to buy land in advance of the Canadian Pacific Railway, Orr and a partner purchased the southwest quarter of Section 14 at Calgary for $10,000. Like many others, Orr believed that the CPR would locate its Calgary townsite on Section 14. He was mistaken, dismayed but undaunted. Instead, he decided to take up permanent residence in Calgary, and work towards raising the commercial value of his land bordering the east bank of the Elbow River.

Orr's entry to the town council in 1888 represented a conscious desire to use his position to effect policies favourable to his vested property interests. The subsequent location of manufacturing enterprises in east Calgary was a tribute to Orr's grand design for the future development of the city. While Orr never lost sight of his private ambitions, they became more longed-for than actual, and as a result he tended to involve himself more heavily in policies of a general nature. He became in effect a full-time civil official, a rarity in those days of temporary appointments and unpaid and often indifferent involvement by young and inexperienced aldermen. Orr's influence was reflected in the early establishment of electric light, water, and sewerage services, the erection of a public hospital and, as has been mentioned, the steps taken to incorporate Calgary as the first city in the North West Territories in 1893.

Wesley Orr also led the city in its promotional ventures in the 1890s. He supported a civic experiment to drill for natural gas in 1892. He also initiated the intensive city lobby for the proposed dominion government's sanatorium for consumptives, the federal experimental farm, as well as the Imperial remount mooted by British military authorities for the Calgary district. Orr worked hard for the cause of irrigation and in 1894 helped organize the first irrigation convention to be held in western Canada. Finally Orr was most prominent in the railroad promotion frenzy of the early 1890s.

Wesley Orr was a man who, in spite of personal diligence and versatility, did not realize his dreams of success. Probably his election as mayor of the city of Calgary in 1894 marked the peak of his personal achievement. He had a lonely private life in Calgary. With the erosion of his marriage he lived at first with his teenage son, and alone towards the end. Then, during his second tenure as mayor in 1897 his health failed.

Wesley Fletcher Orr died in February 1898, a few years before the land boom that would have vindicated his unswerving faith in the future of his adopted city. It is perhaps unfortunate that modern Calgary with its ethos of individual initiative should carry no enduring legacy to the man who was its first unequivocal champion.

Wesley Orr, Calgary's first elected mayor after it became a city, sits at left with various Calgary dignitaries in 1892. Those standing include well-known Calgary defense lawyer Paddy Nolan (left), early Calgary Police Chief English (second from left), prominent early Calgary policeman Constable Fraser (centre), and Senator Lougheed (right), who opened the first law office in Calgary and became the city's biggest property owner. Courtesy, Glenbow-Alberta Institute.

Temperance advocates campaigning for Prohibition in 1915-1916 won success for their cause with the historic referendum of 1916. Courtesy, Glenbow-Alberta Institute.

of social travail was the outstanding negative aspect of the frontier experience. Certainly Calgary's experience was no exception.

As evidenced by their activities in charitable and hospital concerns, public-spirited women provided the most strident challenge to the status quo. One of their activities was spearheading the crusade against the demon drink. The work of the Women's Christian Temperance Union in securing success for the Prohibition cause in 1916 was an outstanding example of the potential force of a hitherto relatively silent voice in public affairs.

Calgary women were also prominent in commercial matters during this period. The Women's Consumers' League was one group formed to combat rising food prices in the city. Due to pressure from women's groups, the Public Market was established in 1910. The activity of the Consumers' League in importing food for sale in competition with local retail outlets was part of an overall plan to use the Public Market as a price leveller. Continued pressure from the Consumers' League led to the incorporation of the Public Market as a city utility in 1915. The Consumers' League also marshalled the support of women in influencing civic elections, and by the end of the period was considering the merits of fielding women candidates for civic office.

At the height of the pre-World War I boom, the intersection of Eighth Avenue and First Street West was the busiest in the city and represented the heart of downtown Calgary. From the Provincial Archives of Alberta.

Perhaps the notion of unrestrained expansion was dominant in, and to a degree synonymous with, the frontier mentality. In Calgary's case it was largely unchallenged except by a few individuals, most importantly by civic-minded women who in fact provided the most strident voice of social conscience in frontier Calgary.

By 1912 Calgarians had much to be proud of. The expanding, vibrant and architecturally harmonious business centre was its best advertisement. The corner of Eighth Avenue and First Street West resembled New York City more than it did the adjacent town of High River. Streetcar lines stretched into the city environs like spokes in ever-widening concentric circles of residential neighbourhoods. The consolidated manufacturing base in east Calgary was evidence of true urban growth. And still people were pouring in from Great Britain, continental Europe, and the United States as the frontier of "the last best west" came into its own. As the largest urban center west of Winnipeg, Calgary reflected the tenor of the times. Its corporate mentality embodied the spectrum of the frontier experience, and was at once aggressive, optimistic, speculative, unstable and non-egalitarian. Few in 1912 realized or cared about the implication of a closing frontier.

Top: *R.B. Nevitt painted* Fort Calgary in Summer *in May 1876. Courtesy, Glenbow-Alberta Institute.*

Above and right: *Superintendent and Inspector William Winder from Ontario was one of the senior officers on the march west in 1874, and in 1876, the time of these paintings, he was in charge of C Troop at Fort Macleod. Courtesy, Glenbow-Alberta Institute.*

Above: Calgary at the Foot of the Rocky Mountains, *sketched by Melton Prior, shows the young town across the river in 1887. Courtesy, Glenbow-Alberta Institute*

Left: *Artist Melton Prior depicted rail travel at its peak of popularity and usage. The colonial sleeping car's well-appointed interior and nicely dressed passengers attest to the degree of exclusiveness available on the CPR's transcontinental trains. Courtesy, Glenbow-Alberta Institute.*

Right: *Probably the most dangerous and exciting of all rodeo events, bull riding pits the cowboy against evil-tempered, specially bred Brahma bulls. Spills occur frequently, and the frantic manoeuvres of rodeo clowns protect thrown cowboys against possible attack by enraged bulls.*

Below: *Chuckwaggon races have thrilled visitors to the Calgary Stampede since 1923. The uniquely Western event is both competitive and dangerous.*

Facing page: *Saddle-bronc riding at the Calgary Stampede attracts competitors from across Canada, the United States, and Australia. The event provides the focal point of interest at Calgary's "greatest outdoor show on earth."*

Right: *Floats emphasizing a central theme, marching bands from all over the continent, and an abundance of horses and cowboys combine to make the annual Stampede Parade one of the city's highlight events. The procession takes about 90 minutes to pass any given viewing point.*

Below: *Rodeo clowns provide half-time entertainment at the Stampede.*

Left: *Each July crowds flock to Calgary's 140-acre Stampede Park for 10 days of exciting events, including saddle-bronc riding. The Calgary Stampede is the oldest regularly held rodeo event in Canada.*

Below: *A popular event at the Calgary Stampede, the wild-horse race originated when early ranch cowboys had to invent their own fun. They would rope, saddle, and ride unbroken horses in something that resembled a race.*

PART II

THE CLOSED FRONTIER: 1914 - 1940

The role of the open frontier in determining Calgary's development ended abruptly with the collapse of the land boom in 1913. A corresponding falling-off in immigration and investment capital indicated that the days of prosperity might be ending. With the outbreak of the First World War in 1914, the open valve of the frontier closed completely, and for more than 25 years the frontier influence was negligible in the city's urban life. In fact, the absence of the frontier element produced an urban mentality much different from the Calgary of the prewar era.

The elements of the open frontier presumed steady growth because of the availability of untapped resources. Calgary's place on the ranching and agricultural frontier was enhanced by the conversion of virgin land to profitable livestock raising and farming. As long as settlers were induced to take part in this conversion, and had surplus capital investment to manage and extend their operations, the frontier remained open and Calgary's continued growth was assured. But the removal of the crucial variables of immigration and capital investment meant an end to externally motivated growth, or in short, to the vibrancy of the open frontier.

The period 1914-1940 was marked by two periods of extraordinary circumstance. The negative effects of the First World War were felt in Calgary as

Facing page: *Calgary City Hall, complete with an impressive clock tower, was opened in 1911 after four years of controversial construction problems. Actual building costs of $300,000 exceeded the original estimate by far.*

Below left: *A steam engine equipped with a water barrel, coal shovel, whistle, and smoke screen is used to thresh wheat on the D.J. Bell farm in Alberta in about 1907. Courtesy, Glenbow-Alberta Institute.*

Right: *Making hay in the years before mechanization was a laborious operation for both people and horses. The cutting and the raking were done with two-horse units, and then workers with hay racks lifted the hay and moved it to stacks. From the Grant MacEwan Collection.*

Below: *Western grain fields saw dramatic changes in threshing equipment, from horsepower to treadmills, then from steam engines to gasoline tractors, and finally to combines. Like the earlier steam tractors, the gasoline outfit required large crews of men and horses. From the Grant MacEwan Collection.*

everywhere else. Similarly, the Great Depression of the 1930s had an awful impact on both rural and urban Canada, and the whole decade in Calgary was punctuated by social and economic dislocation on an unprecedented scale. Not so well understood, however, is that the period 1919 to 1928 was also characterized by generally adverse economic circumstances. A sustained period of drought in the early 1920s drastically affected crop production. Farmers were also faced with lower grain prices and higher production costs. In southern Alberta the cattle industry was hurt: steadily falling prices for finished steers, combined with high feed prices, resulted in heavy herd reductions and many liquidations. In 1923, for example, a knowledgeable Canadian Pacific Railway official commented that 80 percent of Alberta farmers were bankrupt.

These effects were felt in Calgary, and were exacerbated by severe municipal indebtedness. Very simply, between 1914 and the outbreak of the Second World War Calgary existed within a circle of economic constraints,

An old seed drill lies idle, yielding to the eroding forces of time. Once, aided by four farm horses, it made 20 rounds a day on a half-mile stretch, with its shores or drills cutting into the surface of the field. From the Grant MacEwan Collection.

which except for a brief period in 1928-1929 effectively limited urban growth and development.

War and Post-War

Like other major urban centres in Canada, Calgary was directly affected by the war by virtue of its position as a recruiting centre. Between 1914 and 1918, more than 37,000 men enlisted in Calgary for service overseas, while between 5,000 and 15,000 men were quartered in the city either at the Exhibition Grounds or at the permanent Sarcee Military Camp constructed in 1915. Another impressive building constructed during the war was the Mewata Armouries, which was completed in 1918.

The military presence added a volatile element to Calgary's urban life. Soldiers were blamed for displays of moral turpitude, which were viewed as weakening the social fabric of the community. Under a caption "Sunday Orgies Must Cease," the *Herald* once published an account of a Sunday dance on Ninth Avenue disturbed by the irreligious military element. Then in February 1916, the White Lunch restaurant and the Riverside Hotel were damaged by a rampaging mob of soldiers accused of pro-German sympathies by the proprietors. Again in October 1916, another mob of soldiers raided the North West Mounted Police barracks, ostensibly to rescue fellow soldiers imprisoned under the newly enacted prohibition law.

The indirect effects of the war had a much greater effect on the city than the actual presence of the military. First, local commerce and industry tightened considerably. For the first time, the spectre of persistent unemployment raised itself in the city. In September 1914 alone, over 1,200 men were discharged from employment, particularly in the construction industry, which was especially hard hit. Not surprisingly, the value of building permits fell steadily until by 1920 they showed a 90 percent reduction from the peak year of 1912. By February 1915, more than 3,000 unemployed were registered with the Labour Bureau. The cessation of hostilities only worsened an already serious situation. By July 1919, some 15,000 soldiers had returned to Calgary seeking job opportunities. The jobless situation was aggravated by steadily rising prices for staples, which continued through the war period and beyond. Using civic figures as a basis of comparison, $100 worth of goods in 1911 would have cost $235 in 1920.

Things went from bad to worse in the reconstruction period and through the first half of the 1920s. Population growth in Calgary was modest before 1929, and, according to one source, actually fell 6,000 in 1922 from the previous year. The construction industry continued to lag. In 1924, for example, only $1 million were spent on construction, scarcely more than in 1904. As a barometer of urban growth, the real estate market displayed similar bleak signs. Land transactions were negligible in spite of falling prices. In 1923, Calgary's veteran city clerk Jim Miller commented that "conditions have never been so bad," and further, that it was "impossible to secure a permanent position of any kind."

Even the board of trade lost some of its optimism. Its annual reports between 1920 and 1925 were far cries from the exercises in boosterism that

Facing page: "Slim" Moorehouse drove a 32-horse-and-mule team hauling eight waggons and 1,200 bushels of the "world's best wheat" from his district east of Vulcan to the Calgary Exhibition and Stampede in 1924. The spectacle was so popular that he was asked to return in 1925 with the 36-horse team of black Percherons seen in this photo taken on Calgary's Eighth Avenue. The outfit was longer than a city block, and turning corners was a tricky operation. Courtesy, Glenbow-Alberta Institute.

customarily advertised its activities. Typical was the annual report for 1924, which described the year as "disappointing as far as the majority of merchants and manufacturers are concerned." A promotional article published by the mayor's office in 1925 revealed the significant change that had occurred in Calgary's urban mentality since the boom period. Instead of waxing eloquent in typical fashion on the unbounded potential of Calgary and district, the article listed tourism as the prime economic boon in Calgary's future. By 1926 it was freely admitted that the "good old days" were probably gone forever.

A measure of prosperity returned to the West briefly through 1928-29 in the wake of rejuvenated activity in the agricultural and cattle industries, and Calgary reflected this turnabout in increased industrial and retail activity. The Hudson's Bay Company enlarged its premises and cemented its position as Calgary's largest and most popular department store. In February 1929, T.C.

Right: *A heavy steam tractor pulls a threshing machine and sleeping cabooses in about 1920. The steamer was a heavy and slow-moving power unit that broke many country bridges and was helpless in mud, but it furnished steady and the most satisfactory power for operating belts. From the Grant MacEwan Collection.*

Below right: *In about 1908, people attempt to catch fish by a Calgary Waterworks Department water intake and screen on the Elbow River. Prior to the construction of the Glenmore Reservoir in the 1930s, Calgary's water supply was taken from the Bow and then the Elbow rivers. The turbidity and unhealthful nature of this water was the subject of a scathing report by Calgary's chief chemist in 1918. Courtesy, Glenbow-Alberta Institute.*

Eaton and Company opened its million dollar emporium. Substantial manufacturing establishments consolidated themselves, including the Dominion Bridge Company Ltd. and Pioneer Tractor. The long overdue Glenmore Reservoir was also begun in these years.

However, the brief flurry of prosperity was not to last, but was in fact an illusive prelude to the darkest decade in Calgary's history. As everywhere else, Calgary experienced its share of human misery and degradation engendered by mass unemployment. And like other cities across the country, Calgary witnessed collective displays of frustration, anger, and protest. The Depression of the 1930s marked the end of an era in that it demonstrated with stark clarity that the time-honoured system of free enterprise in the classic Adam Smith tradition no longer worked. The result was an increased role for government in the affairs of men.

Water is pumped out of the flooded pool into water tunnels at the Glenmore Reservoir construction site on June 18, 1931, after the peak of high water. Courtesy, Glenbow-Alberta Institute.

Mass meetings were not a new phenomenon when this notice was posted in 1937, but the prevalence of organizations of the unemployed reached a high point during the Depression. Courtesy, Glenbow-Alberta Institute.

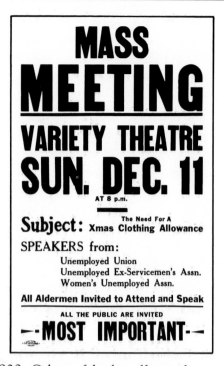

MASS MEETING
VARIETY THEATRE
SUN. DEC. 11
AT 8 p.m.

Subject: The Need For A **Xmas Clothing Allowance**

SPEAKERS from:
Unemployed Union
Unemployed Ex-Servicemen's Assn.
Women's Unemployed Assn.

All Aldermen Invited to Attend and Speak

ALL THE PUBLIC ARE INVITED
--MOST IMPORTANT--

Beginning in 1930, Calgary felt the effects of sustained unemployment on an unprecedented scale. In November 1930, the city had over 1,200 applications for work, and an additional 1,600 single men on file for direct relief. By February 1932, the city was providing food and shelter for 2,600 single men in addition to relief for another 3,200 families. The board of trade estimated in 1934 that over 10,000 people, or approximately 12 percent of the city's population, were on relief. Comparative figures speak for themselves. In the 1920s, the average civic annual expenditure on relief was about $40,000. Between 1930 and 1935, the city spent $2.4 million on relief. The effects of the accompanying social trauma were everywhere as civic and other agencies struggled to handle the innumerable cries for help. Some people requested money to pay pressing bills; others wanted clothes, firewood, and the basic necessities of life. The biggest call, however, was for jobs. Some employers cut wages to minimize layoffs. Others introduced rotating work schedules. It was all too little. Single men were especially affected since they

In 1935 the new Social Credit Party came to power in Alberta with promises of fiscal reform. One of its innovations was the prosperity certificate, which could be traded in for cash after two years if the back was covered with stamps. Courtesy, Glenbow-Alberta Institute.

ALBERTA 1 CENT	ALBERTA 1 CENT	AUG. 6 '36	ALBERTA 1 CENT	ALBERTA 1 CENT	ALBERTA 1 CENT	ALBERTA 1 CENT	ALBERTA 1 CENT	OCT. 7. 1936	OCT. 14. 1936	OCT. 21. 1936	OCT. 28. 1936	NOV. 4. 1936	NOV. 12. 1936	NOV. 18. 1936
NOV. 25. 1936	DE. 2. 1936	DEC. 9. 1936	DEC. 16. 1936	DEC. 23. 1936	DEC. 30. 1936	JAN. 6. 1937	JAN. 13. 1937	JAN. 20. 1937	JAN. 27. 1937	FEB. 1937	FEB. 10. 1937	FEB. 17. 1937	FEB. 24. 1937	MAR. 3. 1937
MAR. 10. 1937	MAR. 17. 1937	MAR. 24. 1937	MAR. 31. 1937	APRIL 7. 1937	APRIL 14. 1937	APRIL 21. 1937	APRIL 28. 1937	MAY 5. 1937	MAY 12. 1937	MAY 19. 1937	MAY 26. 1937	JUNE 2. 1937	JUNE 9. 1937	JUNE 16. 1937
JUNE 23. 1937	JUNE 30. 1937	JULY 7. 1937	JULY 14. 1937	JULY 21. 1937	JULY 28. 1937	AUG. 4. 1937	AUG. 11. 1937	AUG. 18. 1937	AUG. 25. 1937	SEPT. 1. 1937	SEPT. 8. 1937	SEPT. 15. 1937	SEPT. 22. 1937	SEPT. 29. 1937
OCT. 6. 1937	OCT. 13. 1937	OCT. 20. 1937	OCT. 27. 1937	NOV. 3. 1937	NOV. 10. 1937	NOV. 17. 1937	NOV. 24. 1937	DEC. 1. 1937	DEC. 8. 1937	DEC. 15. 1937	DEC. 22. 1937	DEC. 29. 1937	JAN. 5. 1938	JAN. 12. 1938
JAN. 19. 1938	JAN. 26. 1938	FEB. 2. 1938	FEB. 9. 1938	FEB. 16. 1938	FEB. 23. 1938	MAR. 2. 1938	MAR. 9. 1938	MAR. 16. 1938	MAR. 23. 1938	MAR. 30. 1938	APRIL 6. 1938	APRIL 13. 1938	APRIL 20. 1938	APRIL 27. 1938
MAY 4. 1938	MAY 11. 1938	MAY 18. 1938	MAY 25. 1938	JUNE 1. 1938	JUNE 8. 1938	JUNE 15. 1938	JUNE 22. 1938	JUNE 29. 1938	JULY 6. 1938	JULY 13. 1938	JULY 20. 1938	JULY 27. 1938	AUG. 3. 1938	

were routinely the last to receive work.

In Calgary the mounting disaffection was reflected in two separate demonstrations of mass protest and violence. Both the "Red Square" demonstration in 1931 and the Mission Hill disturbance in 1933 were perceived by the press as confrontations between the forces of law and order and anarchy, when they were actually no more than social laments over a world gone crazy. For many, the Depression was to be associated with the dismaying work camps, soup kitchens, hunger marches, and above all, the degrading "dole." Those who lived in trying circumstances through those dark days will probably never forget the experience, and in that sense, the "dirty thirties" marked a watershed in the lives of a whole generation.

In 1935 the United Married Men's Association marched on Second Street East, participating in the social protest associated with the Depression. The banner reads, "We stand behind 12,000 on relief." Courtesy, Glenbow-Alberta Institute.

THE WINTER OF 1932

The following extract appeared in an article submitted by the author to *Alberta History* in 1979 and is reprinted with the permission of the editor.

"By early December 1932, winter held Calgary in its icy grip. The thermometer plummeted to 15 degrees below zero with high winds and drifting snow. A mile and a half of ice floes backed up from the Centre Street Bridge, threatening under-river water mains and power lines. Some schools closed as janitorial staffs could not keep the temperatures above 60 degrees. As the bleak days shortened and Christmas approached, there was little joy in many of the small bungalows that huddled close together on Calgary's snowy streets.

"The effects of the Depression were observable everywhere. The old theatre on Ninth Avenue opposite the YMCA was converted into a refuge for war veterans on relief. Two men, one a young civil engineer, were arrested for begging in northwest Calgary. Some were impatient to join the proposed hunger march to Edmonton to protest inadequate relief measures, that is if they could get transportation and sufficiently warm clothes. Footwear especially was in short supply. Many children were home from school, testing the frayed nerves of harried mothers, because they lacked shoes or boots to wear. Unemployed men were everywhere. Some passed the time in the public library where they read books mainly on the useful arts. The list of jobless was over 7,000, and more than 2,000 applications were expected for Christmas hampers in the *Herald*'s Sunshine Santa Claus Fund. The lavish advertisements customarily associated with Christmas foods were conspicuously lacking. Instead, stores offered boiling beef at five cents a pound, and 'all kinds of soup at 3 for $.25.'

"The Depression's legacy of hopelessness and cynicism was there in Calgary that winter. A new game, 'Millionaires,' was very popular and revealed something of the crumbling work ethic. For example, one received more bonus points for marrying the boss's daughter than for hard work and study, while the quickest route to millionaire status lay not in remarkable ability but in canny investments. A local debating team was victorious over a British rival by successfully arguing that representative government had been a failure. Default was commonplace, with the city of Calgary leading the way. The city council refused to pay the adverse American exchange of $300,000 on bonds maturing on January 1, 1933. Divorces of celebrities were paraded in the press, and people read frequent accounts of whole families being murdered by a deranged parent or child.

"The plight of the Ukrainian girl who lived in a small, draughty building near Chinatown was typical of many. Deserted by her Chinese husband, she was destitute and dependent on relief agencies. Since she was childless, her chances of adequate aid from the city, or of employment, were substantially reduced. The rigours of cold and deficiencies in diet had already undermined her health, and Salvation Army relief workers worried about her condition. More than anything else she was desperately lonely. She had difficulty in the English language and spoke no Chinese. She would like to have gone to Winnipeg where she had a sister, but the train fare was impossible. So she slept a lot and visited the Hudson's Bay department store where efforts were being

While jobs were not always the ultimate reward for the unemployed, welfare agencies and social institutions provided more than the basic necessities of life. A wrestling class for unemployed men was provided by the YMCA during the Depression. Courtesy, Glenbow-Alberta Institute.

made to preserve normalcy and to foster festive gaiety.

"Calgary merchants offered to assume the city's costs in providing for the traditional Christmas lighting. Girls in period costume distributed numbered tags to 9,000 excited shoppers. Three hundred of these numbers were duplicated, and if the lucky ones identified each other, both received a prize. Dancing was a popular pastime as well as a worthy fund raiser for charitable causes. The radio enabled many to enjoy a cheap form of entertainment. The romance of the movie screen held magical appeal, while in the press, Calgarians followed the fortunes of daring aviatrix Amy Johnson, or of speed king Malcolm Campbell and his 2,500 h.p. racing car, *Bluebird*.

"There was also a countervailing tendency to the hopelessness and cynicism mentioned earlier, for the purveyors of optimism were alive and well. People were told that the worst was over, and that economic indices pointed to recovery. Humour assumed a therapeutic dimension. Indeed, the comment by comedian Stan Laurel that he divorced his first wife because they could not laugh together any more was received sympathetically in the press. In defending the capitalist system, economists maintained that the Depression was caused by under-consumption rather than over-production. Calgarians in 1932 were in effect told that they should laugh and make the best out of difficult times, to seek their own solace while waiting for the inevitable upswing. And since they usually tuned in to CFCN radio, and to the pervasive voice of the newly-political William Aberhart, their hopes for the future took a more definite course."

Though employment and business statistics began to improve somewhat after 1936, economic conditions in Calgary remained stagnant until the outbreak of the Second World War. The impact of this second global conflict on Calgary was much different from that in 1914-1918. As a munitions and air training centre, the city experienced an upswing in commercial activity. Its local economy heated in the wake of rising food prices and an emergent housing shortage. Government war contracts helped local enterprises, especially the rising young construction company owned by Fred Mannix. The benefits of the war economy ended with the cessation of hostilities in 1945. But the expected return to normality was not to materialize, for by 1946, the drilling rigs of the Imperial Oil Company had begun to probe the promising Devonian Reef formation near Leduc.

Growth Curtailment

The sustained period of economic stagnation and extraordinary circumstances before World War II resulted in severe financial problems that adversely affected Calgary's growth patterns. In reacting to the realities of financial stringency, civic policymakers and business leaders developed a cautious, pragmatic attitude towards Calgary's future, in effect, an antithesis to the blind optimism characteristic of the frontier ebullience.

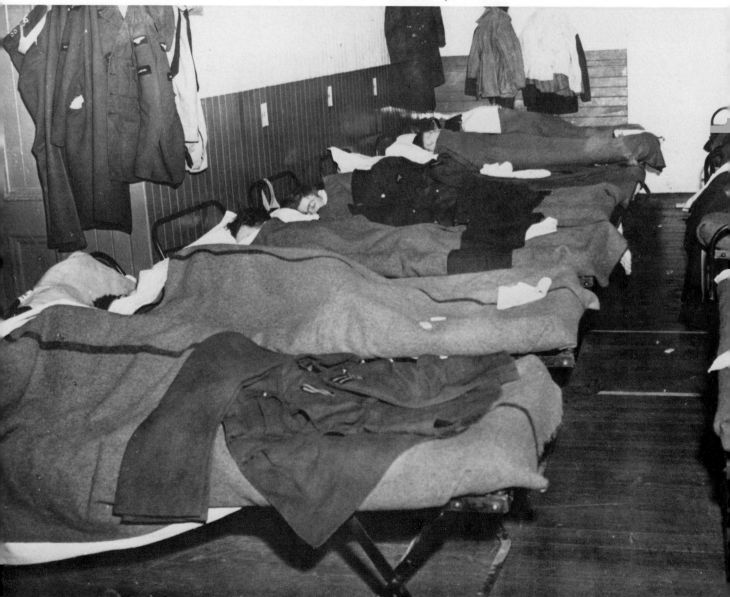

In January 1941 the YMCA was turned into a dormitory for British troops on a weekend pass. The influx of the military into Calgary during World War II strained existing facilities. Courtesy, Glenbow-Alberta Institute.

Between 1914 and 1939, Calgary's corporate growth was negligible. The only capital works project of any magnitude to be completed during this period was the Glenmore Reservoir, which was begun in the brief period of prosperity in 1929 and completed by relief labour during the Depression. Funds were deployed solely for maintaining existing facilities and services. Even then, retrenchment was the order of the day. Relief and other social services were curtailed during the 1920s. Utility, fire, and transportation services were constricted rather than expanded, and consolidation was evident elsewhere. The city was divided into two concentric zones for assessment and development purposes, and people were encouraged to live in the inner area. One result of this was the conversion of larger houses into multidwelling units,

Glenmore Reservoir was the only large capital works project completed during the Depression. Work began during the short period of prosperity in 1929, and relief labour finished the job. Courtesy, Calgary Herald.

especially in the area adjoining the main business centre. The outer area was unserviced, and with the cancellation of many prewar subdivisions, large tracts of city land were converted to agriculture.

The reason for these policies of retrenchment was simply a lack of funds; the city was faced with a perennial shortage in its tax collections. During the boom period, land was assessed at a speculative value, and the resulting inflated assessments meant a higher borrowing limit and a subsequent large bonded indebtedness of over $20 million by 1912. Following the collapse of the boom, many could not pay the high taxes and fell heavily into arrears, and the city was left with extensive shortages in collections. In 1920, over $4.3 million remained uncollected on the tax rolls. Between 1915 and 1923 only about 60 percent of taxable revenue was collected in any single year. Attempts at alternative revenue raising and forcing payment of taxes proved ineffective. For instance, the sale of lands for taxation arrears only resulted in large-scale land reversions to the city. Fixed interest charges and debt repayment procedures meant that the city had substantially reduced monies to run the city. Curtailing services was seen as the only practical solution.

The effect of the taxing policies on many businesses and individuals was staggering to say the least. One market gardener who cultivated 12 acres within the city limits provides an excellent example. In 1917, his assessed tax levy was $1,100, exclusive of the $2,107 in arrears for 1915-1916. Yet he had neither access roads, water, nor electricity. Essentially, his municipal tax burden

Facing page: *Scullers ply Glenmore Reservoir with the Rocky Mountains as a panoramic backdrop. Courtesy, Calgary Herald.*

Above: *Driver Ken Gush poses with the first bus in Calgary's present transit system on the corner of Talon Avenue in 1935. The Leyland gasoline vehicle had a four-speed gear shift, and it serviced the Mount Royal area. Courtesy, Glenbow-Alberta Institute.*

During the spring, summer, and autumn months, migratory geese frequent Calgary's water areas. Birds often delay their southward migration, remaining close to the city area where the feeding is good, until the arrival of winter snow. Courtesy, Calgary Herald.

threatened his livelihood while denying him the most rudimentary of urban services. Small businessmen in the city were also severely affected. Foreclosures and liquidations were common, especially in the early 1920s. Although the idea of business bankruptcies is associated more with the 1930s and the Great Depression, it is also true that the intolerable tax burdens forced many merchants into the amalgamation or even abandonment of their businesses in the lean years of the early 1920s. Furthermore, the land tax burden was exacerbated by a 10 percent business tax, as well as by a system of personal

LEONARD W. BROCKINGTON

One of the most influential civic officials during the 1920s and 1930s was city solicitor Leonard W. Brockington. "Brock," as he was popularly known, represented the type of tough-minded, realistic thinking that characterized municipal policymaking during the interwar period.

The Welsh-born Calgary lawyer received his legal training at the University of Alberta where he earned the gold medal of the Alberta Law Society. After a short period with the eminent Calgary law firm of Lougheed and Bennett, Brockington became city solicitor for the city of Calgary, a post he held for 14 years before resigning in 1935. Brockington made his influence felt through his close association with senior elected civic officials as well as through the clarity of mind he brought to his professional duties. His reports were well-researched, lucid, and above all forthright in their recommenda-

income tax, the latter operating between 1925 and 1932.

By 1925 it was obvious that Calgary's financial dilemma was not going to go away. Tax arrears and land reversions still comprised the most serious problems facing civic administrations. Conservative individuals like long-tenured city commissioner Arthur Graves, the astute and articulate city solicitor, Leonard Brockington, as well as cautious mayors like George Webster and Fred E. Osborne were firmly convinced of the need for continued policies of fiscal restraint.

tions. Brockington was also an eloquent and able debater with a national reputation for public speaking. Naturally, the force of Brockington's arguments rarely went unheeded in civic policy making.

In 1936, Brockington was named first chairman of the newly created Canadian Broadcasting Commission. During the Second World War he acted as special advisor to Prime Minister Mackenzie King, and travelled extensively promoting the Commonwealth war effort. In 1942 he became adviser on Commonwealth affairs to the British Ministry of Information, and by the end of the war, his voice was one of the most recognizable on air waves in Canada, Great Britain, and other Commonwealth countries.

Following the war, Brockington worked in labour relations, and was rector of Queens University for nearly 20 years. A recipient of a Canada Council Medal, which recognized his oratory, Brockington, though crippled with arthritis, managed to live a full life until his death in 1966.

Relief workers labouring in the Bankview area of Calgary in 1931 were participants in the programmes that enabled the city to alleviate some of the massive unemployment resulting from the Depression. Funds were provided on a cost-sharing basis by the provincial and federal governments. Courtesy, Glenbow-Alberta Institute.

The best example of this restricted view of Calgary's future came in 1929 through the city's renewed interest in town planning. Acting on provincial initiative with respect to town planning, the city authorized the preparation of some 30 reports encompassing recreational land use, transportation, civic art, and zoning. A town planner was then hired to oversee the process. The choice of Arthur Doughty Davies, a practical draughtsman from Victoria, provided a functional contrast to the flamboyant utopian Thomas Mawson 17 years earlier. Under Doughty Davies' direction, the newly appointed town planning commission adopted a conservative stance. The proposed zoning bylaw and arterial highway plan were framed on the assumption that Calgary would continue to be a small city. For instance, the zoning bylaw presupposed that the existing commercial land use designation could accommodate Calgary's growth indefinitely. Similarly, the arterial highway plan simply called for the widening of existing thoroughfares as the need arose.

The Depression of the 1930s placed an intolerable financial burden on a city that had scarcely managed to weather the fiscal storms of the 1920s. The city just could not cope, and had no recourse but to turn in total desperation to higher levels of government. Hitherto, such appeals had been largely ignored, and for the most part Calgary had gone it alone. The Depression was different. The notion that municipalities should be responsible for unemployment had been long debated, and certainly never fully accepted at the local level. The Depression underscored the glaring disparity between municipal revenues and responsibilities.

MASS MEETING

OUTLINE OF SOUTHERN'S

WORK FOR WAGES" SCHEME

HEAR THE REPORT OF DELEGATES TO RELIEF COMMISSION IN EDMONTON

VICTORIA PAVILLION

SUNDAY, JUN. 20TH. 2:30 P.M.

Left: In 1937 this handbill appeared, advertising a mass meeting of the unemployed in Calgary, evidence that the times of adversity were not restricted to the first half of the "dirty thirties," but actually extended to the outbreak of World War II. Courtesy, Glenbow-Alberta Institute.

Below: Relief workers level and fill land for recreational use in the Bankview area of Calgary in the early 1930s. During the Depression, the city furnished work on a rotating basis. Preference was extended to married men, and single unemployed individuals found it difficult to secure relief work of any kind with the city. Courtesy, Glenbow-Alberta Institute.

In the early 1930s, Calgary's aggressive labour-oriented mayor, Andrew Davison, carried the city's case to Edmonton and Ottawa. Davison's tough-minded stance made him a provincial spokesman for the municipalities' case for more equitable cost-sharing arrangements. Not surprisingly, Davison was also a dominant figure in city council. His strong influence was put to good advantage when the city adopted the Fortin Plan for consolidating the municipal debt in 1937. Davison believed that future residents should be in part responsible for costs incurred by current capital works projects. The Fortin Plan, by shifting the debt burden further into the future, enabled the city to upgrade power and transporation services to accommodate wartime demands.

The accumulated effects of uninterrupted financial stress on Calgary had

Road crews tear up street-railway tracks in preparation for Calgary's transition to trackless trolleys and gasoline buses. The street-railway system began in 1909. Courtesy, Calgary Herald.

an important implication during the Second World War, and clearly showed how desperate short-run necessities outweighed the merits of long-range considerations in civic policymaking. The occasion was the housing shortage engendered by wartime demands, and involved the virtual disposal of hundreds of acres of city-owned land to private interests.

Between 1911 and 1941, only 6,055 houses were built in Calgary. Indeed, 40 percent of Calgary's occupied dwellings had been erected before 1911. A shortage of houses was a perennial feature in Calgary. In 1930 for instance, the council issued two dollar permits authorizing the erection of tents in the city for dwelling purposes. By 1941, the city was faced with a housing shortage unmatched since the boom period. Rents soared to the accompaniment of hasty and poorly planned conversion of single to multiple dwelling

The board of directors of Canadian Cooperative Wheat Producers, Limited, pose in 1924. Henry Wise Wood (front row, left) came to Alberta with the great wave of immigrants from the U.S. soon after the beginning of the century and homesteaded at Carstairs, not far north of Calgary. Ultimately he became the foremost leader in the Alberta farm movement and the first president of the Alberta Wheat Pool. From the Grant MacEwan Collection.

units. One individual wrote to the council requesting permission to convert his chicken coop to an apartment. In a desperate effort to induce building activity, the city council decided to kill two birds with one stone. The solution involved city-owned lands, which were estimated as being worth $5 million in 1942. Most of these properties accrued to the city in *lieu* of unpaid taxes, and while they stood as equity against the civic sinking fund, they were burdensome in that they generated no taxation revenue.

So in 1941, the city council adopted a policy whereby city-owned land was sold at 50 and later 25 percent of assessed value. Even then the council reserved the right to deal individually with specific cases. Within three years, the city of Calgary had disposed of much of its extensive holdings for a fraction of their market, let alone potential, value. The implications for civic control of future land development are only too obvious. When one considers the price of land in Calgary in 1982, or even in the boom period 1909-12, the bargains secured by those perceptive enough to buy between 1941 and 1944 seem too good to be true. A parcel of 1.6 acres in Spruce Cliff sold for $240. Nineteen acres were purchased in Glendale for $500. The subdivision now known as Mayland Heights was disposed of for $25 an acre. Building lots went as low as $25. Business operations were able to extend their premises economically by purchasing adjoining lots at greatly reduced prices. By 1945, official alarm was expressed at "the speculative evils that had once more been launched on the city," and in 1946 a city lands committee recommended that the policy be discontinued. However, the return to caution might have been somewhat belated.

The Bureaucratic and Collective Dimension

Calgary reflected the closing of the frontier in other ways. The emphasis on individual initiative was weakened in the face of the increased role played by the strengthening forces of bureaucracy and collectivism. In fact, the prolonged period of adversity spurred the establishment of the collective dependency associated with urban living.

The civic corporation became solidly bureaucratized and generally more efficient than in previous years, while the various civic departments extended their scope and operation. In 1919 the city took over the responsibility for hospital management, and in 1923 assumed complete control over relief administration. Utility services were also finally stabilized. Calgary Power Company Ltd. became the sole electricity supplier in the city in 1927, while during the same period the city hammered out satisfactory contracts with the volatile Canadian Western Natural Gas, Heat, Light and Power Company Ltd. The steady refinements in utility contracts during this period stood in sharp contrast to the cavalier, free-wheeling days before 1912 when monopolies, privileges, inefficiency and unreliable service were commonplace.

The static years allowed strong local individuals to fashion institutions to

Junior Red Cross children's hospital, which could accomodate 26 beds, was opened in May 1922 at 522 18th Avenue Southwest. Note the children on the second-storey sun porch. Courtesy, Glenbow-Alberta Institute.

Above: *Calgary Power Company's powerhouse on the Bow River at Horse Shoe Falls was the site of the firm's first hydroelectric project, which began operations in 1910. Courtesy, Calgary Herald.*

Facing page: *Richard Bedford Bennett came from New Brunswick to be a junior member of Senator Lougheed's law firm in Calgary. He soon entered politics and sat in the legislative assemblies of the Northwest Territories, the Province of Alberta, and, later, the House of Commons in Ottawa. Two years after this picture was taken in 1928, Bennett became the Prime Minister of Canada. From the Grant MacEwan Collection.*

their own design. Civic departments, schools, and churches were headed by capable, long-tenured individuals who for the most part ran their operations conservatively and without interference. The more notable included fire chief James (Cappy) Smart, police chief David Ritchie, parks superintendent William Reader, power superintendent Robert A. Brown, and public school superintendent Melville Scott. Their respective departments earned for them a wide measure of respect and prestige, both within and outside the city. The same could be said for other institutional and business leaders whose basic conservatism crystallized more solidly with longevity. Bishop Cyprian Pinkham and the Reverend George Kerby of the Anglican and Methodist churches, respectively, commanded enormous influence and respect, not only from their own congregations but also from the community at large. Pioneer business leaders and employers like A.E. Cross, I.K. Kerr, and Thomas Underwood ran their businesses with a paternal eye. And the idea of tradition was entrenched in other areas. For instance, E.L. Richardson, longtime manager of the Calgary Exhibition and Stampede, was determined that the annual spectacle should always retain its strong agricultural flavour.

Two observable phenomena were part of Calgary's business experience in the interwar period. The first, consistent with the notion of the closed frontier, was the loss of local business autonomy in the face of financial stringency and external pressure. The second is more surprising—the rise of successful business operations during times of relative adversity.

Dave Black arrived in Calgary in 1903, and started his own jewellery business a year later. By 1913 he had the largest watch repair business in Canada. Yet Black's operations were merged with the Montreal-based jewellery firm of Henry Birks and Sons in 1920. The Alberta Flour Mills Company was taken over by the British milling firm of Spillers Ltd. in 1924. Another long-standing enterprise, the Riverside Iron Works, was incorporated into the Dominion Bridge Company Ltd. Large department stores like the Hudson's Bay Company and T.C. Eaton and Sons made it increasingly difficult for smaller, more personalized stores to operate. During the Depression, Canadian

In the 1920s, the average homeowner was accustomed to having milk, bread, produce, and groceries delivered to the door. Shellys Bakery truck is shown at Shaw's Store in the Midnapore district, now a suburb of Calgary. Courtesy, Glenbow-Alberta Institute.

Safeways Ltd. began its transformation of the grocery business, substituting a heavy "walk-in trade" and cash transactions for the more traditional phone-in, delivery and credit operations that had hitherto been characteristic of smaller retail outlets. However, the most significant gesture to the loss of local autonomy came in 1928 when Pat Burns sold his meat packing interests to Dominion Securities Corporation of Toronto for $15 million.

Yet it was during this period that many businesses and names long associated with Calgary first made their presence felt. Operating on shoestring budgets and limited inventories, these interwar entrepreneurs were a diversified lot. A sampling might include the names of automobile dealerships like Brasso, Maclin, and Universal, Niels Weismose in furniture, Henry Marshall Jenkins in the grocery business, Fred Deeves in plumbing, O.J. Hurst in construction, and R.F. (Reg) Jennings, Merv Dutton, Bob Burns, and Fred Mannix in heavy contracting. Then there were the many local enterprises associated with the pioneer oil activity in Turner Valley. Names like William Stewart Herron, Robert A. Brown, Eric Harvie, and Archibald W. Dingman date to this interwar period.

In 1909-1910 this business block housed prominent early Calgary enterprises, such as Curlette's Photo Studio, Black's jewellery, and Neilson's furniture. Black's was taken over by Henry Birks and Sons in 1920. Courtesy, Glenbow-Alberta Institute.

Though the days of the open frontier had closed and the city of Calgary was no longer a boom town, the local business scene continued its evolution toward resident autonomy with mixed results. Most certainly, business entrepreneurship was more restrained than in the earlier days of frenzied expansion. Yet those who were able to wait out the dark days were to reap their rewards in the later years of postwar expansion.

For the working man, some of the rapacities inherent in the frontier experience were modified during this period. Up to the Depression at least, the average worker saw a gradual improvement in job tenure, working conditions, and benefits. For example, the Calgary Police Force adopted a superannuation plan in the 1920s. These advances were due mainly to the collectivization process. Whether through unions, federations, or guilds, the worker was able to use the force of numbers to better his lot. In Calgary, much of the initiative towards improved working conditions was due to the Federation of Civic Employees, which made substantial gains, especially in the years 1918-1921. Although the Depression arrested this advance somewhat, it was more a moratorium than a regression. By 1940, workers' rights had been institutionalized into the familiar adversarial bargaining process between management and labour. Perhaps in Calgary this process was strengthened through a stable, federated body of civic employees, and long-tenured and respected department heads as well as by the mild paternalism of senior policymakers.

The public will was institutionalized in other ways. Civic elections were influenced by the actions of adversarial groups representative of labour and business interests. Service clubs, consumers' groups, and ratepayers' associations pursued pressure policies favourable to their interests. The various religious and recreational agencies organized and ordered the social behaviour of individuals on a collective basis. Educational institutions like the Provincial Institute of Technology began laying the basis for organized cultural activity. The urban environment that existed in Calgary between 1914 and 1940 brought about the interdependent life-style with its emphasis on organized social interaction and group involvement.

An excellent example of the cooperative spirit of public involvement that characterized this whole period of austerity was provided by the formation and early operation of the Calgary Zoo, now recognized as one of the finest in North America.

Three individuals figured prominently in getting the Calgary Zoo off the ground. Dr. O.H. Patrick formed the Zoological Society in 1928 with the idea of a zoo uppermost in his mind. The random assemblage of stray, unwanted creatures then quartered on St. George's Island formed a rudimentary though hardly impressive nucleus. William Reader, city of Calgary parks superintendent, provided the means for an arrangement placing the zoo under loose city auspices. In essence, the city agreed to maintain the animal park if the Zoological Society assumed responsibility for providing animals and pens. The subsequent appointment of Tom Baines as labourer in charge of the animals while also attending to his other duties with the city parks department, was a most fortuitous move. Under Baines' single-minded and able direction, the zoo experiment achieved credibility and permanency through the initial dark years of depression and travail.

Labour was a major problem. Baines was virtually on his own in that no additional permanent staff was assigned to the zoo until 1938. He was helped for a while by casual labour furnished through Depression works programmes, but any specialized or emergent needs had to be supplied by private benefactors, and all construction materials were either scrounged or donated. Luckily the persuasive and resourceful Baines was equal to the task. His friend Lars Willumsen did much to upgrade facilities. Willumsen's construction company donated men and equipment to build pens for foxes, coyotes, bobcats, lynx, and bears. The firm of Trotter and Morton supplied free plumbing services. Crown Lumber, Beaver, and Revelstoke gave lumber and other building materials.

Food was another problem. Baines was given approximately a dollar a day to feed all the animals. Again, public-minded enterprises came to the rescue. Pat Burns and Company donated 100 pounds of meat per week, and continued to do so well beyond the Depression years. The packing firm owned by A.H. Mayland gave all its beef lips to the zoo, and Safeways Ltd. loaded a city truck once a week with produce. A friendly bakery donated all its stale bread, while a local pastry cook saw to it that such delicacies as burnt cake and similar offerings made their way to St. George's Island.

Others helped in different ways. Dr. Gordon Anderson donated veterinary services. Eric Harvie gave free legal advice. Some like Selby Walker and the Cross family contributed animals and money for specific projects. The Finnish-born John Kanerva was responsible for creating many of the famous dinosaur replicas. Noted Banff sculptor Charlie Beile also offered his services.

Special attention should be given to the remarkable Tom Baines. In many ways this gentle English-born animal lover epitomized the spirit of the period. In the years when specialists or experts were developed solely through experience, Baines laboured alone resolutely pursuing his dream of making the Calgary Zoo successful, and in doing so grew immeasurably in professional stature. A friendly, gregarious individual with innate interpersonal skills, he was also able to elicit widespread support and confidence. In 1961 Baines served a term as president of the North American Association of Zoological Parks and Aquariums, the first Canadian to do so, and when he retired in 1964 Baines was an internationally known figure in zoological circles.

Today the octogenarian, much-honoured Baines is a living legend of sorts. Hundreds of thousands of Calgary school children know him for his frequent visits with his travelling museum of assorted artifacts and animal specimens. With his good friend Agnes B. Constrictor often wrapped around his neck, Tom Baines continues to do what he had always done best—communicate with (and for) his fellow creatures.

As has been noted, the sustained period of restricted growth enabled the consolidation of institutions that were in their infancy in the previous decades of frontier expansion. Furthermore, one could argue that as the frontier closed on entrepreneurial activity, so did the more institutionalized environment encourage development in the creative domain. A good example was in the field of art. Here the institutional base was provided by the Provincial Institute of Technology, established in the city in 1916. A personal catalyst arrived in Calgary in 1929 in the form of a somewhat eccentric, compulsive worker, English-born artist A.C. Leighton.

Above: *Tom Baines, former curator of the Calgary Zoo and one of Calgary's best-known personalities, entertains a group of kindergarten children with his display of artifacts. Every year Baines visits thousands of schoolchildren, who become enthralled with his traveling museum. Courtesy, Calgary Herald.*

Below left: *"Dinny," a model brontosaurus—the largest known dinosaur species, resides at the Calgary Zoo. Calgary's proximity to the Red Deer River badlands makes citizens conscious of the many types of dinosaurs whose skeletal remains have been discovered there. Courtesy, E.W. Cadman.*

A.C. LEIGHTON

"Acie" Leighton was 28 years old when he arrived in Calgary in late 1929. A versatile, dedicated and highly productive artist, Leighton was ideal for the position. He came from an artistic family and had had formal training in architectural design. He was by nature a perfectionist with a self-critical eye for detail. Leighton's first big break came in Britain when he was commissioned by the Canadian Pacific Railway to do all the designs, layouts, lettering, and illustrations for its promotional literature. It was in conjunction with this work that he first visited Calgary in 1925. Leighton was enraptured by the beauty of southern Alberta, especially the skies. Later he was to paint a sky a day for practice. Leighton was back in Calgary in 1927, this time at the invitation of the supervisor of art in the Calgary public school system. By this time his national reputation was well established. With no less a patron than Lady Eaton of Eaton's Emporium, herself, Leighton was invited to give an art exhibition at the new Eaton's store in 1929. Soon thereafter, he joined the staff at the technical college.

A.C. Leighton was a well-known artist when he came to Calgary in 1929. In his role as head of the art department at the Provincial Institute of Technology, and later as a prolific and versatile painter, Leighton figured prominently in the development of art in Calgary. Courtesy, Glenbow-Alberta Institute.

Leighton's six years with the Provincial Institute of Technology were eventful and far-reaching in helping to develop art in Calgary. For one, he solidified the growing fraternity of artists by forming the Alberta Society of Artists in 1931. Second, his reputation enticed art students from all over Alberta and the West.

As a teacher, Leighton was both inspirational and exacting. His total commitment to his profession led him to invite his most promising students to join him in extended workshop courses near Seebe in the Kananaskis country. Here, he put them through a Spartan regimen—a sketch before breakfast, painting all day, and lectures in the evening. These summer workshops attracted much public and professional interest, with the ultimate result being the formation of an art department within the Banff School of Fine Arts, itself established by the University of Alberta in 1933.

Students work on creative endeavors at the Leighton Centre for Arts and Crafts near Millarville, southwest of Calgary. The Centre's enduring appeal is due greatly to the efforts of its founder, Barbara Leighton, who named the centre after her late husband, artist A.C. Leighton. Courtesy, Calgary Herald.

"Acie" Leighton both institutionalized and popularized the study of art in Calgary, and his influence extended well beyond his retirement from teaching in 1935, for health reasons. He went on to paint profusely in Alberta and overseas, consolidating his reputation as one of western Canada's leading artists. Some of his students who went on to achieve success of their own included Marion Nicoll, Myrtle Jackson, and Margaret Shelton. He married another student, Barbara Harvey, in 1931. Today, the Leighton Centre for Arts and Crafts initiated by his widow stands as an enduring legacy to his name. Few who have visited the Leighton home, which adjoins the Centre near Millarville, can fail to be impressed. The handsome edifice with its magnificent panoramic mountain view exudes the spirit of the artist who designed it.

When "Acie" Leighton died in 1965, the world lost a character in the fullest possible sense. He symbolized the virtuosity that usually accompanies the advance of the cultural frontier. Equally proficient in pastels, oils, or watercolours, Leighton insisted on painting everything outdoors. He was never satisfied with his work and neglected to hang any of his paintings on the grounds that he would then be forced to relive their failings. He never sold a painting less than a year old, and even then destroyed about 70 percent before the year was up. He evinced all the idiosyncratic behaviour of the true artist, being unpredictable, spontaneous, and unorthodox. For instance he once hauled a canvas to the top of a cedar tree in order to paint an Indian village on Vancouver Island. Those fortunate enough to possess a Leighton own more than just a painting; they have a surviving legacy of an important pioneer in the development of art in Western Canada.

The Provincial Institute of Technology represented the provincial government's compromise to Calgary following its denial of a university for the city. Some art classes were conducted initially, but were later suspended during the war and reconstruction periods. Then in 1926 commercial art courses were introduced. The first head of the art department was Norwegian Lars Hawkeness, and following his death in 1929, the Institute achieved a *coup* of sorts when it hired the highly regarded British artist A.C. (Acie) Leighton to take his place.

During this period, strong efforts were made to further the development of music in the city. Indeed, Calgary had always enjoyed strong public involvement in music. The first Calgary Philharmonic Society was formed in 1904 in an attempt to establish a permanent choral organization. In 1908 the famous Apollo Choir made its debut under P.L. Newcombe in Haydn's *The Creation*. In 1910 the first Calgary Symphony Orchestra was formed to accompany the Apollo Choir, and three years later a second and larger edition of the orchestra first performed under conductor Max Weil at the Sherman Grand Theatre before an audience of 700. The orchestra numbered 55 musicians, and with its inception, Calgary boasted the reputation of being the only Canadian city outside Toronto to support a professional symphony orchestra. Yet by the end of the First World War both the Apollo Choir and the symphony orchestra had passed out of existence.

Facing page: *Artist Jim Nicoll painted* Sicily, *which is on display at the Glenbow Art Gallery. His wife, artist Marion Nicoll, studied with A.C. Leighton. Both Jim and Marion Nicoll are among Calgary's best-known artists and enjoy a wide measure of public popularity. Courtesy, Calgary Herald.*

Below: *The Calgary Concert Band performs for shoppers and visitors at the Stephen Avenue (then Eighth Avenue) Mall. Courtesy, Calgary Herald.*

The Calgary Women's Musical Club was active during the First World War and beyond in sponsoring concerts in the city, including an annual performance featuring world-renowned composers and artists. Due to the efforts of the Calgary Choral and Orchestral Society, a third symphony orchestra was formed in 1928 with Gregori Garbovitsky as conductor. Originally comprising some 50 musicians, the orchestra grew in number to 75 and gave public concerts both indoors and outdoors plus a series of CBC (Canadian Broadcasting Commission) broadcasts before being disbanded in 1939.

An interesting figure in Calgary's musical life during this period was Clifford Higgin, an organist and choirmaster who arrived in Calgary from Brantford in 1920. He conducted the Knox United Church Choir, the Calgary Light Opera Society, and the Institute of Technology Chorale. In 1931 he was instrumental in founding the Calgary Music Competition Festival, the forerunner of the present Kiwanis Music Festival. Higgin's wife, Eileen, also became prominent in musical circles, and among other accomplishments was actively involved in directing the annual production of the Calgary Theatre Singers.

Similarly, Calgary's involvement with sports became more organized and less reflective of the boisterous spontaneity of the frontier period. Before the First World War, local groups were active in horse racing, trapshooting, golf, lawn tennis, curling, cricket, soccer, rugby, polo, boxing, baseball, and hockey. While some leagues were organized, many more were spontaneous with improvisation being the order of the day. For example, prize fighting became popular in Calgary when former heavyweight champion Tommy Burns opened a clothing store in the city and began promoting fights between 1910 and 1913. The city's first golf course was on the bald prairie at Buffalo Wallow, the present day 17th Avenue and 4th Street Southwest. A lot of money was won and lost as a result of the match races held at Calgary's first horse racing straightaway on Third Avenue.

Horses graze in a field south of Highway 22 near Midnapore, prime ranching and horse country. Many riding establishments board horses for Calgary riding enthusiasts in the area south and west of the city. Courtesy, Calgary Herald.

The gradual development of permanent, standardized facilities during the interwar period, plus the wide organization of competitive leagues and the patronage of sports by private businesses, helped institutionalize organized sporting activities. Typical was lawn tennis. It was estimated that in the 1930s there were between 60 and 70 courts in the city. The policies pursued by the Calgary Parks Department under Superintendent William Reader led to improved facilities for baseball, football and community hockey. The Alberta Thoroughbred Horse Breeders Association was established in 1917, and Calgary had its first $1,000 purse two years later. The opening of the Chinook

The historic Blue Rock Hotel in the Mission District meets its end. Courtesy, Calgary Herald.

track in 1925 under the sponsorship of the Speers Corporation formalized thoroughbred racing in Calgary. The Calgary Tigers semi-professional hockey team competed for the Stanley Cup against the Montreal Canadians in 1923-1924, and featured such notable personalities as Red Dutton, Herbie Gardiner, and Harry Oliver. In 1926 the Calgary Team won Alberta's first national junior hockey championships. Success was not confined to hockey, however. Hillhurst won a national soccer championship in 1922.

Between the wars many factors combined to make organized sports more popular with the average Calgarian. Included here was the added media coverage through the development of radio, the greater leisure time afforded by the reduction in the work week, and the many municipal facilities.

In terms of civic action, Calgary surrendered a good deal of local

Old structures were demolished to make way for redevelopment of the Eau Claire area. Courtesy, Calgary Herald.

autonomy in this period to the provincial government. The city lost the power to give inducements to prospective industries in 1913. The Board of Public Utilities, established by the provincial government in 1916, effectively curtailed the city's powers with respect to utilities, assessment, and borrowing procedures. Calgary was put at a disadvantage by provincial action in other areas, as well. For example in the early 1920s considerable civic revenue was derived from the licensing of coin vending machines. Following a tightening of provincial regulations in 1924, the number of such machines in the city dropped from 297 to 15. Similarly, the provincial government aggravated the city's financial problems by accruing increasing revenue from the imposition of new and special taxes. Particularly vexing were the automobile and amusement taxes. The Town Planning Act of 1929 was quite definite in its stipulations respecting subsequent municipal action.

Finally, it is interesting to note that in the lean years of the 1920s, the provincial government actually doubled its revenues while reducing its expenditures, which in 1929 were actually less than in 1921. While it cannot be disputed that the Depression demonstrated graphic disequilibrium between the municipal and provincial domains, the 1920s had an equal effect in widening the gap. It took the wholesale misery of the Depression to drive home a point made clear by Calgary's civic leaders more than a decade earlier.

Calgary's inability to accommodate the demands of the Depression resulted in significant cost-sharing arrangements with the federal and provincial governments. A newer and fairer role for municipalities was established following the historic Royal Commission on Dominion-Provincial Relations. Still, a price was paid for the new deal. After 1935, municipalities like Calgary increasingly found their absolute powers diminished in favour of provincial centralization.

Political and Social Protest

Calgary's tradition of protest continued during this period. Unlike the earlier years of the open frontier, the voices of social and political reform became more institutionalized and definitely more persistent. Indeed, Calgary's most colourful personalities during the years of the closed frontier were not solely associated with commerce or industry. Instead, they also included the social and political reformers who responded to Calgary's urban environment by articulating their case for widespread changes in the status quo.

Some gravitated to the arena of local government where the effects of economic adversity were most observable. In the 1920s and 1930s individuals like Robert Parkyn, Fred White, J.W. Russell, G.D. Batchelor, Walter Little, and Edith Patterson worked hard on the city council to improve general conditions. Parkyn and White were especially interesting figures. Both served terms as MLAs as well as several years on the city council. They were also both heavily involved in local trade unions. Though socialist in orientation, they were not extremists but were basically concerned with formulating specific policies designed to better the lot of the average citizen. The ill-fated municipal housing project of 1929-1930 was probably the best example of their thinking.

In 1929 the Calgary city council gave serious consideration to providing cheap housing for some of its disadvantaged residents. The move marked a radical departure from traditional civic thought, and, though never implemented, gave evidence of the winds of change that soon were to blow over the fields of government activity.

The matter of municipal housing was raised first in April 1929 by Labour alderman Robert Parkyn, who referred to a housing shortage in the city and the accompanying evils of exorbitant rents and slum conditions. A subsequent investigation supported Parkyn's contentions. Severe overcrowding was found in the inner city area. Fully one third of all families surveyed lived in one or two rooms, often with inadequate heating and toilet facilities. Parkyn's suggestion was that the city might alleviate the situation by erecting about 20 houses at $2,500 each for rent at moderate rates to needy families.

Over the next seven months the Special Housing Committee carried the matter to the people and ultimately came up with a specific proposal for a scheme of municipal housing. The city proposed to appropriate approximately $100,000 for the erection of modern, six-room, one-and-a-half storey homes in a desirable part of the city for rent and eventual purchase by deserving, selected residents. A survey revealed that at least 60 interested families were willing to pay the $200 deposit and the $35 monthly rent. As a result, tenders were called and received on the municipal housing project.

But as suddenly as it had been introduced, the housing project died in council. The motion for implementation was defeated amid gathering concern over the future following the dramatic Wall Street crash of 1929. Furthermore, some influential civic officials had never been in favour of the idea. Calgary's housing problem remained. Six months later, in the summer of 1930, two-dollar permits were issued authorizing the erection of tents within the city limits. And then the Depression hit, to compound the misery and travail of Calgary's urban homeless.

The most outstanding example of the voice of reform in local government belonged to the first woman ever elected to Calgary city council. In Mrs. Annie Gale, alderwoman from 1918 to 1923, Calgary received its purest expression of the practical voice of the underdog. Articulate and determined, the dark haired, attractive Mrs. Gale soon made her presence felt around city hall. An outspoken supporter of non-partisan sentiment, Mrs. Gale eschewed party politics and instead called for all able-bodied women to redress inequities by individual and concerted group action. In council, Mrs. Gale focused on public health and consumer protection and produced significant recommendations in both areas.

Below: *In 1929 a Special Housing Committee was formed to deal with the shortage of adequate residential housing. As Calgary has grown, residential subdivisions, such as the one shown under construction, have multiplied with the continuing demand for housing. Courtesy, Calgary Herald.*

Following pages: *Old buildings and new skyscrapers stand side by side in Calgary's transitionary land-use area adjacent to the main business district. Courtesy, Calgary Herald.*

ANNIE GALE: A STRIDENT VOICE OF SOCIAL REFORM

Annie Gale was born in Worcestershire, England, in 1876 or 1877. She received a good Anglican education at the Dudley Proprietary School for Girls, and was married in 1901 to John Gale, a civil engineer. In 1912 the Gales arrived with their two sons in boom town Calgary to begin a new life.

That Annie Gale was not impressed with conditions in Calgary is a gross understatement. She was in fact appalled at the exorbitant prices paid for land, food, and housing. Later she remarked that "we poor immigrants were compelled to pay a quarter for two or three mouldy carrots ... which would only be fed to cows in the Old Country." She perceived the cause to lie in the shortsightedness and cartel mentality of local retail merchants who seemed oblivious to the potential of locally grown products. Mrs. Gale was equally disturbed by the inferior status of women and the seeming indifference of government agencies. For instance, she maintained that expectant cows received better subsidized medical attention than pregnant women. It was not long, therefore, before the hitherto conservative Annie Gale turned her resolute spirit to the world of radical politics and the cause of women.

First she became involved in the Women's Consumers' League where she agitated for direct municipal participation in the public market. Her direct lobbying with various local and provincial government departments began what was to be a continuing crusade to use the force of civic authority to control food prices. During the war her work with the Vacant Lots Garden Club helped prove that Alberta could grow vegetables as successfully as British Columbia. Through the Consumers' League she helped organize the immensely successful Potato Lunch in 1917 to publicize the League's potato exhibition at the city market.

In 1916 Mrs. Gale organized the first Women's Ratepayers' Association in Canada. According to her own recollections, her move in that direction was prompted by the realization that she could do little to redress social inequities through the traditional church-oriented agencies. With this action, Mrs. Gale's radical cast was firmly established. She served two years as treasurer of the Calgary Forum, and by 1921 was identified with the Dominion Labour Party.

With the support of the Women's Consumers' League and Bob Edwards of *The Eye Opener*, Annie Gale was elected to city council in 1918. Though substantive evidence is lacking, Mrs. Gale may well have been the first woman in the British Empire to hold an elected position on a city council. In her subsequent six years on council, Mrs. Gale made her presence felt through her tireless work on behalf of the public welfare. She battled with monopolies and was deeply involved in the movement that led to the municipalization of hospitals in 1919. In 1918 she also held the position of secretary of the Free Hospitals' League. Finally she took on the business community and the city hall bureaucracy when she brought forth her radical proposals for large-scale civic participation in the public market. Her argument was simple: Through the public market the city could exert direct influence to force food prices down.

She lost the battle. The public market issue was dead in 1920, and following Mrs. Gale's subsequent resignation as market adviser, the days of the market were numbered. Within a few short years it had passed out of existence. Mrs. Gale withdrew from civic politics soon after. Following a term as public school trustee in 1925, she left Calgary with her family for the West Coast. She died in 1970.

Annie Gale was the first outspoken champion of the cause of women in Calgary. Her competitive spirit threw her into conflict with vested interests and the status quo, as well as earning for her the position of captain of Calgary's Women's Cricket Team. Whatever the activity, her ringing plea was for women to take their rightful place in society. "We should be free-lancers, steering our course by righteousness and justice of the questions before us. Be perfectly disinterested in our work and we should then be of untold benefit in raising the tone of public service which is generally conceded to be in need of such elevation ... I want to ... plead with women who have the leisure and qualifications to offer themselves for election on all governing bodies ... Oh a woman can do much if she only will ... ." In a way the vivacious and articulate Annie Gale may be perceived as a worthy rational exemplar to those who would pursue similar goals today.

Annie Gale, social reformer and women's rights advocate, was captain of a Calgary cricket team. Annie Gale (second row, seated fourth from the left) poses with her teammates in 1922. Courtesy, Glenbow-Alberta Institute.

William Aberhart came to Calgary in 1910 from Ontario at the age of 31 and died in 1943. A teacher, fundamentalist preacher, and politician, Aberhart became the first Social Credit premier of Alberta. Courtesy, Glenbow-Alberta Institute.

The popular and versatile William Irvine was Calgary's most perennial advocate of wider radical change. First as a spokesman for the Non-Partisan League, then as Calgary's first Labour MP, 1921-1925, and later as a United Farmers of Alberta representative, Irvine was heavily involved in propounding the cause of political and monetary reform. A clergyman by profession, Irvine was also a capable journalist and pamphleteer. His radical weekly, the *Nutcracker,* published in Calgary during the First World War, was a witty complement to Bob Edwards' *Eye Opener,* particularly when they were at odds, which was often enough considering the predictable antipathy between Irvine and Edwards.

During this period, Calgary became a focal point for regional protest. The United Farmers of Alberta operated out of Calgary when building its strength after 1909. Its second president was William J. Tregillus, a Calgary cattle breeder, landowner, manufacturer, and alderman. Tregillus's premature death in 1914 from typhoid ended a promising political career. It was in Calgary after

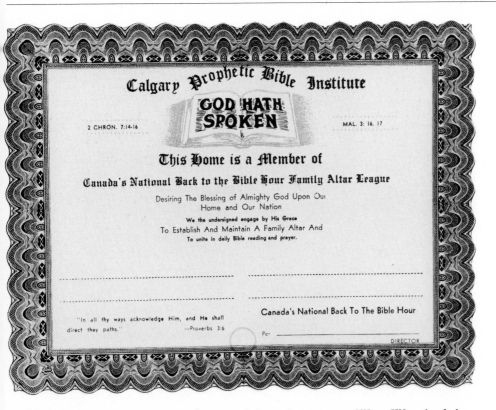

This certificate, issued by the Calgary Prophetic Bible Institute in about 1930, states that "This home is a Member of Canada's National Back to the Bible Hour Family Altar League." The Prophetic Bible Institute was started by William Aberhart. Courtesy, Glenbow-Alberta Institute.

1916 that the American-born farmer-philosopher Henry Wise Wood of the UFA hammered out his doctrine of group government by occupational interests. The much-debated but successful entry of the UFA into politics in 1921 ended the 16-year regime of the Liberal Party as Alberta's governing party.

Similarly, the antidote to depression and the tired policies of the UFA was fashioned in Calgary in the person of the evangelist school principal William Aberhart. The portly Aberhart was a remarkable figure who epitomized the old adage, "the right man on the right spot at the right time." He was a superbly organized person with an uncanny ability to relate to problems in a simple but irresistible and evangelical fashion. These two attributes were blended through the medium of a Sunday radio gospel programme to spawn a political weapon of awesome magnitude. Amid the misery of the Depression in 1935, the appeal of Aberhart's political panacea was all-persuasive, especially when it was couched in the rhetoric of utopian monetary reform. However, the Social Credit doctrine espoused by Aberhart had little relevance for the times. Even Aberhart did not pretend to understand its monetary complexities.

The theory of Social Credit was neither new nor indigenous to Alberta, but was born around 1920 in the mind of a Scottish mechanical engineer, Major C.H. Douglas. Briefly stated, Douglas's theory held that there was never enough money in the hands of consumers to buy back the fruits of production. Banks were the enemy since they held the necessary monetary differential. Social Credit called on governments to redress the inequity by distributing the differential to consumers and by imposing special taxes on banks. The intoxicating appeal of such a solution amid the poverty and misery of the Depression is not difficult to imagine.

Built in 1912-1913, the CPR's Ogden Shops represented the single most important factor in Calgary's industrial development before the oil boom of the modern era. During the Depression the Ogden Shops were closed and railway activity declined drastically. Courtesy, Calgary Herald.

It is interesting that Social Credit's long regime as Alberta's governing party was ended in 1971 by another Calgary-based political organization. This time the alternative was supplied by Calgary scion Peter Lougheed, who fashioned the Conservative Party in a dynamic urban image. In fact Lougheed's success at the polls in 1971 typified the ultimate triumph for urban over rural Alberta in deciding the composition and orientation of future provincial governments.

The policies of discontent were manifested in other directions in Calgary between the wars. The most extreme and utopian national example of trade unionism, the One Big Union (OBU), was born in Calgary in 1919 at the annual convention of the Trades and Labour Congress of Canada. Though short-lived and wildly impractical in its goals, the OBU symbolized the most extreme element in Western Canadian unionism, and for a brief period challenged the conservative mentality of the Canadian labour movement. Thirteen years later in June 1932, the Cooperative Commonwealth Federation (CCF) was also formed in Calgary at the fourth conference of Labour Political Parties. The forerunner of the modern New Democratic Party, the CCF represented the formal political expression of disaffected rural and urban groups.

Locomotive Number 1505 undergoes repairs at the Ogden Shops.

In terms of the formative forces that had characterized the frontier boom period, the years of the closed frontier presented graphic contrasts. Railway activity was moribund, and the closing of the Ogden Shops during the Depression in a way marked the nadir of the city's fortunes and proud heritage as a railway town. The fortunes of the cattle industry went from bad to worse. Early editions of the magazine *The Canadian Cattlemen* in 1938 dwelt at length on how the industry might be rescued from its sad and sorry condition. The real estate market witnessed steadily falling prices for land. The construction industry showed few signs of returning to the 1912 level. The value of building permits in 1940 represented about 35 percent of those in 1912. During this time, as well, the Mounted Police were viewed by many as strong-arm agents of the status quo. The perennial optimism had given way to pessimism. The frontier had indeed closed. It was Calgary's enduring voice of protest that supplied the continuum from the boom period. That maverick quality was part of both frontier experiences.

Above: *Situated on the south bank of the Bow River, the Inglewood Bird Sanctuary is a veritable bird-watchers' paradise. Over the years 217 species of birds have been sighted at Inglewood.*

Right: *Glenmore Park, situated around Glenmore Lake, is one of the largest open-space areas in the city. The lake, completed in the 1930s, is actually a reservoir for Calgary's water supply.*

Above: *A bumper crop of wheat flourishes beneath the deep blue sky just north of Calgary.*

Left: *A Rocky Mountain big horn sheep overlooks the breath-taking view of the mountains.*

Bottom: *The Glenmore Reservoir dam was virtually the only capital works project of any magnitude undertaken during the interwar period. It was begun in 1929 and was completed during the Depression with relief labour.*

Right: *Cows penned in at the Calgary Stockyards are a reminder of the early frontier city's close association with cattle ranching.*

Below: *A farmer harvests barley against a backdrop of blue mountains.*

Far left: *Participants in the Calgary Stampede Parade recall the colourful heritage of the local Chinese community.*

Left: *The Calgary Tower symbolizes the new Calgary to many people. The tower rises over 600 feet and dominates the Palliser Square complex, which includes the CPR station and the adjoining Palliser Hotel.*

Below: *During the summer the SS Moyie is a familiar sight on Glenmore Lake. The 90-foot long Moyie is only a half-sized reproduction of the original paddle-wheel steamer that used to ply the Kootenai Lakes in British Columbia.*

Facing page, clockwise from top left: *When James Short School, located between Fourth and Fifth avenues southwest, was written off by the Calgary Board of Education and the site was cleared for other construction, including the present Greyhound bus depot, the cupola was preserved and placed in Prince's Island Park.*

Centre Street Bridge was constructed during World War I after the original structure had been washed away by flood waters. Three civic officials, including Arthur Graves, were on the bridge when it was overcome by high water.

The A.E. Cross House in east Calgary occupied a position of social prominence in the surrounding working-class district. The building, which was donated to the city by the A.E. Cross family, still stands and houses Calgary's horticultural offices.

Gargoyles decorate the Alberta Hotel Building, one of the oldest structures on Eighth Avenue. It was constructed in the 1880s out of sandstone, the common building material for which Calgary was dubbed the "sandstone city."

Left: *The impressive Permanent Building symbolizes Calgary's position as the financial centre of Western Canada. In 1981 there were 65 general insurance companies, 29 trust companies, 140 mortgage companies, 44 credit unions, and 202 bank branches in Calgary.*

PART III

THE NEW FRONTIER: 1941 - PRESENT

Calgary's phenomenal growth after 1947 has been due almost entirely to its position at the forefront of Canada's burgeoning petroleum and natural gas industry. On the new frontier of fossil fuel extraction, Calgary found the prosperity that was so often promised but denied by the cattle industry and railroad development. The petroleum and natural gas industry enabled Calgary to transcend its dependence on a limited agricultural and pastoral hinterland, and achieve instead a position of national and even international focus. Calgary's extended urban skyline and concomitant urban sprawl are tangible reflections of the ubiquitous influence of "black gold" in the city's development.

The Formative Years

The first reports of the presence of oil and natural gas in southern Alberta were filed by George Mercer Dawson of the Canadian Geological Survey in 1886 when he commented on positive showings in the Waterton area. In 1888 two trappers, William McCandell and Lafayette French, after observing an Indian rubbing a greenish-black mixture on his aching joints, proceeded to discover a small slough of black crude oil, which they named Oil (later Cameron) Creek.

However, the first individual to actually use the discovery was the redoubtable George "Kootenai" Brown, who soaked up the liquid in gunny sacks, bottled it, and sold the containers to nearby ranchers for one dollar each. Other primitive methods of extraction at Oil Creek produced about five or six gallons daily, which made their way into the local market as lamp fuel or lubricants.

The first truly commercial venture in the Waterton area was initiated in 1901 by the Rocky Mountain Development Company, an enterprise owned and controlled by Calgary men including rancher John Lineham, George Leeson, and surveyor A.P. Patrick. The first producing well was completed in 1902 at a depth of 1,020 feet. Transportation costs and slow, inefficient drilling methods hampered operations, and by 1904 that well was yielding only 40 barrels a day. Not surprisingly, Oil City, as it was called, was abandoned.

The beginnings of Calgary's commercial boom in the first decade of the 20th century were accompanied by strenuous local efforts to secure a reliable power source. Natural gas was one logical choice, especially in the light of the Medicine Hat gas discoveries in 1901. In 1905 the city granted an exclusive

Facing page: *One does not have to go far from Calgary to find evidence of the ongoing search for "black gold," the symbol of the new frontier.*

Above: *Eugene Coste was responsible for first supplying natural gas to Calgary in 1912. His home in Mount Royal was considered among the finest in the city and for a while after World War II, it was utilized as Calgary's first Allied Arts Centre. Courtesy, Canadian Western Natural Gas, Limited.*

Above right: *Employees at the C.C. Snowden refinery, located at 1810-1840 11th Street East, stand amid barrels of oil in 1912. Courtesy, Glenbow-Alberta Institute.*

Facing page: *Natural gas entrepreneur Eugene Coste resided in this impressive edifice. The imposing Mount Royal home was for years a symbol of residential exclusiveness. Courtesy, Calgary Herald.*

franchise to local promoter Archibald Walter Dingman for gas supplied to the city. Dingman's company drilled unsuccessfully on the Sarcee Reserve before turning to the Calgary estate of Major James Walker. Here, gas was encountered at a depth of 3,414 feet. Although in limited supply, gas from the Walker well was used to light some east Calgary streets as well as heating the Walker residence and A.E. Cross' brewery.

The first substantial natural gas discoveries with direct effects on Calgary were made by Eugene Coste, an engineer of French descent. In 1909 Coste and a partner brought in the "Old Glory Strike" on the South Saskatchewan River. These reserves of 8.5 million cubic feet per day were supplemented by five other producing wells. In 1912, Coste's Canadian Western Natural Gas, Heat, Light and Power Company Ltd. piped gas through a 16-inch pipe a distance of 170 miles to Calgary from its Bow Island field.

The shift in exploratory interest to the Turner Valley area southwest of Calgary was due entirely to the persistent efforts of local oil pioneer William Stewart Herron, an amateur oil enthusiast and Okotoks farmer. After noticing gas bubbling along the banks of Sheep Creek, Herron bought up promising acreage and filed claims to over 6,000 additional acres in the Turner Valley area.

A.W. Dingman stands by a tap on the pipe leading from the well head of Dingman Number One during the Duke of Connaught's visit on July 28, 1914. T.A.P. Frost holds a mug of oil and W.S. Herron is on the far left. Courtesy, Glenbow-Alberta Institute.

WILLIAM STEWART HERRON

William Stewart Herron was born in Ontario, and was introduced to oil activity in the Pennsylvania oil fields. He worked later in lumber enterprises and railroading, and put his profits into real estate and mineral rights. In fact he once owned the land on which the town of Cobalt, Ontario, was later located, but sold out before the discovery of millions of dollars worth of silver. Eventually Herron located in Okotoks, Alberta, where he purchased a 900-acre farm.

To supplement his income, Herron broke horses, retaining one third of them for his own use. With these he established a cartage service hauling coal from Black Diamond to Okotoks. It was on a lunch break on one of these trips that he encountered the gas seepage on Sheep Creek and was on his way to founding Calgary Petroleum Products—and to seeing Alberta's first oil boom.

Herron maintained his faith in the lean years of the company after 1914, and when company directors talked of selling out in 1919, Herron continued to be optimistic about the future. He once attempted to alert federal authorities of the dangers to Canadian and Imperial interests posed by the looming presence of the leviathan Standard Oil Company of New Jersey.

When the Royalite Oil Company absorbed his company in 1921, Herron briefly went back to farming, only to form the successful Okalta Oil Ltd. in 1925. This was his most successful venture, and his to run since he was both president and the largest stockholder. In the Depression of the thirties, Herron refused to sell and retained his claims and stocks. Meanwhile he went on farming and hauling freight while his wife ran a boarding house. Restless for the venturesome life, he turned to placer mining in British Columbia. He died in Baskerville in 1939.

Herron succeeded in securing financial backing through persuasive and novel methods. For instance, once he fried eggs on a stove over a gas fissure to the astonishment of prospective investors. In any case he was able to form the Calgary Petroleum Products Company with professional geologist Archibald W. Dingman in 1913. Their backers included local business leaders like Richard Bedford Bennett, Sir James A. Lougheed, Alfred Ernest Cross, William Pearce, Judson Sayre, W.H. McLaws, and T.J.S. Skinner.

For two long and frustrating years Herron's company worked 12-hour shifts trying for oil. Then on May 14, 1914, the sweet smell of naptha gas began to flow from a depth of 3,800 feet at the Dingman No. 1 well. With this discovery, the first Alberta oil boom was under way.

One interesting point concerning the early oil interest in Turner Valley involved the Calgary city council, which almost found itself a direct participant in the oil boom.

In 1911, alderman John (Gravity) Watson was journeying through the foothills near Turner Valley when he noticed gas seepage. Following his nose, he discovered a large slough with gas bubbling from it. In June 1911, Watson,

In May 1914 the first oil strike was made at the Dingman Number One well, setting off Turner Valley's oil-producing era. Although the 1914 oil boom met with short-term failure, William Herron's continued faith in the oil potential of Alberta eventually paid off. Courtesy, Glenbow-Alberta Institute.

William Stewart Herron devoted most of his life to proving the existence of oil in Alberta. He was the most persistent of the early oil pioneers, and while he never enjoyed wealth himself, his family inherited the material benefits of his wisdom. The Herron tradition was carried on by his two sons, William Jr. and Harold, who in the 1940s expanded the scope and operations of Okalta. By 1950 the company had 13 producing wells in Turner Valley as well as extensive acreage elsewhere. Over the years the Herron name has continued to figure prominently in local circles, one of the most colourful reminders being that familiar automobile at Stampede time with its plethora of silver plating and assorted western adornments.

Investors line up to buy oil stock in Calgary on May 15, 1914. The discovery of oil in Turner Valley touched off the greatest speculative binge in Calgary's history. Hundreds of Calgarians were caught up in the "quick riches" mentality, conjured up by the discovery of "black gold." Courtesy, Glenbow-Alberta Institute.

Mayor John Mitchell, and other city officials returned to Turner Valley and, on the site later occupied by the Dingman No. 1 rig, erected a sign that read, "Staked for gas and petroleum by the city of Calgary, June 12, 1911. J.W. Mitchell Mayor." A month later they revisited the site to find the sign floating in a pool of oil 50 feet wide, and bubbling gas. Someone then ignited the area, which burst into flames several feet high. The triumphant group extinguished the blaze and left in high spirits after securing a makeshift drilling apparatus. The city fathers' glee soon turned to gloom when they realized that the property had already been surveyed and registered for mineral rights by a homesteader who subsequently assigned them to the Calgary Petroleum Products Company. In any case, the thought of Dingman No. 1 being City Hall No. 1 is almost too much for the mind to handle.

The Turner Valley Era

News of the strike at Dingman No. 1 touched off the greatest surge of excitement ever seen in Calgary. Hundreds trekked to the discovery area in an assorted array of vehicles. It was said that when members of the board of directors of the Calgary Petroleum Products Company visited the well site, they filled their gas tanks with crude naptha and returned to Calgary at a record-

Above: *Placards along Ninth Avenue indicate the promotional zeal prompted by the first oil boom of 1914. Courtesy, Glenbow-Alberta Institute.*

Left: *Intense promotional drives were generated by the oil boom in 1914. Note the low prices of shares that these investors are waiting to buy. Courtesy, Glenbow-Alberta Institute.*

breaking pace. Calgary became a speculators' paradise. The *Herald* reported that "the whole downtown area became a swath of cotton streamers." Over 500 companies were formed, and hundreds of thousands of dollars changed hands. Wild stories emerged of waste baskets overflowing with money, of garbage bins of cash being whisked off to banks for deposit, of exultant individuals rushing about brandishing bundles of random shares bought over the shoulders of a yelling multitude. Then there was the irrepressible former Baptist minister and Calgary alderman T.A. (Tappy) Frost, who hawked bottles of Dingman No. 1 to curious passers-by in downtown Toronto.

Oil rigs were familiar sights on Main Street in Turner Valley in the 1930s. Since Turner Valley was not on a railroad, the town of Okotoks actually filled a more important supply role for drilling operations than did Turner Valley. Courtesy, Glenbow-Alberta Institute.

But in spite of local optimism or Frost's novel publicizing, Eastern Canadian money was not overly attracted to southern Alberta. The outbreak of the First World War dried up further capital investment with the result that the years 1915-1920 failed to advance the fortunes of Turner Valley. By 1918 only 10 wells were producing in the valley, and their 464-barrel average daily flow was a virtual drop in the bucket compared with Canada's annual consumption of 11 million barrels in the same year. Three years later, in 1921, the Imperial Oil Company noted that the total quantity of oil produced in Turner Valley was insufficient to classify it as a proven field.

In about 1924 a team hauls oil-well supplies to Turner Valley from Okotoks. Bill Renard drives the front team, while Adam Schmitke drives the team behind, which was called the bush team and was used to help hold back the load on hills. Courtesy, Glenbow-Alberta Institute.

Many other factors contributed to the failure of Turner Valley to develop as anticipated after 1914. Primitive drilling methods meant long delays and high costs. Drilling time per well averaged two years with a cost of over $50,000. Inadequate transportation links hindered two-way supply as well as marketing efficiency. Finally the lack of suitable refining facilities ensured Turner Valley's continuing pioneer status. By 1919 it was clear that future development in the valley would be increasingly dependent on outside interests. With the stage thus set, the giant Standard Oil of New Jersey was already eagerly waiting in the wings.

The entry of the American petroleum giant into the Canadian scene was part of the escalating battle between U.S. and British interests for control of

This early wooden oil rig in Turner Valley was photographed in the 1920s. Courtesy, Glenbow-Alberta Institute.

the world's potential petroleum reserves. Easily dodging the federal government's crude prohibitory legislation respecting foreign involvement in Canadian petroleum reserves, Standard began to move as early as 1917. Through the Northwest Company, an exploration enterprise organized by its Canadian subsidiary, Imperial Oil, Standard began acquiring crown leases. By 1921, Imperial Oil had control of 392 federal leases totalling 369,537 acres in Alberta. This enviable position was consolidated by an arrangement with the Canadian Pacific Railway which, in return for profit-sharing, agreed to reserve its most promising mineral holdings for exploration and development by Imperial Oil and its new subsidiary, Royalite Company Ltd. In 1921, the latter company was formed to take over the assets of the floundering Calgary Petroleum Products Company. The demise of this feisty Calgary enterprise represented a loss of local autonomy in an increasingly important industry.

Above: On October 18, 1922, this view of the hill north of the CNR mainline was taken, showing the beginning of excavation for the $2.5 million Imperial Oil Company plant at Ogden, Alberta. Courtesy, Glenbow-Alberta Institute.

Right: The Imperial Oil refinery, the most modern refinery in Canada, was completed in 1923 with a capacity of 4,000 barrels a day. The tank shown under construction in January 1923 measured 120 feet by 42 feet. Courtesy, Glenbow-Alberta Institute.

Calgary's proximity to the Turner Valley fields had some positive ramifications even in this early period. Most managerial functions were located in the city, while local merchants profited through the sale of food and equipment to field operations. In 1918 the federal government opened an office in Calgary and employed a resident petroleum engineer to monitor developments. Yet by far the greatest boon to the Calgary economy came in 1923 when Imperial Oil opened Canada's most modern refinery in the city. The 4,000-barrel-per-day plant with its fractional and continuous distillation, and improved product-treating techniques, heralded a new era in refining. It is interesting to note that the civic plebiscite held to approve the building of the $2.5 million plant passed with over 98 percent approval. Indeed, the city's main stipulation regarding construction was that union rates be paid to the workers.

In 1922 Royalite began drilling its famous Royalite No. 4 well about a half mile northwest of the original discovery well, but early signs were not promising. By October 1924, the drilling had gone beyond the instructed limit and was almost 300 feet into the hitherto unproductive Devonian limestone rock. Then the smell of sour gas rose from the derrick floor. The crew closed the valves, and a short time later the casing was blown out of the well. Ignition soon followed and flames roared 100 feet into the air. They were to burn for three months before North America's "wonder well" was brought under control. Over the next 10 years it earned its reputation through a continuous daily production averaging 400 barrels of light, almost pure, naptha oil, and a gas flow of about 20 million cubic feet per day.

Imperial Oil built Calgary's and Alberta's first refinery in the early 1920s. The refinery had a capacity of 4,000 barrels per day. Courtesy, Calgary Herald.

The Royalite discovery stimulated renewed interest in Turner Valley. In 1925 a gas pipeline was built to the Imperial refinery in Calgary. New companies were organized, and speculative activity once again touched the spirits of venturesome Calgarians. Old, long-discarded stock certificates were fished out of attics, trunks, and bureaus. The oil exchange once again became a hub of activity and interest. The high points here occurred in 1925 after the Royalite discovery, and again in 1929 following a promotional deal engineered by a stock brokerage firm and two locally-owned oil companies. Seats on the Calgary Stock Exchange ranged from $200 to $4,000 depending on current conditions and the persistence of Turner Valley oil rumours.

But like the post-1914 boom, Turner Valley promised more than it delivered. Drilling was difficult, slow, and imprecise, particularly given the greater depths being probed. Financing for the most part was dependent on local involvement, and there was simply insufficient capital in Calgary to support large-scale, prolonged exploratory activity in the valley. Furthermore, inadequate conservation measures were of growing concern to potential gas consumers like the city of Calgary. It was said that one could read a newspaper at midnight two miles away from where 350 million c.f.d. waste gas from producing wells was burned. It was called Hell's Half Acre and for years the red night sky and the roar of burning gas proclaimed Calgary's proximity to the oil frontier.

Above: *In 1929 a natural gas pipeline was dug in Turner Valley that helped augment Calgary's domestic and industrial gas supply. Courtesy, Glenbow-Alberta Institute.*

Top right: *Twin Dome Oil Company issued this share certificate to the Burns Foundation on October 19, 1929, during Calgary's second oil boom. Courtesy, Glenbow-Alberta Institute.*

Bottom right: *On December 8, 1914, the Moose Mountain Oil Company, Limited, issued this certificate for 10 shares to D. Young at a cost of one dollar each. Courtesy, Glenbow-Alberta Institute.*

Flaring of waste gas at Turner Valley was a matter of concern from 1924 onward. The glow in Calgary's night sky from "hell's half acre" was a constant reminder to Calgarians of the oil and gas industry's nearby presence. Courtesy, Glenbow-Alberta Institute.

Right: *Imperial Oil company built this float for the historical section of the pageant celebrating Calgary's 50th Jubilee. Courtesy, Glenbow-Alberta Institute.*

Below right: *A truck towing an oil drum across Sheep Creek in the 1930s illustrates the logistic problems facing pioneer oil operations, not the least of which were impassable roads. Courtesy, Glenbow-Alberta Institute.*

In 1925 civic officials in Calgary explored the possibility of using bitumen from the McMurray tar sands to pave city streets, instead of having to rely on asphalt imported from California. The end result was an unsuccessful bid to secure a lease on oil sands property for future development.

The potential of the northern Alberta tar sands was a recognized fact by 1920. As early as 1912, an Edmonton group had been attempting to mine bitumen on a commercial basis, and the first experimental hot water separation plant was established by the Alberta Research Council in 1923 in the basement of the University of Alberta powerhouse. During 1924-1927, over 5,000 tons of bitumen were produced for use by the provincial government mainly in road construction. In 1927, for instance, the Canadian National Railway surfaced its station at Tofield with asphalt produced at the Edmonton

plant. Although production costs were prohibitively high, senior officials with the Research Council and the Dominion Geological Survey were clearly interested in promoting the idea.

Accordingly in 1925, the Mines Branch of the Dominion Geological Survey invited the chief engineers of the cities of Calgary and Edmonton to tour the sands. During the course of the tour, city of Calgary chief engineer A.S. Chapman was led to believe by his hosts that the city should consider direct involvement in the tar sands. Apparently, according to Chapman, allusions were made to municipal use of a projected separation plant financed by the federal government, as well as a direct civic lease in the sands themselves. Encouraged by what appeared to be a covert invitation for civic involvement in the tar sands, the council passed a motion to secure a tar sands lease "for its own use."

Farmers and oil-company representatives meet to negotiate drilling rights and pipeline rights of way. Courtesy, Esso Resources (Canada), Limited.

Actions speak louder than words. The city had no money to follow up development, and certainly any such lease would have benefits only for the future. Similarly, the federal government was not disposed to support any rash statements made by its officials in the Geological Survey. Finally, in its debate with Ottawa over the pending transfer of natural resources from the federal domain, the provincial government was scarcely interested in "sharing the pie" with municipalities. Thus, the civic tar sands lease issue was allowed to die, and Calgary continued to buy its asphalt from California.

Interest in oil exploration dissipated greatly with the onslaught of the Depression. One individual persisted, though, and it was primarily through the single-minded efforts of this remarkable personality that Turner Valley finally came into its own.

Robert A. Brown, a Quebec native and electrical engineer, first visited Calgary in 1906 when he was superintendent of the Northwest Electrical Company. In 1911 he became superintendent of Calgary's Electric Lighting Department, and later assumed the added responsibility for the municipal street railway system. Over the years Brown acquired a reputation for efficiency and diligence. His advice on electrical matters was sought by other municipalities across Western Canada. He was also outspoken in his defence of professionalism. On one occasion when his department was compared favourably with that of Saskatoon, Brown, instead of basking in the glow of praise, lashed out at politicians who used misleading statistics and half-truths to cast aspersions on the reputation and expertise of hardworking professionals.

Brown also had an abiding interest in petroleum development. He was a director of United Oils Ltd. and was in on the much publicized deal of 1929, which saw United Oils transfer a quarter section lease to Jim Lowery's Home Oil Company for an unprecedented one million dollars. Brown decried the general contention by 1930 tha Turner Valley held only salt water and sour gas. He was also aware that the current condensate wells meant the flaring of waste gas and the elimination of byproducts. Instead, Brown believed that conventional crude oil deposits existed at deeper levels in the west flank of Turner Valley. Finding no company to agree with him, he decided to form his own and go it alone. The result was the establishment of Turner Valley Royalties Company, and the subleting of 50 acres in the west flank.

It took three years to raise the $125,000 necessary to purchase the equipment to begin drilling, and even then the only way was to secure funds against the sale of royalties. Besides Brown there were only two major investors: George M. Bell, publisher of the *Albertan* took 9,000 shares, and lawyer Jack Moyer held 998 shares. Drilling commenced in 1934 but needed more support to continue. British American Oil advanced a loan of $30,000, and Imperial Oil secured a 7.5 percent gross royalty in return for a loan of $22,000 worth of

In 1934 workers began drilling for oil at greater depths than had been previously attempted in Turner Valley. In June 1936 a well finally blew at the depth of 6,800 feet. Courtesy, Esso Resources (Canada), Limited.

equipment. Spooner Oils and Calmont Oils also helped. Still, drilling was halted seven times while Brown, Bell, and Moyer peddled royalties. Brown mortgaged his home, sold his car, and borrowed heavily against his insurance policies to keep the operation afloat.

At the site, drilling continued to depths never before encountered by Turner Valley oil rigs. Brown never lost hope, though, and one June day in 1936, at the vast depth of 6,800 feet, the well blew in. Story has it that when Jack Moyer was accidentally drenched by the gushing liquid, he referred to his baptism in the first Turner Valley crude.

Turner Valley Royalties No. 1 had hit the productive Madison limestone and probed it for over 400 feet before the well was complete. Not only was the well the deepest in the British Empire, but for a time it was also the largest producer. With a wellhead flow of between 800 and 1,000 barrels daily, Turner Valley Royalties No. 1 had yielded almost three-quarters of a million barrels of oil by 1950. It certainly vindicated the faith and confidence of Calgary's most intrepid oil pioneer.

Brown's discovery heralded the beginnings of Turner Valley's golden age. By 1939 over 70 wells were producing an annual revenue of more than $10 million, and Calgary shared in this new development. In 1938, the provincial government established Calgary as a permanent administrative centre when it set up the Petroleum and Natural Gas Conservation Board in the city. A year later, British American Oil built Calgary's second refinery.

The British American Oil Company built Calgary's second oil refinery in the late 1930s. Although Calgary continues to be heavily involved in the oil and gas industry, the city has since lost some of its emphasis on refinery to Edmonton. Courtesy, Calgary Herald.

Demand for Turner Valley oil increased during the Second World War. Production peaked in 1942 at 9.7 million barrels, or about 30,000 barrels daily. Yet by 1945, Turner Valley was already a declining field. The exploratory companies led by Imperial Oil had turned away from Turner Valley, and with their newly developed seismic instruments, gravity meters, and magnetometers were outlying hydrocarbon formations in more northerly locations.

The Turner Valley experience was a pioneer venture in the Canadian oil and natural gas industry, and as an oil field it made a small contribution in terms of production figures. As early as 1953, Alberta's annual output of petroleum surpassed Turner Valley's total accumulated production before 1947. Yet, through Turner Valley, Canadian oil expertise was built up and centrallized in Calgary. The potential of the Western Canadian petroleum resources was also recognized through the Turner Valley experience by large international corporations. Very simply, the Turner Valley era helped place Calgary in the forefront of a nascent industry, which by 1945 had not yet evinced its real potential.

The New Frontier

The modern era of the Canadian oil industry really began on February 13, 1947, at Leduc near Edmonton, where Imperial Oil was probing the Devonian Reef formation with Leduc No. 1, its 134th well since 1914. Suddenly the afternoon sky was filled with belching flame and dense black smoke. Imperial's 133 hole drought had ended, and the lid was finally lifted off the enormous oil and natural gas reserves of Western Canada.

Imperial followed its success at Leduc-Woodbend with another discovery at Redwater a year later. Other fields to be discovered in this formation included Wizard Lake in 1951, and Acheson, Bonnie Glen, and Westerose in 1952. Then in 1953 Mobil Oil discovered the highly productive Pembina field southwest of Edmonton. Pembina later became known as the largest stratigraphic oil trap in Western Canada, with the exception of the McMurray oil sands, in that it was hitherto believed that only Paleozoic reefs contained worthwhile exploration possibilities. In the years 1957-1959, the Beaverhill Lake Devonian oil discoveries were made, the most notable field being Swan Hills brought in by Calgary's Home Oil in 1957.

Three more large fields were added to Alberta's proven reserves in the 1960s. Mitsui was discovered by California Standard and Imperial Oil in 1964. Canadian independent companies figured prominently in the other two. The Rainbow Lake field was brought in by the Banff Oil-Aquitaine team in 1965, while Dome Petroleum was involved in the Zama Lake discoveries.

By the 1960s, the oil frontier began to move beyond Alberta to the vast, forbidding Arctic archipelago. As in the earlier pioneer days, local initiative in the form of Calgary-based enterprises showed the way.

The oil potential of the Arctic was being recognized by 1960. In 1959, for instance, a senior official with Dome Petroleum spoke of a recoverable 100 billion barrels lying beneath Arctic ice. Similarly, the International Symposium on Arctic Geology held in Calgary in 1960 aroused some professional interest in the possibility of important oil deposits in the north polar regions.

Still, commercial interest was less than enthusiastic. The federal government had no regulations governing arctic exploration and development, although there was evidence that John Diefenbaker's "Roads to Resources" electoral slogan was about to manifest itself in some clear directives. However, the large oil companies were simply not interested in high-risk exploratory ventures; there were too many profitable areas elsewhere in the world. In addition, the technology needed for arctic work was virtually untried. Logistic problems compounded matters further, and there were few who believed that

Facing page: *Exploration and drilling in the Leduc area in the late 1940s produced an oil boom that greatly boosted Calgary's economy. Courtesy, Esso Resources (Canada), Limited.*

HOME OIL LTD., A HOME-GROWN PRODUCT

In the 1930s Home Oil acquired thousands of acres of land in Turner Valley. This oil rig typifies the wooden structures that dotted the area. Courtesy, Glenbow-Alberta Institute.

Home Oil was formed in 1925 by the colourful, local, former real estate man James Robert Lowery, who had convinced several West Coast businessmen to back him following the Royalite discovery in 1924. Home was not long in gaining publicity. In 1929, Lowery purchased a quarter section lease from United Oils for one million dollars.

In 1936 Home Oil acquired 9,000 acres in the north end of Turner Valley for $36,000 cash, and followed up with a further acquisition of 4,640 acres of Canadian Pacific Railway acreage. Home Millarville No. 2 was spudded in April 1938 and completed in January 1939. It went on to surpass Turner Valley Royalties No. 1, and become the largest producing well in the British Empire. Its accumulated total in 1961 was 1,775,519 barrels of oil and 4.35 billion cubic feet of natural gas. Home Oil was merged with Robert A. Brown, Jr.'s, Federated Oils in 1955 to form Home Oil Company Ltd. Brown Jr. had consolidated his famous father's holdings in the valley into Federated Oils, and had also acquired Imperial Oil's 38 producing wells in Turner Valley.

arctic deposits would yield oil cheap enough to make large-scale exploration ventures worthwhile.

One such individual was Calgary geologist Dr. J.C. (Cam) Sproule, president of the Calgary-based consulting company J.C. Sproule and Associates. Sproule had gained wide experience through his work with the Geological Survey and with major oil companies before forming his own consulting company in 1951. Following survey work in the Mackenzie Valley, Sproule was drawn naturally to the vast promise of the Arctic archipelago. His subsequent work in the islands made him the foremost authority on the geology of the Arctic. He was also an ardent Canadian nationalist who believed that Canadian sovereignty in the Arctic could be best preserved by active involvement. As such Sproule worked hard to convince his many clients that Arctic exploration was both a valid commercial exercise as well as a patriotic gesture.

Through the early 1960s, Sproule continued his survey work in the Arctic islands, isolating the choicest acreages while at the same time desperately trying to interest Canadian investors to finance exploration. He spent over a million dollars of his own money and endless hours in fruitless efforts to build a consortium to secure all significant leaseholders, and to raise the $30 million necessary to mount a large exploratory programme. From 1965 to 1967 Sproule doggedly followed his personal dream. His salesmanship helped convince 75 companies to pledge their lands, but the potential investors still lagged. Twice he had financing as high as $13.5 million, only to see it slip away in the eddies of doubt and hesitancy. The sudden entrance of the federal government saved the project. The formation of Panarctic Oils in 1967 was a

A graduate of the University of Alberta and a naval veteran in World War II, Brown possessed his own brand of entrepreneurship, and it was the Brown daring that characterized Home Oil's aggressive policies after 1955.

Brown's philosophy was simple: using regional geological studies as a base, he would follow up with land acquisitions, geophysical exploration, and exploratory drilling. Home made five important discoveries, including Westward Ho and Swan Hills, in the rich Beaverhill Lake formation. In 1956, Home built the Cremona pipeline from Sundre to Calgary. A year later, the company purchased control of Trans-Canada Pipe Lines for $30 million.

In the 1960s, Home shifted its interests to the international scene, acquiring acreage in the North Sea and drilling successful gas wells in Great Britain. In 1968 the company acquired United Petroleum Corporation, wholesale marketers of natural gas liquids in the United States. In the same year, Brown announced that Home Oil Ltd. had, through its U.S. subsidiary, acquired extensive acreage in the exciting new oil play on the north slope of Alaska.

Unfortunately for Brown and Home, this latest move was both typical and premature. The company overreached itself in Prudhoe Bay by investing huge sums in acreage held by Atlantic Richfield, as well as some $50 million in Arco shares. When exploration efforts proved unsuccessful, the value of Home shares plummeted more than 80 percent. The result was the incorporation of Home into the giant Ontario utility, Consumers Gas Company. Less than a year after the takeover, Bobby Brown, Jr., was dead.

unique experiment in government investment in a private company, and laid the basis for national involvement in the Canadian oil and natural gas industry. The fact that the seeds of government activity were sown in individualistic Calgary is an inescapable irony.

The achievement of the Panarctic project can be traced to Calgary. It was Cam Sproule, operating out of Calgary, who put the proposal together. It probably would have died many times had it not been for Sproule's perseverance. His intimate acquaintance with reliable clients during the difficult days of negotiations helped maintain steady support. A close colleague, Eric Connelly of Calgary, represented the only individual investor in Panarctic. Sam Nickle's company stood by Sproule, and realized it was committing its funds to a long-term investment with little hope of early success. Another Sproule client, Dome Petroleum, was an original investor and functioned as interim operator until Panarctic could organize its own staff.

The current activities of Calgary's Dome Petroleum Ltd. in offshore drilling in the Beaufort Sea may well lead to the elusive Arctic oil bonanza. But while the daring ventures of this high-rolling Calgary company are well advertised, its long involvement with Arctic operations is not so widely known. Dome's interest in the Panarctic project has already been noted. Yet Dome's activities in the Arctic predate Panarctic. It was Dome that drilled the first Arctic well in 1962 at Winter Harbour on Melville Island. Winter Harbour was the brainchild of Dome president Jack Gallagher, a canny Winnipegger who put the deal together on a cooperative basis. While Dome was the operator, it had the backing of some 20 oil companies and mining groups.

THE WINTER HARBOUR EXPERIMENT

Given the current intense exploratory interest in the Canadian Arctic, it is difficult to believe that the first well was spudded only 20 years ago. And like many since then, it failed to verify the oil reserves of the vast Arctic sedimentary basin. It did, however, indicate the feasibility of exploration in high latitude areas, hitherto considered altogether too formidable for either men or technology.

Winter Harbour on Melville Island was considered the best choice for a probe following the issuance in 1960 of the federal government's regulations concerning Arctic exploration because traces of petroleum near Winter Harbour had been recorded by Captain William Parry in 1819-1820. Furthermore, Winter Harbour was free from ice for longer periods than other points in the Arctic. So with Dome Petroleum as operator and Calgary's Peter Bawden supplying the drilling rig, the Winter Harbour experiment began taking shape in the summer of 1961.

Peter Bawden was the operator of Rig 22, which drilled the first Arctic oil well on Melville Island in 1961-1962. The pioneer venture demonstrated that exploratory work was possible under high-latitude conditions. Courtesy, Calgary Herald.

In July 1961, the Danish polar cargo ship *Thora Dan* left Montreal for Winter Harbour. On board was Bawden's Rig 22 and 3,000 additional tons of equipment, including enough food to tide 35 men over for 150 days of work. *Thora Dan* arrived at Winter Harbour on August 20, and by August 24 the supplies had been moved three-quarters of a mile inland to the well site. The extensive preparations included transporting more than 2,000 gallons of water daily from the sea to the well site. Special heaters were installed, three power plants were erected, and an airstrip constructed. The Alberta Trailer Company Ltd. designed and built the camp buildings, while on September 10, 1961, Winter Harbour No. 1 was spudded.

For the next six months the well was drilled to a total depth of more than 14,000 feet before being abandoned in April 1962. Yet in spite of its failure to yield oil, and the high $1.5 million cost, the Winter Harbour experiment was not without merit. For months men had worked in Arctic temperatures as low as 59° below zero, with accompanying winds as high as 60 m.p.h. In fact, following the experiment, Bawden's company stressed the need for clothing to withstand not so much the cold, but the high Arctic winds. The Winter Harbour experiment simply demonstrated that logistic and weather problems were not deterrents to exploration in the Canadian Arctic.

An oil crew leaves Melville Island, where Peter Bawden's Rig 22 drilled the first Arctic well. Courtesy, Calgary Herald.

Local response to the needs and demands created on the new oil frontiers manifested itself in other domains. Peter Bawden's drilling company was the first to operate in the far northerly latitudes, and Calgary-based companies were instrumental in developing the transportation units capable of operating in frontier regions. Bruce Nodwell pioneered the tracked vehicle in the 1950s, working with Imperial Oil around Cynthia, Alberta, and a Nodwell unit proved crucial in the Winter Harbour experiment. The Nodwell-Robinson Manufacturing Company designed and built the world's largest tracked vehicle in 1966. Called the RN 400, this giant could carry a 40,000-pound payload. The Nodwell brothers also produced the "super bugs" of Arctic exploration in 1970. These were basically cabs mounted on tracks, and were equipped with self-powered recorders for seismic work. Capable of holding five men and supplies for five days, these "Sure Go" units greatly facilitated Panarctic's seismic operations. Another Calgary firm, Foremost Developments, landed a $1.2 million order from the Soviet Union for tracked vehicles capable of operating in the Siberian taiga. Arctic Systems of Canada, a Calgary company, was instrumental in helping to produce the world's heaviest-ever air cushion vehicle in 1971. Weighing 144 tons and powered by two 1,280-h.p. engines, the ACT-100 cost $300,000 and had a payload of 112 tons.

Facing page: *Foremost Developments in Calgary produced this large pipe transporter, an example of the adaptations of manufacturing to the needs of frontier industry. Courtesy, Calgary Herald.*

Below: *This tracked vehicle manufactured by Foremost Developments in Calgary is bound for work in the Siberian taiga of Russia. Courtesy, Calgary Herald.*

The need for accommodation units on the oil frontier led to the emergence of a Calgary company that has become a world leader in mobile home construction. Atco Industries Ltd. has had a phenomenal record of success, and in many ways typifies Calgary's part in the frontier experience. From an initial capital base of $4,000 in the late 1940s, Calgary's Ron Southern has built Atco into a complex manufacturing enterprise with 1,700 employees, world markets, and annual sales topping $50 million.

Through a host of colourful individuals of which Dingman, Herron, Brown, Bawden, Robinson, Nodwell, and Southern are representative, Calgary has continually injected daring and initiative into Canada's oil and natural gas industry. In the ongoing debate over the role of multinational companies and foreign ownership in directing the fortunes of Calgary's "oil patch," the crucial and often pivotal function of local initiative is frequently overlooked.

Some idea of the extent and impact of Alberta's post-1947 oil boom can be gained through comparative statistics. There were 502 capable oil wells in Alberta in 1947. By 1960, the number had grown to 9,878, and by 1972 to 14,168. In 1947, Alberta produced 6.3 million barrels of crude oil. In 1960 the figure stood at 133.5 million, and 13 years later had jumped to 522.2 million barrels. A little over $25 million were expended in exploration in 1947. The 1960 figure was $353 million, and the 1974 expenditure exceeded $870 million. Natural gas figures showed similar expansion. In 1947, 48,165,590 million cubic feet of gas were produced. In 1974, the corresponding figure was 2,613,417,000 m.c.f. Estimates of total value of production from oil and natural gas were given at $1.6 billion in 1971, while between 1947 and 1971 some $3.3 billion accrued directly to the provincial coffers in royalties and other payments.

As the national headquarters of the oil and gas industry, Calgary saw its fortunes change dramatically with the sudden upswing in production after 1947. Population figures showed significant and sustained increases. From a population of less than 90,000 in 1941, Calgary had topped 400,000 by 1971, and a decade later had surpassed 600,000. The growth rate was running at 33 percent per decade in 1976 compared with Montreal's 5 percent, Winnipeg's 13 percent, Toronto's 18 percent, Edmonton's 23 percent, or even Alberta's 26 percent.

Much of this growth was directly linked to Calgary's enhanced position following the postwar oil discoveries. The number of companies directly connected with the oil and natural gas industry increased in Calgary from 133 in 1946 to 2,130 in 1974. Of the latter figure, more than 60 percent were related to administration as opposed to operations, giving emphasis to Calgary's emerging status as a head office city. Between 1950 and 1974, over half the head offices established in Canada were located in Calgary, and fully 75 percent of Canada's oil administrative firms were there as well. Contrary to popular opinion, Calgary leads Edmonton in the number of head offices for oil operations. In fact in 1974, in terms of both head and branch offices for oil administration and operations, Calgary was ahead of Edmonton in all categories. Possibly the only area in oil operations where Calgary is losing ground to Edmonton is in refining.

The rise of Calgary as a major financial centre in the past 15 years has

In the late 1940s Alberta experienced an oil boom that boosted Calgary's growth dramatically. Courtesy, Esso Resources (Canada), Limited.

been due entirely to its position on the forefront of the oil and natural gas industry. Some observers see Calgary as a potential rival for the metropolitan hegemony traditionally exerted by Montreal and Toronto. The centrallization of economic power and corporate decision-making in Calgary combined with the focal position of energy both nationally and internationally seem adequate insurance that the foothills city will figure prominently in the labyrinthine machinations that precede political decisions.

Benefits from "Black Gold"

The impact of the oil industry in Calgary's urban life is everywhere apparent. The skyscraper-dominated downtown core is composed mainly of buildings associated with oil and natural gas. The city labour force is vitally dependent on the oil industry; it has been estimated that 50 percent of the entire labour force is derived from needs generated by the oil industry. One source gives the multiplier effect for jobs created a high ratio of seven. This means that as many as seven unrelated jobs are created for every one directly connected with the oil industry itself. If this statistic is accurate, then the staggering implication of Calgary's overwhelming dependency on a single economic sector becomes ominously apparent. In this context, Calgary's position on the new frontier is reminiscent of the boom period of yesteryear.

THE CONTINUING LEGACIES OF ERIC HARVIE AND SAM NICKLE

Eric Harvie was born in Orilla, Ontario, in 1892 and studied law at Osgoode Hall and the University of Alberta. Harvie saw service in World War I, and was wounded on the Somme. On his return to Calgary he joined a local law firm in 1919. A long-time observer of the oil scene, Harvie acquired the mineral rights of the old Western Canada Land Company in 1944, and subsequently leased 480 acres at Leduc to Imperial Oil. Three months later Imperial hit pay dirt, and Harvie was on his way to becoming one of Canada's richest men.

His uncanny intuitions continued. The Redwater and Vermilion strikes were also largely on Harvie's mineral rights. By 1951, Harvie was involved in several companies that wholly or partly operated 82 producing wells. After only 11 years in the business, Harvie divested himself of much of his holdings to Canadian Petrofina for an estimated $50 million. In 1973 another Harvie-

Mr. and Mrs. Samuel O. Nickle celebrate their 50th wedding anniversary on October 11, 1962. Courtesy, Calgary Herald.

controlled company, Western Minerals, was sold to Brascan for $20 million. Eric Harvie died in Calgary early in 1975.

Eric Harvie was a modest, unassuming man who never wore the mantle of wealth with the ostentation or flair so often expected of the immensely rich. He drove an old car and lived privately at his Elbow Park residence. He was, however, a pack rat of formidable magnitude, collecting a vast array of historical objects, in particular, military artifacts. He was instrumental in the formation of Calgary's Heritage Park in the mid 1960s and endowed the Glenbow and later the Riveredge foundations to house and preserve his remarkable col-

lections. The Devonian Group is another Harvie-endowed institution. The present Glenbow-Alberta Institute is generally regarded as one of the nation's finest museums and archival repositories, and owes its existence to the lawyer-oilman who also happened to love history.

Sam O. Nickle was born in Philadelphia in 1889. His father was a shoemaker, and the young Nickle worked with him when the family moved to Winnipeg. Following service in World War I, Sam Nickle rejoined his family in Calgary where he again worked with his father before opening his own store, "The Slipper Shop," on Eighth Avenue where the "Bay" stands today.

Sam Nickle's interest in oil speculation began in the Turner Valley excitement of the mid 1920s, and like many others he acquired leases in the valley. In 1936, following Brown's discovery, Nickle went into the oil business for himself, forming Northend Petroleum. In 1941 one of his wells reached a depth of two miles, the deepest in the British Empire at the time.

Nickle worked hard trying to interest outside investment in Alberta's oil potential. In 1944 he formed Anglo-American Oils, and over the next few years he engaged in exploration in Nova Scotia and obtained extensive mineral rights in Manitoba and Saskatchewan. In 1953 Nickle acquired the refinery and other assets belonging to another resolute oil pioneer, A.H. Mayland. Later he consolidated his businesses into Canadian Gridoil Limited. Sam Nickle died in Calgary in 1971.

The Nickle Arts Museum at the University of Calgary is Sam Nickle's continuing legacy to his adopted city. His donation of one million dollars in 1970 helped launch the project, which was completed in 1979. His son, Carl O. Nickle, himself a noted philanthropist and well-publicized authority on the oil and natural gas industry, later donated his priceless collection of over 10,000 ancient coins dating back 1,500 years. The special numismatic section of the Nickle Arts Museum is a further tribute to the civic spirit of this self-made Calgary family.

Icicles frame the Calgary skyline in January 1969, emphasizing the recently completed Husky (now Calgary) Tower. Courtesy, Calgary Herald.

There is a dynamic quality about Calgary's new-found urban image. The most visible indicator is the city's rising skyline, which in the 1950s was dominated by the Palliser Hotel. Now even the prominence of the 190-meter-high Calgary Tower, built in 1967, is threatened by the towering office and shopping complexes that have dramatically transformed Calgary's skyline over the last decade. In 1980 there were 130 building permits issued for office buildings worth over $3 billion. There seems little likelihood of a slow-down. In 1982, despite a lag in residential construction, due to high interest rates, commercial building is as vigorous as ever. One can still count up to 10 construction cranes from almost any vantage point in the downtown area.

The dynamism of change has affected aspects of development in the

downtown business district. Redevelopment projects slated for the Eau Claire and Victoria Park districts are still in the planning stages. The conversion of busy Stephen Avenue to partial mall use represented an aesthetic attempt to refine shopping practices for greater pedestrian convenience. Unfortunately the results have not all been positive. Far more successful has been the ongoing Plus-15 concept. This consists of the development of a network of elevated walkways to allow pedestrians to move freely from building to building throughout the downtown area. Interspersed with plazas and indoor mini-parks, the elevated indoor linkages provide a novel and utilitarian solution to the vagaries of shopping downtown in inclement weather, a common phenomenon during a Canadian winter.

Devonian Gardens opens to the public in September 1977, offering visitors a one-mile walk along paths that wind between terraces surrounded by natural beauty and placid pools. Courtesy, Calgary Herald.

Construction workers unload a tree for Devonian Gardens on May 27, 1977. Courtesy, Calgary Herald.

Another excellent and successful example of urban adaptation in Calgary has involved the development of large indoor parks and gardens. The city currently has at least three splendid indoor gardens, one of which especially has become the object of international acknowledgement. The oldest indoor garden is the tropical aviary at the zoo, which boasts 1,200 varieties of tropical plants plus brightly coloured birds, rippling streams, and even a waterfall. Constructed in the 1960s, the tropical aviary consists of two main and two smaller units. One of the latter houses an impressive assortment of desert plants and cacti.

The Heritage Square complex reflects the modern vision of commercial space dominated and unified by green areas. Carefully designed and planned to accentuate seclusion, the Heritage Gardens are a delight to weary shoppers and off-duty office workers.

Yet it is the $9 million Devonian Gardens in Toronto Dominion Square that has attracted the most attention. Here, a mile of paths winds through 2.5 acres of indoor park. The visual impact of this park is spectacular. More than 20,000 plants, most of which were carefully chosen for their indoor adaptabilities and resemblance to native flora, abound in the meticulously landscaped terraces that confront the viewer at every turn. Streams, waterfalls, and reflecting pools provide a tranquil complement. Yet human involvement is not ignored. There is seating for 800 people plus a children's playground, a stage area for live performances, and facilities for art and other exhibits. And like Heritage Square, the Devonian Gardens are directly adjacent to major shopping facilities.

The proliferation of suburban Calgary presents a transformation equally as remarkable as the changing downtown skyline. Residential subdivisions, developed for the most part by private companies like Nu-West and Keith, radiate up to 10 miles from the city centre. Initially these new subdivisions duplicated each other with the chief differentials being those of size and quality of construction. However in the 1960s, more imaginative developers in south Calgary came to closer grips with the problem of building exclusiveness into new subdivisions on the bald prairie soil of Calgary's environs. The answer was in man-made lakes using water diverted from nearby Fish Creek. Beginning with Lake Bonavista in 1968 and continuing with Bonaventure, Midnapore, and Sundance, a series of man-made lakes and contoured hills supplied a scenic and social focal point where thousands of Calgarians could enjoy residential exclusiveness. Statistics for Lake Bonavista indicate the magnitude

Children roll up their pants to wade in the refreshing pools at Century Gardens. Courtesy, Calgary Herald.

of the project, which created a water area and a hill on a treeless, featureless plain. The tree-covered hill is 55 feet high. The lake itself is 22 feet deep at its deepest point with 300 gallons of water per minute being pumped in to maintain a consistent level, and to allow boating, swimming, and fishing amenities for community residents.

Calgary's outdoor image is enhanced by its splendid, large recreational spaces, some of which had their origins in early times. For instance in the 1890s William Pearce and the Calgary town council combined to secure the islands in the Bow River where the zoo stands today. Bowness Park owes its existence to a deal between the city and land developer William Hextall in 1912. Most of the large spaces secured for park purposes resulted from the efforts of long-time parks superintendent William Reader, who served Calgary in that capacity for 29 years (1913-42). Currently the city of Calgary has about 5,000 acres in park space with more than 115 kilometres of biking, hiking, equestrian, and cross-country skiing trails. In addition Calgary boasts one of the largest urban parks in the world. Fish Creek Provincial Park in the southern part of the city covers 2,800 acres and shelters many varieties of birds and animals as well as native trees, shrubs, and grasses.

Picnickers at Century Gardens eat lunch surrounded by urban high-rise buildings. Courtesy, Calgary Herald.

There are many new features in Calgary's modern approach to recreational land use. From the development of creative playgrounds to the preparation of trails and pathways, the emphasis has been on active and varied citizen involvement. River beautification schemes and the emphasis on scenic and recreational water areas exemplify an inland city's desire to maximize its water resources. Similarly the awakened interest in heritage is reflected in current park policy. Excellent examples are the Fort Calgary Interpretive Centre and the Fish Creek administrative complex, which includes the original Bow River ranch house once owned by William Roper Hull and Pat Burns. Also, environmental studies are carried out in Fish Creek Provincial Park. The Burns Memorial Gardens feature practical use of the sandstone blocks originally used in Pat Burns' palatial Calgary residence. Douglas fir trees more than 400 years old are preserved in Edworthy Park. Other Calgary recreational areas are incorporated into bird sanctuaries and fish hatcheries.

Left: *Fish Creek Provincial Park in south Calgary, one of the largest urban parks in the world, offers all the advantages of a wilderness area within the boundaries of a large city. Courtesy, Calgary Herald.*

Below left: *Mallards are among the species of native bird life seen on tours of the Inglewood Bird Sanctuary. Courtesy, Calgary Herald.*

Nowhere is Calgary's rapid growth and preoccupation with modernity reflected more than in the field of education. The advance of the public education system and the development of higher learning facilities occurred coincidentally with gross physical expansion and the birth of a new urban society.

In 1945 the Calgary Public School System employed 425 teaching staff at an average annual salary of $2,107 to teach some 13,000 students. Total expenditures amounted to just over $1.5 million. In 1981 there were more than 80,000 students and 4,000 teachers in the public school system. The 1980 budget approximated $200 million. Average annual salary for teachers is pegged at about $32,000.

Today the Calgary Public School System is the third largest in Canada, and over the last 20 years has been engulfed by the revolution in education that has seen new philosophies, ideas, and practices wash over its schools in successive waves. Issues like the place of curriculum, individualized instruction, community involvement, vocational education and the teaching of French have reflected the pluralism characteristic of modern urban life.

Today there is much to indicate that public education in Calgary retains the contemporary flavour present since the turbulent decade of the 1960s. The system boasts one of the best school library programmes and facilities in North America. The pupil-teacher ratio continues its decline, hovering around 20 to 1 for 1982-1983. Individual schools possess a good deal of autonomy to implement special needs programmes and to develop their own educational styles. A stated commitment to the concept of pluralism exists in the Calgary Board of Education's alternative school progamme. Currently the board offers five alternative school programmes to students, and present indications are towards a more solid commitment.

The inception and rapid growth of the University of Calgary is probably the single most tangible manifestation of Calgary's urban maturity over the past 35 years. Today the University of Calgary is a relatively young yet stable institution with a growing number of affiliate and satellite groups under its expanding panoply of influence.

Facing page: *Demolition of the MacCosham warehouse cleared the way for construction of the Fort Calgary Interpretive Centre. Courtesy, Calgary Herald.*

Left: *Located in northwest Calgary, the University of Calgary includes 26 buildings on 314 acres of land. In this view from the men's residence, the Social Sciences Tower is under construction at left centre. Courtesy, Calgary Herald.*

Following pages: *Mount Royal College has served Calgary's secondary educational needs since 1911. In 1972 it moved from downtown to spacious new facilities on an 86-acre campus in Lincoln Park. In mid-1981, over 26,000 full- and part-time students attended classes at the college. Courtesy, Calgary Herald.*

The University of Calgary began in 1945 when the former Normal School (at King Edward School) became a branch of the faculty of education of the University of Alberta in Edmonton. Soon after, the faculty was moved to the campus of the Southern Alberta Institute of Technology. In 1951 a branch of the faculty of arts was established, followed by physical education (1956) and commerce and science (1957). In 1960 the university moved to its present site in northwest Calgary when two buildings, arts and education, and

science and engineering, were opened in September. The university gained academic autonomy in 1964 with a faculty of graduate studies established the same year. The division of engineering became a faculty in 1965 and a year later the University of Calgary gained full autonomy under its first president, Dr. H.S. Armstrong. The University's Gaelic motto, "Mo Shuile Toram Suas" ("I will lift up mine eyes"), in a way symbolizes the beckoning appeal of Calgary: the Rockies and the Chinook Arch in the western sky.

Since that memorable April 1966 date, the growth of the University of Calgary has been phenomenal. In 1980-81, some 10,000 full-time and 2,500 part-time students were enrolled in one of the 15 faculties. The university campus consists of 26 buildings on 314 acres of land. More than 1,000 full-time teaching faculty and 500 full-time and part-time sessional instructors are employed. The University operates the Kananaskis Centre for Environmental Research approximately 80 kilometres west of the city. The University of Calgary Astrophysical Laboratory near Priddis, southwest of the city, contains a laboratory with 18 telescopes plus a rotating dome with the main 18-inch telescope. Other institutes affiliated with the University of Calgary located on or near the campus include the Arctic Institute of North America, the Canadian Energy Research Institute, the Computer Modelling Group, the Institute for Transportation Studies, the Petroleum Recovery Institute, the University Interdisciplinary Sulphur Research Group, and the Vocational and Rehabilitation Research Institute.

These scientific and social institutions, together with the musical, theatrical, literary, sporting, and other special interest groups associated with the various faculties have emphasized the university's increasing role in delineating the focus of Calgary's scientific, intellectual, and cultural life. Before the inception of the University of Calgary in 1966, this dimension was lacking, and in that sense the emergence of modern, forward-looking Calgary has been in some part a reflection of the growth of its senior academic institution.

Facing page: *Santa Claus works on an ice sculpture on the Stephen Avenue Mall. Ice sculpting is a popular pastime during the festive season in Calgary. Courtesy, Calgary Herald.*

Above: *Events such as this Moslem celebration at the Jubilee Auditorium have widened Calgary's cultural image. Courtesy, Calgary Herald.*

Electric lights illuminate Seventh Avenue Southeast in downtown Calgary at night. Courtesy, Calgary Herald.

For all its modernity and nascent sophistication, Calgary's position on the new frontier is evocative of bygone days. The high-rolling mentality is reminiscent of the pre-1914 era. Land speculation is as rife today as it was then, with the exception that houses on the euphemistically named subdivisions reach out 10 miles from the city centre. The notion of bigness and limitless prosperity is alive and well; the difference is only one of degree. Modern boosters look fondly towards the magic million. In 1912, the ambitious could envisage only 200,000.

The construction industry still supplies the chief growth indices. The manifestation of pride and satisfaction in 1980 when the value of building permits hit one billion dollars was similar to the joy expressed in the record-setting construction year of 1912. In its earlier days of frontier ebullience, Calgary saw itself as usurping Canadian rivals, or duplicating the ethos of American urban giants. The modern Calgary is no exception; the targets are just different. Toronto has replaced Winnipeg, while Houston has assumed the mantle of emulation formerly worn by Chicago. Even the legacy of protest is

nurtured through a frontier type defiance. Throughout the years Calgary has found itself in frequent conflict with Edmonton, and even more with Ottawa, over a variety of issues. Whether it was Judge Travis and the federal legal system in 1886, the location of the provincial capital in 1905, the social disrepair of the early 1920s, and the Depression, or the current energy dispute, Calgary has never been reluctant to present its particular viewpoint.

Finally, Calgary's individuality lends itself to the frontier experience as much today as it did, say, in 1886 or 1912. That curious blend of impatience, aggressiveness, and masculine effervescence has become an identifiable hallmark of the city's corporate behaviour. Observers of the Calgary scene in the 1880s were appalled by the town's unkempt, rowdy image. Similarly in the boom period 1909-1912, the same level of sophisticated comment referred somewhat caustically to Calgary's crass urban environment. Today the same selective element is interested in seeing whether or not modern Calgary can overcome its somewhat untamed heritage. And if Canada's frontier city runs true to form, the battle will be a long time in being won—or lost.

Robert the Bruce on the grounds of the Jubilee Auditorium stands out against the Calgary skyline. The Jubilee Auditorium was given to Calgary by the province in 1955 to celebrate the 50th anniversary of provincial status. Courtesy, Calgary Herald.

GRANT MacEWAN, FRONTIER CHARACTER IN THE PRESENT
by LYNWYN FORAN (Age 13)

There are very few true frontier Canadians nowadays. The spirit of the frontier has passed, yet I know one person who continues to display it. Grant MacEwan, who was born in Brandon, Manitoba, on August 12, 1902, is a truly remarkable character. I have heard about many of this man's experiences because he is my grandfather. Gramp has always been a very hardworking and conservative individual. There is never a task too hard to tackle, nor is there any problem that can't be overcome. Frugality is one frontier quality that comes to mind when I think of Gramp. For example any mittens he finds are worn and used until they fall apart. This is partly so because Gramp feels no need for modernness, not in clothing, cars, or appliances. Luxuries added to the plain basic item are wasteful. This was also the philosophy during the frontier era. And he has naturally inexpensive tastes. A store-bought card, for example, isn't as appreciated nearly as much as a homemade one.

Another of Gramp's frontier characteristics is self-reliance. Frontier people could not depend too much on others. Gramp is always willing to attempt things that people say cannot be done. This was proven during the summer of 1981 when Gramp hand-dug with a shovel a 600-square-foot, seven-foot-deep foundation for an addition to our house, which he then built himself. It was astonishing to see, yet it illustrated another important frontier ingredient, and once it was started Gramp had to finish.

Gramp cannot be denied the description of "unique." He always works to maximum capacity; nothing forms a blockade. The physical and mental strength of this man is amazing. While building our garage in the mid 1970s, he cracked a vertebra. Gramp denied the pain and refused to see a doctor. The building went on until the structure was completely erected. This type of behaviour isn't unusual even today for Gramp.

By profession Gramp is an agriculturalist. He loves the land and deep down probably would still like to be a farmer. So, of course, Gramp is very interested in gardens. He enjoys growing fruit trees and vegetables. He built a log cabin at Westward Ho, Alberta, and with a hoe he broke the sod for a large garden. There Gramp's planting takes place. He is always willing to try new things. He is convinced that Alberta's climate can grow a greater variety of crops than those known today. One day I peeled an avocado for lunch, and Gramp took the pit to plant. Gardens were very important during the frontier times, and Gramp still enjoys one.

Gramp is well-known for his frontier personality and for the things he has achieved during his long life. He has written over 30 books. Most of them are to do with history and in them he tells many stories about life on the frontier. He has been a well-known professor of agriculture at the Universities of Saskatchewan and Manitoba. He has been a politician and was mayor of Calgary in 1964-65. When he was lieutenant governor of Alberta he was always visiting and talking to people, sometimes with me on his knee. Even today when he is almost 80 years of age he still lectures and speaks to people in all parts of Western Canada. I can't imagine any pioneer having more energy or love of work than my Gramp.

Gramp has all the qualities needed on the frontier, yet he lives in our modern times. While things around him may change, Gramp's frontier way of life won't be lost.

Facing page: *Lieutenant Governor Grant MacEwan begins one of the many walkathons in which he participated during his eight-year tenure as the Queen's representative in Alberta. This indefatigable Western Canadian covered over 500 miles in countless walkathons, always completing the entire distance. Courtesy, Calgary Herald.*

THE
FRONTIER SPIRIT

The late Johnny Hopkins, former columnist with *The Calgary Herald*, periodically would include a section of his daily column under the caption "Bagdad on the Bow." Those who remember Hopkins' wry wit will doubtless smile as they recall his delightful accounts of local life. But though there is little of the mystical, romantic Bagdad in modern Calgary, Hopkins' analogy is not altogether satirical. The legacy of the past still clings to the city despite its modern and newfound sophisticated image. In fact, it is the merging of old and new in the Calgary of the 1980s that most clearly illustrates an evolving yet historic urban mentality.

The blend of old and new is most blatantly paraded in the annual Stampede festivities. For two weeks in July, Calgary goes on public view, throwing around such terms as "western hospitality" or "the spirit of the frontier" like cowboy lariats. Free pancake and sausage breakfasts, public square dances, and other displays of lusty entertainment represent conscious attempts by private and civic organizations to re-create the frontier nostalgia of the old west. With the famed Calgary Stampede providing the nucleus, these hectic two weeks in July advertise more graphically than any other comparable phenomenon Calgary's conscious effort to reinforce its urban image.

To the casual observer, the new appears to overshadow the old in contemporary Calgary. The sprawling suburbs are neat and modern-looking. Many old buildings have fallen under the demolition hammer to make way for high-rise apartments and office complexes. The regional shopping centres indicate a life-style that has little memory of dependence on corner stores and grocery deliveries. In fact, for a period after the Second World War and especially in the 1950s, the expansionist mentality of the new frontier was hardly interested in preserving legacies of former times.

In recent years however, a growing public appreciation of heritage has reflected itself in Calgary. The result has been a more widespread interest in the value of tradition that transcends mere nostalgic gestures at Stampede time. Older communities like Hillhurst-Sunnyside, Victoria Park, and Ramsay seem determined to preserve their distinctive identities in the face of threats posed by large-scale urban renewal schemes. Heritage Park on the Glenmore Reservoir represents a superb example of how the past can be preserved and turned to social and cultural advantage. Fewer buildings are being demolished; many more are being refurbished and adapted to commercial and other uses. So while Calgary's newness and commitment to growth remain largely unchecked, they are somewhat counterbalanced by a more sensitive public consciousness of the city's heritage.

The old Calgary has been popularly conceived as a city long on individual ruggedness but short on sophistication and cultural amenities. The outdoor ethic cultivated a masculinity that largely eschewed the niceties of civilized liv-

Facing page: *A stone mason repairs the Calgary Memorial Park Library. The facility was provided partly by a Carnegie Foundation grant and was Calgary's first public library. In the 1960s and 1970s it housed the Glenbow Archives and is currently functioning as an art gallery. Courtesy, Calgary Herald.*

Calgary's planetarium was built as a centennial project when Canadians were celebrating the 100th anniversary of Confederation in 1967. Courtesy, Centennial Planetarium.

ing in favour of a more wholesome life-style. Horses, boxing, and steak enjoyed far greater popularity than art, the opera, or escargot. Recently, however, the cosmopolitan tastes of the city's burgeoning population have begun to modify Calgary's traditional image. Intellectual life has been heightened by the establishment and rapid growth of the University of Calgary. Ethnically, the city has reflected less its predominant Anglo-Saxon composition with the influx of more residents from different racial backgrounds. The effects are observable everywhere, from cosmopolitan class lists in local schools to diverse eating places and mystical religions. A more varied cultural life has been enhanced by the increasing number of institutions and organizations associated with the liberal arts.

Yet this emerging cosmopolitanism has also contributed to the merging of old and new in Calgary. In many cases, the cultural baggage of new arrivals to the city includes an awareness of the importance of heritage. Calgary's recent interest in things uniquely Calgarian is not entirely a grass roots movement in that some of the impetus has been provided by recently arrived residents. Here, the positive role of the new British immigrant warrants special mention.

To be sure, Calgary is a youthful city. Its urban atmosphere is punctuated by a drive and aggressiveness usually reserved for the young. In fact some observers continue to associate the city with crass acquisitiveness that has little reverence for precedents or for the casual languor popularly associated with sophistication. Yet one can also look through the softer eyes of reflection and see the meeting of youth and age that symbolizes the modern Calgary.

This kaleidoscope of views reflects very personal contributions. One view could be kindly Tom Baines displaying the relics of the past to eager throngs of fascinated children. Another could be indefatigable Grant MacEwan, striding along a Calgary street in a walkathon accompanied by a milling group of youngsters one-eighth his age. It could be the indomitable Barbara Leighton struggling to maintain the Leighton Centre for Arts and Crafts, in part so that Calgary youth can share in a unique cultural opportunity. It could be aristocratic Mary Dover, OBE, daughter of A.E. Cross, who in spite of physical difficulties insists on presenting her annual history award to a student of Red Deer Lake School. Or it could be gentle Allison Jackson who enthusiastically shares her rich knowledge and unparalleled photographs of historic Calgary with school children of all ages.

Paradoxically, it is because of its youth that Calgary is able to cultivate a distinct urban character. The past is easily discernible in the present through memory, personal embodiments, physical reminders, and of course a growing cultural awareness. With the ethos of the frontier supplying the continuum, Calgary is a historic city in that its urban mentality has evolved through time with a surprisingly consistent development. Though not always alive and well, the frontier has never been far from Calgarians. It has reached into their pocketbooks, intruded into their life-styles, and above all has touched their spirits.

The S.S. Moyie *docks at Heritage Park in preparation for its winter hibernation. The paddle-wheeler plies Glenmore Lake during the tourist season from May to September. Courtesy, Calgary Herald.*

HERITAGE PARK
by FIONA FORAN (Age 14)

Walking into Heritage Park is like going back in time. You see ox-drawn carts, streetcars, a blacksmith bent over his anvil, a livery stable, and you hear the wail of a steam engine as it thunders into the station. Calgary's Heritage Park is known nationwide for its accurate re-creations of a frontier town. Old people come to remember their bygone way of life, and the young to discover how people lived long ago. Anyone interested in history should not miss Heritage Park because its sights, fascinating to some and familiar to others, never cease to delight.

The idea for a park of this type came from Mr. Eric Harvie, a well-known citizen who in 1961 was considering the possibility of a children's park off the Glenmore Reservoir. A sum of $300,000 was donated, $150,000 each by the city of Calgary and by the Woods Foundation. The city also donated the 60 acres of land for the park. City officials and the Glenbow staff were the planners of the park in its early stages, and the Heritage Park Society, formed in 1963, was responsible for all operations, including the construction and supervision.

The park was a cooperative enterprise. The services of a project manager, Bill Pratt, and a field representative, R.G. (Red) Cathcart, were volunteered by Mr. R.F. Jennings of Standard Holdings Ltd. Other personnel were private volunteers, or came from the city and various firms. The park's first manager was Dave Turner. Grant MacEwan, former mayor of the city of Calgary and noted historian, who supported Heritage Park in the city council, opened it officially in July 1964.

Heritage Park is particularly significant because it was the first park of its kind in Alberta. Its main purpose is to preserve old buildings that played a part in Alberta's past, buildings that would have been torn down if Heritage Park had not purchased them.

One of the first buildings in Heritage Park was Sam Livingstone's house. The first farmer in this area, Livingstone was squatting in the vicinity of Glenmore when the North West Mounted Police came in 1875. He moved over the river and built his permanent house there.

A few attractions in Heritage Park cannot go without discussion. One of these is the beautiful Prince house, which Peter Prince built on the banks of the Bow River. It was a lovely house and the plan it was taken from was published in the 1893 edition of *Scientific American* magazine. For its trip to Heritage Park, it was cut into three pieces and the tower was removed. Alberta Natural Gas sponsored the cost of moving as a centennial project in 1967.

The Sandstone House is a smaller reproduction of one built by Calgary lawyer James B. Smith in 1891. He took in tenants and once rented the building to Colonel James Macleod. This house, representing Calgary's sandstone era, which dates roughly from 1890 to 1912, was built by Heritage Park in 1972.

The Burnside Ranch was founded by a Scotsman, Edwin Donald McKay, in 1904. He had come from Scotland to ranch near Cochrane and built this

Facing page, top: *Shonts elevator and Gunn barn are shown in this view of Heritage Park. The elevator, located 250 miles northeast of Calgary, was named after the chief engineer of the Panama Canal, T.P. Shonts. It was built in 1909 by the Security Elevator Company of Winnipeg.*

Bottom: *Chinese laundries were a part of frontier life present in virtually every urban place across Western Canada. The Wing Chong laundry is in Heritage Park.*

home 17 years after he arrived. The name Burnside came about because he had a creek, or burn, flowing through his land. The building was donated by Percy Copithorne and moved by Heritage Park. The complex was then restored with financial aid from Shell of Canada in 1975.

The Weedon School is a favourite with everyone. The Alberta Teachers' Association donated the little school to the park so that students of today could see what school days were like for the children of early Alberta. It was built in 1910, and the typical one-room school was moved by Heritage Park in 1964.

The Claresholm General Store was built in 1904 by Mr. S.A. Mostad, who belonged to one of the many Norwegian families who fled the seven-year Devil's Lake drought in North Dakota. This store had many other uses, as well. It was at times a NWMP barracks, a town hall, a family home, and a boarding house. It was purchased for $400 and moved in 1964.

Originally a roughly-framed, two-story box, the Wainwright Hotel is now a lovely building, tastefully decorated with antiques. It was built in 1906 in the Battle River valley, and it burned down in 1929. The House of Lethbridge and private donors helped Heritage Park with the cost of rebuilding.

The Herschell-Spillman MotorCompany constructed the much-loved Bowness Carousel. It was made in 1905 for Winnipeg Beach Attractions, and was owned by Calgary's Bowness Park in 1917. Donated anonymously, the carousel is housed in Heritage Park, where it is still running today.

Lord Strathcona Street, the main thoroughfare in Heritage Park, was named after Donald A. Smith, a Hudson's Bay Company and CPR official.

Car No. 14 at Heritage Park is a replica of a Calgary electric streetcar built in 1910. The new No. 14 was assembled by retired carpenters and former streetcar men, who helped select the colours. The seat frames are the ones from the old No. 14. The money to build it came from an anonymous donor.

Although quite large, the S.S. *Moyie* is only a half-sized reproduction of a paddle wheeler that ran on the Kootenai Lakes in British Columbia. Constructed in British Columbia, it was tested for seaworthiness in the Pacific. The 90-foot-long and 30-foot-wide boat then was taken apart, shipped to Calgary, and reassembled. It made its first trip on Glenmore Reservoir on August 21, 1965, and now carries about 80,000 people a year.

Midnapore Station was built in 1910 for controlling trains between Calgary and the town of Aldersyde. Heritage Park bought the building for $1.00, moved it in 1964, and used it as the administrative office for awhile.

Heritage Park, a nonprofit organization, is controlled by a 12-member board of directors and administered by a manager and two assistant managers. The park has a year-round staff of roughly 30 people, while its summer staff numbers about 200. Most of the people who make up this figure are high school or university students who are enthusiastic about working in a place such as this. Making the park's atmosphere seem more real are the older people working there.

Heritage Park, the old country town in the big modern city, is an excellent example of how a city can preserve pieces of history so that we of modern times can see how our ancestors carried on their daily lives.

Left: *The fireworks over Midway that end the Calgary Stampede Grandstand show can be seen for miles away in many parts of the city.*

Below: *The showpiece of Calgary's indoor gardens, the Devonian Gardens in Toronto Dominion Square cover over two acres of enclosed space and are internationally regarded as being among the finest indoor gardens in the world.*

Top left: *The Stampede parade gives visitors and Calgarians an interesting look at cowboys, Indians, and the old West, as well as the more traditional parade entries of floats and marching bands.*

Top right: *A ski jumper competes at Paskapoo Ski Hill. Calgary will be the site of ski jumping and other winter sports when it hosts the 1988 Winter Olympics.*

Middle: *The Calgary Flames, a National Hockey League team, thrills fans with action-packed games.*

Bottom left: *A construction worker poses atop the Pan-Canadian Building.*

Bottom right: *Fish Creek Provincial Park in south Calgary is one of the largest urban parks in the world. Trails and bicycle paths meander through the heavily wooded area, affording visitors an ideal opportunity to enjoy the beautiful foothills country. Courtesy, Alberta Recreation and Parks.*

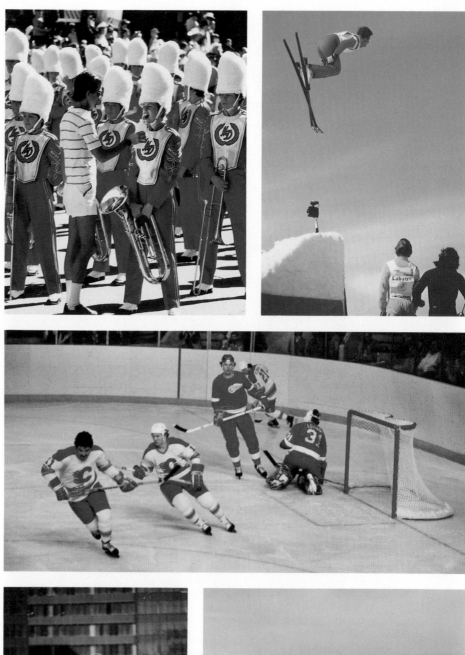

Established on its present site in the early 1960s, first as a branch of the University of Alberta and later as an autonomous body, the University of Calgary has experienced phenomenal growth over the past 15 years. This new library tower is one of the latest physical additions.

Above: *The Centennial Planetarium was Calgary's official project to commemorate Canada's 100th birthday in 1967. Its star chamber provides a unique opportunity for viewers to acquaint themselves with the mysteries of space. The Planetarium also features a rooftop observatory telescope and an aerospace museum.*

Above right: *Dinosaur Park in the Calgary Zoo complex contains over 40 reproductions of prehistoric animals. Displays of the fossilized remains of these creatures also form part of Dinosaur Park.*

Right: *This Siberian tiger is one of the many unusual residents of the Calgary Zoo.*

Left: *Owned and operated by five Calgary cooperatives, Heritage Square features dining and leisure facilities as well as an indoor garden. The five-storey complex is a fine example of functional space made aesthetically pleasing to both workers and visitors.*

Below: *Lake Midnapore in South Calgary is one of the four man-made water bodies that draw their supply from nearby Fish Creek to provide a unique living environment for thousands of Calgarians. Midnapore itself is an old community with historic roots dating back to the 1880s.*

PART IV
PARTNERS
IN PROGRESS

The vital role of the business community in influencing and even determining urban growth in North America is readily acknowledged. Indeed, historians writing at the academic level have isolated the business sector as one of the most crucial formative forces in Canadian urban development. In Calgary, especially in the early years, the dynamism and initiative provided by its business leaders contributed markedly to the city's transition from an isolated police post to a vibrant urban entity.

In the first place, it should be stressed that Calgary owes its corporate existence to an enthusiastic group of businessmen who supplied the initiative which resulted in town incorporation in November 1884. Similarly, the roots of many social, recreational, and even cultural organizations were planted by businessmen either on an individual or group basis. The point is that the interests and energies of the business sector transcended pure commercial endeavour, and extended into every facet of urban life. As such, the founding role of the business community in establishing the young Calgary must stand undisputed.

Calgary's focal position on the transcontinental railroad made it the chief distributing centre west of Winnipeg. The city's emerging commercial and manufacturing base strongly reflected this orientation. Retail services were wide and varied, and in specialty items catered to a wide regional demand.

Wholesaling, too, was important. From the jobbing houses, warehouses, and storage facilities that grew up along the railroad tracks, volume goods from Eastern Canada, Great Britain, and the United States made their way to retail outlets throughout southern and south-central Alberta. Calgary provided the financial and service institutions for its rural hinterland. Manufacturing enterprises processed local raw materials or produced items too bulky to be imported competitively. Particularly prominent have been those businesses associated with the livestock and construction industries.

Calgary's recent position in the vanguard of Canada's oil and natural gas industry has produced a new business dimension to complement its traditional role as a commercial distributing centre. The city has emerged as the nation's oil administrative and management headquarters, as well as the major financial centre of Western Canada. The oil industry has also generated a wide array of related and service business enterprises, with the result that in recent years Calgary's commercial base has become both more specialized and diversified.

Calgary's burgeoning growth is reflected in the depth and scope of its business sector. The following biographical information provides a more personal commentary on some of the prominent participants in Calgary's vibrant business life.

Facing page: *Still the dominant feature of Calgary's downtown skyline, the Calgary Tower reaches 626 feet, the equivalent of 62 storeys, into the Alberta sky. Its revolving restaurant and observation deck provide the best "bird's-eye" view of Calgary and the surrounding area.*

ALBERTA GOVERNMENT TELEPHONES

The independence of the Western Canadian spirit is perhaps no better illustrated than in the growth of its telephone systems. Skeptical of big business, the Prairie provinces evolved their own brand of communications companies. Leading the way with many innovations was Alberta Government Telephones.

Telephones on a national scale arrived in April 1880, when Parliament granted a charter to the Bell Telephone Company of Canada. However, it was 1884 before Parliament voted $675 for Alberta's first telephone from Edmonton to St. Albert. The people themselves had to supply the 288 poles for the wire. At 4 p.m., January 3, 1885, the first Alberta telephone message was relayed: "We wish you a Happy New Year."

Later that year James Walker, who as a member of the Northwest Mounted Police received the first telegraph message sent into Alberta, was the first person to have a telephone in Calgary. The Bell system arrived in Calgary in 1887, with 40 subscribers for its exchange.

By 1900 there were 150 phones in Calgary and three years later Bell issued its first Calgary telephone directory. Long-distance service arrived in Alberta in 1904, when the Calgary-Edmonton line was built at a cost of $45,833.

However, in spite of these achievements, big interests were not popular in the West and Bell fitted that description.

In the Alberta government's first budget a $25,000 figure appeared under "miscellaneous" for preliminary work in establishing a government telephone system. Although Manitoba was the first to declare a government system and the first to buy out Bell, Alberta was the first in North America to build and operate lines.

The first line, completed in 1907, ran from Calgary to Banff. The honor of being the first citizen to speak on the line went to Bob Edwards, editor of the *Eye-Opener*. Banff declared a half-holiday but Edwards' celebration was so lengthy that his newspaper did not appear again for several months.

The spirit of innovation dictated the design of AGT's first building in Calgary, the East Exchange on 9th Avenue East. It was designed in 1909 on the principle of the thermos bottle — two brick walls with air space between to provide a constant temperature for the switching equipment in Calgary's automatic exchange.

AGT began open warfare with Bell on February 14, 1907, when it declared it was in the telephone business to stay. Initially Bell refused to sell out. However, the Manitoba government bought the Bell operation in that province for $3.4 million on January 15, 1908, and two weeks later the Alberta legislature authorized a similar purchase. On April 1 the sale was made for $675,000. At what point the provincial telephone system became known by the initials AGT is not clear, although a Calgary baseball team's uniform shows that the initials were recognized in 1912.

The first full year of World War I had a severe effect on the telephone system; in Calgary alone, 2,000 phones were removed. The 1920s, on the other hand, were a tranquil period — with the emphasis on extending long-distance service. In 1923 Calgarians were able to phone Winnipeg. On October 21, 1925, it became possible to talk to people in all of North America. In 1928 service to the British Isles became a reality. By 1929 Albertans could reach 28 million phones — 80 percent of telephones in the world.

The 1930s began with AGT joining telephone companies across Canada to create the TransCanada Telephone System, a unique exercise in cooperative nation-building which raised a pole line

tretching 4,200 miles from sea to sea. Service opened on January 25, 1932, with celebrations but the 1930s were mostly downhill. In October 1929 AGT had 62,000 phones; by 1933 it had 40,000 and "take-out" orders were soon extended to employees as well. AGT even had to sell its rural lines to farmers to keep the rest of the operation going. A number of mutual companies were established—600 by 1936 and eventually over 1,000.

The telephone business burgeoned following World War II. In Calgary 5,000 were on a waiting list for phones. Fortunately for AGT, a former telephone installer, Jim Watson, was mayor of Calgary from 1945 to 1949 and he was sympathetic to the company's plight in explaining the two-year wait for connections.

AGT had barely caught up to the backlog of orders when it was into the age of microwave. History repeated itself as AGT joined with other regional companies to raise a line of microwave towers from sea to sea. The first tower on the Calgary skyline was atop AGT's new office building on Seventh Avenue. From 1958—when the microwave was com-

plete to the West Coast—to 1971 the firm was the fastest growing in Canada. Revenues during that period rose from $13.5 million to $202 million.

In 1958, on the 50th anniversary of AGT's purchase of the Bell system, it became a Crown corporation. In 1979, to obtain greater representation from the private sector, four members-at-large were added to the commission which governs AGT.

During the 1960s AGT decided that again it should make telephone service available to every rural home—this time via underground cable. The end of an era in rural telephony came on May 30, 1980, when the last mutual telephone company was integrated.

Telephone employees engaged in community service found an unusual use of the telephone. In 1961, at the Children's Hospital in Calgary, there was an experiment to aid in muscle training and speech therapy for disabled youngsters. The resounding success of the Small Fry Telephone Company has led to the creation of hundreds of others throughout North America.

The 1970s introduced a period of exceptional developments for AGT.

Community Antenna Television to 10 cities was introduced. Electronic switching, the first in Western Canada, was installed in the Oakridge exchange in 1972. Altel Data was established to market data services, terminals, and networks. Extended Flat Rate calling came into being in 1974, connecting communities within 30 miles of each other. To give customers a better and more personalized service, AGT regionalized its operations and extended this program to include Calgary in 1978.

Taking advantage of newer technologies, AGT introduced digital switching technology into the network in 1979. Conference TV was another service offered that year. Direct Dialing Overseas was still another service AGT introduced. Design of a fibre optic transmission system was undertaken and brought into service in early 1982. The Calgary-Cheadle link was the first of its kind in North America and contains 12 fibres, each with a capacity for 4,032 conversations.

In 1957 AGT's microwave tower changed the character of the Calgary skyline, vying for prominence with the Palliser Hotel.

ALBERTA ENERGY COMPANY LTD.

Few businesses have received the overwhelming public support demonstrated for the Alberta Energy Company in its first year of existence. Established in 1975 as a special opportunity for Albertans to participate in the development of energy and natural resources, AEC had an initial staff of four, a debt of $1.7 million, and essentially no operations in progress. But by the end of 1975, the firm had 43 employees, $123 million in working capital, more than 50,000 shareholders, and several major projects under way.

One of the more significant events in AEC's first year was the sale of shares, making it a public company. The general public and the Province each purchased $75 million in shares, at a 1982 equivalent price of $3.33 after adjusting for a three-for-one split. Albertans, many of whom were first-time share owners, oversubscribed the issue, which was one of the largest equity offerings in Canadian history and the largest issue of common stock for a new Alberta organization.

The company has grown by an emphasis on new, capital-intensive projects primarily in Alberta. By 1981 it had a billion-dollar asset base and cash flow totalling approximately $92 million. Shareholders totalled more than 50,000 and 55 percent owned 100 shares or less.

Since the Suffield Block shallow gas drilling program began in 1976, the firm's activities in this area have expanded considerably. By 1981 there were 1,681 completed gas wells, and heavy oil production amounted to 334 barrels a day.

In 1978 AEC acquired rights to the Primrose Block near Cold Lake, and within four years 148 wells had been drilled with oil sands reserves estimated at about 17 billion barrels in place. AEC owns 10 percent of the sizable Syncrude Project and two-thirds of the utilities

This illustration provides a graphic record of the growth of Alberta Energy during its seven-year history.

plant which supplies Syncrude. A subsidiary, Alberta Oil Sands Pipeline Ltd., owns and operates the pipeline, which transports the synthetic crude from Fort McMurray to Edmonton.

Alberta Energy owns 33 percent of a 550-mile gas-gathering system in south-central Alberta which gathers ethane feedstocks for processing. Another project is a dual pipeline between Cold Lake and Edmonton for transporting diluted bitumen.

As further indication of its diversified investments in energy, the company has a 25-percent interest in a coal project near Edson which produces over three million tons annually. It also owns 28 percent of a large Canadian integrated forest products company and 100 percent of a forestry complex near Blue Ridge, Alberta. AEC owns a 50-percent interest in Pan-Alberta Gas Ltd., which

contracts for the purchase and sale of Alberta natural gas. The corporation is, as well, a co-venturer in plans for a proposed polyethylene plant and is considering other potential petrochemical investments.

In 1981 AEC expanded its oil and gas exploration activities beyond the Suffield and Primrose Blocks, with programs to include farmins of lands owned by others, purchases of lease rights, or the acquisition of existing operations.

David E. Mitchell, a petroleum engineer who has been the firm's president and chief executive officer since it became active in 1975, is strongly optimistic about future prospects. In 1982 he told shareholders that, despite a difficult economic environment, AEC's outlook is both promising and interesting, with 1982 cash flow anticipated to be in the order of $150 million.

ALBERTA MOTOR ASSOCIATION

In the summer of 1901 motoring arrived in Alberta. Billy Cochrane, son of rancher Senator Cochrane, was the proud owner of the first motor car in Alberta, a 12-horsepower steam Locomobile. But despite this pioneering, Joe Morris of Edmonton ended up with licence number one in 1906 when the government passed the Automobile Act to deal with the province's 41 vehicles. Each owner had to pay $3 for an operator's licence but had to supply his own licence plate. By 1909 there were 275 cars, for which owners paid $499.50 in operating fees to the government.

The first automobile club in Alberta was started in Calgary in 1908 and had 15 members. However, such clubs seldom lasted beyond the summer because cars were usually "put up" for the winter. Calgary, with by far the most active auto enthusiasts because of the lure of Banff, finally saw the successful launching of the Calgary Automobile Club in 1911. Within two weeks 200 people had joined at $10 each.

When the Liberal government was swept out of office by the United Farmers of Alberta in 1921, highways suddenly dropped as a government priority and regional motor clubs emerged as lobbies for better roads. A province-wide organization received a major impetus when clubs successfully fought a move by cities to tax cars. Another boost to unit-ing clubs came in 1925, when the government announced it had no intention of clearing winter roads. The clubs received another jolt when they got wind of plans to create commercial auto clubs.

On November 13, 1926, the Alberta Motor Association incorporation papers were registered and 1,400 Albertans joined at $6.50 each. Charles H. Grant was the first president. Although vehicle use declined during the Depression, by 1936 AMA membership began to grow again.

Services to members have grown steadily over the years. As early as 1920 the Calgary Auto Club had an auto camp "for those who do not wish to stay in a hotel." In 1925 it affiliated with the American Automobile Association which provided for emergency mechanical service. By 1927 the AMA had dispensed its first road maps (100,000 of them), approved six garages for Emergency Road Service, and issued its first road report.

Soon the association had member strength and lobbying power that civic, municipal, and provincial governments could not ignore. Highways were improved and new road construction was begun. The AMA's primary goal for safer and better highways had been realized, and while efforts in this area are not as necessary now as they were over 50 years ago, the club still maintains a watchful eye through its Government Affairs Department.

Today the AMA provides over 30 different services, although Emergency Road Service remains the major benefit. In Calgary and Edmonton it has its own fleet of tow trucks. The AMA is also the parent company of a travel agency, an insurance company, and insurance agency. Its driver education school is among the largest in North America. In more recent years, consumer protection programs have been developed which include a consumer hot-line, a vehicle-inspection service, credit card registry, and an approved auto-repair service program.

By 1982 AMA membership in Alberta exceeded 322,000, of which 105,000 were members of the Calgary region. Through its new Calgary office at 4700-17th Avenue S.W. and its Macleod Trail branch in the Willow Park Shopping Plaza, the AMA expects to continue serving Calgary and area motorists for many years to come.

In 1981 the Alberta Motor Association branch in Calgary moved to new quarters at 4700 17th Avenue S.W. to continue its wide range of services to the over 100,000 AMA members in Calgary.

ALPINE MANAGEMENT CORPORATION LTD.

Austin Henry Ford loved the mountains. For many years he ran a mountain tourist lodge. It was on a mountain hiking trip that he first met his wife, Phyllis. Therefore, it came as little surprise that the name of his company should reflect the high country. Alpine Management Corporation Ltd. traces its origin to 1952 and today owns and manages about three-quarters of a million square feet of downtown high-rise space.

The Ford family moved to Calgary from Bassano during the Depression. In 1932, 19-year-old Austin Ford secured his first job, at a hardware store for $30 a month. He tried farming and other endeavors and then joined the Navy in 1940.

After the war he applied for a civil service job but the very day it came through, he and his accountant father, Henry, bought their own company. It was a small cabinet-making business that manufactured business furnishings and later made bowling and pool hall equipment. Austin named the venture Hayford Limited to reflect the association with his wife's family, the Haylocks. Cabinets they made are still used for display purposes in the Luxton Museum in Banff. Pool tables can still be found in various establishments from Creston, British Columbia, to Red Lake, Ontario. The business had two plants, a leased location near the Calgary Zoo, and a plant and warehouse on Ninth Avenue S.W.

Business was brisk immediately after the war because equipment neglected during those years needed servicing. However, there was quite a downturn in the bowling industry in the early 1950s. In 1951 the leased plant burned to the ground, taking with it most of the machinery and inventory. The combination of events led to the firm being sold to Brunswick in 1952.

Because of his great love of the mountains and a desire to participate in the tourist business, Austin Ford bought four lodges in the national parks west of Calgary with Claude and Bud Brewster of Banff in 1954. The mountain lodges became available from the CPR after the railway realized that tourists were using cars instead of trains to reach these spots. When the partnership dissolved, Ford kept the Lake O'Hara Lodge which he and his wife ran until 1976. It was a six-month job even though the lodge was open for only two months in the summer. At one time staff members were hired only if they had musical talent. Adjacent to the lodge was a lea, called Alpine Meadow, which eventually lent its name to the Ford management company. A Duncan painting of Lake O'Hara still hangs in the corporate head office in the Ford Building.

Alpine Management Corporation Ltd. was initially incorporated as Hayford Building Ltd. in 1952. The name was subsequently changed to Derrick Buildings Ltd. in 1954, and the name Alpine Management Corporation Ltd. was adopted in 1966.

After the sale of the cabinet business the Fords kept the Ninth Avenue warehouse location and formed a new venture, Hayford Building Ltd. Austin Ford saw the need for office space for the fledgling petroleum industry and decided to build on the site. It was a difficult undertaking in that lending institutions required a tenant prior to considering financing of the project and the potential tenants required a building before they would commit to a lease. Ford wore out several pairs of shoes, he recalled, putting the deal together. But with the backing of his father and a great deal of perseverance, the project became a reality. One of the company's first tenants was Dome Petroleum, utilizing about 2,000 square feet of space in this new 1952 project called the Derrick Building.

The firm next expanded to the development of the Alpine Building on the corner of Sixth Avenue and Sixth Street S.W. in 1959. At that time in Calgary it was unheard of to purchase property solely for the land, but in 1959

Harry A. Ford, son of the founder of Alpine Management, took over as president and chief executive officer in 1978.

Austin Henry Ford founded Alpine Management Corporation Ltd. and drew the name from the mountains that were an important part of his life.

Phyllis M. Ford, wife of the founder of Alpine Management, is now chairman of the board and for years managed Lake O'Hara Lodge in the Canadian Rockies.

The 20-storey Ford Tower at 633 Sixth Avenue S.W. houses Alpine Management's offices and is named after the firm's founder, Austin Ford.

tain of the Provost Corps of the Shriners' Al Azhar Temple. He was a director and founding member of the Building Owners' and Managers' Association in Calgary. He was discharged from the Navy in 1946, after serving five and a half years, with a rank of lieutenant commander. He died on October 3, 1981.

Alpine Management now represents three generations of the Ford family since Harry A. Ford took over as president and chief executive officer in 1978. The firm remains a family-held enterprise with Phyllis M. Ford as chairman of the board.

The growth of Calgary since 1976 has been unprecedented and Alpine has grown alongside. The industry now deals with mechanical, electrical, and security systems controlled by computers. Alpine Management has kept pace with new developments in flexible office design, with public amenities being an integral part of commercial complexes. Sophistication in building systems has required the firm to keep pace on professional management as well.

This model of Monenco Place shows the 29-storey office and retail complex started in 1981. Monenco was one of Alpine's early tenants and this project represents their reunion.

three houses were demolished to make way for a two-phase development in the Alpine Building. It was one of the first air conditioned buildings in the downtown core and at the time it stood tall— five storeys was still an imposing and very visible height in 1959.

Another project of Alpine Management was the construction of the Ford Tower, at 633 Sixth Avenue S.W., a 20-storey office structure named after the company's founder, Austin Ford. One of the early tenants of Alpine was Montreal Engineering Company, Limited. The two organizations are once again doing business, this time on a joint-venture basis with the development and construction of Monenco Place, a 29-storey office and retail complex in the downtown core.

During his lifetime, Austin Ford took an active part in community affairs and politics. He was a past president of the Naval Officers' Association and past cap-

ATCO LTD.

ATCO LTD. is an Alberta-based, Canadian-owned holding company for an international group of subsidiaries engaged in energy-related industries. Today the ATCO group has 4,300 shareholders and over 8,000 employees with total revenues reported at over $1.2 billion in its last fiscal year.

But it wasn't always this way. In 1946 it was simply one man's effort to earn a living. Don Southern, who left home at 14, was the original driving force. During the Depression, when his truckdriver's pay dwindled, he joined the Calgary Fire Department, which selected him over several thousand others for a job that offered instant affluence—$98 a month.

In 1946 Don Southern noticed utility trailers for rent and an idea clicked. With his wife Ina's savings, and a $1,200 bank loan cosigned by fellow fireman Slim Farch, he bought 15 trailers and put them up for rent. The new venture was called Alberta Trailer Hire, with 40 percent ownership given to his 14-year-old son, Ron.

Within a year the operation centralized at 805 Third Street S.E., in Calgary, where a bungalow housed the Southerns, a tarpaper shack comprised the office, and the backyard provided space for trailer storage. By 1951 Don quit his job and hired Slim Farch as ATCO's first employee to open the Alberta Trailer Company sales lot in Edmonton.

Ron Southern graduated from the University of Alberta with a bachelor of science degree in 1954; two years later he took over operations, officially leading the company's growth to the multinational billion-dollar status it has today.

During this period, housing unit manufacturing was initiated to honour a drilling company order for seven mobile bunk houses. Increasingly larger orders followed and the limited staff worked themselves into a state of exhaustion. The organization was forced to open a factory in an old RCAF hangar in Airdrie. Suddenly Alberta Trailer Company found itself to be virtually the only firm able to supply instant housing

An 840-man camp and 1,100-man kitchen and recreation complex at Prince George, British Columbia, for Northwood Pulp and Timber Ltd.

Don Southern in front of the 1950 Alberta Trailer Hire sales office.

to resource companies. By 1959 ATCO experienced a sudden change to its feast-or-famine mode of operation due to a successful bid on a multimillion-dollar contract with Boeing. Almost instantly, other large contracts followed.

A subsidiary was established in Australia in 1962 to provide industrial housing to the company's growing resource-related industries. Continuing expansion resulted in the opening of ATCO Industrial Park in 1965 on a 72-acre site in South Calgary. ATCO Industries Ltd., with sales of $42 million, was listed on the Toronto Stock Exchange in 1968 as a public corporation. The Trans Alaska Pipeline project followed and ATCO provided housing and facilities for 15,000 workers in just 16 months. ATCO had become the largest industry of its kind in the world.

Ron Southern, aware of the cyclic nature of shelter manufacturing economies, diversified dynamically into energy-related industries in 1975. He reshuffled ATCO's worldwide subsid-

iaries into semi-autonomous operations. ATCO Metal began to manufacture oil field support buildings and cladding while ATCO Components offered the finest European craftsmanship in millwork, cabinetry, and interiors. ATCO purchased large drilling, well-servicing and oil field equipment companies in Canada and the United States, making it one of the largest oil field service operations in North America. Meanwhile, ATCO Housing & Development became involved in all aspects of land development with commercial real estate being its fastest-growing segment. Today ATCO has completed its first major shopping centre and an office tower with other mega office complexes being completed in downtown Calgary and Edmonton. A customs brokerage and a travel agency complete the service list.

Expansion escalated in 1980 with ATCO's acquisition of 58.1 percent of Canadian Utilities Limited, whose subsidiaries include Canadian Western Natural Gas Company Limited, Alberta Power Limited, and Northwestern Utilities Limited. ATCOR Resources Limited, a recently formed Canadian Utilities Limited subsidiary, has the potential to become a major energy company of the future, actively involved in petroleum exploration, petrochemicals, and engineering.

This is the legacy created by Don Southern and developed by Ron Southern, the boy who started out servicing rental trailers to become the president and chief executive officer of ATCO Ltd. Don Southern continues to serve as chairman of the board of ATCO Ltd.

BANFF LIFTS LTD.

John Jaeggi had a dream and converted it to a spectacular legacy—one of North America's most popular sightseeing lifts. Arriving in Banff from Switzerland in 1924, Jaeggi built a teahouse at the summit of Sulphur Mountain in 1940. For many years previous, hikers had trekked to the top of Sulphur Mountain to reach what had become Banff's most reknowned viewpoint. In 1945 Jaeggi began a unique enterprise that made this arduous trip a little easier. He put a platform on his tractor for 15 persons and started transporting people up the mountain to a halfway house from which they could continue their journey on foot. Billed as "the world's most unique ride," the Alpine Transport took riders "thousands of feet above worry level." Still, not everyone could enjoy the thrill of a mountain-top perch and a cup of tea.

In the mid-1950s, Jaeggi made repeated trips to Switzerland and finally convinced a group of investors, headed by Werner Riesen, a Swiss travel entrepreneur, and Adolf Stettler, a longtime friend of Jaeggi, to back a gondola lift venture. While gondola lifts were familiar enough in the mountains of Switzerland, Banff's local investors were apprehensive about the prospects of a similar lift in Banff—it would be the first lift in North America built solely for sightseeing.

In time, several Canadian investors were found and together with their Swiss partners they incorporated Banff Sulphur Mountain Gondola Lift Company Ltd. in 1958. Adolf Stettler assumed the presidency of the firm with Claude Brewster, a local Banff promoter of the lift, taking the vice-president's chair. In September

world. A second teahouse, known as the "Teahouse in the Clouds," replaced Jaeggi's original log building in 1961 and beckoned visitors to sample a piece of "Pie in the Sky."

Arthur Haenni, a Swiss who came to Canada in 1959 to install the electrical components in the lift—and never left—took over management of the venture in 1974. Now vice-president and general manager, he moved the corporation into a new era of expansion and diversification.

In 1978 the company bought Banff Cablelifts Ltd., operators of the Mount Norquay Ski Area and in 1982 a new circular multi-level building with two restaurants, gift shop, and panoramic viewing terraces was opened at the top of Sulphur Mountain. On November 1, 1981, the firm was reorganized under the name of Banff Lifts Ltd. to incorporate into one body all the lift facilities and supporting services on Sulphur Mountain and Mount Norquay.

The Alpine Transport, a tractor with a platform for up to 15 persons, carried visitors halfway up Sulphur Mountain and was the predecessor of today's gondola lift. Founder and director John Jaeggi is at the controls of the tractor.

A light snow dusts the original teahouse built by John Jaeggi at the top of Sulphur Mountain. Everything—including the furniture—was made of logs and all supplies—including water—had to be brought up on horseback.

1958 construction on the lift was started and on July 17, 1959, the lift's huge bullwheels and 34-ton cables turned with the first passengers—five years after the first application for a license was submitted. What had begun as one man's dream was turned into a proud reality by a young and progressive organization.

Otto Steiner, the lift's first general manager and later vice-president, guided the company during its formative years. Patronage grew steadily as Banff's popularity as a tourist resort drew ever-increasing numbers from around the

Banff Lifts Ltd. operates all the lift facilities on Sulphur Mountain and Mount Norquay.

BANNERMAN INSURANCE LTD.

John "Jack" MacTavish Bannerman was a quiet, shy man who, in the process of building a successful insurance business, earned nationwide recognition for his football contributions. He was named Calgary's Sportsman of the Year in 1963.

In 1917 Jack was selling insurance in Winnipeg for Manufacturers Life. Four years later he entered the general insurance business in Calgary, operating from an office located in the Grain Exchange Building. In 1966 the company built its own offices at the present location, 1915 Fourth Street S.W.

In 1941 Jack formed a partnership with Fred McClelland known as Bannerman and McClelland. It changed back to Bannerman Agencies in 1956, and was renamed Bannerman Insurance Ltd. in 1981.

Jack's chief sports interest was football. He managed the original Calgary Stampeders, then known as the Tigers. After Winnepeg brought the Grey Cup west for the first time in 1935, he organized and was the first President of the Western Interprovincial Football Union, now the Western Conference of the Canadian Football League. In 1941 Jack was President of the Canadian Rugby Union (now the CFL). He was a President of both the Calgary and Alberta Junior Football Leagues, and was instrumental in organizing the first national junior championship.

Jack's son, Bob, became involved in the insurance business in 1949 after graduating from the University of Alberta. Following four years with the Royal Insurance Company, he joined his father's firm as a junior partner.

In 1967 Bob served as President of the Insurance Agents Association of Alberta,

John "Jack" MacTavish Bannerman, founder of Bannerman Insurance Ltd.

and five years later became President of the Canadian Federation of Insurance Agents and Brokers Associations. He has been a Fellow of the Insurance Institute of Canada since 1955, being the first Albertan to obtain this degree by examination, and he was named Canada's Insurance Man of the Year in 1970. In 1972 he was again the first in Alberta to receive the Chartered Insurance Broker designation.

The company, which remains solely involved in insurance and bonding, now includes a third-generation Bannerman. Bob's daughter, Ginny DiGirolamo, obtained her agency license in 1973 — and is now General Manager in charge of the firm's computer programming.

Jack Bannerman passed away on March 7, 1966, at the age of 75, but awards in his memory live on. A trophy in his name is presented to the Most Valuable Player in the annual Canadian junior football championship. A memorial prize is also presented through the Insurance Institute of Southern Alberta to the Most Deserving Independent Agent enrolled in its courses.

Bob Bannerman and his daughter, Ginny DiGirolamo, at one of the firm's computer terminals.

BOW CYCLE & MOTOR CO. LTD.

Bow Cycle & Motor Co. Ltd. was founded by Jim Sibthorpe on June 28, 1957. Twenty-five years later the business was one of the most successful in Canada but the owner still hadn't gotten around to owning a motorcycle of his own—he's been too busy working with them to try playing with them as well.

Sibthorpe has spent his entire life with cycles of one form or another. He started working with bicycles for CCM in Weston, Ontario, at the age of 16. After serving in World War II he was transferred by CCM to its Calgary warehouse as a sales trainee. In 1947 he joined Fred Deeley Ltd. of Vancouver as salesman in its Calgary bicycle division.

He struck out on his own 10 years later. It was a small beginning; the sales and service area totalled 600 square feet. In the first month of selling bicycles, sporting goods, and toys the total income was $793.65. After paying expenses and deducting $26.80 for advertising, it left him and his wife with wages of $20.

To keep things going in the early months, Sibthorpe worked at another job while his wife ran the store. He would return in the evening to do repairs and servicing. Bow Cycle started selling mopeds and scooters in 1958 and sales during the second year jumped to $38,017.55, but personal wages were a mere $691.40.

The business, incorporated in 1965, first started at 6531 Bowness Road N.W. but moved across the street when larger quarters were required. In 1981 the bicycle and sporting goods division moved back to the original site to permit expansion.

Sibthorpe is president of the company's two operations: Bow Cycle and Motor and Bow Sports. Jim Jr. joined the firm full time in 1967 at the age of 17. He grew up in the business—as a six-year-old he used to tag along to help out. He is now the sales manager, assistant general manager, and vice-president. Younger brother Brian is secretary-treasurer of the firm and manager of the

sporting goods store. He was 20 when he came into the family business in 1975.

Bow Cycle was the first Honda dealer in Calgary when it introduced that line in 1959. Honda now holds 40 percent of the Canadian market. In 1961 Bow Cycle became the first Suzuki dealer in Canada.

As a single-store operation, Bow Cycle is probably the largest motorcycle dealer in Canada. In 1981 it sold 1,400 motorcycles and now employs 40 people. The sales in 1981 were over four million dol-

---

A 1965 photograph of Bow Cycle & Motor Co. Ltd.

lars and the payroll was $370,000. The current sales and service area is 28,000 square feet including a storage warehouse for over 600 motorcycles.

The summer months remain the heavy demand months for Bow Cycle products and services but the annual downturn periods are being eased by expansion of product lines into such items as all-terrain vehicles and motorized pumps and generators.

Selling fun and leisure time products keeps Bow Cycle active in the community. The company supports many community activities including the regular sponsorship of two motocross racers.

James Sibthorpe (center) with sons Jim Jr. (right) and Brian.

BENNETT & WHITE WESTERN LTD.

Joseph Garnet Bennett arrived in New York City from England in 1902 looking for the rosy future he'd heard about. Later he headed west looking for the boom the newspapers were describing. He arrived in Calgary in 1910, only to find construction work was very seasonal. But he persevered and formed a partnership which grew to become a major force in Western Canadian construction. By 1981 the company was the 15th largest non-residential construction contractor in Canada, with over $107 million in annual contracts.

Born in England in 1882, Bennett was a marine engineer but shortly after his arrival in the United States he entered the construction business. He became involved in the cut stone business in the Philadelphia area, where sons J.G. (John) and A.G. (Gordon), who followed him into the business, were born.

Deciding he would rather bring up his family under the Union Jack, Bennett moved to Calgary where he helped solve the problem of shaping decorative stone work, including the turned balusters he made for the Legislature Building in Edmonton.

In 1912 Bennett formed a partnership with R.F. Debnam and entered the general contracting business. The pace of construction came to a virtual halt with the advent of World War I and the partners decided to go into farming.

However, in 1916 the Bennett family decided farming was not for them.

Back in Calgary he formed a partnership with a friend, William White, a carpenter who had come west with the construction of the CPR. The firm of Bennett & White, with Bennett as the administrator and White handling the field work, was formed. It had everything but cash. The firm's worth didn't warrant a $1,500 line of credit but it turned out Bennett's reputation did and the partnership was under way.

Their first work was for a farmer — and they slept in a hen house at night. Their next job was in rebuilding the business section of the town of Gleichen after a disastrous fire. In the early 1920s a theatre-building boom hit and Bennett

The Capitol Theatre in Calgary was a Bennett & White project circa 1921. (Photo courtesy Glenbow Archives, Calgary, Alberta.)

& White built the Capitol Theatre in 1921, which remained a Calgary landmark until it was demolished in 1972 to make way for the Bank of Nova Scotia Centre. The excellent quality of the work and the speed with which it was completed advanced the reputation of the company for future ventures.

The firm received another major boost in prestige when it constructed the Chemistry Building at the University of Saskatchewan — a mere six years after the inception of the partnership. It was on this project that sons John and Gordon did their first work for the company. It now became obvious that the venture had grown too large for a simple partnership and Bennett & White Construction Ltd. was formally incorporated on February 25, 1925.

Joseph Bennett was an enterprising man and constantly amazed people with his successes. If his company didn't have the expertise to undertake a specific project, he went out and found it; such was the case in the building of the Glenmore Dam and other major work of the era.

Joseph Bennett went on to become a founding member of the Canadian Con-

Bennett & White were the contractors for the Glenmore Dam project. (Photo courtesy of Glenbow Archives, Calgary, Alberta.)

struction Association, setting a precedent for participation by members of the firm in the affairs of the industry which has been maintained at a high level since his time.

Bennett & White was spared the onslaught of the Depression when it obtained a contract for the extension to the Hudson's Bay Company store. The city's decision to build the Glenmore Dam and the attendant water filtration plant was a major project for the early '30s. It was built over the objection of many citizens that the city would never grow to need such a facility. The firm was awarded the contract even though it wasn't the lowest bidder when Bennett convinced the city council that preference should be given to a local contractor.

In 1932, when Mr. White wanted to retire, the Bennett sons bought his shares and some 50 years later maintain an active interest in the company. During the early 1930s the firm scrambled for whatever work it could obtain. In 1934 it built the Calgary Prophetic Bible Institute, where William Aberhart conducted his early services.

In 1935, in the face of Social Credit construction policies, the firm sent John Bennett to Vancouver to expand operations. With the Campbell brothers, Colin and Bob, they founded Campbell-Bennett Ltd. in 1947. Its projects included many of the major highway projects in the province of British Columbia. It ceased operations in 1958 when the Campbells retired.

Over the years Bennett & White became involved in almost every kind of construction work imaginable. The Bennett brothers, after buying their father's share, have built roads, tunnels, dams, transmission lines, grain elevators, bridges, and railroads, as well as a myriad of other structures. Much of the diversity was inspired by survival instincts, the brothers confess.

During World War II Bennett & White had 8,000 employees. They were instrumental in constructing many of the facilities used by the Commonwealth Air Training Program for Allied Forces air crews. At this time the firm signed its first substantial management contract for the building of an ammonium nitrate plant in Calgary. During the 1950s company projects included the Cold Lake and Namao air bases, plants for such well known firms as Weston, Coca-Cola, Building Products Ltd., and many of the major educational and medical facilities throughout the western provinces.

After the firm's move into Vancouver, it continued to operate in Alberta under two separate branches: the Calgary operation under Ted Walden, and Edmonton under F.W. Forster. The Edmonton operation proved more prosperous and the two branches were merged as Bennett & White Alberta Ltd. with F.W. (Bill) Forster as presi-

High River General Hospital (right) and Midtown Plaza Shopping Centre, Saskatoon, Saskatchewan, are both latter-day projects of Bennett & White Western Ltd.

dent. He subsequently was joined by his two sons, F.W. Forster, Jr., and James E. Forster. These men continue their involvement and participation in the company in the tradition established by their father. In 1974 Bennett & White Western Ltd. was created.

President, general manager, and chairman of the board is E. Steacy Easton who joined Bennett & White in 1946 in Edmonton and held various field and office positions before being transferred to Calgary in 1957 as general superintendent.

In 1970 Mr. Easton was joined in Calgary by Clifford L. Caplette, who played a major role in the completion of Mid-Town Plaza in Saskatoon. Mr. Caplette carries the responsibility of senior vice-president of the company. The corporate headquarters has been located at 1822-10th Avenue S.W. Calgary since 1979, and continues to maintain offices in Edmonton and Saskatoon.

In the latter part of the 1960s the firm developed Mid-Town Plaza in Saskatoon, the first major city centre revitalization project in Western Canada, which brought Bennett & White and its architect a Vincent Massey Award for excellence in urban environmental design.

The company has recorded accelerated growth during the 1970s and early 1980s. Bennett & White's philosophy continues to rest on employee pride and client satisfaction. Success has shown that corporate strength can be measured by the amount of pride its employees take.

BOW VALLEY INDUSTRIES LTD.

The driving force during the past three decades behind Bow Valley Industries Ltd. was Daryl K. (Doc) Seaman, now chairman of the board, past president, and chief executive officer. He and his brothers, Byron (B.J.) and Donald (who were also graduate engineers from the University of Saskatchewan), formed the Seaman Engineering and Drilling Company in 1949. Eight years later the firm drilled wells on its own behalf, and thus entered the oil and gas business as a producer. In conjunction with an institutional investor in 1959 the brothers purchased control of Hi-Tower Drilling Company Ltd.—and three years later changed the name to Bow Valley.

Since then the organization's growth has been dramatic. By 1981 it had a book value of over one billion dollars and employed 2,800 persons in Canada, the United States, Abu Dhabi, Indonesia, the United Kingdom, and Norway. Its proved reserves that year included 72 million barrels of oil, 489 billion cubic feet of gas, 77 million tons of coal, and 6 million pounds of uranium. Listed on the Toronto, Montreal, and American stock exchanges (it was the second most active on the TSE in 1980), the corporation is 77-percent Canadian-owned. The Seaman brothers hold 16 percent of the shares.

In May 1982 Gerald J. Maier was appointed president and chief executive officer and was elected a director of the company. Mr. Maier was formerly the chairman of the board and chief executive officer of Hudson's Bay Oil and Gas Company Limited. He has over 30 years' petroleum experience in Canada and other countries.

Acquisitions that marked the growth of Bow Valley during the 1960s include Cardwell Supply, which provides oilfield equipment and supplies; Flame-Master, which manufactures furnaces in Edmonton; Connors Drilling, a Vancouver-based diamond-drilling contractor; Mainland Foundry and Engineering Ltd., a Vancouver-based

A seismic blast in 1951 exploration work in Alberta.

manufacturer of equipment for the forest-products and mining industries; and Western Research and Development, a firm involved in pollution control.

In 1971 Syracuse Oils Limited, with offshore oil and gas holdings, was acquired. In 1978 Flying Diamond Oil Corporation of Denver, a firm with oil, gas, and coal operations in the United States, came under the corporate umbrella. Apollo Drilling, a four-rig operation based in Denver, was added in 1980. In March of the following year, Bow Valley bought a 50-percent interest in White Motor Corporation of Canada Limited, a heavy-truck assembly plant in

---

Byron Seaman (left) on a seismic drilling operation with his brother, Donald, during work on an Alberta site in 1951.

Kelowna, British Columbia.

Bow Valley Exploration is the company's operating entity dealing with natural resource development. It has five main areas of oil and gas operations: Canada, the United States, the North Sea, Indonesia, and Abu Dhabi.

In Canada the firm is attempting to acquire acreage in more oil-prone areas because of improved oil prices and lowered royalties. Past activity of the company has been Alberta-based but future emphasis is being expanded to offshore sites in Eastern Canada and the Beaufort Sea. Because of its large Canadian ownership, Bow Valley is eligible for government grants in frontier exploration.

In the United States the company has been operating in Utah, North Dakota, Texas, Montana, Colorado, and the ppalachian states. One of the most ttractive acquisitions is a 60,000-acre hallow oil-gas program in West 'irginia.

Bow Valley's biggest asset is its 14-ercent interest in the Brae field in the Jnited Kingdom sector of the North ea. Its participation involves a virtual o-cost arrangement. In exchange for alf of its original 28-percent interest, it vill have all of its development costs in Brae covered. When the field starts to

produce in 1983, the organization will turn over 70 percent of its net proceeds to repay the advances. Production is expected at 112,000 barrels a day, rising to 200,000. While Bow Valley had a total cash flow in 1980 of $100 million, Brae alone is expected to generate about $80 million in 1984.

The Seaman brothers inspect their new offshore drilling rig. From left to right are Donald, Daryl K. (Doc.), and Byron (B.J.).

In the Norwegian sector of the North Sea, Bow Valley has an 8-percent interest in the Heimdal gas and conden-sate field which will go on-stream in 1986. In Abu Dhabi it has a 20-percent interest in a 1.9 million acre little-explored onshore area.

Kentucky is the location of Bow Valley's high-grade bituminous coal mines. With highly automated facilities and non-union employees, the company has contracts with two utilities com-panies running to 1995 and 2004. The 2.2 million tons shipped in 1981 repre-sented the 13th annual increase in mine production.

Bow Valley has a 20-percent interest in the Midwest Lake uranium deposit in northeastern Saskatchewan. Production is expected to start in 1990, once the lake has been drained to permit open-pit mining.

The drilling and manufacturing side of the company is handled by Bow Valley Resources Services Ltd., a 78-percent-owned subsidiary. The oil well-drilling group operates 16 deep rigs and 23 shallow rigs in Canada, making it the largest Canadian onshore drilling con-tractor. In 1981 it bought its first wholly owned semisubmersible oil well drilling rig for $135 million, and ordered two more at $150 million each. Delivery of these will make it the largest Canadian offshore drilling contractor as well. In addition, the company operates nine deep rigs in the United States.

The entrepreneurial skills and the philanthropic works of the Seaman brothers are also evident in civic life. Doc Seaman, a former hockey player with the Moose Jaw Canucks and a fighter-bomber pilot during World War II, emerged with brother B.J. as part owners when the National Hockey League Calgary Flames were incorpo-rated. They structured the operation in such a way that any profits from the Flames' operation would go back into amateur hockey.

Bow Valley's $135-million semisubmersible oil well drilling rig lies off Halifax Harbour prior to being moved to an offshore drilling site.

CALDRAFT (1977) LTD.

Calgary's downtown area owes a great deal to Caldraft, which traces its roots back 75 years to the first decade of the 20th century when it operated, in effect, as the city's drafting department. Floyd K. Beach, who later became chairman of the Alberta Oil and Gas Conservation Board, was one of four civil engineers who were original partners in the Calgary Drafting Company. One map of downtown, which they prepared, is dated November 10, 1909. The firm's offices were on Seventh Avenue.

The venture had a succession of owners in the early years. The Porter family owned it in the early 1930s until

Hugh A. Kerr (left) and Frank Black, holding a map of Calgary (dated 1909) drawn by Calgary Drafting Company.

The Caldraft facilities are located at 5537 One A Street S.W., Calgary.

it passed into the hands of Bern and Leslie Middleton. During this time it became known as Calgary Drafting and Blueprint Company because of the volume of blueprinting.

The modern history of the firm starts in 1951, when Frank Black arrived. A Calgary native, Black had graduated in electrical engineering in 1946. During six months with the CPR he worked on the first railway block signals between Calgary and Lake Louise. For five years he worked for Schlumberger but resigned because oil field work and travelling 50,000 miles annually was not compatible with raising a family.

During this time, Middleton had opened Northern Drafting in Edmonton and offered Black a position in Calgary. Even though his salary dropped by two-thirds, coming to Caldraft was attractive because it was engineering-oriented with the oil industry being the primary customer base. Black purchased a one-third interest in the firm and became its manager.

Caldraft discontinued blueprinting in 1972 and now concentrates on drafting and surveying equipment, ranging from tools to furniture. It also has a repair shop. The company is the city's exclusive distributor for Keuffel & Esser, the world's largest supplier of surveying and drafting equipment. Caldraft also pioneered the distribution of Letraset in Western Canada.

The firm moved to its current offices at 5537 One A Street S.W. in 1982 after 30 years at 615 Eighth Avenue S.W. Prior to that it was on the site of *The Calgary Herald*'s old mechanical building.

In 1977 the company was reorganized as Caldraft (1977) Ltd. An offshoot was created, ProGraphics (1977) Ltd., which concentrated on graphics and art supplies. The reorganization brought in new partners, with David Milne becoming president and general manager and Black becoming chairman. At the same time, J.P. Fournier became president and general manager of ProGraphics.

The corporation's early history had seen it provide a contract drafting service. A number of former draftsmen customers have since become noted artists, including Jim Nicoll, Gerald Tailfeathers, George Horvath, John Herreilers, and Bill Brownridge.

Caldraft is known for its longtime employees. Hugh Kerr has been the accountant for 40 years. Charles Howlett, who joined the firm at the age of 65, was well-known in downtown Calgary as the delivery man with the flower in his lapel and the Caldraft package under his arm for 22 years.

With 45 employees, Caldraft (1977) Ltd. is the largest drafting supplies operator in Calgary. ProGraphics has grown to a similar status in its area.

THE CALGARY CHAMBER OF COMMERCE

Since May 2, 1891, when the Calgary Board of Trade was incorporated, its membership has grown from a mere 45 members to over 4,000. The original certificate of association is dated August 1890. Alexander Lucas, a livery and horse dealer who was also the city's mayor, was the first president. Among the founding members were merchants, traders, bankers, brokers, mechanics, insurance agents, a hotel keeper, a gunmaker, and a chemist.

During the early years the board took an active interest in land settlement in the district—it even distributed maps of available land, freight and passenger rates, construction of government buildings, and the appointment of a police magistrate.

During World War I offices and club rooms for the Calgary Board were located in the basement of the old Lougheed Building. Earlier it had met in the Town Hall meeting hall and shared offices with the Exhibition Association.

Following the war the Board of Trade established itself as a liaison between the urban and rural communities. In 1921, when the United Farmers of Alberta swept the Liberal government from power, their leader was Herbert Greenfield, who later became president of the Calgary Board.

During the 1930s and 1940s the Chamber had a decided influence on government and community activities. It had taken steps to organize the Alberta Wheat Pool, to establish the Tourist and Convention Bureau, to organize the Calgary Community Chest, and to acquire the first airport for the city.

In 1949 the organization's name officially became The Calgary Chamber of Commerce. With the prosperity of the oil fields making the American influence visible, the change was made because confusion existed among U.S. oil men who were inclined to link the Board of Trade with a namesake in Great Britain which was actually a department of the government.

The Chamber had been established as a men's association, but in December 1953 bylaws were amended to admit

women. By 1982 there were over 100 female members. The Calgary Chamber is now one of 115 chambers in Alberta and 850 in Canada.

In October 1978 The Calgary Chamber purchased and began restoring the former Oddfellows Temple in downtown Calgary to establish a permanent meeting place and a physical presence in the heart of the business district. The four-storey building, constructed in 1912, was once considered a skyscraper and is now a heritage site.

The Calgary Chamber operates through a board of directors, an execu-

Major Alexander Lucas was the first president of the Calgary Board of Trade when it was established in 1891. The body has since become known as The Calgary Chamber of Commerce and has more than 4,000 members.

tive committee, and more than 20 volunteer committees. Through this structure The Calgary Chamber of Commerce acts as the primary voice of business in the community to maintain a strong and balanced economy, to preserve the free-enterprise atmosphere, and to promote the quality of community life.

CALGARY CO-OPERATIVE ASSOCIATION LIMITED

Gordon Barker and the Calgary Co-operative Association are inseparable in the minds of many people. He is the only chairman of the board of directors the organization has ever known, and is the only original member of the board still in office.

Barker, a farmer and UFA Co-op petroleum agent in the Chestermere area in the 1940s, has a passion for co-operatives the way others have for golf or fishing. Even when he finally got a salary of $1,000 a year in 1962 all his co-operative commitments often meant that his wife was the full-time farmer.

Under his leadership, by 1982 the Co-op was operating 11 shopping centres—each with a full-service auto centre, three home improvement centres, and a building prefabrication plant. It also owns Co-op Travel Ltd.

The Calgary Co-op traces its roots back to the United Farmers of Alberta (UFA), which branched into the grocery business in the 1940s. The UFA sold its retail stores to the Alberta Co-operative Wholesale Association, but it, too, was unsuccessful. The Calgary operations made money which was used to support other areas.

The first hint of an independent Calgary operation came during the 1954 ACWA annual meeting. By June a questionnaire had been sent to all 4,000 members. Of the 66 replies, 38 said they would support a Calgary Co-op.

The idea kept building, until by mid-1955 shares were on sale. In late 1956 the UFA gave the project a major boost by allowing its members to transfer their equity if they wished. The provisional board decided that it now had enough money to proceed. It bought the stock and fixtures of the ACWA store, at 11th Avenue and First Street S.E. The official opening was conducted by Mayor Don McKay on November 1, 1956.

The board of directors took a bold step in the first year by deciding to pay a patronage dividend every year—a step many believe was the turning point in the organization. The first year's dividend was 3 percent and has never dropped below that. In keeping with Co-op principles, dividends were paid on the amount of purchases, not the amount of share ownership. This rewarded active members.

In its first year, business was so good that the premises had to be expanded. In 1960 the Co-op started construction on store No. 2 on 16th Avenue N.E. After five years of operation, the Co-op boasted of $3.7 million in sales in two stores, a membership of 9,000, and 120 employees. The following year plans were laid for the construction of another centre, at Macleod Trail and 86th Avenue S.—the location of the Co-op' head office.

By 1982 Calgary Co-op was the larges retail consumer co-operative in North America. In its first 25 years of operation it has returned $55 million to its mem bers, of which $39 million has been ir cash. It serves 162,000 active member and had 1982 assets of $56 million. A total of 2,800 people were on the payrol at that time, an increase of 400 over the previous year.

The Co-op will continue to grow with Calgary and move into new areas as they are developed. It is also looking at the possibility of moving into satellite com munities around Calgary.

Calgary Co-Operative Association Limited is now the largest retail consumer co-operative in North America. Pictured are two of its Calgary centres.

CALGARY PUBLIC LIVESTOCK MARKET LTD.

Cattle and the railway were major reasons for the early growth of Calgary. They were also the thrust behind the incorporation of the Alberta Stockyards Company, which was registered in Regina, the territorial capital, on June 1, 1903. The firm holds the distinction of introducing livestock sales by auction to North America; much of what goes on in the markets today is the result of a distillation of procedures developed by The Yards.

Patrick Burns had seen the need for an independent yard to assemble cattle after spending years travelling and buying directly from ranchers. With his guidance, and that of a group of prominent livestock entrepreneurs including R.B. Bennett, F.W. Black, and Henry Pierce, The Yards—located on Canadian Pacific Railway land—became a place not only for trading but also for feeding and watering cattle destined for the East. In 1911 Burns, the company president, sold his majority to other shareholders.

The early years were financially shaky. In 1912 the firm handled 3,828 stock cars; the 1913 profit was $3,923.77. Charges for handling livestock in 1914 ranged from two to five cents a head for all species, and loading a stock car cost 75 cents.

The Depression hit The Yards hard, but the recovery brought on by World War II presented another problem—a manpower shortage. The company improvised by hiring Indians from area reserves, who set up a teepee village while they helped out.

The interest in auction selling was first advanced by I.V. Parslow in 1929. However, the method lacked support until 1950, when Tom Farrell of Burns Ranches began experimenting with it. The idea impressed George Winkelaar, head of a commission firm, who in turn sold the idea to The Yards.

Over the years the firm has handled up to 300,000 head annually with no fewer than 100,000 in any year. Sheep and hogs were a prominent part of the market until sheep were phased out during the 1960s, and hogs moved into a marketing board in the 1970s. The importance of The Yards is further demonstrated by the fact that every CPR president has served on its board of directors.

A dominant figure in the organization for almost 40 years, until his retirement in 1978, was Charlie Kennedy, who guided its destiny through its most significant years. He was also a president of the Calgary Stampede Board and the Calgary and Alberta chambers of commerce, and a driving force behind the 4-H movement.

The Calgary Public Livestock Market Ltd., responding to the need for change in the marketplace, came into existence in October 1981 and leased The Yards from the Canadian Pacific Group. A one-sales-agency concept owned by seven commission and order-buying agent principals, it is carrying on the best market traditions under the presidency of Leonard Friesen.

This aerial view shows The Yards as they were in the late 1940s. The administration building in the lower centre has been replaced by a new structure in the triangular area immediately adjacent. The large structure in the centre of the photo is the Burns packing plant.

CALGARY EXHIBITION AND STAMPEDE

The "Greatest Outdoor Show on Earth" started almost a century ago, in response to demands for an agricultural fair to showcase the area's production. The inaugural fair was held on October 19, 1886, after plans to hold it earlier were stalled by the Riel Rebellion. Prize money of $900 and a crowd of 500 prompted organizers to make the fair an annual event.

Ninety-four acres of land (which would eventually become Stampede Park) were purchased in 1889. However, despite the popular acclaim, the fair was not a financial success. Directors occasionally had to dig into their own pockets, and the city council provided intermittent grants. The ground became city property when the city paid the fair's $7,000 deficit in 1900.

The Calgary Agricultural Society, which had run the previous fairs, was reorganized as a no-dividend, joint-stock company—the Inter-Western Pacific Exposition Company Limited. It enjoyed modest prosperity and even hosted the Dominion Exhibition in 1908. Two years later its name was changed to the Calgary Industrial Exhibition Company Ltd.

The cover of the program of the inaugural Stampede displayed the financial backers of the event: Patrick Burns, George Lane, A.E. Cross, and A.J. McLean.

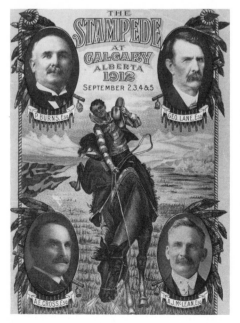

Stampede creator Guy Weadick stands with fire chief Cappy Smart surrounded by Indians in ceremonial dress during an early Stampede.

In 1912 Guy Weadick, a young American cowboy, arrived in Calgary on his second visit with an idea that was to put Calgary on the world's map. A trick roper by profession, Weadick thought that Calgary was the ideal staging point for his "Stampede," a wild-west show extravaganza that would outshine any other. He sold the Calgary Industrial Exhibition on the idea, but frightened off its members with the anticipated $100,000 bankroll. Eventually a meeting was arranged with four prominent Calgarians: rancher George Lane, rancher-meat packer Patrick Burns, rancher-brewer A.E. Cross, and rancher-politician A.J. McLean. These men (later to be known as "the Big Four") agreed to back the project.

The first Stampede in September 1912 was everything Weadick had promised. Press reports say 75,000 people lined the streets to cheer the two-hour kick-off parade. A crowd of over 14,000 attended opening performances.

Despite being a popular success, the event barely recouped its expenses, and Weadick left to work on other shows. World War I interrupted his plans, but with the signing of the Armistice, Weadick reemerged with dreams of a "Victory Stampede."

He went back to the Big Four. His former backers were interested but on the following terms: if 30 other Calgarians could be found to gamble $1,000 each, they would match that $30,000. With little difficulty the funds were raised and the second show proved a tremendous success. The modest profit was divided between the Great War Veterans' Association and the Young Men's Christian Association.

Meanwhile, the annual Calgary Exhibition was not faring well financially. Weadick was elated when, in 1922 he was asked to include the Stampede as a one-year trial attraction with the exhibition. He looked for a new, eye-catching addition—and decided on chuckwagon racing. The Calgary Exhibition and Stampede combination was such a success that the events were permanently united. In 1952 Weadick was the Stampede's special honoured guest and presented the championship trophies—40 years after the first Stampede. He died the following year and was buried in the foothills he had come to love.

In Canada's centennial year, 1967, the Stampede expanded to nine days from six, and the following year yet another day was added. The year 1978 brought a major change in the rodeo format when individual competition gave way to team events. In 1981 the Stampede presented both traditional and team rodeo and 1982 saw cowboys competing for a $.5-million purse in individual events. The prize monies

Indians were a featured part of the 1908 Dominion Exhibition parade and remain a prominent part of Stampede parades today.

offered for the rodeo and chuckwagon events combined have long been the highest in the world.

The success of the Stampede can be attributed to the fact that it is community-based, completely self-supporting, and operates on a nonprofit basis. Although it has a permanent staff of 200, a volunteer structure of committees involves more than 1,200 southern Albertans on a year-round basis.

It adds a definite flavor to the city, and has contributed no small part in Calgary's evolution. Stampede advertising went throughout North America in the '30s and '40s. According to historians, in the late '40s (when the oil boom arrived in Alberta) many oil companies decided to locate in Calgary because they had heard of it through the event's advertising.

Stampede buildings have also turned the park into a year-round playground: a grandstand erected for the 1919 Victory Stampede, with additions in 1924, 1948, and 1959, was replaced by a new $12.5-million structure and race track in 1974; the Agricultural Pavilion was constructed in 1956 to meet growing Agricultural demands; the Stampede Corral was built in 1950 to meet the sporting needs of a booming community; the Big Four Building, completed in 1959 for $1.8 million, is the world's largest indoor curling rink during the winter months; Rotary House, a log hall built in 1979, is a vital tribute to Calgary's history; and in 1981 the Roundup Centre, built for $14.5 million, was opened as an agricultural and trade centre.

The Stampede remains a rarity in annual events in its ability to attract spectators (approximately one million) from all continents. In past years royalty, prime ministers, world leaders, governors-general, and Hollywood stars have all viewed the Stampede and nearly every Canadian prime minister has attended since its beginning.

Wagons round the first turn of the 1956 version of the Rangeland Derby with half a mile to go.

CANADA CEMENT LAFARGE LTD.

It wasn't long after the manufacture of Portland cement in Canada was started in the 1890s that Calgary was receiving a locally manufactured product. Three-quarters of a century later this source was the largest cement plant in Canada.

The Western Canada Cement and Coal Company had acquired rights to property in the Rocky Mountain Park, 60 miles west of Calgary, in 1905. A cement plant was built in 1907 and the town which grew up became known as Exshaw, after Lord Exshaw who had an interest in the company. But markets were saturated with cement and manufacturing stopped in 1910.

By that time it had become obvious that the entire cement industry was in trouble in Canada. It was largely felt that only amalgamation would save the companies still operating. To this end, with Max Aitken—later Lord Beaverbrook—as principal organizer, 10 plants were brought together to form the Canada Cement Company Limited. In 1911 Canada Cement purchased the Exshaw operation. The president of Western Canada Cement at the time was Sir Sanford Fleming of Ottawa, the developer of standard time zones throughout the world. As soon as Canada Cement purchased the Exshaw plant, it installed new machinery and increased the output of the mill to 8,000 bags daily.

In 1914 fire destroyed one of the stockhouses but replacement began almost immediately. Tragedy struck again later that year when three men staged a daring $2,300 payroll robbery and shot and killed paymaster Jack Wilson and wounded assistant Jim Gordon. Police rushed from Calgary in a Model T with track wheels. Indians joined the manhunt and *The Calgary Herald* reported they were "in war paint." Following an all-out manhunt, one robber was caught at Exshaw, one at Morley, and the third was forced out of a Calgary basement when the fire department flooded his hideout. Two of the men were later hanged; the third was sentenced to life imprisonment.

The Exshaw plant is unique among the company's other operations because it involves levelling a mountain rather than digging into the bowels of the earth for limestone. In the early days of the plant, men loaded rock by hand into mine cars. In 1920 a small steam shovel with a stationary boiler was put into operation. The kilns were fired by coal but the plant itself was operated by electric motors with the current being supplied from a steam power plant. In 1913 the steam plant was closed down when electric power became available from the Calgary Power Company's newly finished Horsehoe Falls hydroelectric plant.

World War I brought a sharp decline in demand for cement. By 1918 the country was using only 25 percent of manufacturing capacity. The Depression again stalled the industry's recovery. Not until World War II ended did the total volume approach the 1929 total of 2.15 million tons.

On May 1, 1970, the Canada Cement Company became associated with Lafarge Canada Ltd., thus forming a new venture called Canada Cement Lafarge Ltd. Today Lafarge S.A. of France owns 54 percent of the company's stock.

However, expansions remained a regular part of the Exshaw plant's history. After numerous other expansions, *The Calgary Herald* announced in 1950 the $5-million expansion by explaining: "New outlets for the increased production will be concrete highway bridges, pipe, and blocks. The Alberta government has already started using precast concrete bridges and it is anticipated that 8,000 old-style highway bridges will be replaced in the next 10 years." In that expansion the first dust precipitator in Canada was also installed.

The name "Lafarge" has been intimately linked with the construction

materials industry since 1830, when the Pavin de Lafarge family began to develop a limestone deposit at Viviers on the Rhone River and to produce a Portland cement of the highest quality. During the 19th century, Ciments Lafarge S.A. established itself as one of the principal cement companies in Europe. With the construction of a plant in Richmond, British Columbia, in 1956, the Lafarge group began operations in Canada under the name of Lafarge Cement of North America Ltd.

With the creation of Canada Cement Lafarge, the operations were reorganized and decentralized into five regions. The western region is the largest—stretching from Thunder Bay, Ontario, to the East Kootenays in British Columbia—and also the most profitable. In 1982 it accounted for 34 percent of the sales of the company and 31 percent of the earnings. Regional headquarters is in Calgary with 35 people in the office and another six in sales. Another 17 work in the Calgary terminal, which handles distribution and bagging.

The region has three cement plants besides Exshaw: Winnipeg, Edmonton, and Saskatoon. The latter two are not full cement plants since they merely grind the clinker brought in from Exshaw and Fort Whyte. Vice-president and general manager of the region is J.R. (Dick) Maze, a Calgary-born professional engineer. He started with the firm in 1961 as a sales engineer and worked in various capacities across the country before returning to Calgary in 1980.

Canada Cement Lafarge has a major investment in concrete and construction companies, the largest being Conmac Western Industries in Calgary, a wholly owned subsidiary—formerly Galleli—acquired in 1973. Conmac employs up to 1,000 workers during the summer and operates three ready-mix concrete plants as well as a construction operation for curb, gutter, and sidewalk work.

Recent expansions have made the Exshaw plant the largest in Canada, capable of producing 1.325 million metric tons a year. The 1974 expansion cost $30 million and the 1981 expansion cost $100 million. There are now 155 hourly and 55 salaried employees at the highly computerized plant. The 1974 expansion converted the plant to a dry process which uses far less energy—the major cost of a cement operation.

In 1981 Canada Cement Lafarge acquired Supercrete Incorporated, which employs about 500 people in manufacturing precast and prestressed concrete elements and concrete pipe. That same year Canada Cement Lafarge became the largest cement company in North America by acquiring 97 percent of the shares of General Portland Industries in the United States. The worldwide Lafarge cement operation now ranks as the second largest in the world.

The future seems assured for cement products. In office structures, concrete has acquired the major market share from structural steel and new techniques in road building have made concrete popular—accelerated by the escalating cost of asphalt.

Despite the major changes in the industry, safety has always been a matter of concern and pride for the organization. On July 12, 1939, *The Calgary Herald* noted that only one plant in North America had a better safety record than the Exshaw plant of Canada Cement Lafarge Ltd. "They used to call them 'cement rats'—men who blasted their way into the earth for cement rock. Their chances of being killed were enough to warrant the name. Today they work in safety."

The 1981 expansion of the Canada Cement Lafarge plant at Exshaw made it one of the largest cement plants in Canada, with a capacity of over 1.3 million metric tons a year. In the background is the mountain that provides the raw material.

CANADA SAFEWAY LIMITED

Canada Safeway Limited was a pioneer in the grocery business about the same time Western Canada was extending its own roots. It pioneered the cash-and-carry selling method in many communities, thus eliminating the expensive overhead associated with credit operations then prevalent. Canada Safeway also inititated the use of copper coins in food stores; previously all transactions had been rounded off to the nearest five cents. Later the company introduced open dating to ensure product freshness and unit pricing so shoppers could easily compare prices.

Today Canada Safeway, managed and run by Canadians, operates from Ontario west. It has more supermarkets than any other chain in the country—290—and is employer to more than 3,000 Calgarians.

Canada Safeway Limited was incorporated as Safeway Stores, Limited, on January 14, 1929, in Winnipeg. It received its current name in 1947. Its dominion charter allowed it to "buy, sell, (and) manufacture ... at wholesale and at retail, groceries, meats, fruits (and) vegetables. ..." By December 31, 1929, Safeway operated 127 stores in Canada, with 16 in Alberta. Most of these stores represented acquisitions of existing businesses.

S.J. Pickens, writing in Safeway's house organ *Uno Animo* in May 1929

The first Calgary store.

under the heading "Safeway Goes International," noted: "some of us are inclined to think of Canada as a frigid, barren waste. ... As a matter of fact, climatically the country is not at all disagreeable and far from being barren. It is unquestionably the next big development on the American continent. ... I believe Safeway is indeed fortunate to enter the fields at this particular time. ..."

Canada presented a challenge to Safeway. As L.W. Raley, manager of the Canadian division, wrote in 1932: "The Prairies have the two extremes of climate, cold weather and length of winters predominating. ... In the country ... roads are closed to automobiles in some sections for three months or more in winter on account of snow, and another two months in spring and summer from mud due to thaw and rain, during which time business is spasmodic. ..."

Safeway grew out of a chain founded in 1915 by Marion Barton Skaggs in American Falls, Idaho. He bought his first store from his father, a Baptist minister, and by 1926 his chain numbered 250. Meanwhile, on March 24, 1926, a Maryland corporation was organized under the name Safeway Stores, Incorporated. The name "Safeway" stemmed from a contest held in 1925 by the Sam Seelig Company, a California corporation organized in 1914. On July 1, 1926, the stores of the Skaggs company merged with the Safeway stores with Skaggs as president.

Calgary got its first Safeway store in 1930. Walter J. Kraft opened the first locations and went on to become chairman of the board. The first Calgary store was located at Eighth Avenue and Second Street S.E. In 1936 Safeway acquired Piggly Wiggly (Canadian) Limited, which had nine stores in Calgary. By 1936 the firm operated 258 stores in Canada, a peak that would not be surpassed until 1969.

By 1954 there were 25 Safeway stores in Alberta; a separate Alberta division

An early store's check-out counter.

was created three years later. The following year Canada Safeway had sales of $208 million and the rate of growth was faster than that of the parent company.

To ensure quality control, the firm either purchased or established supply subsidiaries. Polly Ann Bakeries, Ltd., was organized as a subsidiary in 1938. The next year Empress Manufacturing Company Limited began operating as a subsidiary in providing jams, jellies, spices, and related products. In 1947 Macdonalds Consolidated Limited, a wholesale grocery business, became part of the organization.

Today the corporation operates bakeries in Vancouver, Calgary, and Winnipeg; fluid-milk plants in Edmonton, Oakville, and Winnipeg; and egg-candling plants in Vancouver, Calgary, and Winnipeg. Through subsidiaries Safeway also operates a coffee-roasting and tea-packing plant. Through Lucern, the firm employs 200 persons in a box beef plant in Calgary, which breaks down carcass beef for final store cutting in three provinces.

Although the city of registry remains

Winnipeg, and executives are distributed throughout the system, the corporate headquarters is now Calgary. The Calgary division operates 35 stores within the city limits and another 11 in southern Alberta and Cranbrook, British Columbia.

Safeway is active in other countries as well. By 1981 Safeway's non-Canadian operations included 1,947 stores in the

Tony Anselmo, president and chief executive officer of Canada Safeway Limited.

United States, 89 in England and Scotland, 25 in West Germany, and 72 in Australia. Sales at the end of 1981 in Canada totalled $3 billion. The company at that time had more than 24,500 employees.

With an ongoing commitment to one-stop shopping, Canada Safeway has gradually increased store sizes. Those opened in 1980 averaged 38,850 square feet compared to 28,560 square feet five years earlier. The added space has allowed the firm to add specialty departments, such as photo, gift, and natural foods centres. In 1981 the company introduced a "no-frills," warehouse-type store in Calgary under the name Food Barn. It was the first discount store to also sell fresh meat and produce.

Safeway has traditionally promoted from within. It has many longtime employees who, in turn, have also been active in community service. Tony Anselmo, the son of an Italian hard-rock miner, is an example. In 1938, after graduating from high school in Vancouver, he went job hunting and dropped by Safeway. He was put to work stocking shelves, ringing up sales, and sweeping floors.

Safeway gave its employees leaves of absence during the war years and Anselmo returned from duty with the RCAF to take his first management job in 1946. Ten years later he took his first step into senior management as district manager in Victoria. In 1965 he moved to Calgary as Prairie Division manager and became a director. Anselmo was made president in 1971 and became managing director of Canadian operations seven years later. Since 1979 he has held the dual positions of president and chief executive officer.

Very active in community service, Anselmo has strong sporting links, primarily in football, where he served as president of the Calgary Stampeders. He is also an honorary chief of the Blood Indian Band, a reward for helping establish a modern grocery store on the reserve. The example he set has been characteristic of Safeway corporate citizenship.

Today's modern produce section in Canada Safeway.

CANADIAN PACIFIC

Calgary is one of the busiest centres in Canadian Pacific Limited's transportation network, with major activity by CP Rail, CP Air, CP Trucks, telecommunications, and CP Ships container services. As well, it is the headquarters of Canadian Pacific Enterprises Limited, which conducts a diversified international business through subsidiary companies involved in oil and gas, mines and minerals, forest products, iron and

had already been selected. In a letter that has been called Calgary's "birth certificate," CPR's Winnipeg superintendent John Egan wrote to then-general manager William Van Horne: "At Calgary on Section 15, there is a very good location for a town site. No squatters are on this section, as the mounted police have kept them off."

The squatters and speculators encamped on the east bank of the Elbow

town site the following winter.

In the beginning, Calgary was not even a division point on the railway — Gleichen and Canmore were. But it wasn't long before its growing importance was felt. Completion of the Calgary and Edmonton Railway in 1891 and its extension to Fort Macleod the following year made Calgary the area's rail centre. An agreement to locate switching yards east of the new sandstone station was reached in 1898 and the Alberta Stockyards were developed in southeast Calgary in 1903.

Calgary became the administrative centre for the CPR's extensive irrigation projects in southern Alberta in 1904 and, because of this, the railway's colonization branch and land sales administration were moved from Winnipeg in 1910. The department of natural resources, at the time primarily concerned with the CPR coal mines near Banff, at Lethbridge, and in the Kootenays, was organized in Calgary in 1912 — just before the first Turner Valley oil strike in 1914. It was only in the previous few years that Canadian Pacific, following the provincial government's precedent, reserved mineral rights on land it sold.

The westbound Canadian Pacific Railway passenger train No. 11, with locomotive 147, pauses at Calgary station in 1884, shortly after regular service was inaugurated.

River awaiting the railway's arrival could only watch as the first train chugged on to Section 15 and dropped off a boxcar to serve as Calgary's first station. But, wanting to be part of the town, many of them soon followed, skidding frame buildings across the ice to lots in the new

steel, real estate, agriproducts, and other businesses.

Enterprises companies include Pan-Canadian Petroleum Limited, Cominco Ltd., Fording Coal Limited, Great Lakes Forest Products Limited, CIP Inc. (formerly Canadian International Paper), The Algoma Steel Corporation Limited, AMCA International Limited (formerly Dominion Bridge), Marathon Realty Company Limited, Maple Leaf Mills Limited, and Canadian Pacific Hotels Limited.

Moving CP Enterprises' head office to Calgary from Montreal in 1982 not only added considerably to Calgary's stature as a financial centre, but also demonstrated Canadian Pacific's continuing involvement in Western Canada.

When the railway builders reached Calgary in mid-August 1883, a town site

The Alyth marshalling yards when completed in 1969 were the most modern computerized railway yards in North America.

This pre-1929 photograph shows the CPR's Calgary station with the Palliser Hotel, which has had four floors added since, in the background. The station has since made way for the Calgary Tower and Palliser Square.

The years 1912-1914 saw the eight-story Palliser Hotel rise next to an imposing new station, soon surrounded by showcase gardens. At the same time, at Alyth, south of Inglewood, a larger switching yard was built, and still farther south, Ogden Shops took shape—12 buildings on a 213-acre site, with a work force of 1,200—Calgary's first major industrial complex and still one of its largest.

After World War I, Canadian Pacific and the newly organized CNR raced to build branch lines, mainly to handle prairie grain. The CPR added 2,200 miles of track to its system and in 1928, its peak year, carried 370 million bushels of grain to port, a good deal of it through Calgary. The Depression, however, hit hard and in 1937 the traffic was down to 94 million bushels.

Just before the Depression set in the Palliser expanded, adding four floors and a penthouse. In the spring of 1939, when the king and queen visited Canada, they came through Calgary aboard a special

CPR train. They crossed the Atlantic both ways on CP Empress-class ocean liners.

Ogden Shops turned to the production of naval guns and mountings in 1941, producing 3,000 guns and 1,650 mountings by war's end. That same year, Cominco, the British Columbia-based mining and refining firm partly owned by Canadian Pacific since 1898, built a munitions plant for the federal government at the corner of Heritage Drive and Sixth Street S.E. In 1946 it bought back the plant, which remains its Calgary fertilizer operations facility.

Though CP Air was formed in 1942 and ran a service depot for the Air Force at Calgary's Lincoln Park in the early 1950s, it was not until a stop was initiated on the Vancouver-Amsterdam polar flights in the mid-1950s that passengers began boarding in Calgary.

In the postwar years CP Rail converted the motive power on its entire system from steam to diesel. In 1962 CP Investments, now Enterprises, was formed to further Canadian Pacific's diversification in non-transportation fields. Its assets have grown to more than $11 billion. Its activities have spread from Little Cornwallis Island in the Arctic where Cominco has the most

northerly base-metals mine in the world (900 miles from the North Pole), to hotels in Europe and the United States, to smelters in India and Japan, and a mine in Tasmania.

In the late 1960s a computerized "hump" classification yard was built at Alyth, the most modern in North America when it went into service in 1969. In the same period, Palliser Square and the Calgary Tower, perhaps the city's most recognizable landmark, replaced the old station.

When the new Calgary International Airport was built, CP Hotels designed Chateau Airport as an integral part of the structure. It opened on September 18, 1979. Downtown, the Palliser was refurbishing all its rooms and making plans to restore its lobby and public rooms to the elegance of an earlier era.

Across Ninth Avenue, PanCanadian Petroleum occupied its new head office building, PanCanadian Plaza, just about the same time that the CP Enterprises head office staff moved to the city. The Canadian Pacific-Calgary growth partnership promises to continue with a confidence in the future, based on experiences of the past.

This 1982 photo shows the same area, with the Palliser Hotel the only building still in place. It is flanked on the right by the PanCanadian Plaza and on the left by the Calgary Tower and One Palliser Square.

CANADIAN SUPERIOR OIL LTD.

The name "Superior Oil" first arrived on the Canadian scene in 1939, when the U.S. Corporation began geological investigation in Alberta. Four years later Rio Bravo Oil Company Ltd. was created as a Canadian venture with exploration operations headed by N.W. Nichols and A.E. Feldmeyer. That year the two had obtained Mercury automobiles and house trailers and headed north from the United States to look over exploration prospects. However, these prospects didn't materialize and the firm was ready to pull out of Canada by 1946. Feldmeyer had already left and Nichols asked to stay until his second child was born. As it happened, Imperial's Leduc No. 1 came in before the baby and the transfer was forgotten.

Feldmeyer and Nichols were the catalysts that propelled the company into the big leagues. Feldmeyer was conservative and meticulous; Nichols was imaginative and charismatic. Together they mapped out Rio Bravo's future. Nichols left the firm in 1950 eventually

The Wembley Ferry was used by the Rio Bravo pack train to cross the Wapiti River during the summer of 1945.

Andy Janisch came to Canadian Superior as president and chief operating officer in 1982.

Arne R. Nielsen served as president of Canadian Superior from 1977 to 1982. That year he became chairman of the board and remained chief executive officer.

to become president of Great Plains Petroleum. Feldmeyer returned to Canada that year and became president five years later, a position he held for 22 years.

The company's early thrust was in land acquisition because it didn't have the money for an active drilling program. With a good geology staff, it mapped much of Western Canada and went after freehold leases and Crown Land. It ended up with a huge supply of such land and then instituted a farm-out system of drilling so it could spend its exploration capital more effectively. In 1949 the firm drilled its first exploratory well 115 miles northeast of Calgary. This aggressive approach to exploration has given the organization a unique land position which has propelled it to its current status.

The name was changed to Canadian Superior Oil of California Ltd. in 1950 after public interest in the company was invited for the first time with the sale of more than two million shares. This was the first full year of drilling operations, with eight wells completed including the first successful well in the Excelsior field outside of Edmonton. It was also the first year that crude oil production was attained—a net of 19,249 barrels.

Employee ranks swelled from only three in 1943 to 160 by 1950, up from 58 the previous year. The next year's production more than tripled.

The firm began its policy of entering farm-out agreements in 1952, thus providing it with more geological data and greatly increasing its production and reserve potential. Year-end production totalled 171,736 barrels, an increase of 80 percent from the previous year. Of the 18 wells completed, 11 were productive. By 1954 it was producing four million barrels a year.

A year earlier the company inactivated its drilling rig as an economy measure, deciding to contract out all future drilling. In 1955 Canadian Superior became active in the Canadian North. In view of the expanding Canadian gas market, the firm, in association with other operators, invested in gas-processing plants for the first time in 1959.

In 1961 the organization underwent its last name change and became Canadian Superior Oil Ltd. The following year it began an acquisition and expansion program which considerably expanded its territorial and operational horizons. By 1965 the firm had acquired all the shares of the Calgary and Edmonton Corporation, which brought in a substantial amount of fee land. Australian and United Kingdom subsidiaries were formed. The company's shares were listed on the Toronto, American, and Pacific Coast stock exchanges for the first time.

In 1964 Canadian Superior Exploration Limited was formed as a mineral exploration vehicle. The company had entered the gas condensate field during this period and in 1965 became involved in its first sulphur plant. In its first year of operation the Harmattan Leduc Unit No. 1 produced 99,000 long tons of sulphur. Sixty percent of the firm's sulphur sales were destined for foreign markets.

Canadian Superior maintains a fleet of rail cars. In 1968 it had 100 sulphur cars and 71 liquefied petroleum gas cars, which travelled 2.25 million miles

delivering products to foreign and domestic markets. The firm further diversified its interests in 1967 by making a significant investment in McIntyre Mines Limited and its subsidiary, Falconbridge Nickel Mines Limited, companies which were active in hard-rock mineral and coal mining.

The 1970s accelerated the gas-processing plant development program and pointed the way to further growth in the 1980s. Offshore interest also intensified during that decade. North Sea interests had been producing revenues since the first discovery in 1966. In addition, the company had acquired almost 2.5 million net acres in the Arctic Archipelago and the Beaufort Sea-Mackenzie Delta areas in 1968 in the

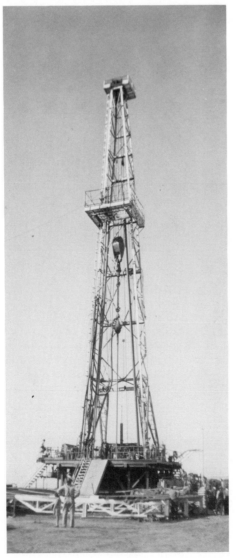

This oil rig drilled Rio Bravo's first exploratory well in 1949.

wake of intensified exploration activities induced by the Prudhoe Bay discoveries.

Canadian Superior's corporate offices were moved from the Brittania Building in 1970 to the newly constructed Three Calgary Place. In 1949 its 700-square-foot office on the third floor of the Canada Life Building housed the entire executive, exploration, and accounting staff.

In 1980 Canadian Superior again became a wholly owned subsidiary of the Superior Oil Company through a share acquisition program. However, although the firm now has only one shareholder, it has genuine autonomy from its parent with its own management and a majority of its board of directors being Canadian citizens.

Arne R. Nielsen, an Alberta-born geologist with a master's degree, became president and chief executive officer of Canadian Superior in 1977 after serving 10 years as the first Canadian president of Mobil Oil Canada. He became chairman of the board and chief executive officer in 1982 when Austrian-born Andy Janisch became president and chief operating officer. A civil engineer, Janisch had been president of PetroCanada and earlier had spent 24 years with Gulf Canada.

Canadian Superior's success story is continuing. Gas production now provides 41 percent of its operating revenues. During 1981 it participated in the drilling of 336 wells. Employing more than 650 people, its revenues that year were $374 million. Its reserves are substantial: 181 million barrels of oil and natural gas liquids, 3.6 trillion cubic feet of natural gas, and 9.8 million long tons of sulphur.

It's no wonder the company is smiling about its future prospects. As Janisch put it: "This is an organization that anyone would be proud to be part of."

CANADIAN WESTERN NATURAL GAS COMPANY LIMITED

Old Glory blew in on a February day in 1909 and proved to be the fuse that ignited the oil and gas industry in Alberta. The Bow Island natural gas discovery well flowed at 8.5 million cubic feet a day—the biggest well in Western Canada up to that time. The success of this well led to the drilling of six more, which convinced engineer Eugene Coste that there was a field large enough to supply natural gas to most of southern Alberta.

Thus began an ambitious project which culminated in the creation of Canadian Western Natural Gas Company Limited. On the basis of these few wells a company was organized, money raised, materials ordered, and a 170-mile pipeline built—all within 13 months. The 16-inch pipeline, itself one of the longest in North America up to that time, was built in only 86 days.

Coste has been called the father of the natural gas industry in Canada for being the first to bring in commercial discoveries in Ontario in 1889 and then in Alberta. He brought in the Bow Island well while on assignment from the Canadian Pacific Railway.

After the discovery, Coste obtained a lease on the field from the CPR and headed off to England to raise money for what he called the "Prairie Natural Gas Company." However, the English found the word "prairie" too foreign and the commodity "natural gas" too mysterious to put any money into the project. Undeterred, Coste changed the name to a more descriptive "Canadian Western Natural Gas, Light, Heat and Power Company Limited" and returned overseas to find no difficulty in raising the required funds.

On July 19, 1911, Canadian Western was officially incorporated, and on August 11, the two existing Calgary gas franchises were assigned to the company. Up to that time, two gas companies had been operating in Calgary. The Calgary Gas Company had an artificial gas plant with some 30 miles of mains and 2,250 customers. The Calgary Natural Gas Company had a small supply from a shallow well in east Calgary and supplied

Top
Four-horse teams were used to haul the 16-inch pipe used in the construction of the Bow Island to Calgary pipeline.

Above
The drilling crew that brought in Bow Island Number 1 in February 1909 poses with Eugene Coste, founder of the company. At left is W.R. "Frosty" Martin and H. Gloyd. At right are Garrett W. Green, who later became general superintendent of Northwestern Utilities, and A.P. "Tiny" Phillips.

gas for street lighting and to 50 customers.

As dusk fell on Calgary on July 17, 1912, some 12,000 Calgarians lined Scotsman's Hill to watch the ignition of the inaugural flare. The *Morning Albertan*, in an editorial on July 19 noted: "If all or even a good measure of what has been promised by the promoters of the enterprise is realized, history may be expected to recite that the industrial development of Calgary dated from the day gas became available in the city."

Service to Calgarians began July 24.

Coste was the first president of Canadian Western. He remained president until 1921 and died in 1940. In his second year as president he built his splendid residence in Mount Royal, which remains a landmark.

Natural gas service to southern Alberta communities expanded quickly. By

Bicycles were pressed into service by Canadian Western's customer service personnel during World War II, when gasoline rationing was in effect. From left to right are "Kit" Fawcett, Ivor Granger, Joe Leslie, Chuck Ross, Oscar Doten, Wally Brailey, and Mar Walters.

Today's Canadian Western serviceman prides himself on the company's motto: "A tradition of service and safety."

the end of 1917 Canadian Western was serving 9,605 customers. Demand for natural gas grew so fast that it soon became apparent that new sources would have to be found. The company's annual report for 1920 noted that its 12,000 domestic customers were taxing reserves and that expansion depended on finding more gas. Between the years 1921 and 1928, three transmission lines were constructed from the Turner Valley Field to the company's 16-inch main line. With these increased supplies, the company was again able to sell to apartment blocks and industrial concerns. The Foremost Field was developed in 1924.

In 1930 Bow Island, the original field, was converted to a storage reservoir to serve as a reserve for peak load requirements in the winter. Jumping Pound Field west of Calgary was connected as a major source of supply in 1951. In 1958 the company acquired reserves in the Carbon Field. The same year gas was purchased from Alberta Gas Trunk Line Company—now NOVA—for the first time. Today gas is purchased from more than 150 different producers.

By 1936 revenue from gas sales was almost $2.3 million. Three years later Canadian Western gained a major concession when, in return for a rate reduction, a city bylaw for the first time gave the company formal use of city streets and lanes for gas distribution.

When the corporation celebrated its 50th anniversary in 1962, it was serving 81 communities and had reached the 100,000 customer plateau. In 1977 it installed its 200,000th meter and by 1982 was providing service in 112 communities and to more than 270,000 customers in a population area of more than 800,000.

As growth continued, Canadian Western became more involved in innovations. Plastic pipe was introduced for the first time in 1964 in rural districts. Two years later the company pioneered the technique of "plowing in" plastic pipe. The Clean Air Fleet was introduced in 1970 with the beginning of a conversion program for service vehicles which would permit them to run on either gasoline or natural gas. By 1974 the fleet included more than 110 vehicles. In 1972 it led in various kinds of research including the fuel cell, a means of producing electrical power directly from natural gas by electro-chemical reaction.

Ownership and organization of the company has changed over the years. In 1925 International Utilities Corporation became agents for the company in the United States. During the period from 1944 to 1947, IU, through various stock purchases, acquired controlling interest of the ordinary shares of Canadian Western. In 1971 Canadian Utilities (owned by International Utilities) offered to purchase all of the outstanding ordinary shares of the company and by mid-1972 had purchased all of these shares, thus becoming the holding company for Canadian Western. Also involved as CU subsidiaries were Northwestern Utilities, Northland Utilities, and a new company, Alberta Power. In 1980 ATCO bought IU International's controlling interest in CU.

A vigorous expansion program is still under way. In 1982 Canadian Western's head office was relocated to 8th Street and 11th Avenue S.W. The company has also developed a number of operations centres—each like a mini gas company—to serve specific areas.

Over the years Canadian Western has shown that it is not only present in the community but it is also active in it. For example, in 1929 it established a home service department. Former publisher of the *High River Times*, Charles Clark, saw it this way: "When Canadian Western talks of 'service' they don't have to shout too loud here in High River to make their point. We see their service in almost every field of community effort by the individuals who to us are the gas company—on the volunteer fire brigade, on the curling club executive, in the service clubs, on the library board, in almost every field of activity that contributes to life's enjoyment in Alberta's smaller communities."

Canadian Western's policy since 1912 has been "to provide safe, dependable natural gas service at the lowest possible cost." It prides itself in living up to its motto: "A tradition of service and safety."

CARMA LTD.

Through the 1950s Calgary home-builders had to line up outside city hall—some of them even brought sleeping bags—to obtain lots to stay in business. The prime source of developed residential land was the city and it simply couldn't keep up. That all changed in 1958 when 45 builders got together and formed Carma Developers Ltd., with assets of $250,000.

Today the story of these builders has changed from mere survival to overwhelming success. In 1981 Carma produced almost 30 percent of the serviced residential lots in Calgary. One-fifth of the city's population now lives in Carma-developed communities. In the process, this home-grown organization has expanded both in geography and diversity to become a billion-dollar firm in just 23 years.

Carma is a unique organization. It is a cooperative of builders who continue to compete against each other for sales of the finished product. Contracts merely assure builders the right to purchase a defined number of lots.

Carma became a public company in 1972 and geographic expansion began quickly. Regional offices were opened in Edmonton and Vancouver. The following year an office was opened in Hamilton. By 1980 the company controlled 17,202 acres of land in Canada.

Carma completed its first commercial project, the Silver Springs Shopping Centre, in 1977 and since has become more heavily involved in revenue-producing properties. That year it also began planning for a 260-acre office-retail complex which became the Deerfoot Business Centre and now houses the firm's corporate offices.

An option on 1,500 acres in Houston took Carma into the United States market in 1977. U.S. operations now represent 27 percent of the firm's assets, which have spread through that country's Sun Belt.

Carma's purchase of Edmonton-based Allarco Developments Ltd. in 1980 for $130 million diversified its interests into such areas as life insurance, a trust company, finance, petrochemicals, automobile dealerships, hotels, and restaurants. The rapid growth prompted a corporate restructuring in 1981, which created Carma Ltd. as the parent company and three operating subsidiaries: Carma Developers Ltd., operating in Canadian real estate; Carma Developers Inc., operating in U.S. real estate; and Allarco Group Ltd., operating in diversified enterprises. Included in these are a 79-percent interest in North West Trust Company, a 70-percent interest in Seaboard Life Insurance Company, 50-percent ownership of Alberta Gas Chemicals Ltd., and a 55-percent share in Redden Construction of Edmonton.

Eighty-one percent of the shares of the company are owned by Carma builders; the rest are traded publicly. Overall, Carma is owned 48 percent by Nu-West Group Limited, of which Ralph Scurfield is chairman and chief executive officer. Other substantial shareholders are Howard Ross and his firm, Britannia Homes Ltd., and Klaus Springer and his organization, Springer Developments Ltd.

The chairman of the board and chief executive officer is C.J. (Joe) Combe, the company's first employee and general manager. Albert Bennett was the founding president and upon his retirement in 1971, Roy Wilson, a founding director, became president and subsequently, chief operating officer.

Community participation is a key aspect of Carma operations, whether it be sponsorship of activities or in the form of advisory committees to guide developments.

The 1962 board of directors of Carma Developers Ltd. included (left to right) C.J. (Joe) Combe, founding president Albert Bennett, A.M. (Tony) Usselman, Robert (Bob) Davies, Howard Ross, Ralph Scurfield, Roy Wilson, and Nado Gallelli.

CASCADE GROUP

The foundation of the Cascade Group was laid in 1959 as a Calgary construction company under the banner of Cascade Builders Ltd. Since that time, A.M. Graham, the founder and chairman of the board, has directed the development of the Group into a fully integrated international company comprised of insurance, development, construction, and leisure operations. The Group, which has its headquarters in Calgary, administers approximately one billion dollars of assets.

Cascade Development Corporation Ltd. was incorporated on June 2, 1970, as the Group holding company and, two years later, the cornerstone of the insurance division was created with the purchase of Family Life Assurance Company. Family Life had its beginnings in 1923 and was founded by J.D. Lalonde in St. Victor, Saskatchewan, as a Death Benefit Assessment Club. In 1954 club members began converting their memberships into life insurance contracts; consequently, Family Life Assurance Company was born.

In 1976 Cascade purchased, through Inland Financial, United Investment Life Assurance Company of Toronto and Westmount Life Insurance Company of Montreal.

The following year the Cascade Group acquired another insurance company by the name of Sovereign Life Assurance Company and Sovereign General Insurance Company. The purchase was made by Inland Financial Company, a Cascade Group holding company. Sovereign Life had sold its first policy in 1903 in Toronto; however, in 1912 the head office was moved to Winnipeg due to the amount of business being written in the West. Sovereign General, on the other hand, had its beginning as Merit Insurance Company in 1953 and sold only car insurance until its agents began selling life policies through Sovereign Life.

The corporate offices of all the insurance companies were subsequently moved to Calgary in 1978, where United Life and Westmount Life were amalgamated, with Family Life being the surviving company. Inland Financial Group purchased Cannon Assurance Limited of Great Britain. This firm has a wide array of products such as The Equity Fund, Property Fund, International Money Fund, and several others. The Group's insurance portfolio stands in excess of $4 billion.

The Real Estate Division, an all-encompassing operation mainly concentrating in Western Canada, develops, constructs, leases, and manages buildings. It recently completed its fourth major downtown office tower in Calgary in 1982. Other projects have included a number of LRT stations, apartment towers and residential complexes, business parks, and shopping centres.

The Group's leisure activities centre around Panorama. The resort is by far the Group's most exciting real estate development. Eventually the project will comprise a $400-million expenditure which, when completed, will create a village for 11,000 vacationers. Cascade purchased the ski area near Invermere, British Columbia, in 1978 and established plans to make it a four-season world destination resort. By 1982, $72 million had been expended, developing the resort into a year-round recreation area, complete with hotel, ski hills, and social and recreational amenities.

The Cascade Group looks upon itself as a team, and prides itself on keeping the majority of operations in-house where one opportunity can build on another. Privately owned, with world corporate offices in the Family Life building in Calgary, the Group has grown to include more than 25 organizations, with Canbrit Holding Ltd. now the Group holding company.

In many ways Cascade typifies the growth of Calgary during the past quarter-century — the city and the organization have grown strong together.

CHINOOK CENTRE

Drive-in theatres were just becoming the vogue in 1946, when three Calgary businessmen—M.A. (Red) Dutton, R.F. Jennings, and Frank H. Kershaw—bought some land on the southern outskirts of Calgary. Three years later the Chinook Drive-in Theatre was open for business. Meanwhile, about eight years later, Woodward's department stores began looking for a location in Calgary. A deal was eventually struck, creating a public company to build a shopping centre on the site of the theatre. To accommodate such a large venture, the adjacent Skyline Drive-in and Driving Range was also acquired.

Sod turning for the $7-million shopping centre took place September 18, 1958, and on August 17, 1960, it officially opened its doors. Ken McGregor, who had been the manager of the drive-in theatre, became the shopping centre manager. He held that post until his death in 1972. Woodward's employed Charles R. Claridge, a Calgary native who had started with the firm as a 17-year-old stock boy, as its first manager.

Chinook Centre opened as a strip centre with 44 other retailers, but unlike most shopping centres it evolved into a much larger complex than anticipated. It now has 225 tenants, with one of the highest incidences of local independent merchants in a shopping centre. It offers 1.3 million square feet and is the second largest shopping centre in Western Canada. In sales performance it is the largest. On a 55-acre site providing 4,070 parking spaces, the complex is used by about 300,000 persons a week.

In a concurrent development, Oxford Development Group had purchased property north of Chinook and in 1963 opened Southridge Shopping Centre with Sears, Loblaws (now Super Valu), and 33 other tenants. Meanwhile, Chinook underwent its first major expansion in 1965 when it doubled in size as 30 tenants and an eight-storey office building were added.

In the early 1970s Oxford Development bought Chinook and in 1974 joined it to Southridge with a 42-store bridge across 60th Avenue. The entire

Top
The 20-year expansion of Chinook Centre is reflected in this recent scene.

Above
This aerial view depicts Chinook Centre as it was in 1960 when it first opened its doors.

complex became known as Chinook Centre. In 1982 a major renovation added 12 food outlets.

Cambridge Leaseholds Ltd., which owns 31 other shopping centres in Canada—from St. John's, Newfoundland, to Calgary where it also manages Deerfoot Mall—bought Chinook Centre in 1981. Lorne Braithwaite is president and part owner of Cambridge Leaseholds with Great-West Life as majority shareholder. Although Cambridge employs 89 persons at Chinook, the entire complex is the work place for over 6,000 persons.

Chinook Centre provides a steady flow of special events, including fashion shows and sidewalk sales. Its annual Stampede Breakfast, attended by 40,000 persons in 1982, is a major event on the entertainment calendar. The Charity Bazaar, which marked its 17th year in 1982, generated $150,000 in revenue for 72 charitable organizations. In addition, during 1981 Chinook provided free space for another 76 organizations to display their activities.

As Calgary has expanded, not only has Chinook Centre—located at Macleod Trail and Glenmore Trail—become near the geographical centre of the city, it remains central to the lives of Calgarians as the most popular place to shop.

CITY BAKERY CALGARY LTD.

To become an accomplished baker or chef, world travel is considered an essential ingredient. So, for many years Austrian-born Fritz Painsi and Hans Wanner travelled to absorb the culinary expertise resident in various parts of the globe. And, when they bought City Bakery, they created another stop on the world education tours of future bakers.

The shop now produces everything from the heaviest rye bread to the finest pastries to the most elegant chocolates. The total volume is 10 times that of 1971. For example, at first the bakery produced only one Black Forest cake a day; by 1982 it produced over 450 cakes

requires only a staff of 30 working five days a week.

The location itself, at 906 First Avenue N.E., has had an interesting history. Constructed in 1908, it housed a grocery store, Sauer & Son, in 1920 and in 1923 became a CPR laboratory. The first bakery was located at the site in 1927, called Calgary Bakery and oper-

This brick oven, which took over six hours to heat up, was one of the last such ovens in commercial use in Canada until 1972, when City Bakery replaced it with a modern version.

Co-owners Hans Wanner and Fritz Painsi show off the edible chess set that the medal winners created at the City Bakery.

a week. Of the 14 different cakes the shop makes, the Black Forest remains the most popular. The bakery delivers to hotels, restaurants, institutions, and clubs, which amounts to 70 percent of the business.

For the first three years the partners virtually took no days off. In 1978 they were still putting in 14-hour days six times a week with Wanner in charge of pastries and purchasing and Painsi handling the bakery, sales, the office, and customer relations.

Specialized European machinery has been imported to cut production time. Initially the partners employed 42 persons and 90 percent of the production time was spent on bread and buns, with the operation running around the clock seven days a week. In four years the volume doubled but 50 percent of the production was now in pastries and tortes. More efficient operation now

ated by the Rosenthal family. In 1935 it operated as the Workingmen's Bakery and five years later became Sunrise Bakery.

In 1948 Harry and Rachel Goresht started operating it as City Bakery. Pierre Macullo bought it six years later, and at that time it became City Bakery Calgary Ltd. The shop is also a training ground. Over the years, under Painsi and Wanner, some 35 pastry assistants from other countries have been employed there.

Both partners have received Alberta Achievement Awards, given to those who have won gold medals in international competition. Their dozens of medals hang in a closet because, as they see it, "Let the people eat our product and judge us that way."

Neither planned to be in Calgary very long, but an opportunity to own their own shop changed that. Painsi, who had apprenticed in Austria, trained as a confiseur (confectioner) in Switzerland, and even spent a year on the cruise ship *New Amsterdam*, arrived in Canada in 1968. Wanner, a konditor (pastry baker) and confiseur who apprenticed in Switzerland, had arrived in Calgary earlier and went to work for City Bakery where the two met later.

The pair took over City Bakery on April 1, 1971, when it was primarily a bakery. Soon they started producing pastries, tortes, and fine chocolates, and created an outstanding name for themselves for their high quality and craftsmanship.

CONSOLIDATED CONCRETE LIMITED

Consolidated Concrete Limited traces its origins to family-run enterprises which grew rapidly in Calgary's postwar construction boom. These companies had been started as early as 1910 by such Calgary entrepreneurs as Jim Jefferies, Ken Paget, Reg Jennings, Red Dutton, and Ernie Lutz. Their businesses included Peerless Rock Products, Jefferies Concrete Products, Consolidated Concrete Industries, and True-Mix Limited. Among the accomplishments of these pioneering organizations were the establishment of Calgary's first concrete pipe plant; the introduction of ready-mix concrete to Calgary, and the successful initiation of Calgary's first lightweight aggregate operation.

The amalgamation of these companies in 1961 formed Consolidated Concrete Limited. The diverse management talents of the merging ventures were combined with the financial expertise of the Standard Holdings Group. This new executive group was led by L. A. Thorssen and included B. A. Monkman, R.M. Jefferies, L.E. Smith, and J.L. Holman. The aims of the new firm were to service the rapidly growing construction industry of Alberta with high-quality concrete and aggregate and to provide the owners with a diverse investment and expanded opportunities for growth.

The innovative traditions of the founding corporations were continued as Consolidated Concrete introduced imaginative new programs in employee safety, quality assurance, and cost control. The company led the industry with the introduction of new production techniques for concrete pipe, concrete block, and ready-mix concrete.

The executives and managers took active roles in the affairs of provincial, national, and international trade associations which were relevant to their business. These included the Expanded Shale, Clay and Slate Institute, the Canadian Standards Association, and the American Concrete Pipe Association.

The organization grew rapidly by expansion and by acquisition during the 1960s. Plants were added in Edmonton, Red Deer, and Grande Prairie. The number of employees increased from 300 in 1961 to 500 in 1967. By that year Consolidated had grown to become Alberta's largest supplier of processed aggregates and concrete materials.

In 1968 a new phase of Consolidated Concrete's history began as it was merged with the B. A. C. M. group, managed by the Simken family of Winnipeg. The following year the merged companies became a part of Genstar Limited, which was expanding its Western Canadian interests in building materials, house building, and land development. Consolidated assumed the role of a senior member in the Genstar family of companies.

Today Consolidated Concrete is an Alberta corporation with 700 employees. In addition to the fixed plants the company operates a large fleet of mobile equipment throughout the province. A number of the executive group from the founding companies now hold senior positions with Genstar Corporation.

In the early days Jefferies employees used horses and wagons to deliver sand, gravel, cement, coal, and wood.

Consolidated Concrete has a large fleet of modern ready-mix trucks to serve the needs of Alberta residents.

COOPERS & LYBRAND

The largest accounting firm in the world started its Calgary office at the same time the Suez Crisis was raging. In October 1956, the month that the Suez Crisis was at its peak, the Canadian accounting firm of McDonald, Currie & Co. sent a young accountant west to open an office in Calgary. Roderick J. Whitehead was fresh from a year's assignment with the firm of Cooper Brothers in London, England.

The "office" turned out to be a room in Whitehead's first home on Third Street S.W. There was a drastic telephone shortage in the city at that time, Whitehead recalls, and for several months the company phone was the telephone booth at the end of the block. The first client was a one-man oil-field contractor, followed by a newly arrived surgeon who was a skiing friend.

Within six months the office moved to its first downtown location in the North Canadian Oil building on Seventh Avenue S.W.

Hustle was the basis of the early growth of the firm in Calgary. According to Whitehead, in addition to "walking Eighth Avenue," the firm obtained work through expansion of client activities into Calgary from eastern Canada.

At the same time, the Canadian firm of McDonald, Currie, & Co., Cooper Brothers in the United Kingdom, and Lybrand, Ross Bros. & Montgomery in the United States concluded an agreement to operate under the name Coopers

Fresh from a year's assignment with the firm of Cooper Brothers in London, England, Roderick J. Whitehead opened the first Calgary office of Coopers & Lybrand in a room in his home shown here).

& Lybrand internationally. This gave the Calgary office access to an even larger pool of clients through international referrals and expansion of energy firms (mostly American) into Calgary. In 1973 McDonald, Currie & Co. officially changed its name to Coopers & Lybrand, and continues to do business under that name.

In 1965 the Calgary practice was merged with Beaton, Mathieson & Company, a strong local firm, which effectively tripled its size. It has grown steadily since that time, spurred by the general growth of the city and the firm's main client base in oil, real estate, and construction. Although Coopers & Lybrand was one of the last "Big Eight" international accounting firms to arrive in the city, it is now one of the larger offices with 14 partners in Calgary in 1982.

As the office expanded and the staff grew, the firm began to offer specialty services to clients. Tax services, followed closely by receivership and bankruptcy, valuations, business interruption

The present office of Coopers & Lybrand is located on two floors in the Bow Valley Square 3 building located at 255 Fifth Avenue S.W.

insurance claim investigation and, most recently, computer auditing, are now offered to clients. Through its associate firm of Currie, Coopers & Lybrand, it has offered management consulting services in the city since 1980.

Today the firm's clients range from large oil conglomerates to suppliers to the oil industry, real estate developers, and provincial governments.

Coopers & Lybrand is a strong supporter of the arts in Calgary, with Whitehead serving a term as president of both the Calgary Philharmonic Society and the Calgary Ballet Company. Other partners have served as president of the Calgary Zoo and Theatre Calgary.

The roots of the Calgary office of Coopers & Lybrand are firmly planted in the Calgary community and the firm looks forward to growing with the city in its dynamic future.

CZAR RESOURCES LTD.

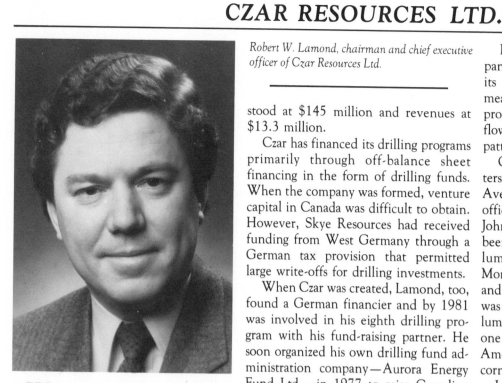

Robert W. Lamond, chairman and chief executive officer of Czar Resources Ltd.

When Scotland-born Robert Lamond decided to form his own oil company, he tried to come up with a short Scottish name that would be easily recognizable on stock exchange printouts. He couldn't, and finally settled for "Czar"—an adaptation of one of his German backers' hometowns of Saarbrücken. His entire career is comprised of similar adaptations to circumstances that have made Lamond and Czar Resources Ltd. spectacular success stories.

Lamond was attending the University of Edinburgh when Imperial Oil lured him to Alberta as a geologist in 1965. Three years later he joined Mesa Petroleum but within one year he started an oil company with a co-worker. During the five years he was chief geologist for Skye Resources, three-quarters of the wells he drilled produced commercial finds. At that point he decided to strike out on his own.

Czar Resources was incorporated as a private Alberta company on April 11, 1974, and went public a year later. It was listed on the Alberta Stock Exchange in 1976 and began trading on the Toronto Stock Exchange three years later. After its first full year of operation, in 1975, Czar had assets of $1.5 million and revenues of $186,206. By 1981 assets

stood at $145 million and revenues at $13.3 million.

Czar has financed its drilling programs primarily through off-balance sheet financing in the form of drilling funds. When the company was formed, venture capital in Canada was difficult to obtain. However, Skye Resources had received funding from West Germany through a German tax provision that permitted large write-offs for drilling investments.

When Czar was created, Lamond, too, found a German financier and by 1981 was involved in his eighth drilling program with his fund-raising partner. He soon organized his own drilling fund administration company—Aurora Energy Fund Ltd.—in 1977 to raise Canadian funds.

Since the imposition of the National Energy Program in 1981, Canadian money has been difficult to raise and most of Czar's activity has been in the United States where it was successful in closing one of the first public drilling funds raised by a Canadian company. In addition, Czar had also started entering joint venture agreements with Canadian and European countries.

Innovation has been a constant companion of Czar. In 1980, Czar negotiated its first discounted gas contract as a means of dealing with the shut-in gas problem and thus developed earlier cash flows. This has since become an industry pattern.

Czar Resources Ltd. has its headquarters on the 10th floor at 333 Fifth Avenue S.W., Calgary, with additional offices in Houston, Texas, and Fort St. John, British Columbia. Operations have been conducted in Alberta, British Columbia, Texas, Louisiana, Arkansas, Montana, and most recently, Oklahoma and Wyoming. During 1979-1980 Czar was the most active driller in British Columbia and now believes it has found one of the larger gas fields in North America in the province's northeast corner.

Lamond, chairman and chief executive officer of Czar, admits to three loves in life: business, history, and an occasional game of tennis. Besides a voracious appetite for books, he now lives in history—as owner of the Coste House, a mansion built in 1912 by one of the area's first successful petroleum engineers, Eugene Coste.

A battery facility and producing oil well operated by Czar Resources in the Twining area, Alberta.

DELTA PROJECTS LIMITED

Bernard Coady felt Canadian expertise in gas processing was being overlooked—and with a keen eye on a business opportunity, decided to do something about it. While other companies simply used Canadian workers, Coady noted that resident abilities in process technology were underutilized. The result was the creation of Delta Projects Limited, with head office in Calgary and now majority owned and controlled by Canadians, which quickly converted its founder's belief into a rapidly expanding corporation.

Coady, born in Alberta and a graduate of the Colorado School of Mines, had joined Delta Engineering Corporation of Houston, Texas, in 1965 but within a year had convinced the U.S. firm that local engineers would be more competitive in the Canadian market. Delta Projects was created in 1966 to provide engineering, procurement, and construction services to the process industry, with Coady as a founding director and one of only two people on staff. By 1970 Coady had proven his point, and using lump-sum turnkey projects as the base in the

Bernard Coady is president of Delta Projects Limited and receives much of the credit for making the firm the influential operation it is in the oil and gas industry.

Delta Projects used its new sulphur recovery process in the Pine River plant in British Columbia to produce 1,100 tons of sulphur a day.

early 1970s—including the 25,000 barrel-a-day Chevron Fort Saskatchewan fractionation facility—the company was ready to diversify.

Coady was made president in 1973, and between 1977 and 1981 was president of Delta Engineering in Houston as well. Building on its initial strength in gas processing, sour-gas treating and sulphur recovery, Delta Projects initiated research to develop new commercial processes.

The MCRC process for sulphur recovery from gas produces a high yield with low emissions. The Pine River project in British Columbia is designed to produce 1,100 tons of sulphur a day through this process. Delta's Delsep Process for sour-gas treatment is unique, separating carbon dioxide from natural gas by the use of membranes.

In 1974-75 Delta Projects became active in in-situ heavy oil development, beginning with the Leming project at Cold Lake. Five other milestone plants have been constructed since then, advancing the technology through new methods including electric pre-heat and steam stimulation. In the early 1980s Delta completed refinery designs for Turbo Resources near Calgary, and in Lloydminster its responsibilities were expanded to include project and construction management of the Husky Oil refinery. Since then, Delta has moved to expand in-house heavy oil upgrading capacity, applying it to such projects as the 1982 Syncrude de-bottleneck at Mildred Lake.

By 1981 Delta Projects was averaging a new plant completion every four months. That year its 300 employees relocated to Heritage Square on Macleod Trail. Many of the employees who joined Delta in 1966 are now among the key employees who own controlling interest in the company. The firm is also involved in a joint program with the Southern Alberta Institute of Technology in the training of engineering draftsmen.

With a history of developing new technology, Delta Projects is taking up the challenge of mastering the needs of the severe environments of the East Coast and the Arctic region. Already it has an impressive capability in design and fabrication of offshore production systems and has on hand a multidiscipline offshore team of engineers and designers ready to take up new challenges.

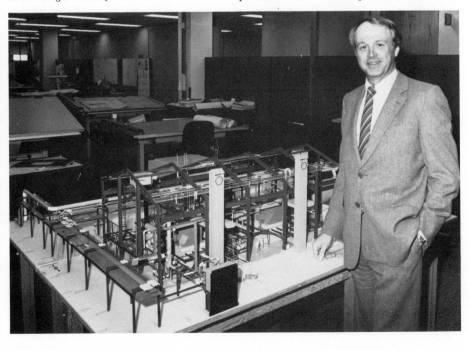

DOME PETROLEUM LIMITED

As Dome Petroleum's first employee, J. P. "Jack" Gallagher has seen the organization grow to become Canada's largest non-integrated oil and gas company. He became president in 1953 and today serves as chairman of the board and chief executive officer.

He was joined in 1957 by W. E. "Bill" Richards, who replaced him as president in 1974. Together they created an enterprise that is known for its distinctive corporate personality. Gallagher, a geologist, and Richards, a lawyer, have combined the flair of an aggressive explorationist with the prudence of a skilled entrepreneur in building their success story.

Dome was formed as a private venture in 1950. Within a year Gallagher developed enough oil and gas reserves to make a public offering of shares for five million dollars. A similar offering was made in 1955.

Dome tasted first success with a wildcat oil discovery in 1951 in the East Drumheller area and the following year drilled its first successful exploratory gas well in the Provost area. In 1958, with oil and gas markets fading, Dome constructed the first flare gas conservation system, which has since made it the largest marketer of natural gas liquids in Canada.

The North looked interesting and in 1961 Dome was the first operator in the Arctic, proving the feasibility of year-round drilling in the area. It was also the initial operator for Panarctic Oils Ltd., in which it still holds an interest.

Dome first filed on Beaufort Sea acreage in 1965 and by 1976 drilling was under way. Canadian Marine Drilling Ltd., a Dome subsidiary, has a fleet of four drill ships, 10 icebreaker supply vessels, one Class Four icebreaker, and support equipment working in the area. Dome is also a 20-percent partner in the Arctic Pilot Project to gather and liquefy natural gas at Melville Island and ship it by ice breaker/tanker to Eastern Canada.

Dome has a diversity of holdings. It has a 40-percent interest in Dome Mines Limited, and with corporate acquisitions such as Kaiser Petroleums Ltd. and Siebens Oil & Gas Ltd. has significantly increased its reserves. Dome Petroleum and Dome Canada share a 47-percent interest in TransCanada PipeLines Limited and in 1981 Dome Petroleum acquired Davie Shipbuilding Ltd.

The acquisition of Hudson's Bay Oil and Gas in 1981 was the largest merger in Canadian corporate history. HBOG, although only 56 years old, has a heritage that goes back to the granting of the Hudson's Bay Charter by King Charles II in 1670. The company started with a handshake in 1926 but was largely dormant until the 1947 Leduc oil discovery. By 1980 HBOG was the third largest producer of natural gas and ninth largest producer of petroleum liquids in Canada.

Dome Canada Limited was formed in 1981 in response to the National Energy Program, which provides incentives that vary with the degree of Canadian ownership.

Today Calgary-based Dome and its subsidiaries employ 9,000 persons. The company remains Canadian owned and controlled and will be a key player in Canada.

W. E. "Bill" Richards, who joined Dome Petroleum in 1957 and became president in 1974, has added his own brand of dynamics to a firm that is recognized for its unique corporate personality.

J. P. "Jack" Gallagher, now chairman of the board and chief executive officer, has played a vital role in making Dome Petroleum the largest non-integrated oil and gas company in Canada.

Canmar Explorer III, one of four drill ships conducting exploratory drilling operations in the Beaufort Sea for Canadian Marine Drilling Ltd., a subsidiary of Dome Petroleum Limited.

EAU CLAIRE ESTATES

In 1886 Peter Prince started the Eau Claire Lumber Company on the banks of the Bow River near a natural bend in the river, a tranquil lagoon and a crescent-shaped island that now bears his name. He had come as a lumber manager from Eau Claire, Wisconsin, and transplanted the name to his new establishment.

Nearly 30 years later renowned architect Thomas Mawson was struck by the natural beauty of the spot. In 1914 he created a master plan for the development of a growing city of Calgary with Eau Claire as the focal point. However, as the city expanded, Mawson's plan was set aside. It wasn't until the early 1970s that a plan again emerged when a group of businessmen began to explore the possibilities of Mawson's concept.

The result was the creation of a downtown community attuned to its natural riverfront setting which developers feel will become one of Calgary's most prestigious neighborhoods. Eau Claire Estates' design provides for a gradual transition from the residential and recreational areas along the river to the commercial buildings in the city centre. Located on a 38-acre site bordering the Bow River between Third and Sixth Streets and south to Third Avenue, Eau Claire Estates provides office, hotel, retail, residential, and recreational facilities in a landscaped downtown location. It is a community of distinct buildings, including elegantly detailed brick residences, clustered around open areas.

When completed, Eau Claire Estates will include 1,250 to 1,750 residential units, 2.4 million square feet of office space, 100,000 square feet of retail space, 3,600 parking stalls, and a 300-room hotel.

The project was undertaken using private investments with no expenditure or dependence on public funds. However, during the four years of negotiations for city approval, the Eau Claire Estates cost went from $150 million to $600 million. Construction began in June 1981, with stage one of phase one completed in the spring of 1983. Prior to that, the site had been virtually vacant and in a state of transition for a number of years.

Eau Claire Estates is an Alberta corporation with Oxford Development Group Ltd. owning 64 percent of the project and a group of Calgary investors holding the remainder. The development team consists of Oxford Development Group Ltd. as developers, the joint venture of Skidmore, Owings & Merrill and the Chandler Kennedy Architectural Group as architects, and PCL Construction Ltd. as general contractors. Project management is by Oxford.

Eau Claire is not only Oxford's largest project, it also represents the firm's first move into residential building. One of Oxford's most outstanding earlier Canadian successes was Calgary's Toronto Dominion Square, which played a major role in revitalizing the downtown area. An acknowledged enthusiast, Calgary-born G. Donald Love is Oxford's cofounder, chairman, president, and principal shareholder.

Eau Claire Estates is an attempt to wed commercial and residential features into a downtown area, and as such, ranks as one of the largest projects of its kind in North America.

ESSO RESOURCES CANADA LIMITED

While Esso Resources is relatively new on the Calgary scene, its parent company has had a long and close relationship with the city. Imperial Oil Limited opened a marketing office in Calgary in 1912, and began refining operations there in 1923. Since Imperial first started exploring for oil in Western Canada, the headquarters of that search has been located in Calgary. These exploration efforts resulted, in 1947, in the discovery of the Leduc field, which has been described as one of the most significant events in Canada's economic history. It marked the beginning of Canada as an important oil-producing nation and the emergence of Alberta as the richest resource province.

Today, as it has been since its earliest days, Imperial is Canada's largest supplier of petroleum energy. Through Esso Resources Canada Limited, it is Canada's largest producer of crude oil and one of the country's largest natural gas producers. Its marketing refining division, Esso Petroleum Canada, operates six refineries and is the leading manufacturer and marketer of petroleum products in the country, with operations extending from coast to coast and from the border to the Arctic.

Through another division, Esso Chemical Canada, Imperial is one of Canada's leading suppliers of primary and intermediate chemicals. In the minerals field Esso Minerals Canada, a division of Esso Resources, has been among the nation's top mineral-exploring companies.

In 1980 the firm celebrated the fact that, 100 years earlier, 16 Canadian businessmen had formed the Imperial Oil Company. By pooling their resources and their talents, the organization's founders were confident that they could compete profitably with ever-increasing imports of United States crude oil and kerosene—the principal oil product of the day.

The Norman Wells refinery, in the Northwest Territories, went into production during World War II to supply much-needed fuel for the U.S. war effort in the Pacific.

Headquartered in London, Ontario, with two refineries in that province and a capitalization of $500,000, the new enterprise moved quickly to broaden its operations. Moving west with the settlers, by the end of its first decade Imperial had a chain of supply depots stretching from the Great Lakes to Vancouver. Operations were expanded in Eastern Canada, and by 1893 the company, with 23 branch offices stretching from the Atlantic to the Pacific, could proudly claim that its products were sold "throughout the Dominion of Canada."

But success brought its own problems. If the venture were to continue to expand, it needed capital. It was not forthcoming in either Canada, then in a depression, or Britain, and Imperial looked for help south of the border. In 1898, in return for the capital it needed,

The site of the Norman Wells oil discovery, which led to the building of a refinery in the area during World War II.

Imperial sold a majority interest to Standard Oil Company (N.J.). The Standard (now Exxon) relationship not only provided capital. Under the new arrangements, Jersey's facilities in Canada became a part of Imperial's assets.

On the domestic scene Imperial was primarily a refining and marketing organization for nearly all of its first four decades. Its refining operations particularly expanded as a result of the demands of World War I—by 1918 the company had five plants in operation and its refining activities spanned the country from Dartmouth on the East Coast to Vancouver on the West Coast. In 1914 it had begun oil exploration in South America through a subsidiary firm, International Petroleum Company Limited, and fields discovered by that organization were a major source of oil for Imperial refineries.

Imperial Oil had begun exploration reconnaissance in Western Canada as early as 1912 and had established an

exploration and production department in 1914. It was not until 1917, however, that the company drilled its first wildcat there. The year 1920 saw its first major discovery—Norman Wells in the Northwest Territories, just 90 miles from the Arctic Circle. The field was, however, too far away from markets and development remained keyed to its local supply area until the late 1970s, when economic conditions made plans for field development and pipeline connection to Edmonton feasible.

Norman Wells seemed to predict the discovery of major reservoirs of oil in Western Canada (as did a 1924 discovery at Turner Valley, southwest of Calgary, by Imperial's subsidiary, Royalite Oil Company Limited). However, the years that followed were anything but encouraging. By the mid-1940s most companies had given up the search for oil in Western Canada, and Imperial had reached the point where it decided it might soon have to close down its exploration effort. Indeed, it was giving serious consideration to building a plant to manufacture gasoline from natural gas. Then, in 1947, Imperial Leduc No. 1 blew in on a farm some 20 miles southwest of Edmonton.

A seismic survey crew refuels its truck in the Leduc area in the early 1940s, when prospects for finding oil looked bleak.

By the late 1940s Alberta had oil to spare. Imperial Oil and others formed Interprovincial Pipe Line Limited to build a line from Edmonton to Superior, Wisconsin. The line was built in a record 150 days during the spring and summer of 1950. It was extended to Sarnia and in 1957 reached Toronto. In 1975-1976 it grew again to Montreal.

Throughout its history Imperial has pioneered not only in exploration and in

---

A crowd gathers around the Leduc No. 1 discovery well, which ushered in the energy prosperity for Alberta, circa 1947.

supplying new product markets, but it has pioneered in technology as well. It introduced Canada's first gasoline service station in Vancouver in 1907, and in 1920 introduced the country's first self-serve station in Edmonton. In 1924 it began a research function that was to develop into the largest research program of any oil company in Canada—at one stage the corporation's advertising pointed out that Imperial was doing more research than all other oil companies in Canada together. That research effort resulted in a number of firsts in the refining field—lubricating oil processes, for example, that came into use in refineries around the world. In the field of petroleum exploration and production the company developed the building of artificial islands to drill in waters offshore in the Arctic that are too shallow for drill ships. It was one of the pioneers in the development of the oil sands of Alberta, and became one of the major participants in the Syncrude project. Indeed, when that project faced collapse after the withdrawal of one of the partners, Imperial played a key role in keeping it alive through determined negotiations with federal and provincial governments. Through its research and pilot projects at Cold Lake in Alberta the company has innovated in-situ production of heavy oil from formations that are too deeply buried to be mined.

During World War II particular demands were placed on Imperial as the country's principal petroleum supplier. During that time the firm also entered into another and associated phase of the oil business—the manufacture of chemicals. In 1942, with supplies of natural rubber cut off, Imperial joined the federal government and a number of other corporations to produce synthetic rubber in Sarnia. Imperial operated through a subsidiary formed for this venture—St. Clair Processing Company Limited, which eventually was absorbed into the Polymer Corporation Limited.

In 1955, with the formation of a chemical products department, Imperial entered directly into the chemical business. Its first plant—to make detergent

The Strathcona Refinery in Edmonton is the largest refinery in Western Canada.

alkylate—went into operation at Sarnia in 1957. This was followed in 1958 by an ethylene plant, the most advanced and largest of its size in Canada. Facilities to produce other petrochemicals were added in Sarnia and in other locations in British Columbia, Quebec, and Nova Scotia. In 1967 Imperial completed what was then the largest single investment in its history—a $50-million fertilizer complex in Redwater, Alberta. By the time it celebrated its 100th birthday, Imperial (operating now through a major division—Esso Chemical Canada) was one of the largest suppliers of chemicals in Canada, with products that included not only primary and intermediate chemicals but building materials, plastic pipe, and binder twine.

In 1965 Imperial's exploration activities took on a new dimension. In a logical extension of its expertise it began to prospect for uranium and other minerals. By the end of the decade the search extended to eight provinces and the Yukon. Coal exploration and development became an important part of the minerals operation by the early 1970s. To conduct its mining operations, Imperial formed Esso Minerals Canada,

that division's activities soon putting the company among the top mineral explorers in the nation.

The immediate postwar period saw a rapid expansion and modernization of Imperial's refining facilities. During World War II the existing refineries had been held together, as one refiner put it, "with baling wire and string." Modernization and expansion to meet a growing demand, and the building of refineries at Edmonton and Winnipeg to use western crude oil, took second place only to continued exploration and field development in Imperial's capital program until the end of the 1950s. In the 1960s modernization continued—major new units at Sarnia, for example, were linked to an on-line computer, the first to be employed in refining operations in the country.

In 1971 the company announced it would spend more than $200 million to build a new petroleum products supply system on the Prairies. Heart of the new system would be a refining complex to be built on the site of the Edmonton refinery. The new (Strathcona) plant would be linked by pipeline with major product terminals in Calgary, Regina, and Winnipeg. With the start-up of Strathcona in 1975, refineries in those cities were closed.

On the upstream side of its opera-

tions—the exploration for and production of petroleum and minerals—Imperial made a major move in 1978 with the formation of a subsidiary company, Esso Resources Canada Limited. Headquartered in Calgary, and formed to expedite prompt and effective investment response to energy and other resource development opportunities, the new venture inherited a petroleum exploration program that covered the western provinces, the western Arctic and the Arctic islands, and offshore in the Atlantic, as well as the exploration and development work of Esso Minerals Canada. Esso Resources became the operator not only of all Imperial's oil and gas production facilities, but of the Cold Lake pilot project. And it took Imperial's place as a major participant in the Syncrude venture.

Esso Resources inherited not only physical assets—it inherited a long tradition of an enlightened and innovative approach to human relations. More than 60 years ago, in 1918, Imperial established Joint Industrial Councils that provided employees with the opportunity to discuss wages, hours, working conditions, and grievances with management. More employee-oriented programs followed in 1919. An eight-hour working day was introduced, the first in Canada. A life insurance policy was introduced. A benefits plan was begun, providing for

Issungnak is an artificial island built by Esso Resources from which to undertake drilling in the Arctic waters of the Beaufort Sea.

illness not covered by workmen's compensation and for injuries that happened off the job. And in that year Imperial established a pension system that, along with other aspects of its benefits program, has been changed and adjusted through the years to reflect changing social and economic conditions.

Imperial adopted the five-day work week in 1932—the second company in Canada to do so. Five years later employees were given holidays with pay. Experiments with working hours were instituted in 1971 when employees in one office location tried a four-day work week. Four-day and even three-day work weeks came into operation at other locations. In 1973 the company began experimenting with flextime, under which employees put in a full working day but come and go at times more convenient to themselves.

On different occasions, the firm has used its resources to help those outside of Imperial. When the price of wheat dropped by one-third during the Depression, Prairie farmers were having trouble paying their debts. Imperial supplied products to them on credit for the first time, then cancelled interest charges on their overdue bills and extended payment time to five years.

The company has led the way in environmental protection, paying attention to this aspect of its operations long before ecology-oriented legislation was introduced. Today that philosophy is reflected in such activities as Esso Resources' reclamation program for its test coal mine at Judy Creek, where 55 acres of land were reseeded and 30,000 trees of improved stock were planted.

What Imperial describes as its "other side" activities has also, for many years, included support of activities of social and cultural importance as well as health, welfare, and community services. In Calgary, Imperial's community relations activities have been carried out primarily by Esso Resources. That company, for example, sponsors Esso Minor Hockey Week in Calgary, which brings 8,000 youngsters together for a tournament. It purchased 1,600 pieces of original Canadian art for employee offices in Esso Plaza. It has made major donations to the Calgary Zoo for the development of a prehistoric park. Esso's combined corporate and employee contribution to the United Way were the first in Calgary ever to top $100,000.

A corporation is more than just a legal mechanism for providing needed goods and services. It can have a personality of its own. Imperial has been not only a major supplier of energy and chemicals for Canada, it has demonstrated that it is innovative, pioneering, willing to gamble, persistent in the face of setbacks, and extremely conscious of its social responsibilities. With its major functions such as Esso Resources Canada Limited, it will continue to play a prominent role in the future of Calgary and of the nation.

This is a seismic survey ship used by Esso Resources in mapping the offshore waters for possible future exploration activities.

Esso Plaza, a twin-tower complex, houses the offices of Esso Resources Canada Limited.

FRANKLIN SUPPLY COMPANY LTD.

Nasie Schnell, president of Franklin Supply Company Ltd.

C.L. "Squire" Maguire admired great men. When he formed an oil company he called it Roosevelt Oil Company after President Theodore Roosevelt. In 1933, in a little red warehouse in Mount Pleasant, Michigan, he expanded into oil field supplies and created Franklin Tool Company, named after Benjamin Franklin. Jene Harper, a 21-year-old employee, soon pointed the way to greater things to come. Within eight years he had purchased the firm and from the Michigan base expanded across the United States and eventually into other countries.

In 1975 Harper sold the business, which now had corporate headquarters in Tulsa, Oklahoma, and Bob Parker of Parker Drilling Company emerged as owner. In 1980 Franklin Supply Company was acquired by Adams Affiliates.

The Canadian operation, which started in 1952, has developed into one of the largest oil field supply companies in the country. Originally it was called Franklin Pipe and Supply Ltd. until 1976, when it dropped "pipe." It is now 80-percent owned by the Franklin U.S. operation and the balance by its Canadian employees.

The company's first office was in Edmonton; in 1953 it opened a sales office in Calgary which became the Canadian headquarters. In the early days it was primarily involved in selling pipe, valves, fittings, and equipment related to the exploration and development of oil and gas wells.

In 1956, when the oil boom hit Saskatchewan, Franklin opened a store in Estevan. It was there that the company's president, Nasie Schnell, joined the firm in 1958. He had been farming with his father and took the Franklin position as a part-time job—and never left. He became general manager in 1975, a vice-president in 1976, and president in 1978.

Franklin has always taken pride in being a frontier company by often being the first supply firm to serve the oil and gas industry in remote areas. In 1959 it opened offices in Swan Hills and Fort Nelson; two years later it opened in Fort St. John. In 1963 a store was opened in High Level and shortly thereafter in Slave Lake.

In 1959 the company opened an Alaska branch, which was operated o of the Calgary headquarters.

By 1982 Franklin Supply had 1 stores in Canada including Fort St. Joh Medicine Hat, North Battleford, Lloy minster, Athabasca, Edmonton Whitecourt, Grande Prairie, Three Hill Brooks, and Peace River.

The Calgary office started with fiv employees and $.5 million in sales in th first year. Today Franklin employs abou 125 persons, of whom 45 are located i Calgary. After operating out of thre prior locations, in 1981 the corporatio moved into new high-rise accommoda tions at 900 Sixth Avenue S.W.

Although Franklin has grown t become a major supply company whic offers the oil field everything fro expendable components to complete ri packages, it is still looking for ne remote outposts to continue its pioneer ing tradition.

GLENBOW MUSEUM

The late Eric L. Harvie, lawyer and philanthropist, was the primary force behind the stature to which the Glenbow Museum has risen.

When the Glenbow-Alberta Institute—now commonly called the Glenbow Museum—moved into its new facilities on September 22, 1976, it marked the first time in its history that all of its departments were housed under one roof. The eight-storey downtown structure adjacent to the Calgary Convention Centre cost almost $8.8 million. In 1981 more than 200,000 persons visited the Glenbow, now considered as Western Canada's foremost museum of art and western history.

As a repository for over one million artifacts, the museum itself has had a dynamic evolution. It began in 1955 as the Glenbow Foundation established by Eric L. Harvie, Q.C., an Ontario native who made a fortune in Alberta oil. A man of eclectic interests, he held a dream of a great museum for Alberta. As a result he set up the foundation to collect paintings, documents, and artifacts illustrating the history of the Canadian West. He even donated many of his books to form the nucleus of a library of Western Canadiana. His collectors gathered armour, weapons, coins, and mineral specimens from around the world. Within a decade these materials filled several warehouses: Artifacts were in an old courthouse, photographs and documents in what was once a library, and paintings in a former Ford assembly plant.

As a pre-centennial gift, Harvie donated the foundation's shares and assets, as well as a $5-million cheque, to form the Glenbow-Alberta Institute, established by an act of the Alberta Legislature in 1966 and administered by a volunteer board of governors. The province matched the $5-million donation and the federal government donated $1.6 million in 1976 to help consolidate the collection.

Glenbow operates as a nonprofit, educational museum-art gallery and library-archives. Located at Ninth Avenue and First Street S.E., the museum has a staff of 160 and is primarily funded by the province and the city. It also operates the Luxton Museum in Banff, which annually attracts 90,000 visitors.

The museum's permanent displays outline Indian life, the developments of the fur trade and exploration, ranching, and settlement, and the 20th century to the discovery of western oil. The art department has about 22,000 works including sculpture, porcelain, crystal, drawings, prints, watercolors, and paintings. Uniforms, flags, and weapons used in the Riel Rebellion are among 60,000 items in the cultural history department. The research library has 45,000 books and pamphlets and the archives houses 250,000 photographs.

In storage areas are countless other items. For example, in 1979 the Glenbow received 40,000 works, valued at $20 million, from the Calgary-based Devonian Group of Charitable Foundations, which will take years to incorporate.

Record crowds attended the international "Treasures of Ancient Nigeria" exhibition in early 1981. Later the same year, "Four Modern Masters: DeChirico, Ernst, Magritte, and Miro," made its only North American stop at Glenbow. These international exhibitions, complemented by displays from Glenbow's own extensive Western art and history collections made history come alive every day at Glenbow.

The Glenbow Museum, seen here from the Eighth Avenue Mall, is visited by more than 200,000 persons a year.

GEORGE & NICK'S MACHINE WORKS LTD.

George Plesa hasn't forgotten how difficult it was to be an immigrant in Canada, desperately looking for work but unable to communicate his intents. He and his younger brother, Nick, learned English while building up their machining business into one of the most successful in Calgary. Now that George and Nick Plesa no longer run the machines and the company that bears their name is a multimillion-dollar-a-year concern, their roots are still reflected by the 13 nationalities that appear on their payroll.

George was 26 when he came from Croatia in 1958. Nick and three other younger brothers, all tradesmen, had escaped from the country a year earlier. George, however, had been caught at the border, spent two months in jail, but fled the country again. The entire Plesa family is now in Canada.

Originally they settled in Montreal, where George got a job in a boiler shop for 50 cents an hour. The others found work with Noranda; Nick became a one-dollar-an-hour machinist. Employment difficulties saw the family head west but again jobs were difficult to find in Calgary. George, wanting to get into his machinist trade, even settled for being a sweeper on the graveyard shift for the CPR Alyth shops in hopes of moving up.

Their break came after they placed an ad in *The Calgary Herald*: "Three brothers from Europe, machinists by trade, are looking for jobs." George and Nick stayed with the machine shop for six and one-half years. During that time, when they saw the need for improved equipment, they decided to make some of it themselves as a sideline. They purchased a small lathe and milling machine and started doing some experimental work after hours. When their employer found out, he promptly fired them.

As a result, George & Nick's Machine Works Ltd. was officially started in September 1965, on a federal election day. The brothers decided to let their company be known on a first-name basis because that's the way everyone referred to the owners. The first location was

Nick (left) and George Plesa.

3802 15th Street S.E., a 100-square-foot portion of a warehouse, to which they added twice.

George and Nick remain the sole owners of the enterprise. Brother Peter has since joined the firm and youngest brother Matt worked for the company until he established his own. George is president and Nick serves as vice-president and treasurer. Early in the organization's history, a nephew, Joe Plesa, worked for the brothers while attending the University of Calgary. After teaching for two years he joined George & Nick's as sales manager in 1975.

Initially all the brothers could offer was their know-how and quality of work. It was a battle of nerves waiting for work to come. George found it difficult seeking customers with his halting English and took a leadership course to gain confidence.

But word of their quality work spread. The willingness to take on any job regardless of size or complexity increased the number of clients dramatically. They quickly established a reputation for expertise and innovation.

In 1977 the company moved to its current location at 4312 Ogden Road S.E. which provides 28,000 square feet of shop area and 10,000 square feet of offices. The company employed 18 people at the time and also installed its first computerized machining units. The industry was booming but qualified machinists were scarce. In fact, since 1977 some 10 former employees of George & Nick's have started firms of their own. To fill the void the brothers started their own training centre, which by 1982 had 18 apprentices in the four-year program.

The firm has a number of departments in addition to the training centre—which has two instructors—including heat treating, electronics, engineering, and computerized machining. However, the backbone remains the machine shop. Its strength is in each individual's pride in his trade, according to the brothers. As a result, the company's biggest asset is its good people. By 1977 there were 37 employees working almost around the clock on a two-shift system. In 1982 the firm employed 120.

George & Nick's has found it wise not to specialize because it avoids industry downturns. Although working primarily for the oil and gas industry, over the years its has produced items for griculture, pulp and paper, mining, civil ngineering, and construction. It is also yeing the aircraft industry.

By 1982 the corporation's biggest narket was in the United States, a narket that started to develop only four ears earlier. The firm believes the uture of the oil industry lies in lectronics and is gearing its efforts in hat direction. For example, the brothers nave developed remote controls for one of the products they manufacture.

Because of the nature of the industry, he company competes worldwide and is a regular participant in trade shows around the globe. George & Nick's has never been afraid to tackle any of the challenges of industry. In fact, it is constantly scouting industry to produce new products as soon as new needs arise. Through research and development, it seeks to create markets by developing products and taking advantage of the lead time that provides. George & Nick's now markets its own line of products.

The owners feel that much of the credit for their success lies with customers who were willing to give the enterprise an opportunity to provide a service. Much of the selling has been done by the customers, they maintain. Some of the company's first customers are still with the firm.

This sense of tribute extends to the country as a whole. The entire Plesa family is thankful to Canada for the freedom and opportunity it has provided. Through their success they hope to show some of that gratitude.

The first location of George & Nick's Machine Works Ltd., at 3802 15th Street S.E.

GREYHOUND LINES OF CANADA LIMITED

Gone are the days when Greyhound buses were escorted by their own snowplows to keep passengers moving through Alberta winters. Gone are the days of gravel highways and hairpin turns. Gone are the days when the Calgary to Edmonton trip took seven hours. By 1981 Greyhound Lines of Canada Limited was carrying 6.5 million passengers over 50 million miles a year.

Operations date back to 1929, when founding president George B. Fay, together with H.B. "Barney" Olson and R.S. "Speed" Olson, formed a British Columbia company, Canadian Greyhound Coaches Limited. The following year they registered the company in Alberta and started the Calgary-Edmonton run.

Fay had been a bus salesman for General Motors whose territory had included Canada and the western United States. He started his Canadian venture without any connection to a similarly named U.S. operation. During the Depression, when financing was not available from traditional lenders, the U.S. firm acquired ownership of the Canadian company.

Passenger service to the Pacific Coast was initiated after the British Columbia and Alberta companies were amalgamated in December 1930 to form Central Canadian Greyhound Lines. Six buses pioneered the service using the hair-raising Big Bend Highway route. The company expanded routes into Saskatchewan in 1934 and Manitoba in 1940, at which point it changed its name to Western Canadian Greyhound Lines. In the meantime, a similar evolution was taking place in Ontario which culminated in the 1944 creation of Eastern Canadian Greyhound Lines Limited. In 1957 the Western and Eastern companies amalgamated to form Greyhound Lines of Canada Limited and stock was listed on the Toronto Stock Exchange. The transcontinental route runs 2,600 miles from North Bay, Ontario, to Vancouver.

Greyhound is both an operator and holding company. It employs more than 3,000 Canadians and has over 4,500

This is one of the 440 buses currently in use by Greyhound in Canada.

The original Calgary Greyhound Bus Depot at Seventh Avenue and First Street N.W. with one of the buses that made the Alberta and British Columbia runs in 1932.

Canadian shareholders. It has grown to become the largest single operator in Canada in terms of route mileage (14,000 route miles) and revenues (over $204 million in 1981). It also serves the largest territory—British Columbia to Ontario plus the Yukon, Northwest Territories, and Alaska—the northern routes being served by a subsidiary, Coachways System.

Motor Coach Industries Ltd. of Winnipeg, a wholly owned subsidiary, produces all the buses used by Greyhound in

Canada as well as exporting coaches to the United States, Mexico, Taiwan, Australia, and Saudi Arabia. In 1981 the plant produced 1,600 buses and with tooling up during 1982 can produce seven buses a day.

In 1965 Greyhound acquired the long-established Brewster Transportation Limited based in Banff, which operates a fleet of sightseeing buses and tourist facilities. One of the biggest revenue producers for the company is package express service. Another service is charter bus tours. Fares remain nominal. The 1930 fare from Calgary to Edmonton was $5. Fifty-two years later it stood at $12.25.

Calgary remains the firm's head office and all of its employees are still Canadians. Fay served as president until 1955. He was replaced by Robert L. Borden, a 45-year employee with Greyhound, who was president from 1955 to 1979 and chairman of the board in 1980. James A. Knight became president and chief executive officer in 1980.

The company's mandate now is to improve the bus travel image. It is actively building new bus terminals across the country and adds 40 to 50 new buses a year. In 1982 Greyhound Lines of Canada Limited ran 440 buses operated by 850 drivers.

GULF CANADA LIMITED

The roots of Gulf Canada's Calgary operations reach back to the very beginnings of the Alberta petroleum industry. In 1912, when local entrepreneurs William Elder, A.W. Dingman, and W.S. Herron formed Calgary Petroleum Products Ltd., they could not have known their venture would one day be part of a major integrated energy company.

Their famous Dingman No. 1 well on the north banks of the Sheep River blew in 1914 and brought to the surface a mixture of natural gas and naphtha. The firm was bought in 1921 by the Royalite Oil Company, which would later become part of Gulf Oil Canada Limited.

In 1962 the British American Oil Company began to acquire an interest in Royalite. Gradually the two enterprises merged operations, with amalgamation completed in 1969 when B-A, Royalite, and Shawinigan Chemicals Ltd. became Gulf Oil Canada Limited.

In addition to Royalite, B-A and Gulf Canada also claim pioneer status. B-A had a refinery at Coutts by 1934 and exploration had been under way for some time in the southern foothills. In 1936 Robert Brown and George Bell, two independent Calgary drillers with B-A funding, brought in the Royalite No. 1 well in Turner Valley to establish a major source of oil and natural gas. Turner Valley crude oil encouraged B-A to build a refinery in Calgary's Inglewood suburb in 1939. With the completion of the Edmonton refinery in the early 1970s, the Calgary plant was converted to asphalt production.

Gulf Oil Corporation was also an early participant in Alberta's petroleum industry, forming the Canadian Gulf Oil Company in 1944 with Calgary as the centre for its operations. Canadian Gulf was an exploration and production company with impressive land holdings. B-A, on the other hand, did not have sufficient oil reserves to meet its refinery requirements. In 1956 it merged into a vastly expanded B-A through the transfer to Gulf Oil Corporation of 8.3 million British American common shares in exchange for the assets of Canadian Gulf. By 1962, 800 B-A staff members were headquartered at the British-American Oil Building in Calgary.

The 1969 merger which created Gulf Oil Canada meant that the Calgary staff, who were spread throughout city-centre offices, began a series of moves. Longtimers recall working in three or four different offices in the following decade.

A corporate reorganization of Gulf Canada Limited in 1979 consolidated exploration and production into a new subsidiary company, Gulf Canada Resources Inc., and resulted in the creation of a refining and marketing division, Gulf Canada Products Company. Calgary became headquarters for Gulf Canada Resources and for the western region of Gulf Canada Products.

Today Gulf Canada ia a fully integrated, nationwide energy organization with over 10,000 employees. Gulf Canada Resources Inc. is an active explorer for oil and gas in the frontiers and Western Canada, is a participant in oil sands and heavy and synthetic oil operations in Western Canada, and operates several gas-processing plants. Gulf Canada Products Company has refining operations throughout the country, and markets a wide variety of petroleum and petrochemical products.

Although the firm's sophisticated Calgary operations bear little resemblance to the simple operations of Dingman, Herron, and Elder—or to the small refinery at Coutts—the beginnings have not been forgotten.

GUNTHER'S BUILDING CENTER LTD.

In 1951 a young and enterprising immigrant couple from Germany stood at the Calgary airport and decided to make a home in that city. Three years later Gunther Kockerbeck had sold his first carload of glass and Gunther's Building Supplies Ltd. was born. From the outset the company philosophy was to provide quality building materials at competitive prices for Calgary's growing housing industry.

An independent man, Kockerbeck was 23 when he and his wife Mary arrived in Alberta. He had heard of the potential of the oil business and was eager to look at expanded opportunities not available in a postwar Germany. His first job was in a warehouse, where he seemed to spend most of his time sweeping. One day Kockerbeck overheard a customer complaining about the difficulties he was having selling an excess carload of glass. The young would-be businessman jumped at this opportunity, sold the material, and promptly started what was to become a thriving business.

The company's first location in 1954 was in east Calgary along the Bow River near the Langevin Bridge. The business outgrew the space very quickly and operations moved to 10th Avenue and 17th Street S.W. Again it wasn't too long before the site was too small and the firm moved to its current location at 2100 10th Avenue S.W. in 1957. At the time it featured only two small buildings. Today it houses a multi-structure complex including a manufacturing plant, warehouse facilities, and showrooms.

Occupied by Gunther's in the early 1950s, this small warehouse housed the entire operation.

The company began operating under its current name of Gunther's Building Center Ltd. in 1971 as the result of an amalgamation of Gunther's Building Supplies Ltd. and Gunther's Interiors Ltd. (formerly Fairway Floor Company). The firm now operates three divisions: building supplies, interior decorations, and door and cabinet hardware. The interiors division is located at 1703 10th Avenue S.W. under the direction of brother-in-law Charles von Muehldorfer and deals in floor coverings, draperies, ceramic tiles, and wall coverings.

The firm is very much a family operation. Kockerbeck's sons participated from an early age—doing odd jobs and helping as counter staff. Today the sons and a number of longtime employees manage the day-to-day operations of the company.

The organization now employs more than 50 full-time workers and a number of subcontractors. Its thrust continues to be the offering of high-quality goods. Today Gunther's supplies Calgary's major builders and contractors (many of whom have grown as Gunther's has from those early years) with a wide range of interior finishing products including domestic and exotic woods, doors, mouldings, plywoods, and hardware. Its own growth has been linked to the growth of Calgary—a city that displays much of the company's products in its living spaces.

Today Gunther's Building Center Ltd. encompasses well over two acres and four warehouses near downtown Calgary.

HENDERSON COLLEGE OF BUSINESS

"New Calgary Business Training School Sets Out To Beat Depression."

That was the headline in the November 1939 issue of *The Beacon*, which continued: "The new school is housed at 509 Eighth Avenue West, Calgary, just opposite the big Eaton store in the heart of the business district. The premises have been entirely remodelled and renovated and a lighting system installed, which makes the classrooms as bright at night as they are by day.

"The very latest in school equipment has been provided so that students are doing work under the happiest and most pleasant surroundings. ... An expert in school supplies, who recently visited Henderson Secretarial School, described it as the best-equipped west of Toronto."

The institute grew from a single classroom in June 1938 to two complete floors and an annex in 1943; eventually it took over the entire building. The founder and principal was C.J. Henderson, a former principal of Garbutt Business College Limited. His daughter, Dorothy, became principal upon his death, and his son, Ernie, assumed the position after his return from World War II service.

In 1972 Ernie Henderson died and Sheila Murphy was hired as principal. Mrs. Murphy had been a business education teacher and secretary in Ireland before going to work in the oil industry in Calgary. In 1976 she bought a majority interest in the business and the following year became sole owner and president.

The school became the Henderson School of Commerce during the 1960s, it was renamed Henderson College of Business in 1972. It relocated in its present site, 1514 Fourth Street S.W., in 1980. The current location and its capacity of 420 students make it the largest and most modern private business college in Canada. It is also unique in operating three separate campuses—with Reliance in Regina and Henderson in Lethbridge.

Accredited by the Association of Canadian Career Colleges, the school is entirely self-supporting. It prides itself on the fact that 90 percent of its students come on the recommendation of previous students. The college has expanded its course offerings to include court reporting, word processing, micro-computer operation, legal and medical secretarial, land and petroleum secretarial training, as well as the traditional secretarial skills. It is the only business college in Canada to provide an assessment centre to determine entry standings.

Emphasis at the school has shifted from clerical to specialization, while electronics has changed not only the secretarial job but also the machines in use. A gradual increase in male enrollment has taken place, and growing numbers of older and more mature students are attending.

Amid these changes two things have remained constant: The college still has a dress code, and absolutely all of its graduates continue to be placed in jobs.

HORNSTROM BROS. CONSTRUCTION LTD.

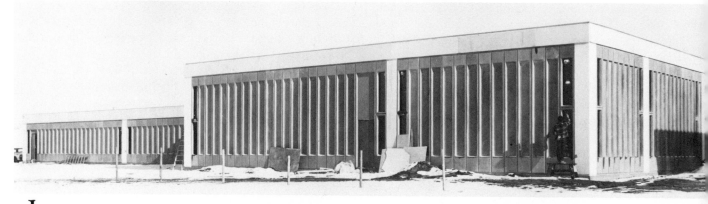

An addition to the government of Canada's Geological Laboratory.

Little did David McMechan suspect that when he took a job as a laborer with Hornstrom Bros. Construction Ltd. he would be its owner and president within a decade. Although his own initial contact with the firm was short-lived, the company's roots go far back into Calgary's history.

Hornstrom Bros. was organized as a partnership in 1917. Walfrid Hornstrom had come to Calgary in 1909 and was followed a year later by younger brother B. Herman. After completing their schooling at Mount Royal College, they started building houses. Many of the hundreds they built were in Mount Royal and were considered among the finest residences available.

With the outbreak of World War II the company became involved in military construction. It built the training building at Currie Barracks in Calgary, as well as much of the Army camp at Red Deer and a number of RCAF stations in the province. Later, during the '40s and '50s, Hornstrom Bros. was one of Calgary's principal school builders.

The second generation in the Hornstrom Bros. operation began unofficially when McMechan obtained a summer job with the firm through mutual friends in 1954. McMechan had attended high school in Thorsby and then left Hornstrom Bros. to spend four years as a laboratory technician with Shell Oil. During this time he married Herman Hornstrom's daughter, Eileen, after meeting her at a summer camp. McMechan later studied geological engineering at Mount Royal College before attending the University of Idaho

in 1961.

By 1962 Walfrid Hornstrom was the only brother remaining in the business—Herman had died in 1957—and he invited McMechan to join the firm. McMechan bought an interest in the organization and became its president in 1962. Today the firm is 90-percent owned by McMechan and his wife through Daveen Holdings Ltd.

Hornstrom Bros. today is primarily involved in medium-size commercial and institutional buildings. Over the years the corporation has erected over 45 different types of buildings—ranging from schools, fire stations, and community halls to banks, dairy plants, arenas, and swimming pools—in 71 communities in Alberta. The company has maintained its great versatility by

choosing not to specialize in a particular type of construction.

McMechan has been active in the construction industry on a professional level as well. In 1968 he was president of the Calgary General Contractors' Association and seven years later served as president of the Calgary Construction Association. In 1979 he was chairman of the board of the Alberta Construction Association and the following year was the Alberta vice-president to the Canadian Construction Association. McMechan continues to be an ambassador of the construction industry, accepting speaking engagements to emphasize the need for a professional approach to the industry.

These two houses, built in 1913 at 1013 and 1015 17th Avenue N.W., represented some of the initial construction ventures of the Hornstrom brothers.

IRVING INDUSTRIES LTD.

The Irving brothers, Donald and Harry, grew up in an entrepreneurial, independent atmosphere. Their father, Frederick Lorne, had come to Calgary as a young man and started Riverside Iron Works Co. Ltd. in 1911, a business he sold to Dominion Bridge Company in 1929. In 1943 he started the Black Nugget Coal Company, a strip mining operation southeast of Edmonton, which his sons acquired later that decade.

With domestic demand for coal dropping, the brothers sold the assets of Black Nugget to create Irving Holdings in 1952. Today the holding company wholly owns the two divisions of Irving Industries—Irving Wire Products Ltd. and Foothills Steel Foundry—and is majority owner of Irvco Resources Ltd.

The brothers knew they were taking a gamble when they created Irving Wire in 1954 but felt they were young enough to recover if their venture failed. Their idea came from hearing a customer complain that he couldn't get locally manufactured wire mesh for reinforcing concrete. As a result, Irving Wire was born on a one-acre lot just south of the city limits—now Glenmore Trail—which even provided a slough for hunting ducks. By 1970 Irving Wire had an annual production of three million dollars. It was the first fully integrated manufacturer of welded wire fabric in Western Canada and a pioneer manufacturer of wire fabric for reinforcing concrete pipe.

In 1958 an adjoining steel foundry became available. It was in financial difficulty but the brothers turned it around; today Foothills Steel is the largest steel foundry in Alberta. Donald took over its active management in 1960 and remains its president. Harry is president of the wire division. The foundry makes custom-steel castings for industrial, construction, oil, and mining machinery. In any month it may produce up to 200 different products with production of up to 300 tons. The plant employs over 100 people.

The brothers had been active in oil and gas investments for some time when they decided to create Irvco Resources Ltd. in 1979, a public company which has annual revenues of about $1.5 million from extensive United States operations. It is controlled by Irving Holdings, a largely passive holding company—with some real estate holdings—jointly owned by the brothers with Harry as president and Donald as chairman. Harry is president and chief executive officer of Irvco.

The brothers complement each other's strong points. Both have degrees from McGill University, Donald in mechanical engineering and Harry in economics. In 1977 Harry also earned a master's degree in resource studies from the University of Calgary.

Football is another family common denominator. Their father was at one time president of the Calgary Bronks—forerunners of the Stampeders—and both brothers played for the University of Alberta Golden Bears. Harry, a captain of the Golden Bears and co-captain and all-star at McGill, spent a year in the professional ranks—as reserve quarterback for the Calgary Stampeders in 1948, the year they went undefeated and won the Grey Cup. Harry has since served as chairman of the Alberta Young Presidents' Organization and has been a vice-president and executive member of The Calgary Chamber of Commerce. He is currently a governor of the University of Calgary as well as a director of a number of Canadian public and private companies. Donald has been chairman of the Alberta branch of the American Foundries Society.

The two divisions of Irving Industries—Foothills Steel Foundry and Irving Wire Products—spent much of their early years on the outskirts of Calgary until the city closed in around them.

Frederick Lorne Irving stands between his sons, Harry (left) and Donald, at the 10th anniversary of Irving Wire Products Ltd.

KAI MORTENSEN

It was natural that Kai Mortensen would come directly to Calgary after leaving his native Denmark. The 26-year-old furniture craftsman, exasperated with Danish moves toward a welfare state, simply followed the trail of stories and Indian relics he had grown up with. During the 1920s many Danes had settled in Calgary, only to return to their homeland as the result of the despair of the Depression. But the stories intrigued Mortensen—and his limited knowledge of Canadian geography brought him to the only Canadian city he had ever heard of.

Within two years of his arrival, Mortensen had his own company, Foothills Upholstering Ltd. Upholstered furniture had been a family tradition. He grew up in a town renowned for furniture making, had apprenticed under his grandfather, and then worked with his father.

His first location in 1959 was a rather strange one for a furniture repair business—the fifth floor of a warehouse. Within six months the firm moved to 12th Avenue S.W. across from the Colonel Belcher Hospital, but that too became cramped.

Mortensen was initially turned down for a $5,000 bank loan to support a new location on Macleod Trail in the downtown area. Finally, he managed to impress a Toronto Dominion Bank employee to note that "this seems to be a hard-working shop" and the business prospered. However, by 1966 the city started talking about urban renewal. Stymied in his efforts to sell and relocate, Mortensen dogged the steps of the city's negotiator and virtually held a one-man sit-in until he received an offer.

Mortensen worked out of a temporary location for a year and in 1968 formed Scandia Holdings with some friends to buy property on 11th Avenue S.W. When that space was outgrown by 1972, he built the firm's current location of 1235 11th Avenue S.W. on the adjacent lot and renamed the company Interiors by Kai Mortensen.

The business by then had developed

Since 1978 Kai Mortensen has also served as Honorary Danish Consul for Southern Alberta, looking after the interests of about 15,000 people of Danish origin.

into a custom shop for new furniture, complete with its own drapery-manufacturing facilities. Today the store is a designer-oriented furniture store with the sales staff consisting entirely of interior designers and decorators.

The furniture manufacturing operation has since left the company and become Kamor Furniture Ltd., jointly owned by Mortensen, his son Johnny, and his brother-in-law John Kristensen. Kamor manufactures all the upholstered furniture sold by Kai Mortensen—as the store is now known—and recently has moved into top-of-the-line executive furniture. In 1979 Mortensen resurrected Foothills Upholstering, which now does all the reupholstering and draperies for the firm under the direction of longtime employee Elmar Petersen.

Mortensen's office is unique in the furniture business—it is the only one that also doubles as a consulate. Since 1978 Mortensen has been the honorary Danish consul for Southern Alberta, looking after the interests of about 15,000 people of Danish origin.

The family tradition in furniture, meanwhile, continues. Wife Birthe has played a key role in the company. Another son, Glen, has shown interest in the furniture business. And the firm, which started with only four employees, now has more than three times that number in furniture sales alone.

The original company-owned location of Foothills Upholstering, at 310 Second Street S.E.

LAVALIN SERVICES INC.

Now firmly entrenched in the West, Canada's largest engineering firm first established itself in Calgary as a result of a visit in 1936 by Bernard Lamarre, grandson of the founder of the Montreal-based Lavalin Inc.

Calgary-born Arthur R. Smith, a former Member of Parliament, well-known executive, and long-standing friend of Lamarre, was instrumental in introducing him to the western scene.

Lamarre returned to the corporate head office in Montreal convinced the West was too vital to ignore. In 1974 Lavalin acquired the Canadian operations of Pipe Line Technologists Inc. of Houston, Texas, now renamed Petrotech Lavalin Inc. and specializing in pipelines. In 1975 Fenco Consultants Ltd. became a member of Lavalin. Its 500 employees specialize in civil engineering and drilling bases including structures resistant to pack ice and icebergs. Another 1975 acquisition was Geocon, a geotechnical engineering company involved in soil mechanics, permafrost, and earthquake engineering.

These acquisitions formed the initial westward thrust of Lavalin Inc., a private, wholly Canadian firm which started as a partnership of Lalonde Lamarre Valois and Associates in 1936 in Montreal. It remained almost totally involved in civil engineering in the Montreal region until Bernard Lamarre took over as president in the 1960s. He developed the corporation's international operations—now Lavalin Interna-

Petrotech Lavalin Inc. had to cross waterways such as Moore Creek in completing a pipeline to the Ocelot methanol plant at Kitimat, British Columbia.

tional Inc., with offices in Africa, Asia, Europe, Latin America, the United States, and the Middle East, and projects in more than 50 countries—and took the organization into the Maritimes and the West. Lavalin Inc. is the holding company, made up of more than 40 technical divisions. Permanent employees now total 6,600. Although it has branch offices across the country, Lavalin directs its operations from four major centres: Montreal, Toronto, Vancouver, and Calgary.

Calgary is the headquarters for Lavalin Services Inc., the coordinating company for the divisions that operate in Western

Canada. The 1,000 employees, now spread among four buildings in the city, comprise one of the largest engineering firms in Alberta.

The western region is headed by Kenneth Fitzgerald, regional vice-president of Lavalin Inc. Arthur Smith (who joined the organization in 1981) is president of Lavalin Services Inc. Smith's duties (beginning in 1982) also incorporated the new position of senior corporate officer for oil and gas, indicating Lavalin's increasingly serious intentions in that field. Fitzgerald is also president of Partec Lavalin Inc., one of the operating divisions formed in 1975 via the succession of Lavalin over the Ralph M. Parsons Co. Ltd. Partec Lavalin Inc. provides engineering, procurement, and construction services for the petroleum and petrochemical industries.

Other western operations include MacLaren Plansearch Services Ltd., consultants on environmental work and oceanography, and MacLaren Engineers, Planners and Scientists Inc., specializing in water systems and waste management. Another firm headquartered in Calgary is Global Trading (1979) Inc., a contractor in equipment and materials for petroleum projects worldwide.

Acquiring the Shawiningan Group in 1982 made Lavalin Inc. a potential world leader in the design and construction of thermal and hydroelectric power projects. Lavalin's stature is also demonstrated by its participation in megaprojects, notably the Olympic Stadium in Montreal and the $16-billion James Bay hydroelectric facility where Lavalin provided the largest manpower involvement.

In Alberta, Lavalin has two major projects under design and construction. One, the largest gas-processing and sulphur recovery plant proposed for Alberta in the past decade, is near Edson; the other is a crude oil-processing plant at Norman Wells. In British Columbia, four divisions of Lavalin are providing EPC services for the Ocelot methanol plant at Kitimat. Lavalin is also undertaking design work for the Foothills Pipeline Project.

Partec Lavalin Inc. designed this gas plant near Waterton Lakes.

A.E. LEPAGE (PRAIRIES) LTD.

The A.E. Lepage real estate company arrived in Calgary in 1955 as Melton Real Estate Ltd., located in a rather inauspicious downtown basement office. Today it is one of the largest real estate firms in the world, the largest in Alberta, and among the top three in Calgary.

A.E. Lepage established the organization that now bears his name across the country in Ontario in 1913. Alberta came under the firm's umbrella on January 1, 1976, when Lepage purchased the brokerage division of Melton. Melton's development arm became Melcor Developments Ltd. and is now listed on the Toronto Stock Exchange.

The original Melton real estate business was founded in Edmonton in 1929 by L.T. Melton, who subsequently sold it to his son Stanley in 1946. Under the son's leadership the firm grew to become the dominant real estate company in Alberta with important representation in Saskatchewan, Manitoba, and British Columbia. Stan Melton, president of the Canadian Real Estate Association in 1963, died in 1973.

Another son, Michael, opened the Melton Calgary office on November 1, 1955, on Eighth Avenue. Al Larsen, now executive vice-president of the Alberta Real Estate Association, was an original Calgary office member.

A.E. Lepage has grown by acquisitions and mergers. It operated initially in Ontario and then moved into Quebec. In 1971 it leapfrogged into British Columbia. In 1975 the business was incorporated as a step into the Prairies. An office-leasing facility was opened in Calgary, followed by an office in Edmonton specializing in industrial, commercial, and investment services. Over the years discussions had taken place intermittently with Melton and in 1976 the Melton brokerage business became part of A.E. Lepage.

Subsequently, in late 1980, the firm was reorganized as A.E. Lepage (Prairies) Ltd. with corporate offices at 933 17th Avenue S.W. The company is now almost totally owned by its employees. Nationally Lepage employs more than 4,000 persons and has annual transactions of $3 billion. Over the years it has grown to become a totally diversified real estate operation. In the early 1980s it continued its expansion by acquiring the brokerage offices of National Trust and Co-op Trust.

In Calgary in 1981 the company's volume was $500 million. There are 340 sales people in southern Alberta. As on the national scene, 60 percent of Calgary's business comes from residential sales.

A.E. Lepage operates a totally diversified commercial department including property management, industrial leasing, and industrial sales. It has residential outlets in every major town and city in the province. In Calgary it has both a corporate relocation office and a home search centre. In addition to operating its own computer service, Lepage provides employees with a 10-day in-house sales training program.

A.E. Lepage not only serves its clients, it also benefits the community. As a good corporate citizen it makes large annual donations to communities and charities. The regional manager and vice-president of the southern Alberta region since 1977 has been Ted Zaharko, who started with Melton in 1971 as a salesman in Edmonton's Jasper Place office—the firm's original office.

MacCOSHAM VAN LINES (CALGARY) LTD.

R.V. "Vic" MacCosham arrived as a 21-year-old in Edmonton in 1906 and over his lifetime left such an impression that he was once asked to be the province's lieutenant governor. He was born in the Ottawa Valley and westerners were frequently surprised that a man with such a Scottish name should claim French as his mother tongue. The local press, in the florid prose of the day, described the founder of MacCosham Van Lines as "a young man come out of the East following a guiding star." Over the next half-century he was to create the largest privately owned company in the moving industry.

The firm was incorporated in 1913 and by the 1920s MacCosham vans were travelling the gravelled highways of the province. In the heyday of the draft horse and the dray wagon, MacCosham built a three-storey horse barn with stables on the second floor. The last two-horse teams were retired in 1947.

While the Prairies were being devastated by the Depression, MacCosham was one of the few businesses strong enough to grow. In 1937 it expanded into Calgary through the purchase of the 1911-established Johnson Storage and Cartage Company Ltd. MacCosham issued a flamboyant press release promising Calgarians unparalleled service and predicting growth in all areas. Privately, however, he wrote to a business associate: "I am not so certain that the man who expands these days is good, bad, or indifferent. In Alberta it is always a gamble."

The gamble paid off despite economics which saw warehouse space rent for five cents a square foot and unloading of box cars go for a flat rate of $15. MacCosham's sense of thrift was notorious. Once, outraged to find lights left burning during the lunch hour in a Saskatoon warehouse, he demanded 60 cents from the offending party. He then hurled the change out the door to prove that waste was costly. In an effort to ease the financial plight of employees, he was instrumental in the formation of the still-successful MacCosham Credit Union.

The Calgary business, operating from

This International Harvester chain-drive truck was one of the early motorized acquisitions of a moving company that also used horses until 1947.

R.V. "Vic" MacCosham had this portrait taken in 1906 when he was 21 years old and had just moved to the West to seek his fortune.

a brick and sandstone warehouse on 10th Avenue S.W. grew steadily. Constructed in 1907, the warehouse was a landmark in the commercial community and in 1980 was restored and redesigned as "MacCosham Place."

In 1945 the firm constructed a new warehouse at the junction of the Bow and Elbow rivers. It turned out to be the site of Fort Calgary, the post established by the Northwest Mounted Police in 1875. In its centennial year the city decided to commemorate Calgary's origins and MacCosham found itself in the midst of an archeological dig. When the company was asked for permission to sink two exploratory shafts in the floor of the warehouse, it was decided that the time had come to step aside for history and relocate on a 10-acre site in the Foothills Industrial Park. This complex is now the largest in the MacCosham group of 26 locations, which nationally has over 26 million cubic feet of warehouse space and operates more than 400 trucks. Of the organization's 600 employees, 100 are in Calgary — swelling to 200 during the busy summer months.

Prior to his death in 1959, MacCosham arranged to sell his firm to his employees. MacCosham Van Lines (Calgary) Ltd. is now wholly owned by all active employees.

LEWIS STATIONERY LTD.

The firm's current premises are located at 240 11th Avenue S.W.

"**E**verything for the office ... with service," is the motto of Lewis Stationery Ltd. Calgary-owned, Calgary-operated, the fiercely independent, community-oriented company has been serving the oil industry capital for 50 years.

Founded during the Great Depression by Jimmy and Mary Lewis, the firm has prospered and grown to become one of the province's largest family-owned office supply companies.

There is scarcely an oil company in Calgary that does not do business with Lewis Stationery, which is jointly owned by Mary Lewis, president, and her daughter, Moira Reid, general manager.

Together they oversee over 100 employees working out of the company's new premises, an 89,000-square-foot structure at 7260 12th Street S.E., and an older seven-storey building at 240 11th Avenue S.W. near the heart of the city.

That is a far cry from the "Dirty '30s," when Mary and her late husband, a World War I veteran, opened a miniscule, 150-square-foot shop near the current Hudson's Bay Company premises at 225 8th Avenue S.W.

"In 1933 we were at the bottom of the Depression," says Mrs. Lewis. "We were operating out of tiny quarters and our inventory was contained in a single display case. When someone ordered 10 pencils, for example, my husband

shed to the supplier and picked up a
zen—10 to fill the order and two for
ock. That's the way we built up our
ventory."

Those were hard days but the Lewis'
termination, optimism, and common
nse approach to business paid off. In
934 the firm moved again to much
rger offices at 405 8th Avenue S.W.
ewis Stationery, which has constantly
ospered, reached its take-off point in
937 when it began an expansion pro-
am that saw it move every 10 years to
ver-more spacious premises in the
uthwest quarter of the city.

In 1937 the business utilized 1,500
uare feet. In 1947, at 532 8th Avenue
W., it occupied 5,000. In 1957, at 620
h Avenue S.W., it used 10,000, and
nally, in 1971, the company moved to
0,000 square feet of space at 240 11th
venue S.W. There, it devotes one-
ird of the space to office furniture
one.

Lewis Stationery has expanded their
remises to a mammoth new building
which is strategically located at the intersection of Glenmore and Deerfoot Trails,
major east-west and north-south traffic
arteries, respectively, in addition to
retaining its downtown store.

That growth in floor space has been
accompanied by a growing work force. In
1933 Lewis Stationery was run entirely
by its dedicated owners. By 1972 it had a
staff of 32, and now, just 10 years later, a
staff of 115.

Today pencils are a minor part of the
retail inventory which, besides the company's Stampede brand stationery products, ranges from office furniture, desk
accessories and file cabinets to electronic
calculators, briefcases and gift items. As
well, Lewis Stationery operates a modern
specialty bindery, producing custom-
made binders, folders and covers.

The loyal, efficient service extended
by the company to its customers during
the hard times of 50 years ago continues
today. Many original customers still come
to Lewis Stationery for their needs and
their ranks have been expanded by thou-

*Mrs. Mary Lewis (left) is President and her
daughter, Mrs. Moira Reid, is General Manager
of Lewis Stationery Ltd.*

sands of private and corporate clients
who have made the Stampede City
what it is today—one of Canada's fastest-
growing business centres.

*Lewis Stationery's new headquarters, at 7260
12th Street, S.E.*

MACLIN FORD

In 1915 if you wanted to buy a Ford car, you had to purchase it directly from the Ford Motor Company of Canada. Chances are that if you bought such a car back then in Calgary, E.A. (Ernie) McCullough sold it to you. In 1916 he sold more cars than any other Ford salesman in the country.

This success so impressed the Ford Motor Company that in 1917, when it decided to set up dealerships rather than use a direct sales force, McCullough was granted the first Ford agency in Alberta. Together with partner T.W. Lines he formed Maclin Motors Ltd.—the name came from the combination of "Mac" in McCullough and the first three letters of "Lines."

Officially incorporated on August 8, 1917, Maclin Motors occupied the corner of 15th Avenue and First Street S.E. and employed 15 people. Lines stayed just a few months.

The new firm had scarcely opened for business when McCullough joined the Royal Flying Corps to train as a pilot. He returned near the end of 1918 to remain as principal owner, president, and managing director. In the mid-1950s he moved up to become chairman of the board. At that time he had already been associated with the automobile industry longer than any other Calgary dealer.

In 1920 the dealership moved closer to the downtown core to 11th Avenue and First Street S.W. a location it occupied for 40 years. With a series of additions, by 1950 the operation occupied almost an entire city block and employed 150 people. Maclin's first sales were of the popular Model T and as models changed by 1950 the firm had already sold over 50,000 automobiles.

McCullough gave freely of himself to the community in many different areas. He had come to Calgary in 1908 and upon graduation from Garbutt's Business College went to work for the Canadian Pacific Railway. Prior to joining Ford he had worked as a clerk for Canadian Oils and as a piano salesman. McCullough served as alderman from 1937 to 1944 and was the founding president of the Glencoe Club.

Not all of Maclin's activities take place on the ground. The firm had the first commercial balloon in Alberta. Pilot Dale Lang has flown the balloons for Maclin since 1974.

The first car in Canada appeared in 1896 and some years later was on display at Maclin Motors. Taking it for a run were Maclin's service manager, Fred Tucker (in top hat), Maclin founder Ernie McCullough, Sr. (the driver), and longtime office employee Freda Gustafson.

His elder son, Ernie J., became president and general manager of Maclin in the mid-1950s. He had graduated from Notre Dame University magna cum laude and was named to the "University Men of the Year" list in the United States. An excellent quarter-miler, he represented Canada in the 1948 Olympics in London, England. Ernie J. was also very involved in community service and was the founding president of the Calgary Olympic Development Association in 1956.

In 1960 younger son Danny became general manager. When the elder McCullough passed away in 1965, the company was reorganized with Ernie J. as chairman and Danny as general manager and president.

Maclin took a bold step in 1960 by leaving the downtown location and becoming the first new-car dealership to be located on Macleod Trail. The move to Macleod Trail at 61st Avenue S.W. was successful as Maclin continues today as the longest established Ford dealership in a major Canadian city.

Maclin has an antique car collection of over 50 vehicles, including three 1903 models—the year Ford started mass production. The company is also well known as the sponsor of the Alberta marathon championships. In addition, since 1976 it has sponsored a chuckwagon outfit with driver Kelly Sutherland who has won both the Canadian and Stampede championships.

THE NORCAL GROUP OF COMPANIES

Hardy Nielsen arrived in Calgary from Denmark in 1951 at the age of 11. After completing his education at Crescent Heights High School and working at several jobs, he spent nine years at Sherwin-Williams where he became sales manager. During this time he started dabbling in real estate by obtaining older houses, renovating them, and selling them. In 1968, to give a formal structure to his growing portfolio of real estate holdings, he established Nelco Corporation Ltd. By 1982 Nielsen was owner of an organization, The Norcal Group of Companies, which had spread into the United States and was active in investment, development, land acquisition, sales and leasing, and property management.

Nielsen's first large project was an apartment on Avenburn Road. Nelco's volume of business in its first year was around $100,000. In 1970 he saw opportunities in residential construction and formed Norcal Construction Ltd., and subsequently in 1972, Nelco Engineering. On land already acquired by Nelco the firm built duplexes and apartments in the growing suburbs of Forest Lawn and Acadia. When the residential market became saturated in 1973, Norcal was already involved in the development of warehouses and was

Hardy Nielsen, president of The Norcal Group of Companies.

entering the field of commercial development.

At this point, because of the scope of endeavors, Norcal's name was changed to Norcal Development Ltd. In 1974 Nielsen bought 50 acres in Franklin Park, a major commercial-retail-warehouse-office development. Norcal's success in building and developing properties for the group and in constructing and project managing for other companies created a need for a real estate team. Consequently, in 1976 Norcal

Real Estate Services was created to handle land acquisitions, leasing, and sales.

In order to strengthen its base and avoid the fluctuations of the Canadian real estate market, Norcal moved into the United States in 1978. Norcal Corporation Inc. was founded as a U.S. holding company, based in Denver and incorporated in six states. In 1980, with expansion into property leasing and sales, Norcal Real Estate Company was founded in downtown Denver.

The five corporations of the group now function under the umbrella of The Norcal Group of Companies. Nielsen's first company, Nelco, now serves some 250 lease clients. The group remains Calgary-based with headquarters at 3016 Fifth Avenue N.E. and all of its non-U.S. operations focused in the city. Some 50 persons are employed in the Canadian ventures.

The Norcal Group is rich in experience in every aspect of real estate and is staffed by a core of professionals. It continues to take on some of the most ambitious projects in western North America and its U.S. expansion plans call for half of its future operations to be located in that country.

Nelco Square—Norcal's prestigious head office in Calgary's Franklin Park.

NOVA, AN ALBERTA CORPORATION

The story of NOVA, AN ALBERTA CORPORATION (formerly The Alberta Gas Trunk Line Company Limited) begins in the early 1950s. With the excitement of the Leduc-inspired oil boom, people started to realize that the sedimentary basins containing petroleum held another potential source of energy wealth—natural gas. Private companies applied to the Alberta government for licences to export this fuel to markets elsewhere, especially in Eastern Canada, but the provincial government was determined that any gas exported should be surplus to the needs of the province. When studies showed there were large surpluses, the concern became how to allow exports and at the same time see that the best interests of the people of Alberta were served.

The provincial government decided its objectives could best be met by establishing a new company, owned by private investors and responsible for the gathering and transmission of all Alberta natural gas to be exported from the province. By specifying that it would operate only in Alberta and that directors had to be Alberta residents, the government ensured that the company would fall exclusively under provincial regulatory jurisdiction and would continue to work for Albertans in the future.

On April 8, 1954, royal assent was granted to a special act of the Alberta legislature, "An Act to Incorporate a Gas Trunk Line Company to Gather and Transmit Gas Within the Province," and The Alberta Gas Trunk Line Company Limited (AGTL) was created. The structure of the company as outlined in the act was unique, giving rise to the mistaken notion that AGTL was controlled by the government. Class "A" shareholders were to have no voting privileges; these rested exclusively with Class "B" shareholders. Class "B" was divided into four groups—utilities, export companies, producers, and government appointees—each of whom had to be from the private sector. However, of the seven-man board of directors, only two were appointed by the government and each of them held only two of the 2,002 Class "B" shares.

Changes in the act have since increased membership of the board to 15. Class "A" shareholders now elect seven directors, Class "B" shareholders elect four, and the government appoints four.

A provisional board of directors appointed by the provincial government met in Calgary on June 5, 1954, to arrange distribution of shares. Later that month William F. Knode, who had been instrumental in setting up the Alberta Petroleum and Natural Gas Conservation Board, was called back from Texas to serve as general manager. James

Alberta Premier Ernest Manning (right) officially opened the initial section of the NOVA system on July 12, 1957.

Pipeline construction today proceeds much as it did in 1962 when this line was laid in southeastern Alberta.

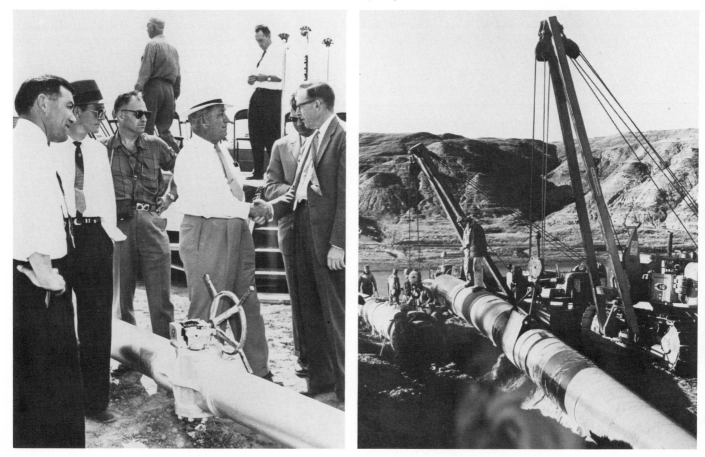

NOVA's world-scale ethylene complex at Joffre, Alberta, is a key element in the province's petrochemical development.

Waste heat from NOVA operations is harnessed and used in such innovative projects as greenhouses at the Princess compressor station site.

C. Mahaffy was appointed secretary-treasurer. AGTL opened its first office on June 20, 1954, in a basement location at 512 Eighth Avenue S.W.

By the end of 1954 the distribution of shares was complete, and an elected board of directors took charge after the first annual meeting in January 1955. The board assembled a management team of seven persons in addition to Mr. Knode and Mr. Mahaffy and, in anticipation of the start of operations, the corporation moved to new offices in the Pacific Building at 320 Ninth Avenue S.W.

By March 1955, however, it appeared that the move was premature and that there was a good possibility the new venture might not be needed. The markets for natural gas were in Eastern Canada, so it was essential that proposed cross-Canada pipeline facilities be given approval before work could begin on the AGTL system. When it proved impossible to arrange satisfactory financing for the cross-Canada project, a delay was announced, and a year later the project was still tied up. By that time, every gas producer but one had stopped calling at the AGTL office, convinced the situation was hopeless. The seven original employees were advised to look for new jobs. Then, in June 1956, after a solid month of acrimonious debate in the House of Commons, Trade and Commerce Minister C.D. Howe invoked closure to clear the way for construction of the cross-Canada system (TransCanada PipeLines Limited). This in turn meant that AGTL could proceed with its mandate.

The company started laying pipe in December 1956 and, to pay for the construction, issued 2.5 million Class "A" common shares in the spring of 1957. The *Financial Post* referred to the offering as "the biggest stock bonanza ever to hit the Prairies." Available only to Alberta residents, the shares were so popular that a rationing system was

devised, with each person restricted to 20 shares. The forms required only family names, and people were eager to become involved in a provincially based company managed by Albertans. There were even stories that some bought extra stock in the names of family pets, goldfish, and canaries. Others went from town to town, making application at different banks, hoping for extra allotments. These early shareholders were almost all Albertans, but shares today are owned very widely, with over 90 percent registered in Canada.

The official startup of the AGTL system came just seven months after the beginning of construction. At a ceremony near Cavendish on July 23, 1957, Premier Ernest Manning opened a valve that allowed Alberta natural gas to flow eastward through the new pipeline.

At first, since the company moved gas

only to eastern export points, the system was built by linking up gas fields close to the Saskatchewan border. Then the provincial government authorized gas exports to British Columbia and the United States, and it became necessary to expand elsewhere in the province. In 1961 the firm placed its Foothills Division into service, and deliveries to the British Columbia and Montana borders began. Also in 1961, the first AGTL compressor station was completed at Princess, Alberta.

By 1963 the company, operating through three divisions, had over 1,500 miles of pipeline moving about 1.3 bil-
(Continued)

The NOVA building, completed in 1982, is a prominent new addition to Calgary's skyline.

Mechanized welding, shown here on a southern section of the Alaska Highway Gas Pipeline, is a modern development.

lion cubic feet of gas per day. In anticipation of this rapid growth, the head office was moved in 1960 to the Alberta Wheat Pool Building at 505 Second Street S.W.

Throughout the 1960s AGTL continued to grow, gaining industry respect for developments in pipeline technology. A 173-mile line from Carstairs to Edson built in 1965 was the first large-diameter pipeline to be installed in winter. That year the company also began a program of automation allowing the entire system to be monitored 24 hours a day from a central control centre. The company was the first in Canada to practice topsoil conservation and one of the first to revegetate pipeline rights-of-way in forested areas.

AGTL employed more than 550 people by 1970 and operated a pipeline system over 3,000 miles long. The board of directors decided that, while the company could continue to provide the services of its utility franchise efficiently and economically, its ability to obtain financing and its active management and professional staff would permit it to take on new challenges serving both regional and national purposes and providing for long-term growth and security. Accordingly, the AGTL act was amended to allow diversification into areas not directly related to the original mandate.

The first steps toward diversification were into petrochemicals, and during the 1970s the firm became involved in the manufacture of methanol, ethylene, and polyvinyl chloride, taking a leadership role in making Alberta a major centre for the manufacture of these products. AGTL's experience in natural gas transmission was also put to use through its co-sponsorship of two large-scale pipeline projects: the Alaska Highway Gas Pipeline and the Trans Quebec & Maritimes Pipeline.

During the mid-1970s AGTL acquired interests in valve manufacturing companies in the United States and Europe and in 1978 became a major force in the Canadian petroleum indus-try with the purchase of majority ownership of Husky Oil Ltd. Husky is a fully integrated Canadian company which is aggressively developing conventional and non-conventional petroleum resources.

Thus in the 10 years prior to 1980 the company had changed from a pipeline utility to a diversified organization with interests in resource development, petrochemicals, and manufacturing added to its gas transmission base. The decade saw another corporate move, this one in 1975 to Bow Valley Square 2 at 205 Fifth Avenue S.W. "Alberta Gas Trunk Line" no longer adequately described the company's varied activities, and in August 1980 the name was changed to NOVA, AN ALBERTA CORPORATION to reflect its diversity while still emphasizing its Alberta base.

Throughout this period of expansion the firm maintained an early commitment to purchasing goods and services from Alberta and Canadian suppliers whenever possible. As an example, pipe purchased from domestic steel producers was used throughout the Alberta system, and in 1980 these companies were awarded contracts to supply pipe for the Alaska Highway Gas Pipeline. The policy is based on recognition of how important procurement activities and development of a strong supply base are in serving the company's needs and in helping the country and its regions achieve economic goals. At the end of 1981 the corporation recorded an annual consolidated net income of $130 million and assets of over $5 billion, and the NOVA companies employed almost 10,000 people.

NOVA's continued growth necessitated one more move and its own addition to the Calgary skyline was completed in 1982. The 37-story NOVA building at 801 Seventh Avenue S.W. provides a dramatic architectural addition to the downtown core. From these new corporate headquarters NOVA expects to continue its activity as a major, independent Canadian-owned company, working toward economic prosperity and future energy supply for Alberta and Canada.

NU-WEST GROUP LIMITED

In 1957 Ralph Scurfield had to sell his house and obtain a bank loan to raise the $15,000 needed to purchase a quarter share in a floundering Nu-West Homes Limited. He has since parlayed his investment and business acumen into his current status as largest shareholder of Calgary-based Nu-West Group Limited, the largest homebuilder in Canada and third largest in North America with 1981 assets of $2.5 billion.

The Saskatchewan-born former teacher entered the construction business by going to work for Chesley McConnell of Edmonton, one of the other three original partners of Nu-West. Mr. Scurfield moved to Calgary to revitalize Nu-West by repairing homes built by former owners and introducing a five-year warranty, the first in Canada. Nu-West managed to complete 65 homes that year—15 more than the previous year—and even finished the year with a profit. The following year Nu-West set the stage for future growth by becoming a founding member of Carma Developers Ltd., now Carma Ltd., a company formed to acquire and assemble land. Nu-West's share of Carma is now 48 percent.

Ralph Scurfield, chairman of the board of Nu-West Group Limited, has been the driving force behind the company since its inception.

This was Nu-West's first model home after the firm was acquired by Ralph Scurfield and partners in 1957.

After spending its early life becoming the largest homebuilder in Calgary, Nu-West moved into Edmonton in 1969 and within 15 months was one of the largest in that city. That year Nu-West went public on the Toronto Stock Exchange and constructed its first apartment building.

Since then Nu-West has grown to include real estate operations in five Canadian provinces and eight U.S. states. In 1981 Nu-West built and sold nearly 6,000 homes across Canada. Ten years earlier it had created Nu-West Realty Ltd.—now Ashford Realty—to serve the resale home market. Nu-West Homes was renamed Nu-West Development Corporation Ltd. and in 1973 moved into Saskatchewan with the purchase of Cairns Homes Limited and a year later acquired a 50-percent interest in an Ontario homebuilder, Mayotte Ltd. It started British Columbia operations in 1971. Nu-West moved into the United States in 1976, when it established a Denver division.

In 1979 the company boldly started its diversification by paying $196 million to acquire Calgary-based Voyager Petroleums Ltd. Although Nu-West's primary business continues to be real estate, almost one-third of its assets and a growing portion of its profits are from energy-related sources.

Nu-West's success is due in part to its entrepreneurial atmosphere which encourages employees—1,400 in Canada and 60 in the United States—to make deals and act as if they were in business for themselves. Nu-West Group Limited is now the parent organization of four main operating companies: Nu-West Development, active in Canadian real estate; Nu-West, Inc., a Phoenix-based real estate operation in the southwestern United States; Voyager Petroleums, with a major natural gas sales contract area in east-central Alberta; and Nu-West Florida, Inc., active in commercial real estate development.

In 1981 Mr. Scurfield gave up the post of president he had held since 1957 but remains the driving force as the company's chairman of the board and chief executive officer. H. Earl Joudrie, who continues to serve as president and chief executive officer of Voyager, became president and chief operating officer of Nu-West Group Limited.

Growth of the firm has been astounding. During the 1970s it grew at the rate of 40 percent annually. People seem to like what Nu-West is doing. Five months after buying a Nu-West home, purchasers receive a questionnaire. Ninety-two percent of the responders say they would recommend buying a Nu-West home to their friends.

PRICE WATERHOUSE

Price Waterhouse arrived in Calgary on the eve of the 1929 stock market crash and faced a struggle for survival before riding the crest of Alberta's oil boom to become one of the largest accounting firms in the city. Founded in London, England, in 1850 and expanding to North America in the 1870s, it arrived in Calgary as the result of a Winnipeg merger with Scott and Company which had a Calgary office—Scott and Stuart.

The office opened on July 1 with Thomas Humphries, who was transferred from Vancouver, British Columbia, as manager. A Humphries note recalls: "Goldie Stuart retired and left Calgary in a hurry. ... He disappeared the day after I arrived and he only had time to introduce me to one of his clients, with whom we had a game of golf. ... It was fortunate indeed that we managed to retain most of the clients whose businesses managed to survive the Depression." Company records of the original staff members include the following remarks: "one senior (not a C.A.), two juniors (who were not articled), and one stenographer (not very competent)." Gross billings for 1930 were $11,000, out of which $700 was paid in rent.

Oil developments in the Turner Valley fields in the mid-1930s brought a change in company fortunes. The staff number stood at 13 when Leduc ushered in an even bigger boom period. By this time the company had moved from its original offices in the Grain Exchange Building to the Canada Life Building, but space remained a premium. Of the 700 square feet available, the manager had a five-by-eight area which housed a desk, chair, and filing cabinet but left no room for a wastepaper basket.

During the 1950s most of the work related to the oil industry with expertise growing in oil accounting and taxation. To accommodate a larger staff, the firm moved to the Bentall Building.

The course of the practice was dramatically changed in 1962 when a merger was arranged with Henderson, Waines and Anderson, an organization founded in 1932 by J. Ross Henderson

who had split his early years between accountancy and operating the pari-mutuels for the Western Canada Racing circuit. The firm's staff of 30 matched PW in numbers but changed what was primarily an oil industry practice into one that covered every aspect of business. Company offices were moved to the Texaco Building.

The firm established Price Waterhouse Associates as a management consulting arm in the 1970s. In addition to the traditional accounting activities, PW has added a special services department to provide business advice geared for the owner-manager.

The firm now employs 180 persons in the 25th-floor offices of Palliser Square One it has occupied since 1971. There

R.E. (Bob) Waller was partner-in-charge for 22 years and played a leading role in solving oil industry accounting problems.

have been six partners-in-charge since PW opened in Calgary. Humphries was named partner-in-charge in 1942 and retired in 1947. Arthur Maw took over and was replaced by William Smith in 1950. The longest term was served by R.E. (Bob) Waller who was partner-in-charge for 22 years beginning in 1952. He played a leading role in solution of accounting problems unique to the oil industry. W.F. (Fay) Anderson, who came over in the 1962 merger, was partner-in-charge for seven years until Bruce Dunlop, a 25-year member of the Toronto office, took over in 1981.

REGGIN INDUSTRIES LTD.

The Depression wasn't an auspicious time to start a business but to L.D. Reggin it was the best way to survive. Reggin was a determined man, unwilling to let hardship defeat him. He had been sales manager for a steel products company but lost his job in 1931 when times got tough. He walked the streets for a couple of days and then bought a failing roofing and sheet metal business. With the purchase came S. W. Keen, a metal worker who was to become the firm's superintendent and vice-president.

Reggin was an accountant by profession but a contractor by choice. In the early years he worked side by side with his employees and did the books at night. The barter system was used widely at the time and it was not unusual to find payment made in cases of beans. An out-of-town job meant sleeping in tents or boxcars.

As needs and industry changed, so did corporate endeavors. The firm entered the heating business as demands for housing increased following World War II under the direction of S. Roberts. Reggin expanded into food-service equipment when that need became apparent and it established an air conditioning division as soon as high-rise buildings started to emerge. The forma-

tion of a refrigeration operation soon followed.

In 1948 the company was incorporated as Reggin Roofing and Metal Works and in 1963 it became known as Reggin Industries Ltd.

O. A. "Os" Reggin, son of the founder, became president and general manager in 1958 upon the untimely death of his parents. He had been with the company since 1946 after four years in the armed services. Earlier, he had attended business college and had

Ted Tucker (left) and John Zacharias inspect the modern refrigeration equipment for one of Calgary's curling rinks.

apprenticed as a sheet metal worker.

Os Reggin now owns the controlling interest in the firm with the balance held by company officers. The management team headed by Reggin includes W. W. Jack as sales manager and vice-president since 1960; Ron Pertl, a director since 1966, as treasurer and operations manager; and Alvin Deines, another longtime employee, as secretary since 1962 and manager of the food service division, the firm's largest division.

The company had three prior locations before moving in 1973 to its current location at 7023 Blackfoot Trail

The air conditioning production shop of Reggin Industries Ltd.

S. E. , which provides 40,000 square feet of manufacturing and office space on a three-acre site. By then the firm had entered into the manufacturing field as well. In addition to custom institutional kitchens, the company found that the age of computers was bringing a large demand for environmental control chambers.

Reggin maintains a fleet of 35 radio-equipped vehicles to provide 24-hour service to its customers. Its 225 employees share a part in most of the major construction projects in Calgary, although products are sent throughout Western Canada and some as far as the Arctic Circle and Saudi Arabia.

The company is still growing. In 1979 it started a subsidiary—Inesko—for the distribution of air conditioning products, gas barbecues, and energy-efficient furnaces. It now has branches in Calgary, Toronto, and Vancouver. In 1981 Don Reggin, eldest son of the president, became manager of Inesko.

Reggin Industries was founded on very basic principles: produce a better class of work, satisfy customer needs, and treat employees properly. Continued growth through the years has proven it to be a winning formula.

PRUDENTIAL STEEL LTD.

Prudential Steel Ltd. came into existence in 1966 as the culmination of a dream of four men well-known to the oil and gas industry. Joe Badyk, a former executive of Canada Cities Service, was largely responsible for arranging the financial end of the project. Rolf Osterkampf, vice-president/production, was already well-respected in the pipe-manufacturing industry through managerial capacities with other pipe mills when he undertook to select men for designing and staffing Prudential. Trev Cullen, Henry Dahle, Martin Dutka, and Jack Cote were among those chosen by Rolf. Glen Peckham, with extensive experience in the steel pipe and tubular steel industry, was appointed vice-president and general manager. Together with Norm French, Prudential's president at the time, they put together an aggressive sales force, headed by Frank Finn.

The original management team was later expanded to include Don Wilson as vice-president/sales, Lee Thompson as vice-president and secretary-treasurer, and Doug McIntosh, comptroller and assistant treasurer. The company's first salesmen were Bud Becksted, later pro-

Intensified industry demands for a highly durable, buried-line pipe coating precipitated the timely introduction of Cardinal Tube Coatings Limited and a comprehensive pipe-coating process—a widely accepted move that has proven a very logical extension of customer services.

moted to sales manager, and Jim Wiles, sales-service coordinator. Herb MacKenzie became personnel manager, assisted by Clarence Rossum.

Prudential Steel was founded as a manufacturer of electric resistance weld (ERW) line pipe. Beginning with a work force of 52 and laboring through three very lean years, the firm drew respect and attention from the quality of its products.

An example of its abilities was demonstrated in 1966, when Osterkampf and his crew produced specification pipe from the very first rolling—a notable achievement in view of the fact that two identical installations in other parts of the world were still trying to duplicate this success 18 months after start-up.

Prudential's main markets are in Western Canada and the northwestern United States and within seven years it had captured almost 40 percent of the available market in its product range. By 1973 Prudential employed 150 persons and ranked among the world's most

A leading producer and supplier of hollow structural steel sections, Prudential Steel operates one of the fastest and most efficient, highly automated HSS plants in the world. The firm's production capabilities, including frequently scheduled rollings plus a representative and functional inventory, assure customers of a readily available, highly dependable materials source.

modern pipe-making facilities, featuring a production rate almost double that of most other installations.

However, within a year it was obvious that another mill was necessary. The 1974 expansion, in which the company's own fabrication division did most of the work, provided an additional 50,000 square feet for the manufacture of casing and tubing and hollow structural steel sections (HSS). With the expansion, Prudential became a major supplier of HSS, a highly versatile product with an almost limitless range of applications in construction, manufacturing, and agriculture.

Valued at $5 million, the new mill was capable of forming and welding skelp at a pace of 250 feet per minute—a rather brisk walk. It had an annual capacity of 50,000 tons of steel on one shift. The plant, highly automated and one of the most efficient in the world, made Prudential one of Canada's most technologically advanced producers and distributors of high-quality tubular steel products.

Through a subsidiary, Cardinal Tube Coating Ltd., a custom pipe-coating service is provided. Harry Langford was hired to develop a market for the new product which was given the trade name "Blue-Gard." Sales increased from a few thousand feet in the first year to over five million four years later.

Prudential also maintains a product development division devoted to product improvement. It was this department that was responsible for developing the first ERW sour-gas pipe in Canada.

On April 17, 1973, Prudential Steel Ltd. became a wholly owned subsidiary of Dofasco Inc. The new support pro-

vided the backing necessary for the major expansions initiated in the mid-1970s and carried on in subsequent years.

Dofasco, with 12,000 employees, is Canada's second largest steel producer, having started as a small operation in Hamilton in 1912 under the direction of Clifton W. Sherman. With an 80-ton daily capacity and a work force of 150, the firm initially supplied many of the castings required by locomotive and freight car manufacturers. The pioneering spirit of Sherman has been subsequently evidenced by such developments as Dofasco's introduction of the revolutionary basic oxygen steel-making process to North America. Dofasco was the first Canadian source for such important products as steel plate, floor plate, tin plate, continuously galvanized steel, and electrical steels. During the 1950s it joined the ranks of Canada's fully integrated steel producers with the installation of a blast furnace and coke ovens. Dofasco's expansion program ultimately led to it securing a western foothold through its acquisition of Prudential.

All of Prudential's manufacturing and inventory storage is accommodated on a

70-acre site in southeast Calgary. Its administrative and sales offices are in the Daon Building at 444 Fifth Avenue S.W.

In 1982 Prudential will have completed a $14-million plant expansion, increasing capacity by 30 percent. The project includes a 24,000-square-foot building to house a "Looper," and a high-speed finishing and inspection line.

The corporation and its officials and employees are active in the community in other ways, as well. For example, Prudential president Badyk is past president and a director of the Calgary Petroleum Club. Langford, general sales manager, is on the board of directors of the Calgary Exhibition and Stampede, while executives Wilson and Thompson are associate directors. As a corporate citizen, Prudential, during 1981 (which was designated as the International Year of the Disabled), made a donation to Foothills Academy, a school for children with learning disabilities. Since 1974 the firm has also sponsored the Steelers, the winningest flag football team in Canada.

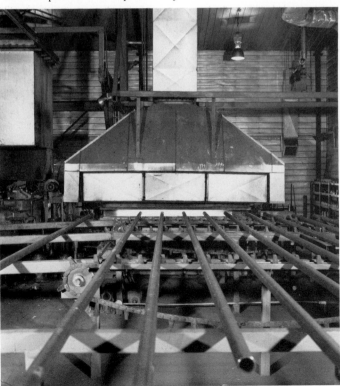

Produced at Prudential's Calgary plant—a general line of casing and tubing for Western Canadian petroleum development companies.

Premium-grade Dofasco skelp is first formed into a continuous tube of precise dimension.

RICHFIELD PROPERTIES LIMITED

The growth of the Richfield Group of Companies has been a reflection of the development of Western Canada. From modest beginnings in commercial warehousing, Richfield has expanded not only by keeping pace but often by setting the pace. Chairman of the board Fred Purich credits this success to "plain old good hard work," a belief in the province's future, and the creation of a product that fulfilled industry needs.

Born in Smokey Lake in 1932, Purich worked at various jobs in Edmonton before coming to Calgary. There he worked for Melton Real Estate—now A.E. Lepage—for four and one-half years but decided to strike out on his own in 1961, initially operating primarily as a real estate broker. The Richfield name was created to incorporate part of the Purich name.

For five years Purich operated Richfield Real Estate Company Ltd. As the firm grew, he created Richfield Building and Design Corporation Ltd., which not only builds for the group but does a high volume in external contracts. Three years later he created Richfield Properties Limited, which subsequently formed a property management division. Richfield Properties is the holding company that owns the buildings. Richfield is unusually successful in property management: Important touches include energy conservation, computerization, qualified service personnel, and well-groomed landscaping.

However, it is in property development that Richfield earned its reputation as an innovator. Enclosed atrium design and development of tilt-up concrete panel construction are among its "firsts." Richfield's specialty has been the design/build concept of construction with projects including shopping centres, supermarkets, office buildings, fast-food outlets, warehouse and distribution facilities, and movie theatres. It is the only company with the capacity to use the tilt-up construction form, which provides speed of erection and all-weather construction capability. Up to 64 feet of wall can be put up at one time in temperatures as low as minus 20 degrees

The Southland Building at the corner of Southland Drive and Macleod Trail features the largest heated parking garage in Calgary as well as a helicopter pad and hangar.

A concrete form is lifted into place as another Richfield project takes shape through the company's unique design/build process, which sees concrete forms made on-site and lifted into place.

Celsius. About half the structures the firm builds are of this design.

The flagship of Richfield's holdings is its 1982-completed Southland Building at Macleod Trail and Southland Drive. The structure offers 600,000 square feet of office space, four movie theatres, and a heated garage for 1,100 cars—the largest in Calgary. It even features a roof-top helicopter pad with the only roof-top hangar in North America.

The company has operated out of a series of offices; the first is now the location of Penny Lane. Since 1977 it has been at Number 220, 7220 Fisher Street S.E. In 1982 Richfield employed 100 persons, including planners, designers, engineers, builders, realtors, financial experts, and technologists. In 1961 Purich had started with only five people.

Since 1981 Herb Reynolds, a professional engineer with a master's degree in business administration, has been the group's president. Purich, a former member of the Young Presidents' Organization, is now a member of the World Business Council.

SCOTIABANK IN CALGARY

The Bank of Nova Scotia, known as Scotiabank to many of its customers around the world, is Canada's second oldest chartered bank. In 1982 the Bank marked its 150th anniversary, and its 100th year of operation in Canada's West.

In 1882, with broad operations in eastern and central Canada, Scotiabank embarked on what was to be a steady and solid expansion westward. The first branch west of the Great Lakes was opened in Winnipeg that year. On March 31, 1903, the Bank's directors recorded in the minute book "the importance of establishing some branches in the Northwest as soon as possible." Three months later, the Bank set up a branch in Edmonton, which was rapidly becoming the centre of the fur trade.

Following a visit by a group of the Bank's directors to the western region in 1903, branches were opened in Wetaskiwin, Fort Saskatchewan, and Calgary. The directors had described much of the province as an uncharted land, with "wolf, coyote, fox, gopher, duck, antelope, and other wild life a-

The Bank of Nova Scotia's main Calgary branch and its regional office are located in the Scotia Centre complex on the downtown mall.

plenty, but little human habitation." Yet many of the towns were already circled with homesteads, and Calgary, built by the ranchmen and made prosperous by the railway, was full of promise.

The Bank of Nova Scotia opened its doors in Calgary on December 16, 1903. The branch's first manager was C.M. Freeman who, because of illness, could not reach Calgary by the time the branch was scheduled to begin business. Undeterred, the Bank sent F.W. Ross from Edmonton to open on schedule.

Between 1903 and 1929 two more Scotiabank branches were established in Calgary, all helping to support the thriving grain industy. The Bank's growth in Calgary, and more broadly, in the West, was particularly impressive considering the distance from the Bank's general office in Toronto and its head office in Halifax, and the relatively primitive communications and transportation systems of the time.

In 1930, despite the Depression, Scotiabank took a further step in its growth in Calgary when it moved its main branch operations from 115 Eighth Avenue West, to a new building at 125 Eighth Avenue West. The new main branch in Calgary was erected by H.G. Macdonald and Company at a cost of $223,722 plus $50,000 for vaults and other furnishings. Scotiabank's main Calgary branch remained there for 46 years until taking up residence in 1976 at the luxurious Scotia Centre, a multistorey commercial complex in the heart of the city.

The Bank has had a long and close association with the province of Alberta, playing an important part in helping Albertans develop their resources—from grain and cattle, to oil exploration and pipelines. In the 30 years since 1952, Calgary has become the home of 33 more Scotiabank branches. That figure indicates the Bank's steadfast commitment to growth and its recognition of Calgary as one of the West's most progressive and successful communities.

Calgary is the centre of Scotiabank's Alberta operations, and the hub of the Bank's commercial and corporate busi-

This is the building that housed The Bank of Nova Scotia when it first started operations in Calgary on December 16, 1903.

ness in the province. Scotia Centre in Calgary houses the Bank's Alberta and Northwest Territories Regional Office, and the Alberta and Saskatchewan International Banking Centre. As part of a network of five such centres across Canada, The International Banking Centre in Calgary provides specialized services to small and medium-size firms, as well as major corporations engaged in import and export trade. The services include foreign exchange, letters of credit, international financing, and advice on all aspects of international trade regulations.

The Bank of Nova Scotia looks forward to serving Albertans in the years to come. With branches throughout the province, Scotiabank is well positioned to meet the needs of a growing population and a burgeoning business community. The Bank will remain an integral part of the province's development. As Tom Cumming, vice-president and general manager of the Bank's Alberta and Northwest Territories Region, states: "We're here. We're committed. And we mean to help Alberta grow."

THE SEFEL GROUP OF COMPANIES

The reception area of the corporate head office of The Sefel Group of Companies.

In 1956 Hungarian refugee Joseph Sefel was working as a janitor in a London, England, department store. A geophysicist with the equivalent of a master's degree, Sefel was awaiting approval to come to Canada to start a new life. Today he is the sole shareholder of a company whose assets stood at $100 million in 1982.

The Sefel Geophysical Ltd. a division of Sefel Group is the largest Canadian geophysical contractor—both internationally and within Canada—and is the ninth largest geophysical corporation in the world. The Sefel Group of Companies, incorporated in 1976 and operating out of its headquarters on the fifth floor of Bow Valley Square II, has three divisions: geophysical, properties, and entertainment. The three arms are not as unrelated as they initially appear. When looking for areas to expand into, Sefel reasoned that energy, housing, and entertainment would remain basic Canadian needs and thus were worthy of pursuit.

Sefel's arrival in Calgary in 1957 followed an unusual chain of events. In London, England, he worked as a department store janitor while applying for jobs in his field of specialty. One of the organizations he applied to was an international geophysical corporation. He was offered a job by them in London but the offer came on the same day he obtained approval to emigrate to Canada. Sefel sent them a letter explaining he couldn't accept the job because he was leaving the country. A few days later he was startled to receive a telegram from this corporation in the refugee camp—saying they had a job opening for him in Calgary. Where was Calgary? He'd never heard of it!

Sefel left them after 10 years to start his own geophysical company. He took some bad advice in buying equipment from a firm that eventually went bankrupt and he lost everything including his health; he spent four months in a hospital. Despite the harrowing experience, Sefel points with pride to the fact that he paid off all his creditors and did not declare bankruptcy.

In 1970 he decided to strike out on his own again. This time he had learned from experience—he was again a geophysical consultant but now there was no investment in equipment. Sefel started as a one-man consultant and a year later incorporated under the name of Sefel J. and Associates. Involved in data processing, the firm bought its first computers thereafter. Incorporation was a major step because almost overnight the company grew to include 30 people. He managed to make the expansion, however, without outside financing. Sefel J. and Associates was the forerunner of the Sefel Group, which now employs over 900 people worldwide.

Sefel Geophysical Ltd. is headed by Saskatchewan-born Frank G. Schweiger. A geologist who had met Sefel in 1964 while both were employed with the same firm, Schweiger worked as a manager of this firm in various parts of the world and eventually became a vice-president. In 1977 Mr. Schweiger formed his own oil and gas exploration company, which he subsequently sold to Sefel in 1979 and he became manager of the Sefel geophysical division.

More than 650 people are employed

M/S Mai, a Sefel seismic exploration vessel.

n the organization's geophysical operations. The company started international operations by opening an office in London, England, in 1973. A Denver office was opened in 1974. Full-scale international operations began in 1979 and currently only 40 percent of the firm's business is of Canadian origin.

Sefel Geophysical Ltd. has had major field operations since 1973, with more recent expansions into the Arctic and South America. The corporation's two ships have seen service in the North Sea, the Mediterranean, and off the coasts of Africa and Canada. Data-processing centres are operated in Calgary, Denver, and London, with a research and development department being an integral part of these offices since the company's inception.

Sefel soon found that diversification was virtually forced upon him. Although the geophysical operations were a good profit producer, the assets of the corporation were not increasing proportionately. The move into properties was made to provide the firm with a growing asset base as well as a cash flow. The asset base was needed to make the business appear more stable—especially in front of financial institution.

Sefel became involved in real estate through the Multiple Unit Residential Building (MURB) program and created its own MURBs by constructing its own buildings. The property operations started in 1975 with the erection of condominiums and apartments. The company's portfolio now includes 800 rental units and it currently also builds accommodations for sale. During 1982 another 200 units were built. Recently the firm has become heavily involved in commercial developments, including high-rise office buildings in Calgary.

Sefel Properties Ltd. has as its president David Carlson, a Saskatchewan-born accountant with an MBA, who joined the firm in his present capacity in 1976 after a mutual acquaintance introduced him to Joseph Sefel. Carlson had been with Abacus Cities for a year and had worked in accounting for Texaco.

The headquarters building of Sefel Properties Development.

The company's move into the entertainment field was "just an evolution of my restlessness," Sefel claims. He describes himself as a good manager who doesn't like details. Once something is going well he starts looking for new areas to conquer.

Since coming to Canada, Sefel has had a dream to create a Canadian indentity through entertainment and culture. His ventures since 1979 have included the full-length feature film, *Kidnapping of the President*, and recordings with internationally acclaimed pianist and conductor Arpad Joo. His record company in Montreal has distributed discs across Canada.

Joseph Sefel's plans don't end there. While personally running the entertainment section, he finds the arrival of pay television in Canada particularly exciting and is determined to be a part of the production houses that will supply the film requirements of this new medium.

Sefel's Calgary data-processing centre.

SHELL CANADA RESOURCES LIMITED

The threat of World War II was looming and oil exploration in Western Canada was just getting under way as Shell Oil Company of New York began an exploration program in the Calgary area in 1939. Earlier in the century, in 1911, Shell Company of Canada Limited—which became Shell Oil Company of Canada Limited in 1931—had been incorporated. Beginning in Eastern Canada, the company had developed retail and refining operations and by 1957, when the American interest had been bought out, the Shell name had spread from British Columbia to Newfoundland.

Shell Oil Company of Canada and its sister organization in the United States both trace their roots to the Royal Dutch/Shell Group formed in London, England, in 1907. The Group in turn is the product of an alliance between Royal Dutch Petroleum Company and the "Shell" Transport and Trading Company. The world-famous symbol of the Shell companies, the pecten, comes from

Calgary division offices of Shell Oil Company, as it was then called, were located in the Canadian Western Natural Gas Building at First Street and Sixth Avenue S.W. in 1957.

the seashells sold as ornaments and buttons in Victorian England by merchant Marcus Samuel through his "Shell" Transport Company.

A major gas field was discovered at Jumping Pound, west of Calgary, in 1944 and seven years later Shell built a gas-processing plant there. The facility still supplies most of Calgary's natural gas needs.

When the firm became Shell Canada Limited in 1963, its activities included all aspects of the oil and gas business. During the 1970s Shell pioneered exploration off the West and East coasts, in the Mackenzie Delta, and in the oil sands regions of Northern Alberta.

In 1976 Shell Canada's exploration and production activities were consolidated into a wholly owned subsidiary, Shell Canada Resources Limited, with its head office in Shell Centre in Calgary. By 1982 it employed 1,500 city residents. Shell started construction of its research centre in University Research Park in 1981, where it will study improved and enhanced oil-recovery techniques and sour-gas technology.

As active members in the community, Shell and its employees have a long

record of support for programs related to health and welfare, education, community and civic affairs, and culture.

In conducting its business activities, Shell has traditionally set social as well as business objectives: Its social performance planning guidelines have been incorporated into the commercial goals. Through employee volunteers, Shell provides funding via a special grant program called the Community Service Fund which makes seed money available for everything from paper supplies for a Brownie pack to a new time clock for a community arena. Shell corporately supports such groups as the United Way; the University of Calgary, Southern Alberta Institute of Technology, and Mount Royal College through bursaries and scholarships; the Centre for the Performing Arts; and theatre and other cultural groups in the city and across the country. The company further supports living Canadian artists through its acquisitions for the Shell Canada Collection.

Shell Centre at 400 Fourth Avenue S.W., completed in the fall of 1977, is the head office of Shell Canada Resources Limited.

SILVESTER BUILDING SUPPLIES LIMITED

Not only has Silvester Building Supplies Limited grown with Calgary, the products it has sold have played a significant part in building it. Its main business today is selling brick, but in the early days a forerunner of the company even manufactured them.

By the time Geoffrey Silvester arrived in Calgary in 1906 he had already established his business and farming credentials in Manitoba. In 1893 he had even been chosen by the Manitoba government to be its commissioner at the Chicago World's Fair that year. He brought nine years of experience in the hardware and lumber business to Calgary when he arrived to become manager and president of Calgary Lime & Cement Co., located at 4th Street and 10th Avenue S.W. —now Gaslight Square. In 1910 he became sole owner of the firm, renamed it the Calgary Silicate Pressed Brick Co., and started manufacturing a sand and lime brick.

He formed G. Silvester Supplies Limited in 1922—a business he retained until 1944—and began handling all types of building supplies except lumber. Plaster was an especially big line in those days. However, despite his business commitments, Silvester remained active in public life, serving as alderman in 1920 and as a member of the school board in 1923.

When he decided to retire, three employees bought Silvester out. Named as the new president and managing director of G. Silvester Supplies Limited was Frank E. Staines, born and educated in

Frank E. Staines was one of three partners who bought Silvester Building Supplies from the founder in 1944.

Douglas J. Staines (left) and his father, John H. (Jack) Staines.

Toronto but a resident of Calgary since 1910. He had joined the firm in 1926 after working as a salesman for Canadian Equipment & Supply Co.—later to become Bell & Morris Ltd.—and serving in the Army during World War I.

Partners in the venture were S. G. Gregg, who had joined the firm in 1922, and C. F. Rannie, who had worked for Silvester in 1907 and then struck out on his own and finally returned in 1935.

The company passed solely into the Staines family's hands after Rannie died in 1948 and Gregg retired the following year. Staines' son, John H. (Jack), bought the two-thirds share left by Rannie and Greg and became the firm's

The Calgary Silicate Pressed Brick Co., forerunner of Silvester Building Supplies Limited, was located at 4th Street and 10th Avenue S.W., where it manufactured a sand and lime brick.

secretary. He had started with the organization in 1947 after serving in the armed forces during World War II. Jack began as a yard worker, progressed to the order desk, and upon the death of his father in 1960 became president.

Silvester's warehouse moved to its current location of 4444 Builders Road S.E. in 1954. Two years later the office moved as well. The firm's name was changed to Silvester Building Supplies Limited in 1954. Jack Staines was instrumental in getting the roadway on which the company is located renamed to Builders Road shortly after its move. It had originally been Second Street S.E., but that name confused everyone because it ran at an angle connecting First and Third streets rather than running parallel to them.

A third-generation Staines joined the firm in 1979 in the person of Jack's son, Douglas J., who is heading up the expansion of its product lines such as natural stone. A total of 14 people are employed by the business, which is one of the city's major suppliers of brick and masonry supplies. Fireplace accessories have also been added in recent years. A unique dimension of the company's operation is the maintenance of a 24-hour, heated and unlocked showroom for displaying its brick and rock products—an idea that is so popular that competitors frequently send clients over for a look.

The year 1982 marked the 60th anniversary for Silvester Building Supplies Limited (April 21, 1922, to April 21, 1982).

STANDEN'S LTD.

The 1920s were an unusual time to become involved in blacksmithing and harness-making businesses. Automobiles were coming of age and the horse-and-buggy days appeared numbered. However, Cyril Standen, with some financial help from his father, William, stuck by their skills, adapted them, and created one of the most successful manufacturing firms in the city. They decided to enter the automobile maintenance field, specializing in springs, since the roads were creating lots of business.

William Standen, a harness maker from England, had come to Calgary in 1912. He went to work for Riley & McCormick and together with his oldest

son, Val, spent that winter in a tent on the banks of the Bow River. His family joined him a year later and it was then that Cyril decided to become a blacksmith.

Cyril Standen obtained much of his early experience in a basement workshop in the Standen home. Here, at the age of 15, he worked on a borrowed anvil, forging steel inserts for cowboy boots. His first business, however, involved sharpening skates for 15 cents a pair to break the boredom on winter evenings. He later went to work at a blacksmith shop, where he was promised a wage of $18 a week but in two and one-half years never received a full paycheque.

The Standens' business officially started as a partnership in July 1924,

with total resources of $600, althoug the father kept his leather work busines going as well. The first location was a the rear of the yard where they lived a 2415 2A Street S.E. It had been a two stall stable. Cyril Standen picked up second-hand forge for two dollars, bor rowed an anvil, improvised a blower and used his skate grinder motor to oper ate it. The bricklayer who built their fur nace warned them they wouldn't last year.

In the early days Cyril and his fathe regularly visited the city dump in searc of springs and scraps of iron and stee The first thing Cyril made in the sho was a set of tools for himself. This was time when any customer who was hel over mealtime would find a place set fo

"1924"

"1974"

him at the dinner table. The shop even had an order from Pincher Creek ranchers for a special grizzly trap for "old Rufe," who was depleting cattle herds but couldn't be held by other traps.

An addition was completed but a fire burned off the roof in 1935, almost destroying a fire truck. In 1938 the business moved to 24th Avenue and 2A Street S.E. Cyril's brother Alec joined the firm in 1929 and 10 years later brothers Sid and Reg joined.

The *Albertan* of July 29, 1938, announced the opening of the new factory with a page-wide headline and noted that the firm, also known as "Little Sheffield" because it used 60 tons of Sheffield steel a year, made springs for all kinds of uses including hair triggers and pipe organ pedals. In 1943 and again in 1953 the building was enlarged. In 1959 a frame and alignment shop was added. The company started to advertise during this period and became a regular radio sponsor of sporting events.

Standen's received a special commendation from the Industrial Relations Board for its contribution to the World War II efforts. In addition to working at peak capacity on war materials, the firm was a leader in war loan drives.

In March 1970 a five-alarm fire occurred, but within six weeks Standen's was under a roof again and installing new equipment. It was, however, becoming obvious that a larger site was desirable. In

1974 the company celebrated its 50th birthday by moving into a new 90,000-square-foot plant on a 7.5-acre site at 58th Avenue and 11th Street S.E. Its employee total jumped from 85 to 120 almost overnight. By 1981 Standen's had grown to a work force of 138 and a payroll of $3.5 million. This new plant represented a $3-million investment.

Steel spring products remain the backbone of the business. Standen's is now the largest and has the most modern equipment of any similar plant west of Montreal. A total of 35,000 square feet is dedicated to spring manufacture, with an annual consumption of 6,000 tons of spring steel. Standen's has a dealer network across Canada and sells to original product manufacturers. Its export sales now stand at one million dollars a year.

The company is also involved in truck bumpers, frame and equalizer hitches, axles, and running gear. The industrial balancing department is the largest and most modern in North America and can balance anything that rotates from six ounces in weight to 10 tons. The firm also has three frame-straightening machines and six wheel alignment racks.

Standen's Ltd. has a growing library of automobile blueprints, which records the original factory equipment of every vehicle commercially manufactured in North America since the 1920s. Substantial increase in warehouse space for about two million dollars in inventory is now

available. The service department has 29 bays. In 1982 Standen's expanded into a radiator distributorship and service facility.

Most of the personnel at Standen's learned their trade at the plant, many of them working up to positions of responsibility. One of the company's largest management moves came in 1967, when Cyril Standen decided to bring two younger men in as directors. One was J. P. Iozzi, who had joined the firm in 1944 and was made vice-president of manufacturing. W. A. Kilbourn, who came with the firm in 1959 as frame and alignment service manager, was made vice-president of operations.

In 1967 Iozzi and Kilbourn bought out Sid and Reg Standen's share of the business when the latter decided to retire. In 1972 they entered a 10-year buy-out with Cyril and Alec Standen. Cyril and Alec are no longer active in the organization but remain involved as directors. Cyril is now involved in model-train engineering as a hobby in a basement workshop, which in actuality is a fully equipped metalworking machine shop.

To all concerned, the company prospects remain bright. As the principals have said for years, "It's always springtime at Standen's."

SUN LIFE ASSURANCE COMPANY OF CANADA

Sun Life Assurance Company has been the largest insurance company in Canada for most of the 20th century. By 1982 it had assets of $8.8 billion and 8,000 employees. Calgary has played an important part in that growth—it was the site of the country's first group life insurance policy.

Sun Life has been doing business in Alberta since 1880, when Roderick MacFarlane was hired to sell life insurance to Hudson's Bay Company employees at Fort Chipewyan. The first office in Calgary was opened in 1902.

The firm had been formally incorporated in Montreal in 1871 with a modest capital of $500,000. The founder of the Sun Mutual Insurance Company was Matthew H. Gault but it was Robertson Macaulay, who assumed the presidency in 1879, who began Sun Life's drive to the top. He took the company into the West Indies and by the turn of the century had reached into Europe, South and Central America, parts of Africa, and the Far East. The organization, whose name was formally changed to Sun Life Assurance Company of Canada in 1882, was the largest life insurance company in Canada by 1908, a position it has never relinquished.

In 1880 it became the first insurance company in the world to offer an unconditional policy by removing restrictions on travel, residence, and occupation. Four years later it introduced the nonforfeiture clause and in the 1920s produced the two-year suicide clause.

Sun Life became the first Canadian firm to sell group insurance in 1919 when it issued a policy to *The Calgary Herald.* Policy No. 17-G has since been "retired" and replaced by one which covers the entire Southam newspaper chain. Strangely enough, the policy bore the number 17 simply because directors in 1919 had created a list of 100 Canadian firms considered as most likely prospects. Thus, although the *Herald* signed first, it had already been allotted its number. Forty-five years later Calgary agent Duke Shaver sold the company's 10,000th group policy—to another Calgary firm, Western Decalta Limited.

In 1962 Sun Life of Canada became a mutual insurance company entirely owned by its policyholders. The firm's corporate seal was moved from Montreal to Toronto in 1979 when it was felt that the Parti Quebecois' desire for provincial control of corporate assets was unacceptable to an international company.

Sun Life's recent approach to insurance has been more consumer oriented. Success is evidenced by the new three-tower, $14-million Sun Life Plaza in Calgary and a mammoth head office complex in Toronto.

Prior to 1963 a single branch office in Calgary handled Southern Alberta and

Sunlife Plaza-Phase 3, Calgary, Alberta, a Sun Life Assurance Company of Canada development.

southeastern British Columbia. By 1982 there were six branches in Calgary alone, employing 100 persons. Not only has Sun Life invested more than $500 million in Calgary, the city's branches have fared well in inter-branch competition. In 1956 the Calgary branch, under manager Gordon Houghton, was named the top branch in Canada. A similar honor went to Calgary's Foothills branch, under manager Joe Driscoll, for three successive years beginning in 1977.

TOOLE, PEET & CO. LIMITED

In 1897 a young Irish immigrant, recently returned from farming in central Alberta, decided to set himself up in a business selling insurance and a little real estate and acting as agent for the Galt Coal Company of Lethbridge. He was George Peet, a lifelong bachelor, who had been in the Calgary area since 1894. He came from the same part of Ireland as Captain John Palliser and it is said he attributed his desire to move to the Canadian West to stories he had heard as a child from the explorer.

In 1905 he met and joined forces with another Irishman, William Toole, a land agent for the Canadian Pacific Railway. Barney, as he was better known, brought to the firm of Toole, Peet & Co. the exclusive agency for townsite properties. He had come to Canada in the late 1880s and had gone to work for the CPR in Winnipeg, moving to Calgary during the next decade.

Archer Toole, Barney's brother, came to Canada in 1908 and started to work for the firm the following year in accounting and clerical work and eventually real estate. The firm was officially incorporated in 1913 with Barney Toole as president and George Peet as vice-president. It was a 60-40 partnership, with Toole owning the majority. By 1925 the firm had grown to include a staff of 17. In 1982 the staff number stood at 50.

Left
William "Barney" Toole was majority partner in the firm of Toole, Peet & Co.

Right
George Peet was a lifelong bachelor who first started the business in Calgary in 1897.

The nature of the firm's business changed over the years. Through the 1920s the company maintained a substantial coal business, complete with delivery service and warehouse. Until 1965 the organization was also a stock broker and investment dealer. It was also involved briefly in mortgages as agent for lenders.

Archer Toole was active in real estate, primarily downtown commercial sites. At one time or another he was involved in the sale of most of the properties along Eighth Avenue.

Among the firm's early real estate deals was the handling of the land for such prestige residential subdivisions as Mount Royal and Scarboro. Today, however, the real estate dimension remains but on a smaller scale. Property management has become a significant part of the business, but insurance constitutes the largest aspect of the enterprise. For example, the company has been Lloyd's agents for marine claims since 1913. It now ranks as the largest locally owned independent insurance broker in Calgary.

The firm has had four locations during its history. Its first site was on Centre Street between First and Second avenues. In 1912 it moved to the Canada Life Building on Eighth Avenue and Second Street. From 1926 to 1980 it occupied its own structure adjacent to the former site. It is now located at 1135 17th Avenue S.W.

Longtime employees are a company tradition. George Eaton joined the firm as an office boy in 1918 and remains a vice-president. Sid Robbins came to the firm in 1919 to build up the insurance portion of the company and is still active.

When Barney Toole died in 1952, Archer became president. George Peet died in 1953. Archer's son Bill joined the firm in 1954 and became president in 1963 after his father's death. He now owns control of the company stock. The family tradition appears to be continuing as Bill's son Larry, a chartered accountant like his father, joined the firm in 1978.

Company principals have been active in the community. Archer Toole was instrumental in the establishment of the Calgary Real Estate Board and was one of its early presidents. Bill Toole is active in the United Fund and has been on the council of The Calgary Chamber of Commerce. Barney Toole was a Chamber president at one time.

TRANSALTA UTILITIES CORPORATION

It all began one dark night in 1887 when, according to the story, the sober and business-like Peter Anthony Prince of Eau Claire Lumber Company fell off a plank sidewalk and severely injured his well-groomed pride. He vowed to bring electrification to Calgary. This (misplaced) step proved to be the first in a complex series of events which eventually resulted in the creation of Calgary Power—the name under which Trans-Alta Utilities operated for more than 70 years.

It was in 1909, the same year the city started its electric streetcar system, that a group in Montreal, headed by W. Max Aitken (later to become Lord Beaverbrook), conceived the idea of Calgary Power Company Limited in the boardrooms of Royal Securities Corporation. On December 27, 1909, the firm came into existence and its assets included water rights on the Bow River.

Calgary Power began service to its first two customers, the city of Calgary and Canada Cement Company, from its Horseshoe Falls power plant on May 21, 1911. The project, including the 45 miles of transmission lines to the city, represented an investment of one million dollars and had a capacity of 13,900 kilowatts.

The Horseshoe Falls hydro-generating plant on the Bow River 45 miles west of Calgary was completed in 1911. It represented an investment of one million dollars and was Calgary Power's first major project.

G. A. Gaherty, who served as president for 32 years, was perhaps the most instrumental in bringing the organization to the position it holds today in Canadian business. With 11 hydroelectric plants operating on the Bow River system, the company took steps to diversify. In 1956 it built the first unit of a steam plant at Wabamun, producing 69,000 kilowatts. A fourth unit, added in 1968, brought the plant's capacity to 569,000 kilowatts.

Perhaps the most significant accomplishment during the 1960 to 1965 presidency of G. H. Thompson was the assimilation of thermal-based power production into the total system. For the first 45 years of its existence the firm had been almost exclusively dependent on hydro production as its source of electrical power. As industrial development escalated in Alberta during the late 1960s, it was A. W. (Bert) Howard during his 1965 to 1973 presidency who primarily was responsible for raising the financial means for a new round of capital projects, including the Bighorn hydro project.

When M. M. Williams became president in 1973, he was to become the last in the line of Calgary Power presidents and the first president and chief executive officer of TransAlta Utilities Corporation. During his term the Sundance coal-fired plant was completed, bringing the company's total generating capacity to 3,349,000 kilowatts.

As the firm's operations grew it became obvious the name "Calgary Power" was no longer appropriate to describe its service area or its scope of activities. Thus on May 14, 1981, the company was renamed TransAlta Utilities Corporation, and was

The Sundance coal-fired generating plant's six units were phased in during the 1970s and the final unit was completed in 1980, bringing the company's total generating capacity up to 3,349 megawatts.

reorganized into three corporate divisions: utilities, resources, and fly ash.

TransAlta Utilities in 1982 employed 2,500 persons and had assets valued at over two billion dollars. The corporation continues to be 99 percent Canadian owned. Except for a few of the very early years, it has been a purely Alberta venture in location, management, and operations. And although the 13 hydro power plants remain a spectacular part of its operations, 90 percent of the generating capacity is now coal-fired. TransAlta Utilities is Canada's largest investor owned electric utility.

TRIMAC LIMITED

What started half a century ago as an operation involving one man, one horse, and one wagon full of coal is today a Calgary-based group of companies doing business internationally in transportation and energy. Trimac Limited is now the largest highway hauler of bulk commodities in Canada and one of the five largest on the continent. In the energy field, almost 100 Trimac rigs are drilling for oil and gas in Canada, the United States, and Europe.

J.W. "Jack" McCaig, the son of a Scottish homesteader, began the haulage business in Moose Jaw, Saskatchewan, in 1929 and traded his horse and wagon for his first truck the following year. With it and hard work he survived the Depression and enlarged his fleet, pioneering methods of two-way bulk hauling that have become basic to the trucking industry.

After World War II McCaig founded Maccam Transport of Moose Jaw with his son, J.R. (Bud), joining him in 1946. Other sons, Roger and Maurice, came into the business in the 1950s. The Maccam fleet grew to more than 100 vehicles carrying petroleum products, cement, and other bulk commodities throughout Saskatchewan and into Alberta and Manitoba.

In 1960 an old friend, Alberta trucking executive Max Trimble, telephoned the McCaigs to say that his family firm, H.M. Trimble & Sons, was going to be sold and that he hoped the McCaigs would buy it. Trimble was in Alberta what Maccam was in Saskatchewan: a major bulk hauler that had grown from strong family roots.

Henry M. Trimble had started a grain-buying company at Lacombe in 1925 and soon had acquired a truck to haul grain from farms to elevators. The family moved to Calgary in 1933 and the firm switched to petroleum hauling in 1935. During and after World War II, Trimble trucks filled contracts up the newly built Alaska Highway. When the founder died in 1949, his wife, Mary Jane, became company president and his sons, Lee and Max, managed the business in Calgary and Lethbridge.

J.W. "Jack" McCaig (left) of Maccam Transport and Max Trimble of H.M. Trimble & Sons meet in 1961 at the Calgary Trimble depot to unite their two family trucking firms. Under the new name of Trimac, the company has since grown into an international organization with diversified interests in energy and transportation.

The firm remained a family business with a close-knit group of loyal drivers. A highlight of each year was the bonus banquet in January, when drivers shared in company profits based on the number of miles they had driven.

Trimble and Maccam merged in 1961 as Trimac, a name built from the first letters of each firm which also recognized "the three macs"—the sons of Jack McCaig. Bud McCaig became president of the Trimble operation in Calgary and assumed overall direction of Trimac when his father retired that year.

Rapid growth during the 1960s dictated a need for capital. After a brief merger with Westburne International Industries, the McCaig family converted Trimac Limited into a public company in 1971.

Diversification into energy services has expanded Trimac's assets and revenues. The 1977 acquisition of Kenting Limited involved Trimac in contract drilling, pipeline and oil field construction, and geophysical and aerial surveying. An Alberta firm born in the 1950s, Kenting concentrated on contract drilling after Tony Vanden Brink became president in 1973; it is now the fourth largest drilling contractor in Canada. Vanden Brink, a 1949 immigrant from Holland, had started as a driller's helper and now is president of Trimac.

With the purchase of the Dallas-based Cactus Drilling companies in 1980, Trimac moved into the American market with 50 additional land rigs, seven offshore rigs, and more than 1,500 new employees. In total Trimac Limited has about 5,300 employees with an annual payroll of more than $100 million. The Canadian Association for Corporate Growth named it Growth Company of the Year in 1981, recognizing its performance in the previous five years: an increase in total assets from $53 million to $439 million and in revenue from $65 million to $309 million.

TRIZEC CORPORATION LTD.

The destiny of Trizec Corporation was placed in the hands of Harold Milavsky in 1976, when he took over as president and chief executive officer. The company was near bankruptcy but since has reemerged as one of the giants in the real estate field with a 1981 book value of $2.5 billion. A chartered accountant, Milavsky is known for his boundless energy and his ability to put deals together—he surprised everyone by creating Bankers Hall in Calgary, a twin-towered complex in which the prime tenants will be two of Canada's largest banks. However, his importance to the firm had filtered out earlier when Trizec moved its head office to Calgary—because the president refused to leave the city.

Trizec has always been known for its landmark buildings in major cities. Its founder was a U.S.-born real estate magnate, William Zeckendorf, who in 1957 conceived of Place Ville Marie, a major redevelopment of downtown Montreal. When financial dealings went sour in 1958, Zeckendorf turned to an English company, Eagle Star Insurance, for help.

The result was the formation of Trizec in 1960, ostensibly to complete Place Ville Marie. The firm's name came from the principals involved: "Tri" for three (Zeckendorf, Eagle Star, and an Eagle Star subsidiary, Second Covent Garden) and "zec" from the first letter of each of Zeckendorf, Eagle Star, and Covent Garden.

Harold Milavsky took over Trizec as president and chief executive officer in 1976 and turned it into one of the world's largest public property companies.

Garden.

Trizec moved into Western Canada through its 1970 purchase of Cumming Properties Limited and its 1971 acquisition of Great West International Equities Ltd. In 1970 it made its first move into the United States with the purchase of three office buildings and the subsequent purchase and development of seven office buildings in the Los Angeles area.

Although it grew to become Canada's largest publicly owned real estate developer by 1972, within four years Trizec had fallen prey to interest rates, inflation, and internal difficulties. Through a complicated financial rescue mission, Peter and Edward Bronfman emerged with controlling interest. They picked Milavsky to head the firm's recovery. Milavsky had worked for them since 1969 as executive vice-president of Great West International Equities and is now the largest individual shareholder in Trizec.

The subsequent growth of Trizec has been remarkable. It has buildings across Canada. In 1980 Trizec acquired Ernest W. Hahn, Inc., of California, a regional shopping centre developer with a portfolio of 25 centres and 28 others in progress. In 1981 Trizec moved into the eastern United States through a 20.5-percent interest in The Rouse Company of Columbia, Maryland, which has 54 shopping centres.

Calgary landmarks in Trizec's portfolio include Calgary Place, Scotia Centre, Fifth & Fifth, Western Canadian Place, and South Centre. Although office buildings and shopping centres comprise 88 percent of assets, Trizec owns 23 retirement lodges and nursing homes through Central Park Lodges of Canada, the largest organization in Canada specializing in accommodations for the elderly. Trizec also owns 32 mobile home parks, the majority located in the U.S. Sun Belt.

The future promises continued growth. In 1982 Trizec had $942 million in projects in progress—the majority in Canada with a focus on Calgary. Trizec's status as one of the world's largest public property companies seems assured.

This is a composite of some of Trizec's buildings in Canada and the United States. In the centre are the bronze and silver towers which make up part of the Bankers Hall project.

TROJAN PROPERTIES LIMITED

In 1971 four men saw a need for a special kind of "design-build" construction, pooled their expertise and $19,000, raised some backing, and formed Trojan Industrial Properties Limited. Today Bill McKay, founder of the firm, has seen Trojan grow into a corporation involved in projects valued in the hundreds of millions of dollars.

The organization obtained its name quite by accident. After a seemingly endless discussion of names, an observer commented that the group seemed to be "working like Trojans." It stuck! An engineer, McKay is chairman and chief executive officer. The Alberta native is also the primary shareholder.

Trojan was formed on the premise there was a substantial untapped market for custom industrial and commercial buildings. Today Trojan is a leader in the design-build concept, a construction approach in which the design is controlled by the builder and the user.

The first Trojan design-build project in Edmonton, led to seven more for the same firm across the country. After months of research into grocery distribution, Trojan's second major project was a large grocery distribution centre in Calgary. About 40 percent of Trojan's design-build business continues to be in grocery distribution construction.

The company has built 35 projects for nine corporations, evidence of its approach to repeat business.

From its industrial development ventures grew Trojan's commercial development division. The firm got into shopping centres and offices. That orderly growth has helped Trojan develop a solid asset base and consistent cash flow.

The company's commercial development division was established in 1975, the same year it dropped "Industrial" from its name. Trojan developed its first enclosed mall shopping centre that year and many neighbourhood centres have followed, primarily in Alberta and Saskatchewan. The firm was nominated for a design award for its Willow Park Village in Calgary.

Trojan's special projects division was formed to deal with the larger com-

Bill McKay, founder of Trojan Properties Limited, is its chairman and chief executive officer.

prehensive projects, which required a "special" approach. One of these projects undertaken in joint venture with a Toronto developer is Prince's Court in the Eau Claire district in Calgary and is a unique one-million-square-foot mixed-use development. The company's most important special project, St. George's Technology Park, is a world-class 2.6-million-square-foot office project in "near downtown." The project is 100-percent owned by Trojan and its 22 separate parcels will be developed over a six-year period.

Believing it prudent to start U.S. operations, Trojan opened a commercial development office in Denver in 1980 and began the long process of duplicating its Calgary operations.

Trojan has an office staff of 80 with up to 200 field personnel. Its headquarters are at 517 10th Avenue S.W.

Bill McKay is most proud of the exceptional team of professionals that run the day-to-day operations of the corporation. He is extremely growth oriented and likes to maintain a family-type atmosphere in the company. As a result, Trojan Properties Limited sponsors a great deal of employee programs. In recent years, almost three percent of its revenues have been spent on education programs and community services.

TROTTER & MORTON LIMITED

In the Arctic it was the bitter cold of the total dark of winter. In the Antarctic it was equally cold although the sun shone around the clock. But to Calgary-based Trotter & Morton Limited it was business as usual. The company has grown used to meeting challenges in the plumbing, heating, air conditioning, and process piping fields, and having its crews working poles apart was merely an interesting diversion.

Its polar projects one year included a U.S. Navy research station at the South Pole, a research camp on the 11,000-foot elevation of the Antarctic, and a Utilidor system for servicing the water, sewage, and utility needs of a 3,000-man construction camp at Prudhoe Bay, Alaska.

The firm traces its origin to 1927 when two employees of James Ballentine Company, a plumbing contractor, were faced with the prospect of unemployment when their employer suddenly curtailed all non-Toronto ventures. Instead, W.B. Trotter and Howard Morton incorporated their own venture on August 5. Today hardly a major structure goes up in the city without Trotter & Morton leaving its imprint.

In 1955 the two founders retired and the company passed into the hands of William Watson, his two sons E.H. (Bud) and Don, and fellow associate Bob Worden. Watson, an original employee of the firm, had the distinction of holding Certificate No. 1 for being the first indentured apprentice in the Alberta plumbing apprenticeship course. In 1972 he was elected chairman of the board and replaced as president by son Bud, a mechanical engineer, who also holds the title of general manager. Brother Don, a journeyman plumber and gas fitter, is a vice-president and the secretary-treasurer. The brothers are the majority shareholders although employees own a portion.

The company runs a very diversified operation. Projects have included refineries, hospitals, gas plants, dairies, breweries, office buildings, schools, and colleges from the West Coast to the Ottawa River. It has been involved in water and sewage treatment facilities and pioneered the single-stack, no-vent plumbing system through regulatory bodies. Part of its facilities includes a 2,500-square-foot pipe fabrication shop. In recent years the firm has used the design/build concept, a team approach which makes it possible to start building a project while planning is still taking place. In 1982 it had 150 people in the field and another 20 in the office.

Trotter & Morton started its life on 12th Avenue across from the Colonel Belcher Hospital but eventually moved to the Eau Claire district. In 1962 it moved to its current location at 323 Forge Road S.E.

The firm's standing in the industry was demonstrated in 1968 when fire destroyed its files. With accounts receivable exceeding $750,000, the company was left with only a list of names—but no amounts. Relying on the goodwill of customers, suppliers, and employees, the files were rebuilt so successfully that less than $500 was unaccounted for. A competing firm even offered Trotter & Morton the use of its facilities.

The Watsons have also played important roles in professional organizations. Bud was president of both the Calgary and Alberta construction associations and was vice-president of the Canadian association. Don has been president of the Calgary and Alberta mechanical contractors' associations. Their father had been similarly active.

Trotter & Morton Limited

W.B. Trotter

William Watson

Howard Morton

TURBO RESOURCES LIMITED

Turbo Resources' new 30,000-barrel-per-day Southern Alberta Refinery, located five kilometres north of Calgary, is completed and was constructed in only 18 months. The refinery will produce a full range of high-quality gasolines, diesel fuels, and other petroleum products.

In 1970 Turbo Resources Limited was born. In its first year of operations, sales reached one million dollars. By 1982, only 12 years later, Turbo has sales of some $600 million and assets of over one billion dollars, including a brand-new, state-of-the-art crude oil refinery near Calgary, some 300 service stations from British Columbia to Ontario, 50 drilling rigs, and interests in a variety of other affiliate and subsidiary companies—impressive growth for a business that had started with just three service stations and a waste oil recycling plant that cleaned used crankcase lubricants.

Today Turbo stands as one of the most amazing stories ever recorded in the Canadian energy business, a field dominated by mega-sized, fully integrated petroleum resource development corporations. Through its operating subsidiaries, Turbo is currently involved in such activities as oil and gas well drilling, well servicing, oil field rentals and supplies, oil and gas exploration and production, mining, manufacturing, refining, marketing of petroleum and related products, transportation, heavy equipment sales, and real estate.

Since the company's founders, Bob Brawn and Ken Travis, joined forces in 1970, Turbo Resources has been built largely through the process of acquisition. Names that are well-known in North America's oil patch and mining sector—such as Challenger, Pine Well, Heath and Sherwood, Bankeno Mines,

and Merland Explorations—all became part of the Turbo group through the many acquisitions made by the firm since its inception. With those acquisitions has come diversification, and more recently full integration as an energy company.

Bob Brawn and Ken Travis met in 1959, when Brawn began working for Travis' "mud" company, Drilling Fluids Ltd. in Saskatchewan. In 1965 Travis was offered the chance to purchase an oil recycling plant in Edmonton, which re-refined old, used crankcase oil. Travis offered Brawn the chance to run the plant, which Brawn declined. "After thinking about it for three months, I decided I'd buy it myself," says Brawn, "and Ken gave me his blessing."

The two men took separate paths until 1970, when they combined Travis' operations with Brawn's by-then 35 ser-

vice stations in Alberta and Saskatchewan. They formed Liberty Resources Ltd., the forerunner to Turbo, and listed on the Alberta Stock Exchange. As the two men got together, the acquisitions and diversification began. In 1971 they bought Parkland Oil Products and Freeway Transport, a trucking company. The Parkland deal added another 33 service stations in small towns across Alberta and Saskatchewan.

By 1972, when Turbo Resources was listed on the Toronto Stock Exchange, the company owned 109 stations, all in Alberta and Saskatchewan. That same year a decision was made to enter the exploration and production side of the petroleum industry and 23 wells were drilled, of which seven were oil wells and eight were gas. In 1979 Turbo completed its first major purchase, Upper Canada Resources Ltd., a custom oil well contract drilling company, which also owned an interest in a small company called Bankeno Mines Ltd. Today Turbo holds a 90 percent interest in Bankeno Mines, which as a publicly owned resource company holds significant oil, gas and mineral assets, including a majority interest in Merland Explorations Limited, a major Western Canadian gas explorer and producer.

Turbo, a Canadian owned and controlled company has promoted and proven the value of free enterprise and hard work. Its activities now are worldwide, with no end in sight to its growth or success.

This new Turbo station on Parkvale Boulevard in southwest Calgary is one of the more than 300 retail outlets Turbo operates from British Columbia to eastern Ontario.

WESTERN ROOFING (1977) COMPANY LTD.

Western Roofing Company's first office was located at 1417 24th Avenue S.E.

Old-time roofers enjoyed a unique rapport with their customers. Jack French, for example, once put on a roof and then refunded five dollars to the lady and told her to get an Easter bonnet. Although the times and styles have changed, the quality and reputation of Western Roofing has remained.

John Falconer started the firm in the early 1960s, operating out of his house. He had come to Calgary from Saskatchewan and learned the roofing business with French Roofing. When he entered the real estate business he sold the firm to brother-in-law Stan Pawchuk. He, too, went into real estate and in 1967 Herb Imler, Falconer's other brother-in-law, became the new owner.

Imler's organization was an amalgamation of Western Roofing and French Roofing, which had been run by Jack French since the 1940s. Born in Golden, British Columbia, Imler came to Calgary in 1949. He had been a long-distance truck driver prior to the purchase of Western Roofing but a desire to be home with his family prompted the change in careers. His new prospects were not considered good—business was slow and he knew little about the industry. He decided, however, that whatever he did, he would do well.

Imler's first office was at 1417 9th Avenue S.E. In 1970 he moved operations to 828 24th Avenue S.E. and three years later moved across the street to the current location, 839 24th Avenue S.E.

In the first years Imler's business centred primarily on residential housing and the re-roofing of older homes. It grew to become one of the city's largest shingle re-roofing companies. In 1970 Western Roofing branched out into commercial and flat-roof applications. Its first piece of equipment was a small 500-pound tar kettle, which has since been replaced by 20-ton and 28-ton asphalt bulk carriers.

In 1967 the company had sales of $100,000 and Imler was the sole estimator, accountant, and superintendent. By 1981 sales exceeded $5 million and the firm had grown from only one person in the office to a payroll of 100. The business is also no longer seasonal. For example, in February 1968, Western Roofing's sales were only $300, but 14 years later the same month produced sales of $250,000.

In 1977 Imler took in two minor partners who had been with the business for a number of years. Mike Murphy has since left the company but Elwood Hensch remains. Family members are also active. Imler's wife, Marg, is in charge of accounts receivable. Son Al has been with the organization since 1976 and is in charge of the shingling division.

Imler has been very active in community affairs. He has been a director of the Canadian Cancer Society in Calgary for 20 years. Active with the Fraternal Order of Eagles, Imler has been a Calgary president six times, as well as serving with the national body. He is also a charter member of the Chinook Rotary Club.

In 1973 Western Roofing Company moved to its present location at 839 24th Avenue S.E.

WHITE SPOT RESTAURANTS

Steve Pappas arrived in Halifax on October 9, 1951, from his native Greece—a penniless mechanic determined to escape the poverty he had known. A cousin loaned him $20 in spending money to go to Montreal, where relatives found him a job with the Canadian Pacific Railway. Driven by a desire to own a business, he left after five years and headed north to make some quick money. In six months on the DEW line he survived temperatures of 76 degrees below Fahrenheit and managed to save $7,000.

Together with a partner, Pappas made his first move in Montreal into the restaurant business. He lost his investment, and in 1957 he headed west to work as a welder in Kitimat, British Columbia, and Saskatoon. After a year in Thompson, Manitoba, working seven days a week, 12 hours a day at $2.75 an hour with no overtime, his doctor told him the strain was too much.

Again Pappas went looking for a business, and in August 1960 he and two partners bought the White Spot at 11th Avenue and 4th Street S.W. Business was good but the profits weren't high enough to sustain three partners. Pappas became sole proprietor by giving his associates everything he owned.

To encourage more business the restaurateur installed a charcoal broiler in a window and introduced the steak sandwich to Calgary. He even donned a chef's hat and apron and cooked the steaks himself; he couldn't afford a cook. By 1965 the White Spot was the busiest restaurant in town, once serving a record 1,100 steaks on a single Friday night.

At that point Pappas decided to expand, and he purchased two small downtown eating houses calling them White Spot No. 2 and No. 3. In 1967 he entered the nightclub business by opening the El Morocco in the basement of his original White Spot. Four years later he opened No. 5 on Macleod Trail, and the following year built No. 4 in northwest Calgary. He relocated No. 2 to Forest Lawn when an expired lease forced him to move.

For a while Pappas operated

Steve Pappas chats with his son and partner, Gregory, at one of the White Spot Restaurants.

restaurants in Edmonton and Medicine Hat, but found out-of-town ventures too difficult to control. In 1979 he opened an operation on Richmond Road, and another location on Macleod Trail and Heritage Drive in 1982; plans call for yet another in northeast Calgary. Pappas was forced to sell the original White Spot site in 1981; the land had become too valuable for strictly restaurant use. Thus ended 46 years for White Spot on that corner.

Although Pappas has been the driving force behind the business—at one point he hadn't taken a day off in 10 years—his family is very much involved. His wife Chareklea worked as a cashier and controller before retiring in 1981, after 10 years as the company's sole buyer. Son Gregory, who started as a cook, is now a partner and is being groomed to take over the business.

White Spot owner Steve Pappas sits beside actor Burl Ives, who referred to his host as one of Calgary's best ambassadors.

CALGARY PATRONS

The following individuals, companies, and organizations have made a valuable commitment to the quality of this publication. Windsor Publications and The Calgary Chamber of Commerce gratefully acknowledge their participation in *Calgary: Canada's Frontier Metropolis.*

Alberta Energy Company Ltd.*
Alberta Government Telephones*
Alberta Motor Association*
All-West Construction Ltd.
Alpine Management Corporation Ltd.*
R. Angus Alberta Limited
ATCO Ltd.*
Banff Lifts Ltd.*
Bannerman Insurance Ltd.*
Bennett & White Western Ltd.*
John Blain Engineering Ltd.
Bow Cycle & Motor Co. Ltd.*
Bow Valley Industries Ltd.*
Burns Foods Limited
Caldraft (1977) Ltd.*
Calgary Co-Operative Association Limited*
Calgary Exhibition and Stampede*
The Calgary Herald
Calgary Public Livestock Market Ltd.*
Canada Cement Lafarge Ltd.*
Canada Safeway Limited*
Canadian Pacific*
Canadian Superior Oil Ltd.*
Canadian Western Natural Gas Company Limited*
Carma Ltd.*
Cascade Group*
CEP Consultants Ltd.

Chinook Centre*
City Bakery Calgary Ltd.*
Eric Connelly
Consolidated Concrete Limited*
Coopers & Lybrand*
Czar Resources Ltd.*
Davies Electric Company Limited
Delta Projects Limited*
Digital Perspectives Ltd.
Dome Petroleum Limited*
Dr. William A.J. Donald
Eau Claire Estates*
Esso Resources Canada Limited*
Foothills Hospital
Franklin Supply Company Ltd.*
Genstar Cement Limited
Geophysical Service Inc.
George & Nick's Machine Works Ltd.*
Glenbow Museum*
Clarkson Gordon
Woods Gordon
Greyhound Lines of Canada Limited*
Gulf Canada Limited*
Gunther's Building Center Ltd.*
Henderson College of Business*
The Highlander Motor Hotel
Home Care Medical Center
Hornstrom Bros. Construction Ltd.*
Irving Industries Ltd.*
Kai Mortensen*
Lavalin Services Inc.*
A.E. Lepage (Prairies) Ltd.*
Lewis Stationery Ltd.*
MacCosham Van Lines (Calgary) Ltd.*
Maclin Ford*
Marvelite Industries Ltd.
Milner & Steer
Mobil Oil Canada, Ltd.
The Norcal Group of Companies*

NOVA, AN ALBERTA CORPORATION*
Nu-West Group Limited*
Palliser Hotel
Pangaea Petroleum Limited
Price Waterhouse*
Prudential Steel Ltd.*
RCA Inc.
Reggin Industries Ltd.*
Richfield Properties Limited*
Scotiabank in Calgary*
The Sefel Group of Companies*
Shell Canada Resources Limited*
Silvester Building Supplies Limited*
Standen's Ltd.*
Sun Life Assurance Company of Canada*
Toole, Peet & Co. Limited*
Total Petroleum (North American) Ltd.
TransAlta Utilities Corporation*
Trimac Limited*
Trizec Corporation Ltd.*
Trojan Properties Limited*
Trotter & Morton Limited*
Turbo Resources Limited*
Twin Richfield Oils Ltd.
Walsh, Young
Wells Fargo Bank Canada
Western Roofing (1977) Company Ltd.*
White Spot Restaurants*
Royden D. Whitney

* Partners in Progress of *Calgary: Canada's Frontier Metropolis.* The histories of these companies and organizations appear in Part IV, beginning on page 273.

BIBLIOGRAPHY

Although almost the entire manuscript was researched from primary documents, the following list includes relevant publications on the history of Calgary. Not included are the many excellent master's and doctoral theses available on microfilm at both the Glenbow-Alberta archives and the University of Calgary. Also not mentioned in this bibliography are the many excellent articles on the city which have appeared regularly in such journals as *Alberta History*, its predecessor, *The Alberta Historical Review* or the many other scholarly journals on Western Canadian and urban development.

Baine, R.P. *Calgary: An Urban Study.* Clarke Irwin, Toronto, 1973.

Barr, B.M. ed. *Calgary: Metropolitan Structure and Influence.* Western Geographical Series, Vol. II. University of Victoria, Victoria, 1975.

Cunniffe, Richard. *Calgary in Sandstone.* Historical Society of Alberta, Calgary, 1969.

Dempsey, Hugh A. ed. *The Best of Bob Edwards.* Hurtig Publishing, Edmonton, 1975.

Foran, M.L. *Calgary: An Illustrated History.* History of Canadian Cities Series, Vol. II. James Lorimer and the National Museums of Man, Toronto, 1978.

Kelly, L.V. *The Rangemen.* William Briggs, Toronto, 1913.

Kennedy, Grant H., and Stanton, James B., eds. *The Albertans.* Lone Pine Publishing Co., Edmonton, 1981.

MacEwan, J.W. Grant. *Calgary Cavalcade.* Institute of Allied Arts Ltd., Edmonton, 1958.

_____ *Pat Burns: Cattle King.* Western Producer Prairie Books, Saskatoon, 1979.

McNeill, Leishman. *Tales of the Old Town: Calgary 1875-1950.* The Calgary Herald, Calgary, 1950.

Morrison, E.C. and Morrison, P.N.R. eds. *Calgary 1875-1950: A Souvenir of Calgary's Seventy-Fifth Anniversary.* Calgary Publishing Co., Calgary, 1950.

Morrow, E. Joyce. *Calgary Many Years Hence: The Mawson Report in Perspective.*

Morton, A.S. *The History of the Canadian West to 1870.* Thomas Nelson & Sons, London, 1939.

Rasporich, A.W. and Klassen, Henry C. eds. *Frontier Calgary: Town, City and Region, 1875-1914.* University of Calgary and McClelland Stewart West, Calgary, 1975.

Ward, Tom. *Cowtown: An Album of Early Calgary.* McClelland and Stewart West, Calgary, 1975.

Calgary, Alberta. Calgary Chamber of Commerce, Calgary, 1979.

Calgary in Fact: A Profile of Canada's Most Dynamic City 1981-82. City of Calgary Department of Business Development Service to Business, Calgary, 1982.

Century Calgary Historical Series. 6 Vol. and 2 photographic Vols. Calgary Historical Series, Calgary, 1975.

ACKNOWLEDGEMENTS

We would like to thank the staff at the Glenbow-Alberta Institute for the courtesy and many assistances extended to us during the preparation of this volume. Our thanks and appreciation are also extended to Mrs. Deirdre Slater for her work in typing all drafts of the manuscript and for her meritorious efforts in interpreting some indecipherable scrawl.

Max Foran

Heather MacEwan Foran

Calgary

INDEX

Italicized numbers indicate illustrations

THIS BOOK WAS SET IN
GRECIAN OLD STYLE TYPE,
PRINTED AND BOUND BY
D.W. FRIESEN & SONS, LTD.
HALFTONE
REPRODUCTION BY
ROBERTSON GRAPHICS